D1563393

Samuel Johnson
and the Art of Sinking
1709–1791

Samuel Johnson
and the Art of Sinking
1709–1791

FREYA JOHNSTON

OXFORD
UNIVERSITY PRESS

OXFORD

UNIVERSITY PRESS

Great Clarendon Street, Oxford OX2 6DP

Oxford University Press is a department of the University of Oxford.
It furthers the University's objective of excellence in research, scholarship,
and education by publishing worldwide in

Oxford New York

Auckland Cape Town Dar es Salaam Hong Kong Karachi
Kuala Lumpur Madrid Melbourne Mexico City Nairobi
New Delhi Shanghai Taipei Toronto

With offices in

Argentina Austria Brazil Chile Czech Republic France Greece
Guatemala Hungary Italy Japan South Korea Poland Portugal
Singapore Switzerland Thailand Turkey Ukraine Vietnam

Published in the United States
by Oxford University Press Inc., New York

British Library Cataloguing in Publication Data

Data available

Library of Congress Cataloging in Publication Data

Data available

ISBN 0-19-925182-7

1 3 5 7 9 10 8 6 4 2

Typeset by Laserwords Private Limited, Chennai, India

Printed in Great Britain
on acid-free paper by
Biddles Ltd, Kings Lynn, Norfolk

For my mother, Dale, with love and thanks

Acknowledgements

PART OF MY INTRODUCTION and the last paragraphs of Chapter 1 have been published together as one section of 'Little Lives: An Eighteenth-Century Sub-Genre', in *Cambridge Quarterly*, 32 (2003), 143–60. Part of Chapter 3 first appeared as 'Diminutive Observations in Johnson's *Journey to the Western Islands of Scotland*', in *Age of Johnson*, 12 (2001), 1–16. The concluding paragraphs of Chapter 4 were published as 'Samuel Johnson and Robert Levet', in *Modern Language Review*, 97 (2002), 26–35. None of these is reproduced exactly, but I am grateful in all cases for permission to reprint.

Thanks are long overdue to the colleges of Cambridge University in which the work for this book was carried out—Trinity, Newnham, and Christ's. I also want to thank everyone who provided help, criticism, or information, particularly those who commented on different sections of the book at various stages: the three anonymous readers of my initial proposal and draft chapters; Matthew Bevis, Cathal Dowling, Howard Erskine-Hill, Sophie Goldsworthy, Mina Gorji, Nicholas Hallam, Paul Korshin, Fred Parker, Tom Perridge, Clare Pettitt, Jackie Pritchard, Elizabeth Prochaska, Claude Rawson, Felicity Rosslyn, Dale Thatcher, Jessica Thatcher, and Frances Whistler. Only the errors are entirely mine.

This book is partly about teaching. I hope it answers some of the questions about Johnson and the eighteenth century that my students have raised over the past few years. My greatest debt is to my best teacher, Eric Griffiths.

F. J.

Contents

Note on Texts and Short Titles

Full citations are provided for most works when they first appear and abbreviated versions thereafter. The following works, more frequently cited or with appearances scattered across the book, are referred to throughout by abbreviations. Variant spellings and punctuation have been reproduced from the original texts without notice of a '[*sic*]'. Except where the context requires a differentiation of one speaker or source from another, I have not reproduced speech within double quotation marks thus: ' "Sir . . ." ' but in the singular form: 'Sir . . .' Much of what I cite is Johnson's spoken word rather than his writing; at such moments, James Boswell and Hester Thrale/Piozzi are often quoting someone else who is in turn quoting Johnson, so that it would be necessary to write: ' " 'Sir . . .' " ' or even, at some points, " " " 'Sir . . .' " " " For the sake of consistency, I have applied this rule throughout; always making it clear, however, that I am quoting (say) Imlac's words rather than his author's. Citations from the Bible are from the King James Version.

Austen, *Works*	*The Works of Jane Austen*, ed. R. W. Chapman, 6 vols., 3rd edn. (Oxford: Oxford University Press, 1988). Volumes cited are as follows: ii: *Pride and Prejudice* iii: *Mansfield Park* iv: *Emma* v: *Northanger Abbey and Persuasion* vi: *Minor Works*
Burke, *Enquiry*	Edmund Burke, *A Philosophical Enquiry into the Origins of our Ideas of the Sublime and the Beautiful*, ed. James T. Boulton (Oxford: Basil Blackwell, 1987)
Dictionary	Samuel Johnson, *A Dictionary of the English Language*, ed. Anne McDermott (Cambridge: Cambridge University Press, 1996) (on CD-Rom). Unless otherwise stated, references are to the first edition of 1755

Early Biographical Writings	*Early Biographical Writings of Dr. Johnson*, ed. J. D. Fleeman (Farnborough: Gregg International, 1973)
Fielding, *Tom Jones*	Henry Fielding, *The Wesleyan Edition of the Works of Henry Fielding* (Oxford: Clarendon Press, 1967–): *The History of Tom Jones, A Foundling*, introd. Martin C. Battestin, ed. Fredson Bowers, 2 vols. (1974)
Goldsmith, *Collected Works*	*Collected Works of Oliver Goldsmith*, ed. Arthur Friedman, 5 vols. (Oxford: Clarendon Press, 1966)
Hazlitt, *Complete Works*	*The Complete Works of William Hazlitt in Twenty-One Volumes: Centenary Edition*, ed. P. P. Howe (London: J. M. Dent, 1930–4)
Letters	*The Letters of Samuel Johnson*, ed. Bruce Redford, 5 vols. (Princeton: Princeton University Press, 1992–4)
Life	*Boswell's Life of Johnson; Together with Boswell's Journal of a Tour to the Hebrides*, ed. George Birkbeck Hill, rev. and enlarged L. F. Powell, 6 vols., 2nd edn. (Oxford: Clarendon Press, 1971)
Lives	Samuel Johnson, *The Lives of the English Poets*, ed. George Birkbeck Hill, 3 vols., 2nd edn. (Oxford: Clarendon Press, 1996)
'Longinus', *On the Sublime*	*Aristotle: The Poetics, Longinus: On the Sublime, Demetrius: On Style*, trans. W. Hamilton Ffye and W. Rhys Roberts (Cambridge, Mass.: Harvard University Press, 1927; repr. 1991). References to *Peri Hupsous*, or *On the Sublime*, are given by chapter and (where relevant) subsection (e.g. Longinus, *On the Sublime*, IX. 7)
Miscellanies	George Birkbeck Hill (ed.), *Johnsonian Miscellanies*, 2 vols. (New York: Barnes & Noble, 1966; repr. 1970)
Poems	Samuel Johnson, *The Complete English Poems*, ed. J. D. Fleeman (Harmondsworth: Penguin, 1971; repr. 1982)
Pope, *Correspondence*	*The Correspondence of Alexander Pope*, ed. George Sherburn, 5 vols. (Oxford: Oxford University Press, 1956)

Pope, *Dunciad*	*The Twickenham Edition of the Poems of Alexander Pope*, ed. John Butt, 11 vols. (London: Methuen, 1939–69), v: *The Dunciad*, ed. James Sutherland, 2nd edn. (1953)
Pope, *Essay on Man*	*The Twickenham Edition of the Poems of Alexander Pope*, ed. John Butt, 11 vols. (London: Methuen, 1939–69), iii/1: *An Essay on Man*, ed. Maynard Mack (1950)
Pope, *Prose*	*Selected Prose of Alexander Pope*, ed. Paul Hammond (Cambridge: Cambridge University Press, 1987)
Prefaces	*Samuel Johnson's Prefaces & Dedications*, ed. Allen T. Hazen (Port Washington, NY: Kennikat, 1937; repr. 1973)
Prose and Poetry	*Dr Johnson: Prose and Poetry*, ed. Mona Wilson (London: Rupert Hart-Davis, 1969)
Savage	Samuel Johnson, *An Account of the Life of Mr Richard Savage, Son of the Late Earl Rivers*, ed. Clarence Tracy (Oxford: Clarendon Press, 1971)
Spectator	*The Spectator*, ed. Donald F. Bond, 5 vols., 2nd edn. (Oxford: Clarendon Press, 1987). References are given by essay, volume, and page number (e.g. *Spectator* 6, i. 29)
Swift, *Prose Works*	*The Prose Works of Jonathan Swift*, ed. Herbert Davis, 16 vols. (Oxford: Basil Blackwell for Shakespeare Head, 1939–74). Volumes cited are as follows: iv: *A Proposal for Correcting the English Tongue, Polite Conversation, Etc.*, ed. with Louis Landa (1957) v: *Miscellaneous and Autobiographical Pieces, Fragments and Marginalia* (1962) viii: *Political Tracts 1713–1719* (1953) x: *The Drapier's Letters and Other Works* (1941) xi: *Gulliver's Travels* (1959) xii: *Irish Tracts 1728–1733* (1955)
Tatler	*The Tatler*, ed. Donald F. Bond, 3 vols. (Oxford: Clarendon Press, 1987). References are given by essay, volume, and page number (e.g. *Tatler* 47, i. 341)
Thraliana	*Thraliana: The Diary of Mrs. Hester Lynch Thrale, Later Mrs Piozzi, 1776–1809*, ed. Katherine C.

	Balderston, 2 vols., 2nd edn. (Oxford: Clarendon Press, 1951)
Tour	*Boswell's Journal of a Tour to the Hebrides with Samuel Johnson, LL.D*, ed. Frederick A. Pottle and Charles H. Bennett (London: Heinemann, 1936)
Watts, *Divine Songs*	*Divine Songs attempted in Easy Language for the Use of Children: Facsimile Reproductions of the First Edition of 1715 and an Illustrated Edition of circa 1840*, introd. J. H. P. Papford (London: Oxford University Press, 1971)
Watts, *Guide to Prayer*	*A Guide to Prayer. Or, A Free and Rational Account of the Gift, Grace and Spirit of Prayer; with Plain Directions how Every Christian may attain them* (London: for Emanuel Matthews and Sarah Cliff, 1715)
Watts, *Humility*	*Humility Represented in the Character of St. Paul, the Chief Springs of it opened, and its Various Advantages display'd; together with some Occasional Views of the Contrary Vice* (London: for R. Ford and R. Hett, 1737)
Watts, *Hymns*	*Hymns and Spiritual Songs. In Three Books. I. Collected from the Scriptures. II. Composed on Divine Subjects. III. Prepar'd for the Lord's Supper*, 19th edn. (London: for R. Ware, et al., 1755)
Yale	*The Yale Edition of the Works of Samuel Johnson*, ed. John H. Middendorf et al. (New Haven: Yale University Press, 1956–). Volumes cited are as follows:

i: *Diaries, Prayers, and Annals*, ed. E. L. McAdam, Jr., with Donald and Mary Hyde (1958)

ii: *The Idler and The Adventurer*, ed. W. J. Bate, John M. Bullit, and L. F. Powell, 2nd edn. (1970)

iii–v: *The Rambler*, ed. W. J. Bate and Albrecht B. Strauss (1969)

vi: *Poems*, ed. E. L. McAdam, Jr., with George Milne (1964; repr. 1975)

vii–viii: *Johnson on Shakespeare*, ed. Arthur Sherbo (1969)

ix: *A Journey to the Western Islands of Scotland*, ed. Mary Lascelles (1971) x: *Political Writings*, ed. Donald J. Greene (1977)

xiv: *Sermons*, ed. Jean Hagstrum and James
    Gray (1978)

xvi: *Rasselas and Other Tales*, ed. Gwin J. Kolb (1990)

Quotations from *The Rambler, The Idler*, and *The
    Adventurer* are sourced by essay, volume, and
    page number (e.g. *Rambler* 198, *Yale*, iv. 160);
    other works by Yale volume number and page
    reference alone.

References to Pope: for ease of reference, citations are given by poetic
book, canto, epistle, or dialogue (where relevant) and line number (e.g.
The Rape of the Lock, I. 132; *Arbuthnot*, ll. 161–72). Unless otherwise
stated, references to *The Dunciad* are to the final 1743 text, the 'B' version
in Sutherland's edition.

The commerce between Man and his Maker cannot be carried on but by a process where much is represented in little, and the Infinite Being accommodates himself to a finite capacity.

(William Wordsworth)

'Sir,' said he, 'there is nothing too little for so little a creature as man. It is by studying little things that we attain the great knowledge of having as little misery and as much happiness as possible.'

(Samuel Johnson to James Boswell)

There are those ... who devote their lives to writing the Lord's Prayer in little.

(William Hazlitt)

Introduction

Bidding a gleeful adieu to constraint and propriety, Becky Sharp flings his dictionary out of a carriage window. Elizabeth Gaskell's Captain Brown (a Dickens man) abhors his harmonious triads. William Hazlitt found his style 'unmeaning' and 'artificial', lacking in 'discrimination', 'selection', and 'variety', its habitual abstraction resistant to 'the immediate impressions of things, for fear of compromising his dignity'. Owen Ruffhead complained of the remoteness of his 'tumid and pompous' expressions.[1] From his own day to ours, the standard caricature of Dr Johnson presents him as a generalizing, canon-building, language-fixing, neoclassical tyrant who had no time for detail or for inferiority. As the literary Colossus, Hercules, and Great Cham of his age, he must have dismissed those little, awkward things and people that impinge on the peripheries of a work of art, soliciting admission. Thus Terry Eagleton feels confident that 'Johnson thought ... the particular was tedious and the universal exciting', while Marilyn Butler claims that 'the view of literature' which emerges from his *Prefaces Biographical and Critical* (1779–81), or *Lives of the English Poets*, is that of 'a limited canon of great works written by exceptional individuals'.[2]

---

[1] William Thackeray, *Vanity Fair* (1847–8; Harmondsworth: Penguin, 1994), 6; Elizabeth Gaskell, *Cranford* (1853), ed. Elizabeth Porges Watson (Oxford: Oxford University Press, 1980), 8–10; William Hazlitt, *Lectures on the English Comic Writers* (1819), V: 'On the Periodical Essayists', and *Table-Talk* (1821–2), Essay XXIV: 'On Familiar Style', in *Complete Works*, vi. 102; viii. 243; Owen Ruffhead, 'The Prince of Abissinia. A Tale', *Monthly Review*, 20 (1759), 428–37 (p. 428).

[2] Terry Eagleton, *After Theory* (London: Allen Lane, 2003), 75; Marilyn Butler, 'Oxford's Eighteenth-Century Versions', *Eighteenth-Century Life*, 12 (1988), 128–36 (p. 131). Butler sees Wordsworth as 'denigrating the tradition of Dryden and Pope and its apologist Johnson, while clearly identifying a preferable alternative tradition in the nature-poet and Spenserian James Thomson'. *Romantics, Rebels and Reactionaries: English Literature and its Background, 1760–1830* (Oxford: Oxford University Press, 1981; repr. 1990), 57. Yet it was at Johnson's request that Thomson, in spite of being a Scot, was included in the *Lives of the English Poets* (*Letters*, iii. 20; *Lives*, iii. 281 n. 1), where he is singled out for 'the eye which Nature bestows only on a poet, the eye that distinguishes in every thing presented to its view whatever there is on which imagination can delight to be detained, and with a mind that at once comprehends the vast, and attends to the minute' (*Lives*, iii. 298–9). See also Chapter 4.

Such views tell only half the story of Johnson's authorial character. Clichés about the hauteur, exclusivity, and abstractness of his style have been challenged by recognition of its haphazard, associative qualities, and of its concrete attention to particulars.[3] My argument here is that, during a century exercised by social and literary hierarchies, catalogues, and taxonomies—specifically, by such complex marginalizing labels as 'little', 'mean', 'trifling', 'low', and 'dunce'—Johnson's works maintain a defining relationship to materials variously upbraided or prized as beneath their regard. That such a relationship involves committing himself to a series of contradictory positions is hardly surprising: 'imputed to man', as Imlac tells Rasselas, 'Inconsistencies ... may both be true' (*Yale*, xvi. 33). This book spends less time on the Johnson who, in Goldsmith's wary reformulation of Colley Cibber, 'when his pistol misses fire, ... knocks you down with the butt end of it' (*Life*, ii. 100) than it does on the Johnson who felt called upon to examine, and unable to decide between, two or more competing things: 'Such is the uncertainty, in which we are always likely to remain with regard to questions, wherein we have most interest, and which every day affords us fresh opportunity to examine: we may examine, indeed, but we never can decide, because our faculties are unequal to the subject: we see a little, and form an opinion; we see more, and change it' (*Adventurer* 107, *Yale*, ii. 444).

The four chapters of this book track the fluctuations of Johnson's uncertainty across his career. An admirer of Pope, he intensely disliked the derogatory conflation of private with public character, of poverty with artistic incompetence, which fuelled *Peri Bathous: or, Martinus Scriblerus, His Treatise of the Art of Sinking in Poetry* (1727) and *The Dunciad* (1728–43). A champion of poetic excellence, he was concerned to elevate the standing of unaccomplished versifiers—frequently on ethical rather than on literary grounds, thereby giving the lie to Pope's assertion that 'each *Ill Author* is as bad a *Friend*' (*An Essay on Criticism* (1711), l. 521). Famed for his weighty, universalizing style, and for ornamenting topics of permanent applicability, he repeatedly called for writers (himself included) to abase themselves to the grubby and transient necessities of

[3] On his elevation of low subjects and minutiae, see, for instance, Howard Erskine-Hill, 'Johnson and the Petty Particular', *Transactions of the Johnson Society of Lichfield* (1976), 40–7, and Isobel Grundy, *Samuel Johnson and the Scale of Greatness* (Leicester: Leicester University Press, 1986), 62–78. On his style as exploratory, incomplete, empirical, and loose, see, for instance, Paul Fussell, *Samuel Johnson and the Life of Writing* (London: Chatto & Windus, 1972), 35–61; Cyril Knoblauch, 'Samuel Johnson and the Composing Process', *Eighteenth-Century Studies*, 13 (1980), 243–62; Fred Parker, *Scepticism and Literature: An Essay on Pope, Hume, Sterne, and Johnson* (Oxford: Oxford University Press, 2003), 232–81.

everyday routine. I would like to claim for Johnson that principled variety of indecisiveness that Peter Robinson has discerned in Wordsworth, and Seamus Perry in Coleridge. Poetry, according to Robinson, 'may arise from the many circumstances in which no appropriate action is possible, when the desire to make reparation which remains is expressed through the activity ... of making poems'. This attempt to make reparation, which exemplifies 'the responsibility of art towards the world', involves 'a turning of attention out from the vicissitudes of the poet's inner life, to the complexity of life in nature, in a society, and in history'.[4] Coleridge's thought, Perry argues, is 'best understood, not as the solution to a *problem*, but as the experience and exploration of a *muddle* ... to experience or embrace an intellectual contradiction, while perhaps untidy and difficult, need not be simply disreputable'; indeed, in certain scenarios, '*not* to be in a muddle, *not* to be caught between irreconcilables, is the truly disreputable state'.[5]

In *Rambler* 66, Johnson finds himself in a reputable muddle when considering the responsibility of art towards the world. He speculates of Greek and Roman authors that 'It seemed, perhaps, below the dignity of the great masters of moral learning, to descend to familiar life', or to 'the passions of little minds, acting in low stations' (*Yale*, iii. 351). Although 'no man had a higher notion of the dignity of literature than Johnson' (*Life*, iii. 310), he swiftly ridicules the deficiencies of such elevation. 'The gratifications which affluence of wealth, extent of power, and eminence of reputation confer, must be always, by their own nature, confined to a very small number.' The contests of 'petty ambition' and of provincial domesticity, on the other hand, since they 'destroy private quiet and private virtue, and undermine insensibly the happiness of the world', were 'not unworthy of the longest beard, and most solemn austerity' (*Yale*, iii. 351; see also 'Life of Pope', *Lives*, iii. 234).

It should give a reader pause, however, that Johnson writes 'not unworthy' rather than 'worthy'. His litotes displays a tussling, continuing irresolution in the face of two rival claims. A double negative might, in some contexts, indicate a mere hedging of bets, but here it seems to derive from a genuine reservation about preferences. If something is 'not unworthy', we move from a 'worthy' that is not quite articulated to the 'unworthy' which is articulated, and then, because that is denied,

---

[4] Peter Robinson, *In the Circumstances: About Poems and Poets* (Oxford: Clarendon Press, 1992), 1, 9, 8.

[5] Seamus Perry, *Coleridge and the Uses of Division* (Oxford: Clarendon Press, 1999), 7, 9, 10.

back towards 'worthy' again. And there, in view of the waggish, beard-
stroking irreverence of 'the longest beard, and most solemn austerity', we
might be tempted to stop (the comic undercurrent of 'not unintoxicated'
lies in its strong implication of 'blind drunk'; 'not unworthy' could
similarly appear to be emphasizing, beneath the surface of tempering,
the 'worthy' aspect of what it describes). But we do not know at what
point to conclude the evaluative process, and nor does Johnson. Like
other negatives, only more so in this instance because the negative is
itself negated, his litotes reveals a specific cast of mind: one that restlessly
considers both sides of a question. Critical and persuasive by virtue of
its determined mobility, it invites us to balance two equally compelling
alternatives—common everyday life on the one hand, dignified classical
precedent on the other—in terms of how worthy or unworthy they might
be of literary representation. Mapped out on a larger scale, this essay's
energetic rebounding from antique heroism to daily existence, from the
glamorous solemnity of generalization to a bathetically tenacious real
world (and back again), is typical of Johnson—as is an unwillingness
to shoehorn the double-mindedness from which it derives into a single-
minded conclusion.

By rehearsing and testing the claims of great and little, dignified and
familiar subjects on his attention, Johnson weighed up the tenets of pagan
rhetoric,[6] criticism, and ethics that persisted into the eighteenth century
and beyond. Among the many projects left unaccomplished at his death
was a 'History of Criticism, as it relates to judging of authours, from
Aristotle to the present age. An account of the rise and improvements of
that art; of the different opinions of authours, ancient and modern' (*Life*,
iv. 381 n. 1). Such an account, rising from Greek and Roman originators
to Johnson's contemporaries, would necessarily have recognized that
ancient critics, like their eighteenth-century descendants (and in spite
of many differences of opinion among themselves and with each other),
approximate a consensus in their repeated emphases on decorum.

---

[6] By 'rhetoric' I mean the study of a particular discipline in the Greek and Roman
schools from the 5th century BC onwards, repeatedly modified and revived in Britain by the
time of the 18th century, whose goal is to persuade an audience of the speaker's argument
through the judicious choice and disposition of words and figures. Ancient theories of
style emerge from rhetorical handbooks, largely the work of teachers aiming to instruct
the fledgling practitioner, so that it is impossible to separate classical literary criticism
from its pragmatic contexts. The art of effective advocacy sprang from a litigious society:
it depended on the skill to convince listeners by a well-contrived attack, not by sincere
personal testimony or self-expression. For an overview, see Brian Vickers, *In Defence of
Rhetoric* (Oxford: Clarendon Press, 1988), 1–82.

This central rhetorical principle required that a subject and its expressive vehicle be aptly fitted one to another. Little topics called for a low or humble medium; great topics for a sublime or elevated manner. Laying the foundations of linguistic decorum, Aristotle argued that: 'Propriety of style will be obtained ... by proportion to the subject matter. Style is proportionate to the subject matter when neither weighty matters are treated offhand, nor trifling matters with dignity, and no embellishment is attached to an ordinary word.'[7] Cicero's hierarchical division of styles into a tripartite scheme of plain, tempered, and grand ('parva', 'modica', and 'magna') similarly insists that the orator strive for congruence between subject matter and expression. He considers it as discordant to narrate a commonplace transaction in the sublime manner as to demean a grand subject by phrasing it in workaday language. His ideal speaker will accordingly 'discuss commonplace matters simply, lofty subjects impressively, and topics ranging between in a tempered style'. Or, as he swiftly reformulates it: 'trivial matters in a plain style, matters of moderate significance in the tempered style, and weighty affairs in the grand manner.'[8] Cicero's *Orator* contains a straightforward demonstration of how important decorum was for antique writers, speakers, and thinkers:

In an oration, as in life, nothing is harder than to determine what is appropriate ... let us call it *decorum* or 'propriety.' Much brilliant work has been done in laying down rules about this; the subject is in fact worth mastering. From ignorance of this mistakes are made not only in life but very frequently in writing, both in poetry and in prose. Moreover the orator must have an eye to propriety not only in thought but in language. For the same style and the same thoughts must not be used in portraying every condition in life, or every rank, position or age, and in fact a similar distinction must be made in respect of place, time and audience. The universal rule, in oratory as in life, is to consider propriety. This depends on the subject under discussion, and on the character of both the speaker and the audience. The philosophers are accustomed to consider this extensive subject under the head of duties ...; the literary critics consider it in connexion with poetry; orators in dealing with every kind of speech, and in every

[7] Aristotle, *The 'Art' of Rhetoric*, trans. John Henry Freese (London: Heinemann, 1926; repr. 1947), III. vii. 1–2.
[8] Cicero, *Brutus and Orator*, trans. G. L. Hendrickson and H. M. Hubbell, rev. edn. (Cambridge, Mass.: Harvard University Press, 1939; repr. 1962), *Orator*, XX. 69–70; XXIX. 100–1. See also William Edinger, *Samuel Johnson and Detailed Representation: The Significance of the Classical Sources* (Victoria: English Literary Studies, University of Victoria, 1997), 15–72; Vickers, *In Defence of Rhetoric*, 80–2; D. A. Russell, *Criticism in Antiquity* (London: Duckworth, 1981), 137–9.

part thereof . . . the poet avoids impropriety as the greatest fault which he can commit. [9]

Another Latin treatise of this period, the anonymous *Ad Herennium*, provides its own examples of the three styles—the grand, the middle, and the simple ('Gravis', 'Mediocris', and 'Adtenuata' or 'extenuata')—and details the incongruities that result from clumsy attempts to deliver them.[10] For Dionysius of Halicarnassus, such a scheme did not preclude local variations within a performance couched in one prevailing tone: low, mean, and insignificant things, the 'minor happenings of everyday life' and 'commonplace, humble words', had their place in the sublime writings of Homer. Even this opinion, however, assumed an underlying gradation of subjects and a general symmetry between form and content: 'no word should be grander than the nature of the ideas.'[11]

Initially one of numerous stylistic virtues, decorum eventually became (as in Cicero's account) a governing concept for rhetoric as a whole. If ideas are appropriately embodied, arranged, and presented—according to the orator's character, occasion, and audience—it follows that speech will be persuasive, fulfilling the goal of all ancient rhetoric. Decorum, the overarching principle of aptness, thus invokes a wide range of social, linguistic, aesthetic, and ethical properties for classical and eighteenth-century authors and critics. Anthony Blackwall's limp *Introduction to the Classics* (1718), the sort of textbook survey Johnson might have encountered at school, typically emphasizes that the authority of pagan writers stems from their decorum and elevation. Homer is to be savoured for his 'Sublimity' and 'Propriety', Virgil for his 'Propriety and Sublimity', Herodotus and Livy for their 'complete Decorum', Xenophon for a style 'suitable to every Subject', Cicero for his 'proper Language', and the entire corpus of ancient literature for its 'beautiful Propriety of Language'.[12]

The purchase of ancient rhetorical theory on classical or eighteenth-century literary practice was not as commanding as such remarks might imply (Cicero's *Orator* describes an ideal of appropriate speaking, not a reality): the precepts of decorum, a stimulus to disagreement and to conformity, have always been honoured in the breach as well as in the

[9] Cicero, *Orator*, XX. 70–4.

[10] Anon., *Ad C. Herennium: De Ratione Dicendi (Rhetorica ad Herennium)*, trans. Harry Caplan (Cambridge, Mass.: Harvard University Press, 1954; repr. 1989), IV. viii. 11–xii. 18.

[11] Dionysius of Halicarnassus, *The Critical Essays*, trans. Stephen Usher, 2 vols. (Cambridge, Mass.: Harvard University Press, 1974–85), 'On Literary Composition', 3.

[12] Anthony Blackwall, *An Introduction to the Classics: Containing a Short Discourse on their Excellencies; and Directions how to Study them to Advantage*, 4th edn., with additions (London: for Charles Rivington, 1728), 13, 17, 23, 28–9, 30, 57.

observance. Classical notions about propriety and sublimity may have been codified on the basis of Homeric practice, but they could easily be turned against him. Criticisms of the absurdity or offensiveness of ancient epic run from the Greeks up to and beyond Pope, Homer's generally admiring translator, who confesses himself 'at a loss how to justify' *The Iliad*'s foul-mouthed, sluttish, and bloodthirsty divinities—including Juno, who calls Diana 'an *impudent Bitch*' before boxing her into a tearful pulp (*Iliad*, XXI. 566n.).[13]

The influence of decorum, and of its infractions, pervades countless spheres of eighteenth-century life. Hester Piozzi, reporting Johnson's advice on clothing and manners, observed that his 'demands of propriety' were 'rigorous': 'Learn (said he) that there is propriety or impropriety in every thing how slight soever, and get at the general principles of dress and of behaviour; if you then transgress them, you will at least know that they are not observed' (*Miscellanies*, i. 337–8). The point holds good for such literary transgressions of propriety as mock-heroic that exhibit an identifiable awareness of the rules they are flouting: the reader then knows 'at least . . . that they are not observed'. John Cleland's review of *The History of Pompey the Little; or, the Life and Adventures of a Lap-Dog* (1751) concluded that Francis Coventry's literary venture, improperly combining the dignity of history with the indignity of a lapdog, was an exception that proved a rule:

There are, to the great disgust of the public, too many productions of the press, beneath giving a character of: This one is, however, so far of a different kind, that it is not easy to do justice to the merit of it. The author, whose name is not to the work, takes for his subject, a *Bologna* lap-dog, brought from *Italy* to *England*, where he often changes masters, by several accidents, which furnish the writer with a handle to introduce a variety of characters and situations; all painted with great humour, fancy, and wit: and, indeed, he every where displays a perfect knowledge of the world, through all its ranks, and all its follies. These he ridicules, with a fineness of edge, unknown to the sour satyrist, or the recluse philosopher. Even his negligences are pleasing. The gentleman, in short, breaths throughout the whole performance, and the vein of pleasantry, which runs through it, is every where evenly upheld, from the beginning to the end . . . All his characters are natural. His language easy and genteel.[14]

[13] See Russell, *Criticism in Antiquity*, 18–19; Howard D. Weinbrot, *Britannia's Issue: The Rise of British Literature from Dryden to Ossian* (Cambridge: Cambridge University Press, 1993), 193–236, 296–328; Claude Rawson, 'Heroic Notes: Epic Idiom, Revision and the Mock-Footnote from the *Rape of the Lock* to the *Dunciad*', in Howard Erskine-Hill (ed.), *Proceedings of the British Academy*, 91: *Alexander Pope: World and Word* (Oxford: Oxford University Press for the British Academy, 1998), 69–110.

[14] *Monthly Review*, 4 (1751), 316–17.

Cleland's observation that there are 'many productions of the press, beneath giving a character of' might apply to the character of ungentle-manly authors as well as to the works they produce. Both are vulnerable to accusations that they are below literary and social attention. Yet Coventry's mock-heroic performance is thought to be unusually 'gen-teel', '*evenly* upheld' in spite of the flagrant inequality between style and subject on which it is founded. To lend cohesion to the indecorous, picaresque medley shows a redeeming literary and ethical orderliness that, in turn, reveals innate nobility. Shaftesbury's mingling of informal genres, homely idioms, and colloquial locutions with philosophical abstraction, weighty Latinisms, and studied periods in his *Characteristics of Men, Manners, Opinions, Times* (1711) implies a privileged capacity to move 'from the minutest ranks and orders of beings to the remotest spheres', from 'that common world of mixed and undistinguished company' to elevated reverie and solitude. Polished grammatical subordination conveys a social and literary vantage point over heterogeneous mate-rials—a gentleman's ability to govern and subdue life's promiscuous miscellany—hence the confidence with which Shaftesbury can employ and defend a variety of styles and subjects.[15] Cleland's claim that 'the gentleman *breaths throughout* the *whole* performance' suggests a similarly refined alertness to disorder: Coventry shows in every word he writes that he is aware of the legitimate rules he is affronting. His style has a dynamic relation to its topic, a reflex identifying function that Cle-land recognizes as a self-conscious infringing and restoring of decorum. Coventry's manner of disregarding propriety is really a commitment to observe it—not least because his *Pompey*, written in the third person, makes a firm distinction between its subhuman fictional protagonist and its knowing, superior author.

Johnson abided by a gentlemanly conception of rhetoric when he defined it in his *Dictionary* (1755) as 'The act of speaking not merely with propriety, but with art and elegance', and, secondarily, as 'The power of persuasion; oratory'.[16] By casting 'propriety' alone as insufficient to the act of speaking persuasively, he aligns himself with Aristotle's suggestion (to poets and orators) to spurn the merely 'prosaic' whenever possible, without violating clarity: 'The merit of diction is to be clear

[15] Anthony Ashley Cooper, third Earl of Shaftesbury, *Characteristics of Men, Manners, Opinions, Times*, ed. Lawrence Klein (Cambridge: Cambridge University Press, 1999; repr. 2001), 275, 249.

[16] See also Steven Lynn, 'Johnson's *Rambler* and Eighteenth-Century Rhetoric', *Eighteenth-Century Studies*, 19 (1986), 461–79, and Wilbur S. Howell, *Eighteenth-Century British Logic and Rhetoric* (Princeton: Princeton University Press, 1971), 259–98, 441–7.

and not commonplace.'[17] The ornamental and selective additions of 'art' and 'elegance' imply a habitual elevation of the speaker above his target audience.[18] On this view, it is not enough to employ a low style in accordance with the demands of particular, low occasions. Such occasions ought generally to be avoided, as inherently indecorous.

William Edinger distinguishes three complementary approaches at work within ancient views of decorum: lexical, rhetorical, and ontic. Lexical decorum censures words or descriptions that appear too mean for their occasion. Rhetorical decorum involves style as a whole, as it is affected by considerations of subject matter, audience, and speaker. Ontic decorum concerns itself with the inherent dignity or grandeur of whatever topic a speaker chooses to represent.[19] In practice, classical and eighteenth-century attacks on literary inappropriateness often combine, confuse, or make rapid transitions between these three categories. For Johnson and his immediate predecessors, the first-century critic known as Longinus was an especially influential commentator on the high style and its disruptions, since it was from his *Peri Hupsous,* or *On the Sublime*—as filtered through the French translation of 1674[20]—that John Dennis derived the principles outlined in *The Advancement and Reformation of Modern Poetry* (1701) and *The Grounds of Criticism in Poetry* (1704). It was also from *Peri Hupsous* that Pope (Dennis's bitter enemy) took the hint for a mock-handbook of stylistic abuses, *Peri Bathous,* a forerunner to *The Dunciad* that attacks many of the same authors. *Peri Hupsous,* which does not employ the tripartite stylistic scheme, at once pointedly and obscurely censures 'The use of trivial words' that seem 'beneath the dignity of the subject', 'paltry words' and those 'too colloquial . . . to be dignified', as well as excessively inclusive lists, in terms of their attenuating effects on sublimity: 'One ought not in elevated passages to have recourse to what is sordid and contemptible' (Longinus, *On the Sublime,* XLIII).

Eighteenth-century critics 'not only emulated this sensitivity, they made it a hallmark of good taste':[21] Johnson followed Longinus when

[17] *Aristotle: The Poetics, Longinus: On the Sublime, Demetrius: On Style,* trans. W. Hamilton Ffye and W. Rhys Roberts (Cambridge, Mass.: Harvard University Press, 1927; repr. 1991); Aristotle, *Poetics,* XXI. 22.

[18] See Russell, *Criticism in Antiquity,* 5.

[19] Edinger, *Samuel Johnson and Detailed Representation,* 27, 36, 51.

[20] See *Longinus, On the Sublime: The Peri Hupsous in Translations by Nicholas Boileau-Despréaux, 1674, and William Smith, 1739: Facsimile Reproductions,* introd. William Bruce Johnson (Delmar, NY: Scholars' Facsimiles & Reprints, 1975).

[21] Edinger, *Samuel Johnson and Detailed Representation,* 15.

he defined sense 4 of 'LOWNESS' in his *Dictionary* as 'Want of sublimity;
contrary to loftiness'. (W. K. Wimsatt observed that 'low' was 'perhaps
[Johnson's] most generic term of censure'.[22]) In the wake of Addison's
Spectator (1711–12, 1714) papers on Milton,[23] the recurrence of little, mean,
and degraded words became a focus of disapproval including Johnson's
in *Rambler* 168: 'every man, however profound or abstracted, perceives
himself irresistibly alienated by low terms . . . debased by vulgar mouths'
(*Yale*, v. 126–7). He repeated the last phrase over twenty years later in his
'Life of Cowley': 'the most splendid ideas drop their magnificence, if they
are conveyed by words used commonly upon low and trivial occasions,
debased by vulgar mouths, and contaminated by inelegant applications'
(*Lives*, i. 58–9).

But for 'splendid ideas' to 'drop their magnificence' was not necessarily a bad or undesirable thing. Noting Johnson's gruffly affectionate,
conversational use of the low word 'dog', William Empson concluded
that 'a great deal of the thought of a man like Dr. Johnson, and probably the parts of his thought which are by this time most seriously and
rightly admired, were not carried on his official verbal machinery but on
colloquial phrases . . . that he would have refused to analyse on grounds
of dignity, even if he had been able to'.[24] Hazlitt, too, thought 'Johnson's
colloquial style was as blunt, direct, and downright, as his style of studied
composition was involved and circuitous' (*Complete Works*, vi. 103). It
does retain the capacity to pull a reader up short that the man who,
in *Rambler* 133, sonorously lamented 'gloomy privation, or impotent
desire', when 'the faculties of anticipation slumber in despondency, or
the powers of pleasure mutiny for employment' (*Yale*, iv. 342), baldly
rephrased the point by asserting (reputedly) that 'the greatest pleasure'
in life was 'fucking'—closely followed by 'drinking': 'And therefore he
wondered why there were not more drunkards, for all could drink tho'
all could not fuck.'[25]

---

[22] W. K. Wimsatt, Jr., *The Prose Style of Samuel Johnson* (New Haven: Yale University
Press, 1941; repr. 1963), 104.

[23] See especially *Spectator* 285, iii. 10–11.

[24] William Empson, *The Structure of Complex Words* (1951; Harmondsworth: Penguin,
1995), 174.

[25] Norman Page (ed.), *Dr Johnson: Interviews and Recollections*, (Totowa, NJ: Barnes
& Noble, 1987), 86 and *Boswell: The Ominous Years, 1774–1776*, ed. Charles Ryskamp and
Frederick A. Pottle (London: Heinemann, 1963), 114 and n. 3. Pottle and Ryskamp plead
that Arthur Murphy, from whom this anecdote derives (via David Garrick), is an unreliable
witness (p. 114 n. 3). But there is no reason to think him less accurate than, say, Hester
Piozzi. In Scotland, Johnson told Boswell that 'nobody talks more laxly than I do' (*Tour*,
350). Speaking to Captain McLean, he said, ' "How *the devil* can you do it?" but instantly

'What words to come from the great moralist and lexicographer!' (Hazlitt, *Complete Works*, vi. 103). Some of Johnson's contemporaries, however, were alive to the potential reciprocity between a periphrastic, intellectually 'circuitous' style of writing and its 'blunt, direct, and downright' physical origins. In 1767, Archibald Campbell parodied *Rambler* 133, which narrates 'The condition of a young woman who has never thought or heard of any other excellence than beauty' (*Yale*, iv. 342), by dramatizing it as Johnson's hapless encounter with a prostitute: 'Perdita eagerly co-operated to ripen barren volition into efficacy and power. But alas! such helpless destitution, such dismal inanity, such gloomy privation, such impotent desire! the faculties of anticipation slumbered in despondency, but the powers of pleasure mutinied not for employment; and vain were all her fascinating charms, and equally vain all my artificial stimulations to effectuate a proper and adequate reciprocation of civilities.'[26]

In writing, as in conversation, Johnson frequently set 'official verbal machinery' against 'colloquial phrases', thereby deliberately confronting high ideas with 'inelegant applications' to common life. His *Dictionary* citation from Roger L'Estrange under 'PROPRIETRESS' stands out for its coarseness, as well as for its Empsonian reference to dogs. Illustrating the brute fact of contested ownership in the real world comically outweighs the implied association of 'PROPRIETRESS' ('A female possessor in her own right; a mistress') with linguistic propriety: 'A big-bellied bitch borrowed another bitch's kennel to lay her burthen in; the *proprietress* demanded possession, but the other begged her excuse.' 'Begged her excuse', like '*proprietress*', retrospectively overlays L'Estrange's crude fabular scenario with a veneer of deference—dogs cannot speak, although they can beg—and at the same time unmasks the brutish origins of human civility. The first part of Johnson's definition, 'A female possessor in her own right', similarly refuses to distinguish between animals and people. What might strike us as a comparatively unobtrusive term in L'Estrange—'big'—was seen in the eighteenth century as a low word, one for which Boswell was attacked when he quoted Johnson as saying 'I wish thy books were twice as big'. As Boswell noted in his own

corrected himself, "How can you do it?"—I never before heard him use a phrase of that nature' (*Life*, v. 306; this section of Boswell's *Tour* is missing in MS).

[26] [Archibald Campbell], *Lexiphanes, a Dialogue. Imitated from Lucian, and suited to the Present Times. Being an Attempt to restore the English Tongue to its Ancient Purity, and to correct, as well as to expose, the affected Style, hard Words, and absurd Phraseology of many late Writers, and particularly of our English Lexiphanes, The Rambler*, 2nd edn., corrected (London: for J. Knox, 1767), 70.

defence, however, his friend 'often used' it in conversation (*Tour*, 293; *Life*, iii. 348; app. C, v. 425). In slang terms, 'a big-bellied bitch' could be 'A name of reproach' ('BITCH', sense 2, Johnson's *Dictionary*) for a fallen, pregnant woman, so that the sense in which a proprietress is also a 'mistress' begins to sound morally suspect; a 'kennel' is not only a doghouse, but also the urban sewer, or 'water-course of a street' (sense 4 of 'KENNEL' in Johnson's *Dictionary*). This wilfully indecorous splicing of an apparently neutral definition with its squalid practical application resembles, in modified form, the collapse from expectations of sublimity to the '*impudent Bitch*' Pope was dismayed to find in *The Iliad*. While Homer's gods are reduced to men and women, in the *Dictionary* human beings are sometimes degraded to the level of beasts.

Mrs Digby and Frances Brooke may have congratulated Johnson on 'the omission of all *naughty* words' from his *Dictionary*—to which 'the moralist' replied: 'What, my dears! then you have been looking for them?' (*Miscellanies*, ii. 390). But they must have been broad-minded readers, or in search of something especially naughty, to count as acceptable the words 'ARSE', '*To hang an* ARSE' ('A vulgar phrase, signifying to be tardy, sluggish, or dilatory'), 'BAWD', 'BITCH', 'BORDEL', 'BUBBY' ('A woman's breast'), 'BUM', 'BUMBAILIFF', 'CLAP' ('A venereal infection', sense 5), 'DUG' ('A pap; a nipple; a teat: spoken of beasts, or in malice or contempt of human beings'), 'FART' (exemplified by John Suckling: 'Love is the *fart* | Of every heart; | It pains a man when 'tis kept close; | And others doth offend, when 'tis let loose'), 'FUNK' ('A stink'), 'HARLOT', 'ITCH' ('A cutaneous disease extremely contagious', sense 1), 'ITCHY' ('Infected with the itch'), 'LECHER' ('A whoremaster'), 'LEWDSTER', 'MUCKSWEAT' ('Profuse sweat'), 'PIMP', 'PISS', 'PISSBURNT', 'PRIAPISM', 'POX' ('The venereal disease', sense 2), 'PUKE', 'PUNK' ('A whore; a common prostitute; a strumpet'), 'STEW' ('A brothel; a house of prostitution', sense 2), 'RUT', 'RUTTISH', 'SATYRIASIS', 'SCRUB' ('A mean fellow, either as he is supposed to scrub himself for the itch, or as he is employed in the mean offices of scouring away dirt', sense 1), 'STINKPOT', 'STRUMPET', 'TROLLOP', 'TURD', 'WHORE', 'WHOREMASTER', 'WHOREMONGER', and 'WHORESON' ('HUSSY' and 'SLUT' indicate only 'slight disapprobation' or 'slight contempt').

Beginning his putative critical survey with Aristotle, Johnson was singling out an author distinguished for the range and depth of his moral and psychological enquiries, for an 'ability to get at essentials, to discover the determining factors or actual modes of operation in human life'. It is not surprising that, having thus described Aristotle, Brian

Vickers's thoughts turn naturally to Johnson, who praised Bacon's *Essays* (1601) in terms equally applicable to his own works: as 'the observations of a strong mind operating upon life'.[27] Johnson remarked that 'Books without the knowledge of life are useless'—'for what should books teach but the art of *living*?' (*Miscellanies*, i. 324). His *Dictionary* definition of 'DECORUM' therefore speaks primarily to the realm of action, not to that of writing: 'Decency; behaviour contrary to licentiousness; contrary to levity; seemliness.' In so doing, it conforms with the silent reference from aesthetic to moral sensibility that crops up throughout Greek and Roman writing.[28] But it also raises a potential challenge to the ethical probity of 'the great masters of moral learning', and therefore to the rules of decorum as laid down by 'despotick antiquity' (*Rambler* 156, *Yale*, v. 67).

Empson highlights the nature of that potential challenge to antiquity, and the divided thinking behind Johnson's attitudes to low, humble words and occasions. In *Seven Types of Ambiguity*, he summarizes Thomas Gray in terms that hold equally true of Johnson (whom Empson is also discussing at this point): 'after all he was a Christian trained in Pagan literature; he is playing off against one another . . . two different standards of morality.'[29] As with Johnson's definitions of 'PROPRIETRESS' and 'DECORUM', which gesture towards behaviour in the real world and not towards the seemly conduct of writing, there is something more at stake in comparing these 'two different standards of morality' than 'playing off' might imply. The pagan ethical tradition elided moral excellence with worldly success: what *Rambler* 66 sums up as 'affluence of wealth, extent of power, and eminence of reputation'. Romans employed the same term—'honestas'—for both.[30] When Cicero associates 'propriety' with 'rank' and 'duties' in the *Orator*, he invokes the performance of distinct public roles within a social hierarchy (Johnson is thinking of the same kind of appropriateness when he includes the phrase 'suitable to a character' in his *Dictionary* definition of 'DECOROUS', although his citation from John Ray immediately refers this to what is '*decorous*, in respect of God').

Antique decorum governs the relationship between, say, a speaker and his audience, or between a patron and his client—according to which the donor preserves the power and dignity of his official 'character'

[27] Vickers, *In Defence of Rhetoric*, 22, 24; *Miscellanies*, ii. 229.
[28] See Russell, *Criticism in Antiquity*, 1–33.
[29] William Empson, *Seven Types of Ambiguity* (1930; London: Hogarth Press, 1991), 122–3.
[30] See Tom Holland, *Rubicon: The Triumph and Tragedy of the Roman Republic* (London: Little, Brown, 2003), 5–6.

as he gracefully unbends towards the inferior objects of his regard, while the client is expected humbly to acknowledge whatever favours the patron might bestow, thereby reinforcing the division between the two figures. In *Idler* 4, Johnson duly criticized the 'beneficence' of the Roman emperors as 'occasional' and uncharitable: 'these distributions were always reckoned rather popular than virtuous: nothing more was intended than an ostentation of liberality, nor was any recompence expected, but suffrages and acclamation'; 'no man thought it either necessary or wise to make any standing provision for the needy, to look forwards to the wants of posterity, or to secure successions of charity'; 'Those antient nations who have given us the wisest models of government, and the brightest examples of patriotism ... have yet left behind them no mention of alms-houses or hospitals, of places where age might repose, or sickness be relieved' (*Yale*, ii. 13). A staged, public, Roman decorum (like its stylistic equivalent) stems from a rigid separation of dignity from meanness, of the high from the low. It is bound up with a heathen ethic of continual striving for glory, greatness, and the recognition of one's social peers—and with a corresponding contempt for servility, failure, and the plebs.[31] Gibbon has in mind this ethic, as well as Cicero's idea of the 'duties' that belong to the preservation of social status, when he mildly censures Marcus Aurelius Antoninus' lapse from 'the dignity of an emperor': 'he even condescended to give lessons of philosophy.'[32]

Pope followed Longinus when he upbraided Homer for having 'sunk' the characters of his gods 'down to Men' (*Iliad*, XXI. 566n.).[33] New Testament writers, however, repeatedly celebrate the spectacle of Christ's exemplary condescension, or 'drop' from 'magnificence', in precisely these terms: '[He] made himself of no reputation, and took upon him the form of a servant, and was made in the likeness of men' (Philippians 2: 7). His incarnation, suffering, and passion, his 'vulgar' and 'inelegant' manner of teaching the most sublime truths, set a simultaneously unique and imitable example of descent to the humanly little: 'Mind not high things, but condescend to men of low estate' (Romans 12: 16). A sense of this moral imperative leads Johnson to adopt a charitable approach to some of the low and poverty-stricken targets of Pope's satirical

---

[31] See John Casey, *Pagan Virtue: An Essay in Ethics* (Oxford: Clarendon Press, 1990), pp. v–ix, 199–210; Grundy, *Samuel Johnson and the Scale of Greatness*, 176–232.

[32] Edward Gibbon, *The History of the Decline and Fall of the Roman Empire* (1776–88), ed. David Womersley, 3 vols. (Harmondsworth: Penguin, 1995), i. 102.

[33] 'Homer has done his best to make the men in the *Iliad* gods and the gods men.' Longinus, *On the Sublime*, IX. 7.

condescension in the *Art of Sinking in Poetry* and *The Dunciad*. On Roman terms, humility inheres in the public show of deference towards a social superior, or in the rhetorical performance of modesty that is designed to win over an audience and has nothing to do with the orator's private feelings. On Christian terms, however, humble behaviour towards our fellow human beings should derive from the conviction that we share finite, creaturely, and dependent natures beneath an all-seeing deity. As Isaac Watts put it: 'Indeed there is no Possibility of lessening our selves comparably to the Self-abasement of the Son of God; and yet the nearer we are like him the more shall we partake of the Father's Love, and we shall be in the Way of Divine Advancement, in a humble Imitation of the Advancement of Christ himself'; 'Never was any Religion founded in so much Humility as that of the Gospel'; 'As Humility towards God is a necessary Qualification of every Christian, so humble Thoughts of our Selves in Regard of our fellow-Creatures belong to the Profession and Character of this Gospel' (*Humility*, 21–3).

From the vantage point of ancient decorum, such a deliberate compound of divinity with self-abasement, of the high with the low, represents a shockingly inappropriate and therefore comic degradation. *Peri Bathous* sarcastically enquires: 'Will not every true Lover of the *Profound* be delighted to behold the most vulgar and low Actions of life exalted in this manner?' (Pope, *Prose*, 201). Yet there is, on Christian terms, no definitively mean subject: 'in the Christian context humble everyday things . . . lose their baseness and become compatible with the lofty style', while, conversely, 'the highest mysteries of the faith may be set forth in the simple words of the lowly style which everyone can understand'.[34] Erich Auerbach's analyses of commonplace people and things in the Gospels thus explain Christian descent to everyday life as compatible with the greatest dignity of style, its loftiest truths as reconcilable with humble expressions. Peter's repeated denial of Christ, one of many quotidian occurrences populated with low and mean characters, gains for New Testament authors the importance of an epoch-making event (see Matthew 26: 34–75; Mark 14: 30–72; Luke 22: 34–62; John 13: 38, 18: 25–7). They will, here as elsewhere, necessarily reject the classical assumption that each category of subject possesses or requires a corresponding level of style: 'the rule of differentiated styles cannot possibly apply in this case. The incident, entirely realistic both in regard to locale and *dramatis personae*—note particularly their

[34] Erich Auerbach, *Literary Language and its Public in Late Latin Antiquity and in the Middle Ages*, trans. Ralph Mannheim (London: Routledge & Kegan Paul, 1965), 37.

low social station—is replete with problem and tragedy.' The Gospels' 'mingling of styles', or 'to and fro of the pendulum', Auerbach argued, 'was graphically and harshly demonstrated through God's incarnation in a human being of the humblest social station, through his existence on earth amid humble everyday people and conditions, and through his Passion which, judged by earthly standards, was ignominious'. And the events leading up to Peter's denial portray 'something which neither the poets nor the historians of antiquity ever set out to portray: the birth of a spiritual movement in the depths of the common people, from within the everyday occurrences of contemporary life, which thus assumes an importance it could never have assumed in antique literature'.[35]

Since the Christian message permeated everything in life, there could be no established hierarchy of themes, such as classical rhetorical theory required. It is characteristic of Johnson that he should capture with fine economy the division between Christian and classical perspectives on lowness of style, behaviour, or station in his *Dictionary* definitions of the adverb 'LOWLILY': '1. Humbly; without pride'; '2. Meanly; without dignity.' The order of priorities (1. Christian: praiseworthy. 2. Pagan: farcical/reprehensible) is reversed in the definitions he provides for the apparently synonymous adverb 'LOWLY', displaying a fundamentally mixed reaction: '1. Not highly; meanly; without grandeur; without dignity'; '2. Humbly; meekly; modestly.' As Isobel Grundy has shown, Johnson retained throughout his life an attraction to the antique ideals of success, grandeur, heroism, and greatness, matched by a powerful sense of the Christian necessity to stoop to the poor, the mean, and the lowly.[36] By staging Johnson's 'dismal apprehensions' of divine wrath in the Roman arena, Boswell rightly saw his friend's mind as a theatre of pagan ambition and as a theatre of Christian self-renunciation: 'His mind resembled the vast amphitheatre, the Colisæum at Rome. In the centre stood his judgement, which, like a mighty gladiator, combated those apprehensions that, like the wild beasts of the *Arena*, were all around in cells, ready to be let out upon him. After a conflict, he drove them back into their dens; but not killing them, they were still assailing him' (*Life*, ii. 106).

This book dwells on such collisions and occasional reconciliations between two different scales of moral and aesthetic values, as they evolve from the year of Johnson's birth and the inception of *The Tatler*

---

[35] Erich Auerbach, *Mimesis: The Representation of Reality in Western Culture*, trans. Willard R. Trask, 10th edn. (Princeton: Princeton University Press, 1991), 41–3.

[36] Grundy, *Samuel Johnson and the Scale of Greatness*, 62–78, 176–232.

(1709–11) to the publication of Boswell's *Life of Johnson* (1791). Chapter 1 examines some of the difficulties Boswell encountered in commemorating Johnson's littleness as well as his greatness. It sees in his *Life* a combination of classically allusive, heroic diction with low, trifling subjects (such as Johnson's hoard of orange peels, or his abortive endeavour to learn how to knit): a combination that might be cast as a prose version of Pope's *Rape of the Lock* (1712–17). This chapter also considers the ambiguously inclusive and exclusive aspects of Pope's attitude to his dunces; the ways in which literary taxonomies may alert us to what they have left out, as well as to what they have accommodated; how Johnson's *Vanity of Human Wishes* (1749), as a catalogue poem, sets particularity against generalization; and, finally, the uses of recognizing our own littleness. Chapter 2 concentrates on Johnson's prefaces and dedications, especially those contributed anonymously to other people's works, as forms of writing in which humility is at a premium. A dextrous vocabulary of mock-humility recurs throughout the eighteenth century as a means of simultaneously obeying and resisting the call to descend to everyday things, particularly in the context of journalistic writing (although the *Dictionary*'s renovation of low, inconsiderable, and beggarly objects or people also comes into play here). Johnson's early journalism is read alongside that of his predecessors, Addison and Steele, whose *Tatler* and *Spectator* papers set an example of how to familiarize heroic grandeur to private life—an example to which Johnson responded throughout his career.

Chapter 3 traces his pursuit of domestic particulars in *A Journey to the Western Islands of Scotland* (1775), and the challenges they pose to the dignity of his style. It examines 'little' as a complex word which unites the impulses to elevate and to depreciate the low detail or character; Johnson's use of the terms 'elegance' and 'inelegance' as an index of the Scots' advance towards English standards of civility (one proof of such an advance being the capacity to attend to little things); and his employment in the *Journey* and in the *Life of Savage* (1744) of litotes, one instance of which has already been discussed, in order to suspend before the reader his scrupulous indecision about the gains and losses of social and intellectual progress. Chapter 4 interprets some of Johnson's *Lives of the Poets* as non-satirical, corrective responses to Pope's *Peri Bathous* and *The Dunciad*: Richard Blackmore, for instance, 'Father of the *Bathos*' and loudest of the braying dunces (Pope, *Prose*, 180; *Dunciad*, II. 268), gains a moral advantage over the author who had ridiculed him. This chapter also elicits the competing senses of eighteenth-century

'condescension' as a good and as a bad quality, dependent on whether
the writer has Christian or classical precedents in mind. It attempts to
tease out the motives behind Johnson's solicitous reactions to Blackmore
and to Watts, and concludes by discussing his commemoration of a
semi-literate, indigent physician, 'On the Death of Dr. Robert Levet'
(1783): an example of his distinctive art of sinking.

The self-styled 'new Augustan age'[37] in which Johnson began his
career saw authors espousing, combating, and attempting to reconcile
contrary influences, producing forms of writing that responded to the
prescriptions of ancient decorum and to what most of them viewed as
the ethically superior claims of Christianity. (Blackwall himself, keen
promoter of ancient sublimity, ranked the classics well below the Psalms,
which 'raise the soul to the highest heavens; and are infinitely more
marvellous and transporting than the noblest and most happy flights
of Pindar and Horace'.)[38] That 'new Augustan age' was and is often
presented as relentlessly ascending towards a peak of social and aesthetic
refinement, a second Rome.[39] But there is nothing unique to the eighteenth century about such myths of perfectibility, nor did contemporary
ideas of progress necessarily derive from the example of the ancients.
Howard Weinbrot's *Britannia's Issue*, the amplest study to date of a
recurrent contempt as well as a reverence for the classics throughout this
period, suggests 'an uncertain, indeed slovenly "progress" ' founded on
'necessary departures from' as well as on 'continuity with' ancient precedent.[40] Norbert Elias remarked that the terms 'civilized' and 'uncivilized'
represent 'stages in a development which . . . is still continuing. It might
well happen that our stage of civilization, our behavior, will arouse in our
descendants feelings of embarrassment similar to those we sometimes
feel concerning the behavior of our ancestors.' The 'civilizing process',
he argued, is characterized by the manner in which those who describe

[37] 'Th'approaching times my raptur'd thought engage: | I see arise a new Augustan age',
Leonard Welsted, *An Epistle to his Grace the Duke of Chandos* (1720), ll. 43–4, in *The Works,
in Verse and Prose, of Leonard Welsted, Esq*, ed. John Nichols (London: for the editor,
1787). 'Produce your Labours on the public Stage, | And she [Queen Caroline] shall raise a
new *Augustan* Age', Stephen Duck, 'Upon Her Majesty's Bounty to the Thresher' (1730),
ll. 27–8, in *Poems on Several Occasions* (London: for the author, 1736).
[38] Anthony Blackwall, *The Sacred Classics Defended and Illustrated: Or, An Essay humbly
offer'd towards proving the Purity, Prosperity, and true Eloquence of the Writers of the
New-Testament* (London: for C. Rivington and W. Cantrell, 1725), 4.
[39] See, for instance, David Spadafora, *The Idea of Progress in Eighteenth-Century Britain*
(New Haven: Yale University Press, 1990).
[40] Weinbrot, *Britannia's Issue*, 10, 76.

it 'include certain areas and exclude others as a matter of course, the hidden evaluations which they implicitly bring with them'.[41]

All human works, necessarily partial and finite, are informed by what they leave out. But T. S. Eliot thought there was 'reason for feeling that too much was excluded' in 'the English eighteenth century'.[42] This book tries to bring about a critical shift from examining what literature of this period excludes to consider its modes of including recalcitrant material. The two issues are not entirely separate, for both touch on matters of allusion, rejection, condescension, and abjection. Eighteenth-century treatments of literary, moral, social, and intellectual hierarchies reveal an allegiance uncertainly divided between pagan and Christian tradition—although such uncertainty or division does not characterize this century alone. Much of the writing I discuss might be said to arrive at an embattled compromise between including and excluding low or mean things, permitting the author to grant attention and importance to a little subject at the same time as formally dismissing it. Johnson's style is often interpreted as disconcertingly studied, polished, and enclosed, yet his works demonstrate a consciousness not of their own finitude but of the infinity of the world from which they select and abstract, prompting a deliberate inconclusiveness. Often worrying at the ethical and literary nub of inclusion, Johnson's commanding stature in the period makes such inconclusiveness about social, linguistic, and aesthetic boundaries especially fertile and influential.

Donald Davie's study of late eighteenth-century poets, *Purity of Diction in English Verse*, was triggered by what he perceived as a series of rejections and selections occurring at the 'disputed margin' of their compositions: 'there are poets, I find, with whom I feel . . . that a selection has been made and is continually being made, that words are thrusting at the poem and being fended off from it, that however many poems these poets wrote certain words would never be allowed into the poems, except as a disastrous oversight.'[43] The experience of certain words and occasions thrusting at, and being fended off from writing lies at the heart of a literary culture informed by antagonistic conceptions of the professional author's role, character, and status. Should he or she be elegantly selective or inelegantly inclusive, above or beneath his or her

---

[41] Norbert Elias, *The Civilizing Process: The History of Manners and State Formation and Civilization* (1939), trans. Edmund Jephcott (Oxford: Blackwell, 1994), 47, 4.

[42] T. S. Eliot, 'What is a Classic?' (1945), in *Selected Prose of T. S. Eliot*, ed. Frank Kermode (London: Faber and Faber, 1975), 115–31 (p. 121).

[43] Donald Davie, *Purity of Diction in English Verse and Articulate Energy* (1952, 1955; London: Penguin Books, 1992), 11, 6.

audience, rhetorically aloof from or sincerely committed to a topic, concerned with the high or with the low? Pondering the likely reception of his edition of Shakespeare, its immersion in minutiae confined to the printed margins of the text, Johnson handsomely conceded that:

The greater part of readers, instead of blaming us for passing trifles, will wonder that on mere trifles so much labour is expended, with such importance of debate, and such solemnity of diction. To these I answer with confidence, that they are judging of an art which they do not understand; yet cannot much reproach them with their ignorance, nor promise that they would become in general, by learning criticism, more useful, happier or wiser. (*Yale*, vii. 107–8)

Elevating and diminishing his efforts, he portrays his concern for textual detail in two conflicting ways: grandly, and in terms of his higher comprehension of the art, then wryly, and with a salutary shrug of the shoulders, in terms of its remoteness from common experience. Intellectually superior readers might repudiate any association with trifles, but the bulk even of literate humanity is more likely to be baffled by the sheer laborious irrelevance of editing. The public appears as a single body, not as a dispersed multitude, opposing the capricious plurality of editorial quibbles. Johnson reveals a sharp consciousness of the tendency of his own stylistic 'importance' and 'solemnity' to enlarge minutiae. The goal of persuasion yields to the comically mournful, pragmatic, and generous admission that criticism may not turn out to be especially helpful to real life. He translates his potential rebuke into the potential for self-reproach, broadening his field of enquiry and deliberately unsettling his editorial confidence. He thereby reinforces our faith in his character as a man of the world, not as a man of letters. The adversative but non-adversarial 'yet' turns outwards and upwards from the minute adjustments of textual emendation to the general claims of the common reader in everyday life: as if to say that we are perpetually moralists, but we are critics only by chance.[44]

---

[44] Johnson wrote that 'we are perpetually moralists, but we are geometricians only by chance' ('Life of Milton', *Lives*, i. 100).

1
Inclusion and Exclusion

On April Fool's Day, 1775, James Boswell—the biographer whose name was to become 'a byword for a fool'[1]—finally dared to investigate the orange peels that Johnson was known to conceal in his pockets:

I saw on his table the spoils of the preceding night, some fresh peels nicely scraped and cut into pieces. 'O, Sir, (said I,) I now partly see what you do with the squeezed oranges which you put into your pocket at the Club.' JOHNSON. 'I have a great love for them.' BOSWELL. 'And pray, Sir, what do you do with them? You scrape them, it seems, very neatly, and what next?' JOHNSON. 'I let them dry, Sir.' BOSWELL. 'And what next?' JOHNSON. 'Nay, Sir, you shall know their fate no further.' BOSWELL. 'Then the world must be left in the dark. It must be said (assuming a mock solemnity,) he scraped them, and let them dry, but what he did with them next, he never could be prevailed upon to tell.' JOHNSON. 'Nay, Sir, you should say it more emphatically:—he could not be prevailed upon, even by his dearest friends, to tell.' (*Life*, ii. 330–1)[2]

The tone of 'mock solemnity', which Boswell's stage direction tells us he adopted once Johnson had (eventually) declined to enlighten him, informs his retrospective account of this exchange in its entirety. Indeed, Fanny Burney noticed Boswell's 'odd mock solemnity of tone and manner' four years after the incident and thought it not assumed at will, but 'acquired imperceptibly from constantly thinking of and imitating Dr. Johnson'.[3] (In Scotland, Boswell wrote that 'I find myself insensibly acquiring some of Mr. Johnson's expressions, such as beginning a sentence with "Why sir." . . . I have even learnt a more curious expression, which is to resume a subject with "No, sir," though there is no negation in the case', *Tour*, 292.) Entering on his perilous mission, the young

---

[1] Adam Sisman, *Boswell's Presumptuous Task* (London: Hamish Hamilton, 2000), 'Introduction', p. xxii.

[2] For the draft version of this scene, see *James Boswell's Life of Johnson: An Edition of the Original Manuscript*, 4 vols. (Edinburgh: Edinburgh University Press, 1994–   ), ii: *1766–1776*, ed. Bruce Redford with Elizabeth Goldring (1998), 144.

[3] *Dr Johnson & Fanny Burney: Extracts from Fanny Burney's Prose 1777–84*, ed. Nigel Wood (Bristol: Bristol Classical Press, 1989), 113.

detective gravely clocks, in mock-heroic vein, 'the spoils of the preceding night'—perhaps recalling Swift's 'Behold the Ruins of the Night!' or Pope's 'glitt'ring' domestic 'Spoil', which derives in its turn from Dryden's *Aeneis* (1697).[4] It is unlikely, however, that Boswell had any particular example in mind. 'Spoils' was at the forefront of a mobile linguistic armoury of comic and grave classical allusion throughout the eighteenth century; Pope has sixty examples of the noun, thirty-eight of which occur in his *Iliad* (1715–20) and seventeen in his contributions to *The Odyssey* (1725–6).[5] The word is hospitable, on the one hand, to the lurid expanses of martial hyperbole (the scraped peels are spoils of war that Boswell determines to apprehend, against their owner's will and for the public good, in all their hinting significance). On the other, it appeals to the fastidiously confined domain of a literary connoisseur; the *Oxford English Dictionary* traces this sense of 'spoils' back to Gray: 'That which is or has been acquired by special effort or endeavour; esp. objects of art, books, etc., collected in this way. Sometimes with slight suggestion of the primitive sense' (see 'spoil', senses 1 a.–c.).

Johnson's biographers, rehearsing their efforts at commemoration, frequently invoked the warlike or dilettantish associations of culling precious literary spoils. Boswell noted his own tendency to 'pick up fragments' and soon thought of himself as 'a kind of virtuoso. When I espied any singular character I would say, "It must be added to my collection." '[6] He did not rest content with fragments. His life's work, the title page proclaimed, would exhibit 'A VIEW OF LITERATURE AND LITERARY MEN IN GREAT-BRITAIN, FOR NEAR HALF A CENTURY'. Johnson himself would 'be seen in this work more completely than any man who has ever yet lived' (*Life*, i. 30). Hester Piozzi, unhampered by such a task, thought that 'we who produce each a score of his sayings, as proofs of that wit which in him was inexhaustible, resemble travellers who having visited Delhi or Golconda, bring home each a handful of Oriental pearl to evince the riches of the Great Mogul'. Her fragmentary *Anecdotes of the late Samuel Johnson* (1786) might be a 'despicable . . . specimen of Johnson's character', yet she surmises with the leisured equanimity of an amateur

---

[4] *The Poems of Jonathan Swift*, ed. Harold Williams, 3 vols., 2nd edn. (Oxford: Clarendon Press, 1958), II, 'A Beautiful Young Nymph Going to Bed' (1731), l. 68; Pope, *The Rape of the Lock*, I. 132 and n.

[5] See Emmett G. Bedford and Robert J. Dilligan, *A Concordance to the Poems of Alexander Pope*, 2 vols. (Detroit: Gale Research Company, 1974).

[6] *Boswell: The Ominous Years*, 203; *Boswell on the Grand Tour: Germany and Switzerland, 1764*, ed. Frederick A. Pottle (London: Heinemann, 1953), 263.

collector that 'every body naturally likes to gather little specimens of the rarities found in a great country' (*Miscellanies*, i, 346, 308–9). During the Scottish tour, Johnson told her that he had been 'claimed by a Naturalist, who wanders about the Islands to pick up curiosities' (*Letters*, ii, 72). But vestiges of the *OED*'s 'primitive sense' remain strong in Boswell's 'spoils', in order to underline (only half-jokingly) the heroic 'effort or endeavour' involved in his strenuous gleaning of materials for the *Life*, a point made plain by the 'Advertisement' to the first edition:

I must be allowed to suggest, that the nature of the work, ... as it consists of innumerable detached particulars, all which, even the most minute, I have spared no pains to ascertain with a scrupulous authenticity, has occasioned a degree of trouble far beyond that of any other species of composition. Were I to detail the books which I have consulted, and the inquiries which I have found it necessary to make by various channels, I should probably be thought ridiculously ostentatious. (Life, i. 6–7)

Boswell audibly struggles with irritation as well as with fatigue. The biographer '*must be allowed to suggest*', in general terms at least, the pains which it would '*probably be thought ridiculously ostentatious*' to enumerate. The self-doubt (and the doubt about his audience) involved in that '*probably*' is telling, in broader terms, of the uncertain criteria employed to classify some kinds of literary investigation as estimable disciplines and others as worthless nitpicking.[7] An emphasis on laborious accuracy in '*particulars ... even the most minute*' courts the accusation of 'a vain Curiosity and Diligence in Trifles', even of 'a promiscuous inclusiveness' breaching 'the criteria of discrimination and relevance', which would conflict with the impartial curation many thought it Boswell's duty to perform: 'It is not enough that Johnson be a monument, we need to be discreetly assured that Boswell is a reputable mason.'[8] As Johnson himself put it in *Idler* 84: 'He that recounts the life of another,

---

[7] On 18th-century arguments (including Johnson's) about the merits and utility of editorial practice, for instance, see Simon Jarvis, *Scholars and Gentlemen: Shakespearian Textual Criticism and Representations of Scholarly Labour, 1725–1765* (Oxford: Clarendon Press, 1995), 17–87. On Johnson's view of editing as 'marginal', see Thomas Reinert, *Regulating Confusion: Samuel Johnson and the Crowd* (Durham, NC: Duke University Press, 1996), 132–6 (p. 132).

[8] Henry Fielding, *The Wesleyan Edition of the Works of Henry Fielding: The Covent-Garden Journal; and, A Plan of the Universal Register Office* (1752; 1750), ed. Bertrand A. Goldgar (Oxford: Clarendon Press, 1988), 157; Bruce Redford, *Designing the Life of Johnson: The Lyell Lectures, 2001–2* (Oxford: Oxford University Press, 2002), 11; Donald Greene, ' "Tis a Pretty Book, Mr. Boswell, But—" ', in John A. Vance (ed.), *Boswell's 'Life of Johnson': New Questions, New Answers* (Athens: University of Georgia Press, 1985), 110–46 (p. 123); Kevin Hart, *Samuel Johnson and the Culture of Property* (Cambridge: Cambridge University Press, 1999), p. 29.

commonly dwells most upon conspicuous events, lessens the familiarity of his tale to increase its dignity, shews his favourite at a distance decorated and magnified like the ancient actors in their tragick dress, and endeavours to hide the man that he may produce a hero' (*Yale*, ii. 262). If the life-writer 'commonly dwells on conspicuous events', to dwell on 'the common incidents of common life' becomes conspicuous ('Life of Pope', *Lives*, iii. 234). Boswell, once seen to be pursuing such incidents, might be deemed incapable of fulfilling the great task of doing justice to his subject.

The Irish clergyman Thomas Campbell, hearing later on the same April Fool's Day of Boswell's bold enquiry about the peels, observed that it was 'ridiculous to pry so nearly into the movements of such men — yet Boswell carries it to a degree of superstition . . . I verily think he is as anxious to know the secret as a green sick girl.'[9] The 'spoils of the preceding night' seeks to avoid such distaste by increasing our familiarity with Johnson at the same time as preserving the dignity of Boswell's tale (although it necessarily compromises that of the biographer). It registers but does not dwell on the labour of ascertaining '*with a scrupulous authenticity*' the provenance of exiguous particulars. The phrase introduces, after all, a rare example of Boswell's failure to elicit information from Johnson. It counterbalances brute pillage and tender care on behalf of both men's attitudes to a pile of leftovers, and facilitates the scene's poised inflections of disdain and regard for trifles — a regard that Johnson advances by teasing Boswell about the peels' 'fate'.[10] (This was not the first time that he had celebrated the fruit in mock-solemn strain: his 'Prologue to Garrick's *Lethe*' (1740) mentions the playwright's fear of hecklers wielding 'the indignant Orange', l. 9.)[11] Johnson counselled Hester Thrale and Charles Burney (amongst others) against 'Mysteriousness in trifles', and 'encouraged an openness of conduct' (*Miscellanies*, i. 326; *Letters*, iv. 431), yet he himself 'loved to be mysterious in little matters'.[12] He maintained, on this occasion, a gentleman's right to hold something in

[9] Boswell asked Johnson about the peels on the morning of 1 April 1775; that evening, he dined at the Thrales', where Campbell was among the guests. Page (ed.), *Dr Johnson: Interviews and Recollections*, 86.

[10] Johnson may have saved the peels for medicinal reasons: he recommended to Hill Boothby 'one Scruple' of 'dried orange peel finely powdered' with 'a glass of hot red port' as 'a very probable remedy for indigestion and lubricity of the bowels' (*Letters*, i, 120).

[11] The Folger Library text provides an alternative reading — 'the poignant orange', describing the author's rather than the audience's response — which the Yale editors follow (*Yale*, vi. 67).

[12] *James Boswell's Life of Johnson: An Edition of the Original Manuscript*, ii: *1709–1765*, ed. Marshall Waingrow, 137. See also *Life*, iii. 324–5.

reserve. The tone created by such decorous fencing ('pray, Sir', 'Nay, Sir') forecloses too solicitous an investigation in advance of Boswell's disappointment—apparently gilded by Johnson's stylish compliment, which neatly transforms a refusal to comment into an occasion for proclaiming his friendship to the world: 'Nay, Sir, you should say it more emphatically:—he could not be prevailed upon, even by his dearest friends, to tell.'

Campbell, however, reported a more succinct rebuttal, one that may come closer to the truth of the original exchange: 'The Doctor's reply was that his dearest friend should not know that. This has made poor Boswell unhappy.'[13] Campbell's version might imply that Boswell, as Johnson's dearest friend, 'should not know that'; or, less comfortingly, that he had no chance of getting at the truth of what even Johnson's most intimate companion would not discover (which would indeed make 'poor Boswell unhappy'). In the *Life*, this ambiguity disappears. Since Boswell, included as one of Johnson's dearest friends, will not be informed, nor shall posterity learn his precious secret. Might Boswell have massaged 'friend' into 'friends'? By reporting his enquiry as determined by what 'the world' might wish to know—thus drawing the reader into the processes of research and composition—and by narrating the scene as if it were an occasion to display Johnson's dignity in the slightest transactions ('Trifles themselves are Elegant in him'),[14] Boswell rises above the impression of mere grasping curiosity.

Johnson's evasiveness recalls a point in his own biography of a much-loved older friend, Richard Savage, at which he mentions his subject's behaviour on receipt of his pension: 'No sooner had he changed the Bill, than he vanished from the Sight of all his Acquaintances, and lay for some Time out of the Reach of all the Enquiries that Friendship or Curiosity could make after him; at length he appeared again pennyless as before, but never informed even those whom he seemed to regard most, where he had been, nor was his Retreat ever discovered' (*Savage*, 87). Savage's fairy-tale vanishing act, at once inevitable and inexplicable ('No sooner had he . . . than he . . .'), finds a counterpart in Johnson's. A pair of animated abstractions ('Friendship or Curiosity') and the passive voice, eternally unresolved and equally fairy-tale-like ('nor was his Retreat ever discovered' having the opposite effect to 'they all lived happily ever after'), stand in for the anonymous author, securing his own retreat from the

[13] Page (ed.), *Dr Johnson: Interviews and Recollections*, 86.
[14] Pope, 'Epistle to Miss Blount, with the Works of *Voiture*' (1712–35), l. 4.

indignity of exposure. As Thomas Reinert notes, personifications rather than human beings dominate the *Life of Savage*.[15]

The separation of friendship from curiosity—perhaps the progression from one to the other—might suggest, in addition, a hardening of the heart, or a perceptible transition from the role of companion to that of biographer. The fact that the two feelings are described as interchangeable makes it sound as if Johnson is conjecturing cause from effect, where he might have introduced direct evidence of his own efforts to track down Savage. Instead, his words imply no more than that enquiries were made, and that it is reasonable to assume that either friendship or curiosity prompted such endeavours.[16] The result, peculiarly impersonal yet far from equivocal, is true to Savage's character, as well as to the distinction between friendship and life-writing: 'always disengaged' yet 'a warm Advocate', Savage was simultaneously 'remote' in 'his Interest' and 'concerned . . . so nearly' (*Savage*, 120, 83). Were Johnson an indifferent observer, he would not deploy the intensifying words and phrases 'No sooner . . . than', 'all his Acquaintances', 'all the Enquiries', 'never', 'even', and 'ever'.

He might have phrased his pursuit in the more anguished terms employed (in 1765) to describe Shakespearian textual emendation: 'when the truth to be investigated is so near to inexistence, as to escape attention, its bulk is to be enlarged by rage and exclamation' ('Preface to Shakespeare', *Yale*, vii. 102). Even here, however, his arguments are couched in a lofty passive and a timeless present tense that guard against personal implication without attempting self-exculpation; 'rage and exclamation', like 'Friendship or Curiosity', remain at arm's length from their source. An intricate network of words demonstrates the velleities and niceness of the work under discussion. The lexical proximity of 'investigated' to 'inexistence' (strengthening the claim that the object of investigation is 'near to' inexistence); the shading of 'to . . .' from an unaccomplished intention ('to be investigated' and 'to be enlarged' describe, without achieving, action, while 'to escape' refers to the object of enquiry rather than to the enquirer) into a vaguely spatial co-ordinate ('to' borders on 'inexistence'); the ambiguity of 'to be enlarged' (will the truth to be investigated also, inevitably, be enlarged? Or is this enlargement merely a possibility?); the outward movement from petty

[15] Reinert, *Regulating Confusion*, p. 106.

[16] Johnson distinguishes 'friendship and curiosity' as '*generally* praised' amongst the 'adscititious passions' in *Rambler* 49 (*Yale*, iii. 265; my emphasis), underlining his abstract treatment of a personal subject here.

*inv*estigation to broad *exc*lamation, itself an enlargement in the sense of a release: such features write small the permeations of self-doubt and write large a sense of general human impotence. (This lack of specific culpability extends to Johnson's unusually lenient treatment of previous editors: 'They have all been treated by me with candour, which they have not been careful of observing to one another' (*Yale*, vii. 102).[17])

Johnson habitually describes those things that might elude his attention, and that of humanity, in simultaneously self-involved and self-abstracted terms. Like Boswell, he must remain sufficiently above petty details to protect himself from ridicule, and to formulate general reflections on the business of writing about them, sufficiently close to those details to convince us of the pains he is discussing, and of the value of undergoing them. It should not be forgotten that Johnson is pursuing a 'truth', however minute, rather than mere whim. One pervasive concern of his and Boswell's arguments about great and little things is that an 'enlarged' truth may cease to be a truth at all. Their joint aspiration, like Austen's, is therefore to be not only 'more at large', but 'likewise more at small—with equal perspicuity & minuteness':[18] 'we pitched upon the elephant for [Johnson's] resemblance', Piozzi writes; 'the proboscis of that creature was like his mind most exactly, strong to buffet even the tyger, and pliable to pick up even the pin' (*Miscellanies*, i. 287).

Bruce Redford recently noted the double sense of the final verb ('regard') in Boswell's *Life*, which compels us 'to read the inner through the outer man' and 'might be said to sum up not only Boswell's goal but his method . . . We complete the Character and close the biography understanding that our regard *for* Johnson depends upon our regard *of* him.'[19] A muted play on the same potential of 'regard' to mean 'see' and 'revere' (not as cheap a species of dexterity as punning, which Johnson despised, *Life*, ii. 241) serves briefly to animate the *Savage* passage, offering only in order to retract a potential *rapprochement* between two friends, between human wishes and reality. '[He] never informed even those whom he seemed to *regard* most', echoing 'the *Sight* of all his Acquaintances', reneges on the general hope that close friendship will facilitate perfect intimacy (those whom Savage regarded most should have been able to regard him more fully than this). Over thirty years later, in conversation with Boswell about the orange peels, Johnson is

---

[17] See also Jarvis, *Scholars and Gentlemen*, 159–81.

[18] Jane Austen to Cassandra Austen (10–11 Jan. 1809), *Jane Austen's Letters*, ed. Deirdre Le Faye, 3rd edn. (Oxford: Oxford University Press, 1996), 163.

[19] Redford, *Designing the Life of Johnson*, 75, 79. See *Life*, iv. 429–30.

caught in the oddly self-detached act of advising his biographer how he should posthumously narrate a transaction which Johnson himself refuses to communicate in full. Yet his own inability to fill in the gaps of Savage's life was accompanied by the at best dubious consolation that he was among those whom Savage '*seemed* to regard most'. Whatever the truth of his original answer may have been, 'his dearest friends' leaves Boswell's reader in no such doubt.

1. 'LADIES, I AM TAME; YOU MAY STROKE ME'[20]

Johnson's notorious fear of an afterlife in which he would be found wanting should be weighed against the playful detachment with which he regarded the composition of his own biography. Such occasions, when he considered secular rather than divine judgement, were the only times at which he could happily think of himself in the past tense.[21] Boswell's rampant curiosity was well adapted to probe his subject's mysterious nicety, while Johnson in response chose to frame the odd teasing omission from the comprehensive view Boswell sought to present in his *Life*. By the 1770s, the biographical project was no secret, and Boswell—at once to solicit approval for his minute endeavours, and to exhibit knowledge that their minuteness laid him open to ridicule—liked to formulate mock-solemn responses to snippets of information fresh from the horse's mouth: '[JOHNSON.] "a man would never undertake great things, could he be amused with small. I once tried knotting. Dempster's sister undertook to teach me; but I could not learn it." BOSWELL. "So, Sir, it will be related in pompous narrative, 'Once for his amusement he tried knotting; nor did this Hercules disdain the distaff.' " JOHNSON. "Knitting of stockings is a good amusement" ' (*Life*, iii. 242).[22]

---

[20] 'at one of the late Mrs Montagu's literary parties, . . . Mrs Digby herself, with several still younger ladies, almost immediately surrounded our Colossus of literature (an odd figure sure enough) with more wonder than politeness, and while contemplating him, as if he had been some monster from the deserts of Africa, Johnson said to them "Ladies, I am tame; you may stroke me." ' Page (ed.), *Dr Johnson: Interviews and Recollections*, 119.

[21] On his fear of death, see, for instance, *Life*, ii, 106–7. For light-hearted conjectures about his biographers ('the rogues'), see *Miscellanies*, i. 165–6 (p. 166).

[22] On the construction of this scene, see Redford, *Designing the Life of Johnson*, p. 92. As punishment for murdering Iole's brother, Hercules was forced to serve Omphale, queen of Lydia, who made him spin and wear female dress. See *Statius*, trans. J. H. Mozley, 2 vols. (London: Heinemann, 1928; repr. 1957), i. 367; *Seneca: Tragedies*, trans. Frank Justus Miller, 2 vols., rev. edn. (London: Heinemann, 1929; repr. 1968), ii. 213.

Both men, in Boswell's account, are labouring a point: the overworked
alliteration of 'did', 'disdain', and 'distaff' mimics the amusingly lopsided
gravity with which he envisages the Great Cham's attempt to master
a trivial female accomplishment.[23] The endeavour to knit, comically
beneath the talents of 'a Herculean genius, just born to grapple with
whole libraries'[24]—but at the same time a mark of his determinedly all-
encompassing character—also replicates the accents of Judaeo-Christian
descent to the lowly: a descent which would, on a purely heroic view,
constitute a shameful indignity.[25] Hence the absence of Hercules and the
distaff from ancient Greek sculpture and painting. Later ages were not
so wary about shaming their heroes: Elizabeth Montagu lamented the
fact that, in Corneille and Racine, 'Many of the greatest men of antiquity
. . . were exhibited in this effeminate form. The poet dignified the piece,
perhaps with the name of an Hercules, but, alas! it was always Hercules
spinning that was shewn to the spectator.'[26]

'His maxims', Boswell wrote of Johnson, 'carry conviction; for they
are founded on the basis of common sense, and a very attentive and
minute survey of real life', knitting not excepted (*Life*, iv. 428): a point
which endorses Boswell's 'minute survey' of Johnson himself, including
'all the little peculiarities and slight blemishes which marked the literary Colossus' ('Dedication', *Life*, i. 2). To complete 'an exact likeness',
Boswell observed in the *Life* MS, 'he who draws it must not disdain the
slightest strokes'.[27] But the knitting passage is humorously fraught with

---

[23] 'Needle-work had a strenuous approver in Dr. Johnson, who said, "that one of the
great felicities of female life, was the general consent of the world, that they might amuse
themselves with petty occupations . . . A man cannot hem a pocket-handkerchief (said a
lady of quality to him one day), and so he runs mad, and torments his family and friends.
The expression struck him exceedingly' (*Miscellanies*, i. 328). Perhaps Johnson was struck
by the thought that Othello would not have been tormented by a handkerchief, had he been
able to hem one. When Sir John Hawkins admitted that he had briefly pocketed Johnson's
private meditations, the latter told him: 'You should not have laid hands on the book; for
had I missed it, I should have roared for my book, as Othello did for his handkerchief, and
probably have run mad' (*Miscellanies*, ii. 130).
[24] Dr John Boswell in James Boswell, *Boswell in Search of a Wife: 1766–1769*, ed. Frank
Brady and Frederick A. Pottle (London: Heinemann, 1958), 277. Boswell altered 'Herculean'
to 'robust' in the *Life* (iii. 7).
[25] 'She layeth her hands to the spindle, and her hands hold the distaff. She stretcheth out
her hand to the poor; yea, she reacheth forth her hands to the needy' (Proverbs 31: 19–20).
[26] *An Essay on the Writings and Genius of Shakespear, Compared with the Greek and
French Dramatic Poets* (1769; London: Frank Cass, 1970), 4. Hercules with the distaff was a
popular subject for 18th-century French painters such as François Lemoyne ('Hercules and
Omphale' (1724), Musée du Louvre).
[27] *James Boswell's Life of Johnson: An Edition of the Original Manuscript*, i: *1709–1765*, ed.
Marshall Waingrow (1994), 340.

uncertainty about the properties of a hero: should a Hercules disdain the distaff? Should his biographer disdain to report that he did not? By presenting the subject in the form of a conversation (which begins when he mentions that he cannot content himself with small matters, *Life*, iii. 241), Boswell dramatizes his own indecision about the tone and orientation of his biography—an indecision that Johnson ignores. He has already cast the faithful record of Johnson's conversation as a commemorative end in itself. This allows him to illustrate his formally unfinished concerns about heroic representation in a dialogue with the object of those concerns—a dialogue that is, of necessity, formally closed. (This exchange is itself, however, vulnerable to the charge of being a mere trifle. Boswell states early on that 'the peculiar value of the following work, is, the quantity that it contains of Johnson's conversation; which is universally acknowledged to have been eminently instructive and entertaining', but quickly proceeds to equate conversation with 'minute particulars', 'happily ... adapted for the petty exercise of ridicule', and defends its inclusion by citing Plutarch, Johnson, Secker, Caesar, and Bacon, *Life*, i. 31–4.)

The 'pompous narrative' device shields the biographer's real laboriousness beneath a pointed consciousness of what it means to be laboured. Yet, like '*It must be said* ... he scraped them, and let them dry ... ', Boswell's 'So, Sir, *it will be related* ... ' (my emphases) reminds Johnson in earnest that he is talking on record. Although his mythical formulation styles itself 'pompous', it nonetheless borrows its terms direct from Johnson: 'amused' becomes 'amusement', 'I once tried knotting' translates as 'Once ... he tried knotting'. Even here, Boswell is showing that he is accurate, and his mock-heroic calibration of great and small (Hercules and the distaff) takes its cue from Johnson's remark that 'a man would never undertake great things, could he be amused with small'. Boswell conflates Johnson's general reflection and the example from his own life for which it serves as evidence—'amused' loses its place in the maxim and becomes Hercules' personal 'amusement'. But he omits, in the 'pompous' version of events (a selective kind of biography, countenanced alongside Boswell's), his *inability* to practise the art of knotting.

Johnson's attempt to master it exemplifies his claim that 'The true strong and sound mind is the mind that can embrace equally great things and small ... I would have a man great in great things, and elegant in little things' (*Life*, iii. 334). The last phrase is asymmetrical, in spite of an appeal to equality of embrace ('great in great things' but not 'little in little things'), no doubt to avoid the suspicion of pettiness when attending to trifles. But Johnson's 'elegant' is also an allusion to the etymology of the word: it derives from the Latin 'eligere' (to choose) and hence from 'elegans' (tasteful, refined, elegant, choice); strong minds should take care to be selective in their descent to little things. Yet Boswell's inelegant and determined inclusiveness registers the fact that, while Johnson may on this occasion have sought to compass the minute as well as the great, he could not, just as Boswell's Herculean pursuit of the orange peels was finally and literally fruitless. Neither failure is concealed in the finished *Life*. The mock-solemn vein in which Johnson readily co-operated with Boswell over the orange peels shielded him from his vulnerability, Boswell from the imputation of puerility, and both men from the corrosive ironies of a wholly acquisitive/resistant exchange.[28] It is, after all, from a defeated enemy and not from a revered friend that spoils are wrested by force.

Boswell compared his *Life* to Homer's domestic epic *The Odyssey* and, at the other end of the scale, to a 'Flemish picture' detailing 'the most minute particulars' ('Advertisement to the Second Edition', *Life*, i. 12; iii. 191). His tremulous advance towards the peels entails a self-conscious diminution of the epic panorama to a particularized realm of sociable, bloodless, and domestically contained thrust and parry, a diminution signalled by 'spoils' that Pope might have admired. Boswell resorts to martial language (deprived of actual slaughter, yet resonating with heroic fortitude and resilience in the face of inevitable death) throughout the *Life*, employing 'the vast amphitheatre, the Colisæum' as a Roman figure for Johnson's ceaselessly self-opposing mind, the 'mighty gladiator' for his judgement combating 'dismal apprehensions' of 'this aweful change' (*Life*, ii. 106). Such an approach recalls Pope's heroic versification, machinery, situations, and diction, subdued to a coterie atmosphere of quotidian contemporary subjects, in *The Rape of the Lock*, which has been seen as a serious attempt to write epic 'sanitised *ab initio*'—divested, that is, of the uncomfortable presence of bloodshed.[29] Thus 'The conqu'ring Force of unresisted Steel' felt by Belinda (III. 178) is merely the impudent snip of the Baron's scissors, while Sarpedon's speech urging Glaucus to war, which Pope translated in 1709, becomes (in 1717) Clarissa's exhortation to Belinda to be good-humoured—because death is unavoidable, not because a warrior's glorious self-sacrifice is to be actively embraced (V. 9–34). This late insertion was intended '*to*

---

[28] See also Empson on Dryden's 'mutual comparisons which benefit both parties; the natural act is given dignity, the heroic act tenderness and a sort of spontaneity'. *Seven Types of Ambiguity*, 220.

[29] Rawson, 'Heroic Notes', 80.

open more clearly the MORAL *of the Poem*' (V. 7n.), a moral concerning
the importance of trivial actions which Pope at once divulges and coyly
refuses to press home, and which (with equal indeterminacy) governs
Boswell's *Life*.

It might be argued that, in the second half of the eighteenth century,
biography replaced mock-heroic verse as a means of investing the low
occurrence, trifling detail, or domestic setting with a wilfully overstated
literary significance (the overstatement sheltering a genuinely high regard:
Boswell insisted that he should not be attacked for descending to
particulars of Johnson's appearance, yet was once again driven to invoke
Hercules in order to justify mentioning the great man's oak stick).[30] This
would partly explain the life-writer's residual fidelities to epic furniture
and to epic tradition. Yet to claim that biography gradually superseded
mock-heroic could suggest that mock-heroic once constituted a finite
genre in itself. It seems better to describe it as a consciousness of the
limits of the heroic mode—a consciousness that might manifest itself in
biography as well as in poetry. Both forms are dedicated, throughout this
period, to readjusting 'false measures of excellence and dignity' (*Rambler*
60, *Yale*, iii. 320).

Such a readjustment half-abandons the 'uniform panegyrick' and
heroic domain in which great agents might otherwise be celebrated in
favour of, say, a Belinda's dubious elevation to our regard via 'those
petty qualities, which grow important only by their frequency, and which
though they produce no single acts of heroism, nor astonish us by
great events, yet are every moment exerting their influence upon us'
(*Rambler* 60, *Yale*, iii. 323; *Rambler* 72, *Yale*, iv. 12). By writing of such
'petty qualities' *as if* they produced 'acts of heroism' or 'great events',
Pope bids us simultaneously to mind the gap between the two and to
acknowledge the compatibility to 'Little Men' (I. 11) of small occasions
with disproportionate effects: 'What mighty Contests rise from trivial
Things' (I. 2). Or, as Johnson put it in *Rambler* 156, where he objects
to the neoclassical theory of the unities: 'The connexion of important
with trivial incidents, since it is not only common but perpetual in the

[30] 'Upon this tour, when journeying, he wore boots and a very wide brown cloth greatcoat
with pockets which might have almost held the two volumes of his folio dictionary, and he
carried in his hand a large English oak stick. Let me not be censured for mentioning such
minute particulars. Everything relative to so great a man is worth observing. I remember
Dr. Adam Smith, in his rhetorical lectures at Glasgow, told us he was glad to know that
Milton wore latchets in his shoes instead of buckles. When I mention the oak stick, it is but
letting Hercules have his club; and by and by my readers will find this stick will bud and
produce a good joke' (Boswell, *Tour*, 8–9).

world, may surely be allowed upon the stage, which pretends only to be the mirrour of life' (*Yale*, v. 68–9). The 'Preface to Shakespeare' makes a similar case for 'the mingled drama': it 'approaches . . . to the appearance of life, by shewing how great machinations and slender designs may promote or obviate one another, and the high and the low co-operate in the general system by unavoidable concatenation' (*Yale*, vii. 67). Pope's heroine, and his poetry, gain and lose in stature by comparison with ancient precedent: epic simile 'differentiates as it aligns'.[31] Pope is neither wholly mocking, nor wholly heroic; Belinda is by turns an empty-headed minx, an 'awful Beauty', and a 'Goddess' decked with international spoils (I. 139, 132), the lock at once a trifling object of dispute between two noble families and an attribute of Belinda's celestial beauty that is worthy of elevation among the stars.

If mock-heroic verse is 'dedicated to downgrading the ethos of war' by focusing on bloodless domestic conflict,[32] then biography—encouraged by Johnson's *Rambler* 60, which suggested that 'there has rarely passed a life of which a judicious and faithful narrative would not be useful' and promoted the inclusion of 'domestick privacies', and of 'the minute details of daily life' (*Yale*, iii. 320–1)—develops along similar lines, arguing for the valuable proximity to readers' experience of humdrum routine rather than of singular achievement. Life-writers were urged to descend to everyday detail about the private characters of their subjects, and thereby to a realistic view of mere mortals. As Goldsmith put it in his Johnsonian *Life of Richard Nash* (1762): 'I chose to describe the man as he was, not such as imagination could have helped in compleating his picture' (*Collected Works*, iii. 289).[33] Earlier still, *The Tatler* had mused, in terms which Johnson would echo and perpetuate in *Rambler* 60, that literature should turn its thoughts 'to Cares and Griefs, somewhat below that of Heroes, but no less moving' (no. 47, i. 341).

Yet Boswell, although at pains to defend the inclusion of domestic particulars in the *Life*, seems (unsurprisingly) to have felt that Johnson's colossal stature called for an appropriately epic gravitas, while his own microscopic investigations benefited from a knowing breach between grand style and little subject (as did *The Tatler*'s: 'I am undertaking, methinks, a Work worthy an invulnerable Hero in Romance, rather than a private Gentleman', no. 25, i. 193). Not everyone

---

[31] Redford, *Designing the Life of Johnson*, 6.   [32] Rawson, 'Heroic Notes', 80.

[33] See also Robert Folkenflik, *Samuel Johnson, Biographer* (Ithaca, NY: Cornell University Press, 1978), 19–55, 97–117.

would his 'pen's *minutiæ* bless', even in the *Journal of a Tour to the Hebrides* (1785):

> O! whilst amid the anecdotic mine,
> Thou labour'st hard to bid thy hero shine,
> Run to Bolt Court, exert thy Curl-like soul,
> And fish for golden leaves from hole to hole:
> Find when he ate and drank, and cough'd and sneez'd—
> Let all his motions in thy book be squeez'd:
> On tales, however strange, impose thy claw;
> Yes, let thy amber lick up ev'ry straw:
> Sam's nods, and winks, and laughs, will form a treat;
> For all that breathes of Johnson must be great![34]

The Popean references to Edmund Curll, a prominent scandalmonger in *The Dunciad* (see, for instance, II. 57–184), and to the *Epistle to Dr. Arbuthnot* (1735)—'Pretty! in Amber to observe the forms | Of hairs, or straws, or dirt, or grubs, or worms; | The things, we know, are neither rich nor rare, | But wonder how the Devil they got there?'—firmly locate Boswell amongst the dunces and piffling 'small Critics' of the 'Comma's and points' school, prone to be 'earnest upon Trifles' and to 'dispute on the most indifferent Occasions with Vehemence' (*Arbuthnot*, ll. 161–72; *Tatler* 29, i. 220). While Pope quizzically observes the amber as an impersonal repository for detritus, wondering how such tat came to be enshrined there, Boswell on the Scottish tour is, according to Peter Pindar, *himself* the amber, actively seeking out worthless ephemera on which to bestow an unwarranted immortality ('lick up ev'ry straw' also points to the servility involved in such a pursuit). In the *Life of Johnson*, however, an ironic guard defends from epic pretensions the author who wishes to elevate trifles to significance, and simultaneously preserves his aspirations to heroic pronouncement. Thus Boswell opens by delaying the entrance of his clinching verb ('is') and of his clinching noun ('task'), in periodic syntax designed to create suspense and an appetite for great event, but the sentence ends on a hesitant note: 'ᴛᴏ write the Life of him who excelled all mankind in writing the lives of others, and who, whether we consider his extraordinary endowments, or his various works, has been equalled by few in any age, is an arduous, and may be reckoned in me a presumptuous task' (*Life*, i. 25).

---

[34] Peter Pindar (John Wolcot), 'A Poetical and Congratulatory Epistle to James Boswell, Esq. on his Journal of a Tour to the Hebrides with the celebrated Doctor Johnson', ll. 223–32, in *The Works of Peter Pindar*, 4 vols. (London: for Walker et al., 1816), i.

2. TYPES AND INDIVIDUALS

Boswell's pursuit of the orange peels may have ended in frustration, but he won 'a small bet' by putting the 'bold question' in the first place—something which, he reported, Lady Diana Beauclerk 'laid I durst not do' (*Life*, ii. 330). His embarrassment at descending to subjects beneath the province of letters, or a 'little fear of the shame of falling' (in Johnson's phrase), is an eighteenth-century literary hallmark ('The Life of Sir Thomas Browne' (1756), *Early Biographical Writings*, 467). Christopher Ricks observes with reference to Keats that 'English life and literature have had the advantages and the disadvantages of embarrassability', while 'the French have had the advantages and disadvantages of unembarrassability'.[35] His suggestion remains apt: the English (and the Scottish, if Boswell is anything to go by) have long been touchily responsive to the charge that their intellectual life is characterized by a hopelessly empirical attention to low or irrelevant particulars. *The Tatler*'s effeminate trifler, Ned Softly, is said to be 'a true *English* Reader'—'incapable of relishing the great and masterly Strokes' of poetry, or the 'Genius and Strength' of 'the Ancients'. Instead, he is 'wonderfully pleased with the little *Gothick* ornaments of Epigrammatical Conceits, Turns, Points, and Quibbles, which are so frequent in the most admired of our *English* Poets' (*Tatler* 163, ii. 407). During the course of the eighteenth century, this sensitivity about paying attention to trifling particulars is brought into literary prominence, with all *The Tatler*'s instinctive opposition of 'the Ancients' to a native preference for 'little ... ornaments'. Boswell's tireless pursuit of *Johnsoniana*, and Johnson's alternate co-operation and 'strange unwillingness to be discovered' (*Life*, ii. 330), herald by the end of the century a self-consciously cumulative 'relaxation of [...] embarrassment' at 'writing or reading about objects, occupations and people regarded at the start of the century as too "low", "minute" or "mean" to be worthy of literary attention'.[36]

A relaxation of embarrassment has been equally apparent in criticism of the period, at least since the publication in 1957 of Ian Watt's *The Rise of the Novel*, in which a perceived eighteenth-century demand for literary representations of 'all the varieties of human experience' (including

[35] Christopher Ricks, *Keats and Embarrassment* (Oxford: Clarendon Press, 1974; repr. 1984), 6. See also Peter Ackroyd, *Albion: The Origins of the English Imagination* (London: Chatto & Windus, 2002), 274–8.

[36] John Barrell, *English Literature in History 1730–80: An Equal, Wide Survey* (London: Hutchinson, 1983), 21.

' "low" subjects' and 'low life') was related to the emergence of a middle-class readership and to the decline of patronage.[37] More recently, Peter Stallybrass and Allon White have documented a 'production of identity and status through a repudiation of the "low" ' alongside a 'shift in the cultural threshold of shame and embarrassment' during the course of the period.[38] Roger Lonsdale's *New Oxford Book of Eighteenth-Century Verse* aspired to be 'more representative of the full range of eighteenth-century verse than most collections'; his anthology duly makes room for poets lower down the social scale and outside London whose verse addresses the trials and pleasures of daily life. Lonsdale hoped that this inclusiveness would challenge the received interpretation of eighteenth-century verse as a polite endeavour to eschew 'the homely' and 'the crude', to quell 'the "low" and potentially disturbing immediacy of the real world'.[39]

In recent years, literary-critical studies have also been characterized by pursuit of 'the other', or of that which you define yourself by when you say what you are not. Numerous re-evaluations of Johnson have lately sought to cast him as a writer interested in marginal or neglected groups and individuals (critics have scrutinized his purported misogyny in this light).[40] Pat Rogers notes in his contribution to *The Cambridge Cultural History* that scholars of the eighteenth century are now 'ushered

[37] Ian Watt, *The Rise of the Novel: Studies in Defoe, Richardson and Fielding* (Harmondsworth: Penguin, 1972), 10–11 (and *passim*, pp. 9–65).

[38] Peter Stallybrass and Allon White, *The Politics and Poetics of Transgression* (Ithaca, NY: Cornell University Press, 1986), pp. ix, 85.

[39] Roger Lonsdale (ed.), *The New Oxford Book of Eighteenth-Century Verse* (Oxford: Oxford University Press, 1984), 'Introduction', pp. xxxix, xxxiv.

[40] See James G. Basker, 'Dancing Dogs, Women Preachers and the Myth of Johnson's Misogyny', *Age of Johnson*, 3 (1990), 63–90, 'Myth upon Myth: Johnson, Gender, and the Misogyny Question', *Age of Johnson*, 8 (1997), 175–87, and 'Radical Affinities: Mary Wollstonecraft and Samuel Johnson', in Alvaro Ribeiro and James G. Basker (eds.), *Tradition in Transition: Women Writers, Marginal Texts, and the Eighteenth-Century Canon* (Oxford: Clarendon Press, 1996), 41–55; Annette Wheeler Cafarelli, 'Johnson and Women: Demasculinizing Literary History', *Age of Johnson*, 5 (1992), 61–114; Norma Clarke, *Dr Johnson's Women* (London: Hambledon, 2001); Isobel Grundy, 'Samuel Johnson as Patron of Women', *Age of Johnson*, 1 (1987), 59–77; Eithne Henson, 'Johnson and the Condition of Women', in Greg Clingham (ed.), *The Cambridge Companion to Samuel Johnson* (Cambridge: Cambridge University Press, 1997), 67–84; Charles H. Hinnant (ed.), *Johnson and Gender: Special Issue of South Central Review*, 9/4 (1992); Kathleen Nulton Kemmerer, '*A Neutral Being between the Sexes': Samuel Johnson's Sexual Politics* (Lewisburg, Pa.: Bucknell University Press, 1998); Irma S. Lustig, 'The Myth of Johnson's Misogyny in the Life of Johnson: Another View', in Thomas Crawford (ed.), *Boswell in Scotland and Beyond* (Glasgow: Association for Scottish Literary Studies, 1997), 71–88; Catherine N. Parke, 'Samuel Johnson and Gender', in David R. Anderson and Gwin J. Kolb (eds.), *Approaches to Teaching the Works of Samuel Johnson* (New York: MLA, 1993), 19–27; Sarah R. Morrison, 'Samuel Johnson, Mr. Rambler, and Women', *Age of Johnson*, 14 (2003), 23–50.

in the direction of outsiders in society', a state of affairs to which his own *Grub Street: Studies in a Subculture* contributed.[41] There is an identifiable awareness in many eighteenth-century authors of an affront presented to the organization or even to the survival of literary culture by certain kinds of people and things; the dunce, for instance, is 'a servant of literature whose practice threatens the very existence of literature'.[42]

Many authors—including Henry Fielding—found the idea of a servant heroine such as Richardson's Pamela transparently comic, and their reaction cannot merely be dismissed as a conservative reflex (although it was sometimes that). The novel's apparent encouragement of social levelling, its flagrant confounding of hierarchies, insulted a given order of things and at the same time offered a tempting precedent: *Pamela* (1740) inspired not only *Shamela* (1741) but *Joseph Andrews* (1742).[43] The latter response gradually ceases to be parodic of its original; Joseph's heroic resistance to Lady Booby renders him on balance steadfast rather than ludicrously acquisitive, since he is guarding his chastity for another woman. *Shamela* had mocked a gentleman's condescension to a woman of superlatively low birth by recasting Mr B's predatory attempts on Pamela as cretinous impotence, her 'Vartue' as pert mercenary deceit. However, Lady Booby's genuinely threatening social and physical assaults on Joseph (she lusts after him as an inferior who refuses to be abjectly complying and is herself, like Fielding, both attracted and repelled) are more in tune with *Pamela*. They make her seem grotesquely beneath him: 'Ha! and do I doat thus on a Footman! I despise, I detest my Passion.—Yet why? Is he not generous, gentle, kind?—... curse his Beauties, and the little low Heart that possesses them; which can basely descend to this despicable Wench.'[44]

By this point, Fielding has already gone out of his way to upbraid those (including Lady Booby) who 'think the least Familiarity with the Persons below them a Condescension, and if they were to go one Step farther, a Degradation': a position apparently recommending a limited social mobility which might sit slightly uncomfortably with the zestful and

[41] Pat Rogers, 'Literature', in Boris Ford (ed.), *The Cambridge Cultural History of Britain*, v: *Eighteenth-Century Britain* (Cambridge: Cambridge University Press, 1992), 159–201 (p. 160).

[42] Pat Rogers, *Grub Street: Studies in a Subculture* (London: Methuen, 1972), 201.

[43] See T. C. Duncan Eaves and Ben D. Kimpel, *Samuel Richardson: A Biography* (Oxford: Clarendon Press, 1971), 126–32, 152–3.

[44] *The History of the Adventures of Joseph Andrews and of his Friend Mr. Abraham Andrews and An Apology for the Life of Mrs. Shamela Andrews*, ed. Douglas Brooks (Oxford: Oxford University Press, 1971), 336–44, 295.

resolute baseness of Shamela's character. Yet Joseph is made amenable
to fiction by virtue of wishing to marry his social equal, 'a poor Girl,
who had been formerly bred up in Sir *John*'s Family; whence ... she
had been discarded'. Unlike the implausibly accomplished Pamela, 'poor
Fanny could neither write nor read'. Lady Booby is chiefly to be ridiculed
because she seeks to disrupt the propriety of this match, to replace it with
another wildly asymmetric pairing of the sort that concludes *Pamela*:
'Marry a Footman! Distraction! Can I afterwards bear the Eyes of my
Acquaintance? But I can retire from them; retire with one in whom I
propose more Happiness than the World without him can give me!'[45]
Joseph himself objects in a strain highly reminiscent of his sister that such
a coupling would be unacceptable; by marrying within his own class,
he preserves that attitude intact, while Pamela is driven from reviling
to celebrating Mr B's socially outrageous condescension, once sanctified
by marriage, as an act of Christian self-abasement.[46] Only while his
intention was to violate her has his conduct been truly low. An attitude
of vexed semi-inclusiveness, of sympathy and reliance on as well as
antipathy towards social and literary sub-groups, surfaces throughout
this period (and in 1747, Fielding married his own housekeeper, Mary
Daniel).[47]

   Brean Hammond argues that: 'Although *The Dunciad* tries to fight
a rearguard action for the separation of "low" art forms and popular
writing from "high" art forms and writing informed by the classic
tradition, the poem is clearly nurtured by the demotic forms it ostensibly
despises'; 'demotic and high cultural forms, low-brow and high-brow art,
are mutually dependent even in Pope's own writings and even though
there are intellectual forces at work making for their separation.'[48] At the

---

[45] *Joseph Andrews*, 141, 43, 295.
[46] Joseph tells Lady Booby that, were she to marry him, 'I should think your Ladyship
condescended a great deal below yourself' (ibid. 35). Compare Pamela on Mr B, before
and after their marriage: 'if he can stoop to like such a poor Girl as I ... What can it be
for?—He may condescend, may-hap, to think I may be good enough for his Harlot'; 'Every
Hour he makes me happier, by his sweet Condescension.' Samuel Richardson, *Pamela;
or, Virtue Rewarded*, ed. Thomas Keymer and Alice Wakely (Oxford: Oxford University
Press, 2001), 41, 353. Pamela's first use of 'condescend' is removed from the final version
of the novel (replaced by 'He may, perhaps, think I may be good enough for his harlot'),
as if Richardson, considering its later uses to celebrate Mr B's humility, wished from the
start to keep a praiseworthy sense of the word in the foreground. Richardson, *Pamela;
or, Virtue Rewarded*, ed. Peter Sabor, introd. Margaret Anne Doody (Harmondsworth:
Penguin, 1985), 73.
[47] Pat Rogers, *Henry Fielding: A Biography* (London: Paul Elek, 1979), 150–6.
[48] Brean Hammond, ' "Guard the Sure Barrier": Pope and the Partitioning of Culture',
in David Fairer (ed.), *Pope: New Contexts* (Hemel Hempstead: Harvester Wheatsheaf,

origin of this book has been a similar wish to understand the impulses to exclude and to include some kinds of material from and in literature not as irreconcilable (most authors, like Fielding, had a foot in both camps), but as a set of literary and ethical affiliations informing the lowest and highest writing of the period.

Johnson squarely addressed the question of sub-literary and socially peripheral materials with frequency, contempt, anxiety, self-contradiction, and lasting influence on public opinion. His principled desire to improve the posthumous reputation of some of Pope's dunces, especially that of Blackmore, is evident in the *Lives of the Poets*. Yet Hester Thrale well understood the warring elements of charitable solicitude and critical disdain that combined in Johnson's brand of literary condescension. Anticipating with relish the forthcoming 'Life of Blackmore', she hazarded a guess that the much-maligned Father of the Bathos would be 'rescued from the old wits who worried him, much to your disliking'—primarily on grounds of Johnson's 'love of his Christianity', but also 'a little for love of his physick, a little for love of his courage—and a little for love of contradiction'. Yet if Johnson were planning to 'save him from his malevolent cricks', it was perhaps only to 'do him the honour to devour him yourself—as a lion is said to take a great bull now and then from the wolves which had fallen upon him in the desert, and gravely eat him up for his own dinner'.[49]

Recent literary-critical efforts to bring 'the other' into prominence might be read in the light of Pierre Macherey's distinction between the two functions of 'criticism' (including Johnson's, as here envisaged by Thrale): the term on the one hand denotes 'a gesture of refusal, a denunciation, a hostile judgment', on the other 'the study of the conditions and possibilities of an activity . . . The discipline of criticism is rooted in this ambiguity, this double attitude.'[50] Criticism, in other words, may be as exclusive or inclusive as the writing it criticizes. Macherey's 'double attitude' shows up in Rogers's chapter on the criteria for duncehood in *Grub Street: Studies in a Subculture*. Answering the recommendation that we should consider authors immortalized in *The Dunciad* as perennially applicable types rather than as historically specific

---

1990), 225–40 (pp. 228, 230–1). See also Brean Hammond, *Professional Imaginative Writing in England, 1670–1740: 'Hackney for Bread'* (Oxford: Clarendon Press, 1997), 195–302 (especially p. 209).

[49] Hester Lynch Piozzi and Samuel Johnson, *Letters to and from the late Samuel Johnson, LL.D.*, 2 vols. (London: for A. Strahan and T. Cadell, 1788), ii. 122.

[50] Pierre Macherey, *A Theory of Literary Production*, trans. Geoffrey Wall (London: Routledge & Kegan Paul, 1978), 3.

individuals, Rogers argues that such a stipulation is unhelpful. Ignoring
the original reasons for their inclusion in or exclusion from the poem
curbs our ability to respond to it, just as the notion that Pope randomly
selected his dunces or lent them an existence no more than symbolic
misrepresents the nature of his invention and the real effect it had on his
victims' livelihoods.[51]

It seems clear that we lose a good deal if we are denied the ability to
size up the dunces' aptitude for their parts, to compare what we know
of the real hacks with the world of half-truths ('dark and deep', 'motley',
'mazy', and 'jumbled') they are styled to inhabit in *The Dunciad* (I. 55,
65; II. 21; I. 68, 70). But there is a sense in which maintaining uncertainty
about the motives for their presence represents a truth about the poem's
composition (and the mixed feelings it stages): if nothing else, it is to
co-operate with its author's wishes. Pope tried at every opportunity to
forge an equivalence between insignificance and worthlessness, to make
the never entirely convincing point that, in spite of their appearance
in his work, the dunces were 'neither rich nor rare'. But the wonder
nonetheless remains 'how the Devil they got there'. Defoe, classed as an
ostrich in chapter VI of *Peri Bathous* (see below), may appear 'Earless on
high' as 'unabash'd De Foe' in *The Dunciad* (II. 147), yet Pope remarked
equivocally to Joseph Spence in 1742: 'The first part of *Robinson Crusoe*,
good. DeFoe wrote a vast many things, and none bad, though none
excellent. There's something good in all he has writ'[52] (perhaps he is
called 'restless Daniel' in the 1729 *Dunciad Variorum* because Pope cannot
quite place him; a footnote admits that he 'had parts', I. 101 and n.). If
the dunces embody everything that poetry should not be, how do they
come to figure in a poem? Might we say of them, individually, that 'none
[is] bad, though none excellent'? What adjustments need to be made to
their lives and writings to convert them into Pope's agents?

Rogers's attempt to answer these questions succeeds in throwing light
on the process of Pope's composition and the effect it had on some of its
victims, but it reconstructs an ideally informed reader of *The Dunciad*.
Swift told Pope he had 'long observ'd that twenty miles from London,
no body understands . . . town-facts and passages; and in a few years not
even those who live in London' (Pope, *Correspondence*, ii. 504; see also
'Life of Pope', *Lives*, iii. 146). Richardson remarked in 1748 that Pope
'could not trust his Works with the Vulgar, without Notes longer than

---

[51] Rogers, *Grub Street*, 176–213.

[52] Joseph Spence, *Observations, Anecdotes, and Characters of Books and Men Collected
from Conversation*, ed. James M. Osborn, 2 vols. (Oxford: Clarendon Press, 1966), i. 213.

the Work . . . to tell them what he meant, and that he *had* a Meaning, in this or that Place'.[53] Three months after the appearance of the 1728 *Dunciad*, the anonymous author of *Characters of the Times* was confused by Blackmore's prominence in the poem: 'Sir *Richard* has not for many Years been so much as nam'd, or even thought of among Writers, as such; and whom no one except *P–pe*, would have had Ill-nature enough to revive.'[54] Pope must have registered this accusation of a cruelly renovated interest, since he incorporated a version of the comment in a footnote to *The Dunciad Variorum*, at the conclusion of the noise contest in which Blackmore triumphs (II. 256n.). As Thomas Jemielity notes, however, the final part of the quotation—'and whom no one except *P–pe*, would have had Ill-nature enough to revive'—is omitted, thus translating a criticism of Pope's malice into an apparently concurring judgement about Blackmore's literary inconsequence.[55]

Eighteenth-century readers seem as likely as modern audiences to have found Pope's selection of victims baffling or inconsistent, and to have responded to many duncies as little more than indistinct 'types'. Rogers acknowledges that Pope 'inherited certain models when he came to anatomise literary folly', but goes on to make the claim that 'equally the firm historical reality' of the duncies 'stands out'.[56] Stands out from where? From the poem itself? Can we say that each of the duncies has a claim equally to mythical status and to 'firm historical reality'? 'No period has writers who play more difficult games with fact and factuality than the Augustan. This helps to make Pope the most interesting and problematic of subjects.'[57] It seems odd, in view of his emphasis on the reality of Pope's victims, that Rogers makes nothing of the fact that some were alive and some were dead even at the time that *The Dunciad* first appeared in 1728, a crucial distinction when assessing the poem's impact on its targets. Susannah Centlivre, Thomas Durfey, Richard Flecknoe, Charles Gildon, Luke Milbourne, Francis Quarles, George Ridpath, Abel Roper, Elkanah Settle, Thomas Shadwell, Nahum Tate, John Toland, and John Tutchin all died before 1728. They all appear in a more or less open

---

[53] Richardson, *Selected Letters of Samuel Richardson*, ed. John Carroll (Oxford: Clarendon Press, 1964), 100.

[54] Cited in Albert Rosenberg, *Sir Richard Blackmore: A Poet and Physician of the Augustan Age* (Lincoln: University of Nebraska Press, 1953), 145.

[55] Thomas Jemielity, 'A Mock-Biblical Controversy: Sir Richard Blackmore in the *Dunciad*', *Philological Quarterly*, 74 (1995), 249–77 (p. 249).

[56] Rogers, *Grub Street*, 177.

[57] Barbara Everett, 'Tibbles: A New Life of Pope', in *Poets in their Time: Essays on English Poetry from Donne to Larkin* (Oxford: Clarendon Press, 1991), 120–39 (p. 122).

form of identification in the 1728 *Dunciad*, with their names spelt out in the *Variorum* of 1729 (the year in which Blackmore died—a fact that did not prevent him from remaining one of the chief targets of the poem).

When the last *Dunciad* was published in 1743, a year before Pope's own death, the sense in which this pantheon of incompetence was attacking live abuses must have felt still more remote. Anthony Alsop, Richard Bentley, Thomas Bentley, William Bond, Abel Boyer, John Durant Breval, Peter Burmann, Daniel Defoe, John Dennis, George Duckett, John Dunton, Thomas Hearne, Philip Horneck, Ludwig Kuster, Bernard Mandeville, Nathaniel Mist, John Oldmixon, Edward Roome, James Moore Smythe, Elizabeth Thomas, Ned Ward, Joseph Wasse, and Thomas Woolston, all of whom appear in this version of *The Dunciad*, were dead by 1743. Five of them (Alsop, Burmann, Richard Bentley, Kuster, and Wasse) were first introduced to the poem in 1742—when Book IV of *The Dunciad* was published by itself, prior to its incorporation into a revised poem in four books the following year. Then, only the Bentleys and Oldmixon had died as recently as 1742; Alsop and Kuster—both 1742 additions—were dead as long ago as 1726 and 1716.

Pope's neatly chiastic suggestion that 'the *Poem was not made for these Authors, but these Authors for the Poem*' ('PREFACE *prefix'd to the five imperfect Editions of the* DUNCIAD, *printed at* Dublin *and* London, *in Octavo & Duod.*', *Dunciad*, 205) is, as Rogers observes, 'double-edged': it could mean that 'the Dunces were mere instrumentalities, unidentified lackeys of a higher poetic cause' or it could 'confer a new importance and a new individuality on these special, custom-designed antitypes'.[58] This ambiguity allows James Sutherland to claim that 'such a comic butt as Tom Durfey is introduced, not because Pope felt spiteful towards him, but because almost every one was prepared to treat Durfey as a joke' (*Dunciad*, p. xlv)—a point which fails to disprove Pope's spite—while Rogers can plausibly object to the casting of Durfey as an ahistoric type that 'Pope's decision to use notorious figures of this kind among his cast serves to *fix* the developing narrative within a historical context, rather than to liberate it from such a context'.[59]

Pope's actors gain individual significance above all from the fact that (in post-1728 versions of *The Dunciad*) they are named. Swift may have insisted that 'you must have your Asterisks fill'd up with some real names of real Dunces', but he also warned Pope to: 'Take care the bad poets do not outwit you, as they have served the good ones in every

---

[58] Rogers, *Grub Street*, 179.   [59] Ibid. 177.

Age, whom they have provoked to transmit their Names to posterity . . .
Gildon will be as well known as you if his name gets into your Verses'
(Pope, *Correspondence*, ii. 343, 505). Gildon had died by this time, which
alters the implications of transmitting his name 'to posterity'; the poem
could no longer strangle his career, only his posthumous reputation.
And if other duces (living or dead) were understood as types rather
than as individuals, this might be said to contribute to the dynamic of
the work. For if Pope's original readers sometimes did not register a
continuity between seemingly mythical beings and real people—if they
failed to make Rogers's immediate reference from literature to life—then
the murky division between traditional and newly fashioned dunces
supports the conclusion Pope sought to drive home. Contemporary
hacks would one day be relegated to the status of their predecessors,
becoming unidentifiable components of an amorphous dullness.

Blackmore may stand out from the poem as the noisiest and most
persistent dunce, 'Who sings so loudly, and who sings so long' (II. 268),
yet 'his name', as Johnson writes, 'was so long used to point every epigram
upon dull writers that it became at last a bye-word of contempt' (*Lives*, ii.
252)—as Boswell became, in Adam Sisman's phrase, 'a byword for a fool'.
The author of *Characters of the Times* could not understand his inclusion,
since by 1728 he had already faded from public consciousness. Indeed,
Johnson's comparatively brief 'Life of Blackmore' (eleven pages in G. B.
Hill's edition of the *Lives of the Poets*) is informed by a sense that it is
impossible to reconstruct the historical reality of its subject: 'Blackmore
is one of those men whose writings have attracted much notice, but of
whose life and manners very little has been communicated, and whose lot
it has been to be much oftener mentioned by his enemies than by friends';
'of his private life and domestick character there are no memorials' (*Lives*,
ii. 235, 253). In the case of many of Pope's targets, it was *The Dunciad*
itself which ensured that 'no memorials' would remain of their lives,
other than the infamy conferred by the poem. Eliza Haywood, forced
into anonymous publication by Pope's demeaning reference to her 'Two
babes of love' and 'fore-buttocks to the navel bare' in the first version
of *The Dunciad* (II. 150, 154, *1728a–f*), was said 'from a Supposition of
some Liberties being taken with her Character after Death' to have 'laid
a solemn Injunction on a particular Person, who was well acquainted
with all the Particulars of it, not to communicate to any one the least
Circumstance relating to her'. Haywood's first biographer, who wrote
these lines, could discover nothing of his subject other than that her
father 'was in the Mercantile Way, that she was born in *London*, and that,

at the Time of her Death, which was, I think, in 1759, she was about sixty
three Years of Age'. And this in spite of the fact that Haywood had died
only eight years before he attempted to write her memoir.[60]

A certain kind of ambiguity, then (between one critical argument that
we should think of the dunces as types, and another that we should
reconstruct them as individuals; between Pope's assertion of the dunces'
unimportance and the fact that they are important enough to be included
in his poem) implies the existence of a literary middle ground that is
neither wholly exclusive nor wholly inclusive. There is a case to be made
for the way in which writers allude to what they reject without thereby
quite including it; certain works can exhibit a latent consciousness or
indirect representation of what they are not. The world of 'nonsense'
constructed in *The Dunciad* (I. 60, 123, 241; II. 194; III. 59, 201) is half-
truth, half-fiction; 'non' calls up 'sense' as the standard from which it
deviates, and without which it would not make sense. The poem, 'now
to sense, now nonsense leaning' (*Arbuthnot*, l. 185), inhabits a region
between two poles. Pope liked to do things by halves. He issues in
Book IV of *The Dunciad* with the lines 'Of darkness visible so much be
lent, | As half to shew, half veil the deep Intent' (ll. 3–4), and in other
contexts gives a posthumous existence to the apparently defunct—as in
the compounds 'half-viewless' and 'Half-breathless' from his translation
of *The Odyssey* (VIII. 304; XVI. 65). These combinations are, so to speak,
half-empty rather than half-full. They pull back something from the brink
of becoming nothing, the categorically not-breathing or not-viewed. The
dunces, creatures of an intermediate kind, similarly inhabit a shady zone
on the borders of attention and at the threshold of literary consciousness;
'scarce quick in embryo', they are the 'hints, like spawn' of the poem,
named but also 'nameless Somethings' or 'Nothing' personified, a 'half-
form'd' combination of reality and fiction, of sense and nonsense, that
affronts species divisions as well as literary categories: 'a monster of a
fowl, | Something betwixt a Heideggre and owl' (*Dunciad*, I. 59, 56; II.
110; I. 61, 289–90. John James Heidegger, 'Master of the Revels' under
George II, was notoriously ugly. See note to *The Dunciad*, 443–4).

A related effect is created by amalgamation of opposites in Pope's
famous portrait of the androgynous Lord Hervey as 'Sporus' ('Half

---

[60] [David Erskine Baker], *The Companion to the Play-House: or, an Historical Account
of all the Dramatic Writers (and their Works) that have appeared in Great Britain and
Ireland, from the Commencement of our Theatrical Exhibitions, down to the present year 1764.
Composed in the form of a Dictionary*, 2 vols. (London: for T. Becket and P. A. Dehondt;
C. Henderson, and T. Davies, 1764), ii, entry under 'HEYWOOD, Mrs. *Eliza*'.

Froth, half Venom') in his *Epistle to Dr. Arbuthnot*: 'Amphibious Thing!
that acting either Part, | The trifling Head, or the corrupted Heart! | Fop
at the Toilet, Flatt'rer at the Board, | Now trips a Lady, and now struts a
Lord' (ll. 320, 326–9). Sporus' crime, his 'Amphibious' nature resembling
the semi-aquatic and wilfully dubious characterization of bad writers in
Peri Bathous (see below), is to elude and hence to insult conventional
definition. Such indeterminacy is at once a mark of moral depravity,
and a poetic opportunity. It would be wrong to consider the dunces'
and Hervey's incursions on propriety simply as forces Pope wished to
eradicate—although this is in one sense true—for his verse worries at and
revels in the task of giving full expression without full accommodation
to their singularity. One of the complicated pleasures of such writing is
that it is only in partial accord with its own professed disgust.

The marginal region of hybrids which Sporus and the dunces inhabit is
a reflection of that 'area of shadow in or around the work', the recognition
of which Macherey calls 'the initial moment of criticism'. He goes on to
argue that 'we must examine the nature of this shadow: does it denote a
true absence, or is it the extension of a half-presence?'[61] We might gloss
Pope's 'half-viewless' as the extension of a half-absence, but whether
he is conferring a half-absence or a half-presence on the dunces or on
Sporus is complicated by the fact that he is dealing to a greater or lesser
extent with actual identities. Perhaps we can say that *The Dunciad* seeks
to confer a half-presence on the dunces as types, a half-absence on the
dunces as individuals. They exhibit 'a curious mixture of unimportance
and of generic or exemplary status'.[62] This is true, in a broad sense, of all
fictional characters. The *British Critic*, acknowledging that Austen 'gives
no definitions' of her actors, nevertheless concluded that we 'instantly
recognize among some of our acquaintance, the sort of persons she
intends to signify', while one recent critic discerns in *Emma* (1816) a
method that primarily associates Miss Bates with 'universal standards'.[63]
Henry James, revisiting *Roderick Hudson* (1875), concluded of his hero
that: 'The very claim of the fable is naturally that he *is* special, that his
great gift makes and keeps him highly exceptional; but that is not for a
moment supposed to preclude his appearing typical (of the general type)

[61] Macherey, *A Theory of Literary Production*, 82.
[62] Claude Rawson, *God, Gulliver, and Genocide: Barbarism and the European Imagination* (Oxford: Oxford University Press, 2001), 270.
[63] Anon., *British Critic* (1818), cited in C. B. Hogan, 'Jane Austen and her Early Public', *Review of English Studies*, NS 1 (1950), 39–54 (p. 47); Norman Page, *The Language of Jane Austen* (Oxford: Basil Blackwell, 1972), 57.

as well; for the fictive hero successfully appeals to us only as an eminent instance, as eminent as we like, of our own conscious kind.'[64]

The 'claim' described here has two aspects: it is both the assertion of the story and its hold on our attention that Roderick is a special character; yet the counter-claim (the other side of the fable's 'appeal') is that he attracts us as a recognizably typical one. James's argument might be adapted to sublimely awful characters, 'highly exceptional' in dullness or, as Pope has it, 'distinguish'd in the *true Profound*' (*Prose*, 175). The stature of the duncess is 'as eminent as we like', as dependent on our own consciousness of their importance (and on how seriously we take the threat of their unabashed professionalism and vulgarity) as it is on their part-creator's. But it should not be forgotten that these dunces, unlike Roderick Hudson, were also real people.

3. CATALOGUES

Literary productions are of necessity finite, informed by the materials they omit as well by those they include. Freud, as Macherey notes, recognized these necessary omissions and accordingly relegated the '*absence of certain words* to a new place . . . which he paradoxically *named*: the unconscious'.[65] Pondering the nature of jokes and their reliance on the unconscious, Freud observed that one 'kind of allusion consists in "omission" . . . Actually, in every allusion something is omitted, viz. the train of thought leading to the allusion.' This omission is inevitable; it only 'depends on whether the more obvious thing is the gap in the wording of the allusion or the substitute which partly fills the gap. Thus a series of examples would lead us back from blatant omission to allusion proper.' In a literary context, we might question Freud's confidence of the ability to determine intermediate stages between 'blatant omission' and 'allusion proper' (he goes on to say that 'A joking allusion . . . emerges without my being able to follow these preparatory stages in my thoughts'),[66] but it is in tune with Pope's Scriblerian propensity to foster hierarchies of literary sub-groups, breezily indicating the stages by which bathetic writers ascend to and sink beneath the level of our attention.

---

[64] Henry James, *Roderick Hudson* (1876), introd. Tony Tanner (Oxford: Oxford University Press, 1980; repr. 1988), 'Preface', pp. xlvii–xlviii.

[65] Macherey, *A Theory of Literary Production*, 85.

[66] *The Standard Edition of the Complete Psychological Works of Sigmund Freud*, ed. and trans. James Strachey et al., 24 vols. (London: Hogarth Press and the Institute of Psycho-Analysis, 1953–74), viii. 77, 168.

The complex descent to bad writing in *Peri Bathous* is at once prissy and careless, orderly and nonchalant, comically dramatizing the impulses of a divided mind. Scriblerus sets out to 'range these confin'd and less copious Genius's under proper Classes, and (the better to give their Pictures to the Reader) under the Names of Animals of some sort or other' (Pope, *Prose*, 179). To call such writers 'confin'd and less copious' (even when one of the chief complaints about Blackmore, 'the most celebrated Amplifier of our Age', was his rampant prolixity, as Scriblerus goes on to display, *Prose*, 183–5) suggests in advance that their limited capacities are ripe for the imposition of categories. The vigorous toing and froing of the Sporus passage, on the other hand, cries out for settled categories whilst showing awareness that settled categories cannot accommodate such deviance. The unrestrained and incursive aspects of bad writing are not mentioned at this point in *Peri Bathous*, since the question of classing is involved, while the airily unspecific 'Names of Animals of some sort or other' suggests that the appropriateness of those classifications to the authors they describe is not especially important. Scriblerus hints at the fact that Pope cannot quite decide whether it is more culpable to elude or to be encapsulated by categorical description (discussing Pope, Empson commented that 'one belittles a man merely by classifying him', while T. S. Eliot has a character remark on the assumption that 'A man is only important as he is classed'):[67]

I SHALL range these confin'd and less copious Genius's under proper Classes, and (the better to give their Pictures to the Reader) under the Names of Animals of some sort or other; whereby he will be enabled, at the first sight of such as shall daily come forth, to know to what *Kind* to refer, and with what *Authors* to compare them.

1. THE *Flying Fishes*; these are Writers who now and then *rise* upon their *Fins*, and fly out of the *Profound*; but their Wings are soon *dry*, and they drop down to the *Bottom*. G. S. A. H. C. G.
2. THE *Swallows* are Authors that are eternally *skimming* and *fluttering* up and down, but all their Agility is employ'd to *catch Flies*. LT. WP. Lord R.
3. THE *Ostridges* are such as whose Heaviness rarely permits them to raise themselves from the Ground; their Wings are of no use to lift them up, and their Motion is between *flying* and *walking*; but then they *run* very fast. D. F. L. E. The Hon. E. H.
4. THE *Parrots* are they that repeat *another's Words*, in such a *hoarse, odd* Voice, that makes them seem *their own*. W. B. W. H. C. C. The Reverend D. D.

[67] Empson, *The Structure of Complex Words*, 85; T. S. Eliot, *Eeldrop and Appleplex* (London: Foundling Press, 1992), 3.

5. THE *Diadappers* are Authors that keep themselves long *out of sight*, under water, and *come up* now and then where you *least expected* them. *L. W.*—*D.* Esq; The Hon. Sir *W. Y.*

6. THE *Porpoises* are unweildy and big; they put all their Numbers into a great *Turmoil* and *Tempest*, but whenever they appear in *plain Light*, (which is seldom) they are only *shapeless* and *ugly Monsters. I. D. C. G. I. O.*

7. THE *Frogs* are such as can neither *walk* nor *fly*, but can *leap* and *bound* to admiration: They live generally in the *Bottom of a Ditch*, and make a *great Noise* whenever they thrust their *Heads above Water. E. W. I. M.* Esq; *T. D.* Gent.

8. THE *Eels* are obscure Authors, that wrap themselves up in their *own Mud*, but are mighty *nimble* and *pert. L. W. L. T. P. M.* General *C.*

9. THE *Tortoises* are *slow* and *chill*, and like *Pastoral Writers* delight much in *Gardens*: they have for the most part a *fine embroider'd Shell*, and underneath it, a *heavy Lump. A. P. W. B. L. E.* The Rt. Hon. *E.* of *S.*

THESE are the chief Characteristicks of the *Bathos*. (*Prose*, 180–1)

The Dunciad's ambivalence about naming and thus immortalizing its targets is here rehearsed in early form. Pope's list combines a scrupulous titular deference ('Lord', 'The Hon.', 'The Reverend', 'Esq.', 'The Hon. Sir', 'Gent.', 'General', 'The Rt. Hon.') with more or less cryptic initials (when these initials appear in a long list, it is hard to tell how many individual characters they are describing, or at what points those individuals should be demarcated one from another). He ensures the potential at once for readers to specify his authors and for him to claim (or to provoke) a broader satiric applicability. Certain identification of every individual is impossible: the groupings remain sufficiently fluid, in a literal and metaphoric sense, to harbour further examples (the reader will be enabled 'to know to what *Kind* to refer, and with what *Authors* to compare them'), sufficiently directed to seem as if they must be appropriate to the instances they cover. The fact that we cannot pinpoint most victims might prompt the endeavour to establish fixed identities, and at the same time lead us to think that any writer who fits the bill should be classed as this sort of creature. Are these elusive authors types, or are they individuals?

Rogers's arguments about *The Dunciad*'s historical specificity, or lack of it, are equally appropriate to *Peri Bathous*, but the fact that this is the case raises further questions about the historical specificity of either work. For Martinus Scriblerus, who also introduces *The Dunciad*, is himself characterized (like Sporus), in half-watery terms which approximate those of his subjects: as 'a man of capacity enough that had *dipped* in every art and science, but injudiciously in each' (i.e. his own incompetence is also a butt of the joke, but not necessarily at the same time or in the same manner as that of his bathetic authors).[68] The categories mediate between vague generalization and diffused particularity—both faults attributed to bad writers, and both as applicable to their critic: Scriblerus exclaims that 'A great Genius takes things in the Lump, without stopping at minute Considerations', and, virtually in the same breath, 'How inimitably circumstantial! . . . *Amplification* . . . is the spinning Wheel of the *Bathos*, which draws out and spreads it to the finest Thread' (*Prose*, 183–5).

The semi-aquatic creatures in *Peri Bathous* are, like Scriblerus and Sporus, capable both of rising and of sinking. This passage depicts a water mark above which such authors make their presence felt, thus constructing a threshold of literary attention, and 'thresholds symbolise beginnings of new statuses':[69] the fishes 'now and then *rise* upon their *Fins*, and fly out of the *Profound*'. Once these authors '*rise*' above their denominated sub-realm, 'the *Profound*', they stake a legitimate (albeit brief) claim to our regard, so that Pope's catalogues cannot be said merely to enshrine creative abuses. They are mixed repositories of intermittent success and predominant failure, classifications of an unclear kind registering interest and delight as well as repugnance. Pope's unwillingness to categorize his targets as simply or straightforwardly inept registers in Scriblerus' own semi-competence; the mask shields a genuine indecisiveness.

Mary Douglas argues that, in some cultures, penguins might prove anomalous 'because they swim and dive as well as they fly, or in some other way they are not fully bird-like'.[70] Pope's bathetic writers do indeed swim and dive, as well as fly—they are not fully author-like in the sense that they cannot always write up to the mark; not fully dunce-like in that they are not always beneath that mark. Of the non-aquatic creatures, the ostrich, as a land-bound bird, cannot fly nor inhabit the elevated sphere for which it seems designed (the implications for poetic flight and elevation are obvious—these authors are not properly classifiable as such); parrots mimic another species for their unnatural powers of speech. They affront a received order of things, yet also belong to a '*Kind*', prompting the simultaneous formation and confusion of distinctions. The very nature of Pope's subjects means that they obstruct as well as encourage the impulse to classify them, and *Peri Bathous* thus 'defies, or

---

[68] Pope in Spence, *Observations*, i. 56 (my emphasis).
[69] Mary Douglas, *Purity and Danger: An Analysis of the Concepts of Pollution and Taboo* (London: Routledge & Kegan Paul, 1969; repr. 1976), 114.
[70] Ibid. 56–7.

complicates, or undermines, certain clarities of demarcation on which
[it] simultaneously insists' (the confusion is catching).[71] According to
Douglas, the Lele tribe separates 'animals of the above (birds, squirrels,
and monkeys) from animals of the below: water animals and land animals.
Those whose behaviour is ambiguous are treated as anomalies of one
kind or another and are struck off someone's diet sheet. For instance,
flying squirrels are not unambiguously birds nor animals, and so they are
avoided by discriminating adults.'[72]

   Like the flying squirrels, Pope's flying fish might be shunned, by aesthetically discriminating adults, because they constitute a mixed category
(mostly they write badly; occasionally—perhaps accidentally?—they
write well). His taxonomies promote an exchange between natural
historical and literary classification. Italics draw attention to key characteristics of an authorial and creaturely kind: '*slow*' and '*chill*' might
apply as much to mental plodding as to constitutional phlegm; dropping
'down to the *Bottom*' is equally interchangeable. But other references are
slightly less so. What does Pope mean when he writes that ostriches can
'*run* very fast'? Is the comment more applicable to real ostriches than
to authors? Or is he hinting at an ability to evade capture and reprisal?
The murkiness of the criteria is yet another aspect of the satire, mocking the solemn pedantry of scientific enumerations[73] and what Henry
Knight Miller called the 'terminological vagueness ... of the period'.
Henry Fielding's 'Some Papers proper to be read before the R—l Society, Concerning the Terrestrial CHRYSIPIUS, GOLDEN-FOOT OR GUINEA'
(1743), published in the same year as the last version of *The Dunciad*, is
a Scriblerian-type parody of Abraham Trembley's investigations into an
'aquatick Insect', the polypus. Fielding is alert to the humorous potential of such categorical indeterminacy: 'I have not, after the minutest
Observation, been able to settle with any degree of certainty, whether
this be really an Animal or a Vegetable, or whether it be not strictly
neither, or rather both.'[74] The impossibility of identifying Pope's victims,
thanks in part to the combination of literal muddiness and figurative
obscurity, means that we are unable to confirm either that these authors
are made for their categories, or vice versa. It is a nice irony that Spence,

[71] Rawson, *God, Gulliver, and Genocide*, 161.

[72] Douglas, *Purity and Danger*, 166–7.

[73] See also *The Tatler*'s '*Will of a Virtuoso*' (no. 216, iii. 133–5).

[74] Henry Fielding, *The Wesleyan Edition of the Works of Henry Fielding: Miscellanies*, ed.
Henry Knight Miller, Bertrand A. Goldgar, and Hugh Amory, 3 vols. (Oxford: Clarendon
Press, 1972–97), i. 195 and n. 3, 254, 196.

Pope's great admirer, considered the 'worst Fault of any Language' to be 'Ambiguity'.[75]

Taxonomies may succeed merely in hinting at a realm of promiscuous detail beyond their defining terms; their display of finitude then ceases to appeal by comparison with the niggling object or character that 'at first sight, seems not to belong to the domain of the *notable*'.[76] A highly developed consciousness of such peripheries is compatible with a period that witnessed so many literary projects laying comic or serious claim to unexceptionable applicability and exactitude—Swift's satirical *Tale of a Tub* (1704) is, as the subtitle informs us, 'Written for the Universal Improvement of Mankind'. Too particularized an attempt at universality paradoxically fosters the impression of a lack of coverage, drawing attention by its specificity, as does the rhetorical figure of paralipsis (e.g. 'not to mention the weather . . . '), to what has been left out, not to what has been included:

A prayer followed, of the catalogue type which by attempting to get everything in only succeeds in focusing attention on what has been omitted. 'For all miners, steel-workers, farmers' (the boot and shoe trade?), 'for all mothers in childbirth, sufferers from cancer' (herpes? Scarlet fever?), 'for all doctors, nurses, surgeons, for all whose business lies upon the great waters' (does this include submarine crews? Does it include them when *submerged*? And if it doesn't, what have *they* done to deserve being left out? And if you can't mention *everyone* specifically, why mention *anyone* specifically?), 'for the King and Queen and all the royal family, for the sick and the homeless, for all those . . . ' It lasted for nearly a quarter of an hour, persons eventually unsupplicated for including, by Mr Datchery's estimate, musicians, tailors, greengrocers, and Mr Aneurin Bevan.[77]

Prayers 'of the catalogue type' trigger Mr Datchery's counter-catalogue, 'including' a group of professions which belong together by virtue of their omission from a different one. The joke about his 'estimate' wryly suggests the flawed thinking behind attempts at exhaustiveness—as if there might be less in the world than in a catalogue prayer of sufficient length, and that you might set about calculating what has been overlooked. Edmund Crispin borrowed the titles of two of his novels

[75] Joseph Spence, *An Essay on Pope's Odyssey: in which Some Particular Beauties and Blemishes of that Work are Consider'd*, 2 vols. (London: for James and J. Knapton et al., 1726–7), ii. 25.

[76] Roland Barthes, 'The Reality Effect', in Tzvetan Todorov (ed.), *French Literary Theory Today: A Reader* (Cambridge: Cambridge University Press, 1982), 11–17 (p. 11).

[77] Edmund Crispin (Bruce Montgomery), *The Long Divorce* (1951; Harmondsworth: Penguin, 1958), 65–6.

from Pope[78] ('Mr Datchery' is itself a pseudonym for the Oxford English Literature don-cum-detective, Gervase Fen), and there is a connection between Datchery's simultaneously whimsical and energetic concern for submarine crews, who lie beneath rather than 'upon the great waters' ('Does it include them when *submerged?*'), and Pope's bathetic '*Diadappers*', 'Authors that keep themselves long *out of sight*, under water, and *come up* now and then where you *least expected* them.' Pope and Crispin project their common interest in diving beneath superficial categorization into literalized form: what of those below the surface? To what kinds of pressure do submerged or marginal presences subject the groupings they are not meant to inhabit, but with whom they share certain characteristics? Pope told Spence in 1736 that *Peri Bathous*, 'though written in so ludicrous a way, may be very well worth reading seriously as an art of rhetoric':[79] a point which suggests the straightforward truth of his assertion (and its applicability not merely to bad writers but to himself, as the author of this work, of *The Rape of the Lock*, and of *The Dunciad*) that 'few can arrive at the Felicity of falling gracefully . . . for a Man . . . to descend *beneath himself*, is not so easy a Task unless he calls in Art to his Assistance' (*Prose*, 175). As in Boswell's sketch of a Herculean Johnson stooping to the distaff, the discernible accents of a charitable descent 'infinitely below' oneself (*Prose*, 177), or of a mock-heroic skilfulness in elevating the lowly to our regard, prevent this from being read solely as an satiric reversal of Pope's attitudes. *Peri Bathous* is, finally, ambiguous as to whether the emphasis falls on contempt or on praise for 'an Art of *Diving* as well as of *Flying*', or 'the Skill to bring it down' (*Prose*, 175, 186). It is not only a recommendation of how *not* to write, since it might also be interpreted as a suggestive description of its author's own methods. Like Boswell, Pope adopts an ironic guise in order to sanction the inclusion of what his writing simultaneously rejects.

Pope's ambiguous catalogues and Mr Datchery's instinctive resistance to prayers 'of the catalogue type' prompt the thought that there might be such a thing as a literary sensibility directed primarily at what has been left out of its own productions, and of those by other authors. Franz Kafka, as reader, writer, and theatregoer, was acutely aware of his gravitation towards the margins:

---

[78] Edmund Crispin (Bruce Montgomery), *The Moving Toyshop* (London: Victor Gollancz, 1946), from *The Rape of the Lock* (I. 100), and *Frequent Hearses* (London: Victor Gollancz, 1950), from *Elegy to the Memory of an Unfortunate Lady* (1717), l. 38.

[79] Spence, *Observations*, i. 57.

Dieses Verfolgen nebensächlicher Personen von denen ich lese in Romanen, Teaterstücken u. s. w. Dieses Zusammengehörigkeitsgefühl, das ich da habe! In den 'Jungfern von Bischofsberg' (heißt es so?) wird von zwei Näherinnen gesprochen, die das Weißzeug für die eine Braut im Stücke machen. Wie geht es diesen 2 Mädchen? Wo wohnen sie? Was haben sie angestellt, daß sie nicht mit ins Stück dürfen, sondern förmlich draußen vor der Arche Noah unter den Regengüssen ertrinkend zum letztenmal nur ihr Gesicht an ein Kajütenfenster drücken dürfen, damit der Parterrebesucher für einen Augenblick etwas Dunkles dort sieht.

This pursuit of the secondary characters I read about in novels, plays, etc. This feeling of our belonging together that I have then! In the *Virgins of Bischofsberg* (is that what it's called?), there is talk of two seamstresses, who sew the linen for the play's one bride. What happens to these 2 girls? Where do they live? What have they done that they may not also enter the play, but stand, as it were, outside, in front of Noah's ark, drowning in the torrents of rain, and may only press their faces one last time against a cabin window, so that the audience member in the stalls sees something dark there for a moment.[80]

This entry is an expansion on a cryptic note, made around seven months earlier, about Kafka's disgusted response to authors (or the business of authorship, with its attendant selections and rejections), and his interest in their discarded by-products: 'Schriftsteller reden Gestank | Die Weißnäherinnen in den Regengüssen' ('Writers talk rubbish. | The seamstresses in the torrents of rain').[81] Kafka's 'Zusammengehörigkeitsgefühl' ('feeling of belonging together') predominates over his ability to remember with confidence the name of the play in which his subordinate characters fail to appear—although he was right about the title. There is, initially, a colloquial urgency to his questions about them: 'Wie geht es diesen 2 Mädchen?' means not only 'What happens to these 2 girls?' (i.e. 'why are they not permitted to appear on stage?'), but, more simply, 'How are they?' (i.e. 'what are they up to in real life?'), which, followed by the question 'Where do they live?', has a disconcertingly vitalizing, everyday quality. The conventional present tense in which Kafka is discussing the play's action extends beyond its confines, at once startlingly and unobtrusively, to bestow a present existence on characters the play has not deigned to include. Left out of a fictional world, they inhabit a real one that makes the closed province of the drama seem at once inert and hostile. Central characters are excised by a passive construction ('[es] wird von zwei Näherinnen gesprochen',

---

[80] Franz Kafka, 16 Dec. 1910, *Tagebücher*, ed. Hans-Gerd Koch, Michael Müller, and Malcolm Pasley, 3 vols. (Frankfurt a. M.: Fischer, 1983), i. 132 (my translation).
[81] Kafka, May (?) 1910, ibid. 13 (my translation).

'there is talk of two seamstresses'); the 'play's one bride' is syntactically subordinated, in a diametric reversal of the playwright's attention, to the humble seamstresses who produce her linen.

Kafka's unwieldy 'Zusammengehörigkeitsgefühl' is played off against the brief, spatio-temporal density of 'da' ('then', but also 'there'), pinpointing his identification with characters that reside in the margins of other literary works—hence the title of the novel we now know as *Amerika*, but which Kafka called *Der Verschollene*, or *The Man who Disappeared*. His diary entry bucks against the sort of authorial arbitration over great and little, primary and secondary characters, which Fielding genially foregrounds (and hence dissipates) in *Tom Jones* (1749): 'As our History doth not ... give great Characters to People who never were heard of before, nor will ever be heard of again; the Reader may hence conclude, that [Miss Nancy] will hereafter appear to be of some Importance in our History' (*Tom Jones*, ii. 705).

Considering what usually happens to Kafka's fictional protagonists, the 'pursuit' he mentions in his diary has overtones of harassment as well as of solicitude. Is it as much in the sense of being pursued as of being secondary that Kafka, in chasing the seamstresses, feels at one with them? The paradoxical condition of subsisting on the peripheries of attention while at the same time being actively sought out might sum up one dynamic of his writing, as well as one of Pope's. Kafka's fictional protagonists, humdrum clerks such as Gregor Samsa in *Die Verwandlung*, or *The Metamorphosis*, seem themselves to be secondary to their own narratives, bewildered at the experience of performing centre stage as much as they are bewildered at being hunted to extinction. Kafka has moved from being a reader, in the opening sentence of his diary entry, to being a spectator not merely of Hauptmann's play but of his own reconstructed version of it, which looks from the inside outwards rather than from the outside inwards, dwelling on a brief glimpse (within the confines of the ark, the theatre, and of the work itself) of 'something dark' pressing against its outer reaches.

There is something particularly 'dark' in the Jewish Kafka's 'feeling of belonging together' with characters excised from the world of the stage, prefiguring Hitler's progressive exclusion of the Jews from artistic, social, and political life prior to their mass extermination.[82] But Kafka had his

---

[82] Point Four of the Nazi Party's 1920 programme, which was never altered, stated that: 'Only those of German blood, whatever their creed, may be members of the nation. Accordingly no Jew may be a member of the nation.' See Daniel Jonah Goldhagen, *Hitler's Willing Executioners: Ordinary Germans and the Holocaust* (London: Abacus, 1996), 85.

blind spots too: there are, in fact, *three* seamstresses mentioned in *Die Jungfern von Bischofsberg*.[83] It is as a pair of characters, however, that they hold his attention, and prompt the expansive chronological reversion from Hauptmann's twentieth-century play to Noah's ark, that sanctuary for privileged couples from which this twosome is excluded.[84] As a figure for what happens to the numberless characters conceived in the literary imagination yet finally discarded, it would be hard to improve on this expression of a sudden, decisive rift between creature and creator.

Literary works might, then, be approached by focusing on their peripheries because they themselves suggest such a distribution of emphasis—satirical writers often permit themselves to countenance in allusive mode the very arguments, ideas, and interests they also wish formally to repudiate. As Brean Hammond argues, the Scriblerians were 'able to draw energy from the cultural forms that they simultaneously despised'.[85] A catalogue may proffer the vision of order, yet none remains hermetically isolated from the examples it rejects (in Pope's case, the extent to which he is rejecting anything remains unclear). Such examples may begin to demonstrate a creative order of their own, as in negative catalogues like Mr Datchery's: 'Granted that disorder spoils pattern; it also provides the materials of pattern.'[86]

Since books and paintings always omit something, it makes sense to ask, as John Barrell does, what a work suggests (rather than says straight out), or what it does not say—which is itself a form of suggestion. Reflecting on 'a number of unwritten but binding rules which governed the terms on which the poor could appear in landscapes', rules 'for the most part recognised only when they were broken', Barrell advises that 'It is not often intended or explicit meanings that I shall be pointing to . . ., but meanings that emerge as we study what can *not* be represented in the landscape art of the period'. ('May *not*' would be better than 'can *not*', since the sense in which an eighteenth-century painting cannot represent a peasant is different from the sense in which it cannot represent a twenty-first-century factory-worker.) The evidence for an ambiguity tends itself to be ambiguous, yet this emphasis on implicit rules for omission results in explicit conclusions. Of the 'necessary distance' between Constable

---

[83] Gerhart Hauptmann, *Die Jungfern von Bischofsberg* (Berlin: Fischer, 1907), 25.

[84] Two years later, Kafka wrote to Max Brod of the difficulties involved in omitting another pair of characters from his own work; like the seamstresses, they gained in vivacity by their expulsion. Franz Kafka, *Briefe*, ed. Hans-Gerd Koch (Frankfurt a. M.: Fischer, 1999–   ), i. 229.

[85] Hammond, *Professional Imaginative Writing*, 11.

[86] Douglas, *Purity and Danger*, 94.

and the figures who appear in his landscapes, Barrell writes that the artist (in common with many late eighteenth-century poets) 'is *excluded*, and reduced to envying a condition that he cannot attain'; '*Excluded* from the society of the inarticulate, Constable retaliates by *excluding* them from the society of those with a true appreciation of the universe.' Wordsworth's relationship with nature 'must *exclude* guide, traveller, poet . . ., who are *excluded* therefore also from the natural community of the valleys'; his language 'must *exclude* the articulate poet from the inarticulate community of nature'. Gray's *Elegy Written in a Country Churchyard* (1751) is 'a particularly early dramatisation of what is a ubiquitous sense of *exclusion* in the later eighteenth century'.[87]

'Ubiquitous' is an exaggeration; Barrell does not mean more than that a sense of exclusion is widespread, or it would cease to be comprehensible as such (except in terms of our common expulsion from Eden). He rapidly concludes from the absence of a particular the wholesale banishment of a class. But the fact that something is unmentioned, or unmentionable, does not entail that it has been excluded: how can Barrell tell so clearly what has been omitted, unless his examples provide compelling inferences that oblige him to supply it? In which case, 'exclusion' is too strong a word for the way in which these works both gesture towards and fail to accommodate certain people and things.

Human communication depends on the recognition of intent. There are many everyday scenarios in which the mere fact that an intention is understood results in its accomplishment. Communication might be said to occur not when we apprehend the linguistic sense of an utterance, but when we deduce the speaker's intended meaning from it. Hence the fact that when people notice someone has misused a word or made a slip of the tongue, they tend to disregard the wrong meaning. The interpretation they discount may not be nonsensical on its own terms; it is false only insofar as it provides misleading evidence about the speaker's intentions.[88] Norman Page argues that *Emma* relies 'on the normal susceptibility of the commonplace remark or action to be open to more than one interpretation';[89] thus, when Mr Knightley is reported as saying 'He had just looked into the dining-room, and as he was not wanted there, preferred being out of doors', Emma understands that 'He

---

[87] John Barrell, *The Dark Side of the Landscape: The Rural Poor in English Painting, 1730–1840* (Cambridge: Cambridge University Press, 1980), 17, 18, 156–7, 159 (my emphases).

[88] See Dan Sperber and Deirdre Wilson, *Relevance: Communication and Cognition* (Oxford: Basil Blackwell, 1986), 21–31.

[89] Page, *The Language of Jane Austen*, 42.

meant to walk with her' (*Works*, iv. 424). The ways in which we discuss poetry and painting rely on this model of obliquely communicating and acknowledging intent, and Michael Baxandall observes that criticism accordingly requires 'concepts of . . . indirect or peripheral kinds': 'many of the thoughts we will want to explain are indirect, in the sense that they are not pointed quite directly at the picture'; indeed, 'Most of the better things we can think or say about pictures stand in a slightly peripheral relation to the picture itself.'[90]

Description of any kind involves limiting a field and choosing what matters under specific circumstances, and what matters always points to more than we see at present. It cannot register all that lies before us, although it may give the impression of doing just that. As James put it: 'Really, universally, relations stop nowhere, and the exquisite problem of the artist is eternally but to draw, by a geometry of his own, the circle within which they shall happily *appear* to do so.'[91] A wholly inclusive view of society representing what Ian Watt identified as '*all* the varieties of human experience' (my emphasis) is, as Johnson well knew, an unfeasible standard by which to judge any work of art: 'what is obvious is not always known, and what is known is not always present . . . when it shall be found that much is omitted, let it not be forgotten that much likewise is performed' ('Preface to the Dictionary', *Prose and Poetry*, 323).

4. THE GENERAL AND THE PARTICULAR

One of Ivy Compton-Burnett's characters expresses the Johnsonian view that 'small things have their importance. They may have more meaning than bigger ones. Trifles make perfection, and perfection is no trifle.'[92] Perfection may be 'no trifle', yet it summarizes a host of imperfect, trifling constituents. As Compton-Burnett's chiastic phrasing makes plain, a modulation between the local and the universal may take the form of dignifying particulars by combining them into a single, elevated generalization (perfection), or of dissecting a generalization into its various elements (trifles): 'Sublimity is produced by aggregation, and littleness by dispersion. Great thoughts are always general, and consist in positions not limited by exceptions, and in descriptions not descending to minuteness' (Johnson, 'Life of Cowley', *Lives*, i. 21).

---

[90] Michael Baxandall, *Patterns of Intention: On the Historical Explanation of Pictures* (New Haven: Yale University Press, 1985), 6, 5.
[91] James, *Roderick Hudson*, 'Preface', p. xli.
[92] Ivy Compton-Burnett, *Two Worlds and their Ways* (1949; London: Virago, 1990), 185.

Reinert argues that the 'difficulty of generalization' or an 'ambivalence in the relation between exemplars and what they are supposed to exemplify' manifests itself in the 'disconnected, open-ended' sequences of catalogue poems such as *The Vanity of Human Wishes*, which alights (like *The Dunciad*) on socially and historically specific rather than on mythical actors for its purposes. Simultaneously arousing pathos for their exemplarity and scorn for their paltriness, Johnson's agents 'are meant to illustrate the most general principle of human life . . .—the fatal insistence of vanity—but they also have the mock heroic's tough, inert particularity'.[93] That tough particularity, and (at a still further stage of particularization) the synecdoche which destines a ruler's or a statesman's rise and fall to a mere 'Nod', 'Smile', 'Glance', 'Eye', or 'Hand' (ll. 103, 104, 110, 111, 100, 220)—a counterpart to what Peter Pindar saw as the undignified emphases on 'Sam's nods, and winks, and laughs' in Boswell's *Tour*—repeatedly challenges the status and applicability of elevated, public generalizing:

> In full-blown Dignity, see *Wolsey* stand,
> Law in his Voice, and Fortune in his Hand:
> To him the Church, the Realm, their Pow'rs consign,
> Thro' him the Rays of regal Bounty shine,
> Turn'd by his Nod the Stream of Honour flows,
> His Smile alone Security bestows:
> Still to new Heights his restless Wishes tow'r,
> Claim leads to Claim, and Pow'r advances Pow'r;
> Till Conquest unresisted ceas'd to please,
> And Rights submitted, left him none to seize.
> At length his Sov'reign frowns—the Train of State
> Mark the keen Glance, and watch the Sign to hate.
> Where-e'er he turns he meets a Stranger's Eye,
> His Suppliants scorn him, and his Followers fly;
> At once is lost the Pride of aweful State,
> The golden Canopy, the glitt'ring Plate,
> The regal Palace, the luxurious Board,
> The liv'ried Army, and the menial Lord.
> With Age, with Cares, with Maladies oppress'd,
> He seeks the Refuge of Monastic Rest.
> Grief aids Disease, remember'd Folly stings,
> And his last Sighs reproach the Faith of Kings.
>   (*The Vanity of Human Wishes*, ll. 99–120)

---

[93] Reinert, *Regulating Confusion*, 76–7.

Wolsey's 'full-blown Dignity' might be read as a figure for generalization itself, and for its failure to accord with the fate of a specific human
being (however great): as an individual ceases to stand for something
representative, so the language conveying the decline of a 'sinking Statesman' (l. 79) becomes fractured. Prepositions reinforce the apparently
immovable solidity and transparent vacuity of Wolsey's eminence: he
stands *in* dignity, law is *in* his voice, fortune *in* his hand; church and
realm consign their powers *to* him, the stream of honour is turned *by*
his nod. Yet the rays of regal bounty shine *through* him; the emphasis
falls on a display of largesse for which the swollen Wolsey serves as mere
vehicle, and whose object may change. Johnson might be describing a
stained glass window: exemplary, but diaphanous. The juxtaposition of
intangible ('Law . . . Fortune') and corporeal ('Hand . . . Nod . . . Smile')
nouns produces comically portentous and internally discordant effects.

As Wolsey's fortunes change, the tense reverts to the past for one
couplet (ll. 107–8), perhaps to show that he is in the process of being
transmuted into a historically illustrative failure, and that the poet has
become a chronicler. Back to the present tense, 'the Train of State'
initially seems to be an unelaborated abstract idea—state's generic
retinue—as is usually the case in Johnson's verse,[94] so that it comes as an
appropriate surprise (echoing Wolsey's) to find it dispersed into actual
royal attendants by the following line's first word, the admonitory 'Mark'.
As he comes under suspicion, the company of words clustering around
Wolsey becomes particularized into former 'Suppliants' and 'Followers';
he can no longer assume the support of a collectively submissive body.
Similarly, the potentially abstract and imposing 'Pride of aweful State'
translates into six enumerated possessions, the single human collective
'liv'ried Army' following 'the luxurious Board', as if (until now) Wolsey
has not needed to tell the difference—the army was as easy to command
as a meal. His fundamental mistake seems to have been that he had too
general, too elevated, and too grandiose a view.

The final line is ambiguous as to whether or not it is an embedded
quotation: did Wolsey's 'last Sighs' actually 'reproach the Faith of Kings'?
Or do his sighs indirectly reproach that faith, in the sense that they serve
perpetually to upbraid royal fickleness (thus acting as a parallel to the
'regal Bounty' of l. 102, which will continue to 'shine' through one vessel

---

[94] As in, for instance, 'Soft Pleasure with her laughing train' and 'the labouring train'
('An Ode' (1747), l. 6; 'Prologue to Goldsmith's *The Good Natur'd Man*' (1768), l. 3). See
also *Rambler* 165 on truth 'when she intrudes uncalled, and brings only fear and sorrow in
her train' (*Yale*, v. 111).

or another)? Is Johnson periphrastically expressing a final, spoken rebuke, or is he extrapolating a moral from Wolsey's death? Is he writing in particular, or in general terms? Johnson does not directly state that Wolsey died. The narration of his decline elides retirement, arrest, and death in a different manner from Juvenal's brutally detailed lines on Sejanus' fall. Similarly, Johnson's description of old age (*The Vanity of Human Wishes*, ll. 299–310) resists Juvenal's lengthy, vicious catalogue of physical and sexual indignities,[95] although he defended its veracity in terms which show he may have pondered the question of a general or a specific portrayal: 'one day, in a conversation upon the miseries of old age, a gentleman in company observed, he always thought Juvenal's description of them to be rather too highly coloured—upon which the Doctor replied—"No, Sir—I believe not; they may not all belong to an individual, but they are collectively true of old age"' (*Miscellanies*, ii. 166–7).

An exemplary decline cannot be made unambiguously 'To point a Moral' (l. 222) in Wolsey's case, and the portrait is the better for it. What we are made aware of, instead, is the process of determinedly mediating between an individual's specific fate, its applicability (or lack of it) to the rest of us, and the reason for writing about such things at all. The ensuing fourteen lines pose stern questions to the reader about his or her own 'safer Pride', and the potential usefulness or uselessness of attending to Wolsey, Villiers, Harley, Wentworth, and Hyde (ll. 121–34). Here, Johnson again closes his verse paragraph ambiguously, on a question whose sense is as deliberately undecided as that of 'The conclusion, in which nothing is concluded' in *Rasselas* (1759) (*Yale*, xvi. 175). Asking what caused the downfall of these men, he reworks the 'consign'/'shine' rhyme of ll. 101–2: 'What but their Wish indulg'd in Courts to shine, | And Pow'r too great to keep, or to resign?' (ll. 133–4). 'Indulg'd' faces in two different directions here. We might read it as a participial adjective generally describing those who shine in courts, or as a past participle in the passive voice, tied to specific historical instances. The line could mean 'they wished to shine, indulged, in courts' (as you or I may do), or that 'their wish to shine in courts was indulged' (as yours and mine has not been). Such indeterminacy, on a crucial point, seems to say that it is equally disastrous to dream of such pre-eminence and to achieve it.

It is a strength of the writing in this context that we gain the impression that Wolsey, rather than his author, 'loses the grandeur of generality, for of the greatest things the parts are little; what is little can be but pretty,

---

[95] See Niall Rudd (ed.), *Johnson's Juvenal: London and The Vanity of Human Wishes* (Bristol: Bristol Classical Press, 1981; repr. 1988), 64–9.

and by claiming dignity becomes ridiculous' ('Life of Cowley', *Lives of the Poets*, i. 45). William Mudford wrote that *Rasselas* 'no where falls off from its dignity', and the same holds true of Johnson's style in this poem: he often seems to be alerting us to the distinction between synecdoche and bathos, implying that a subject's descent need not entail authorial degradation. When Mudford proposed that *The Vanity of Human Wishes* sometimes 'laboured into dignity', he was not necessarily disparaging Johnson (although he thought his 'claim to poetry' was 'very doubtful').[96] One of the poem's great achievements is the sense it conveys of a mind labouring to translate mucky, particular truths into resonant, piercing generalities, and vice versa—or rather, *almost* vice versa. As the above lines demonstrate, Johnson's descent to specifics remains ambiguous enough to allow for a general interpretation of one man's fate, as Byron recognized: ''tis a grand poem—and *so true*! . . . The lapse of ages *changes* all things—time—language—the earth—the bounds of the sea—the stars of the sky, and every thing "about, around, and underneath" man, *except man himself*, who has always been, and always will be, an unlucky rascal. The infinite variety of lives conduct but to death, and the infinity of wishes lead but to disappointment.'[97] Burke proposed that one 'source of greatness is *Difficulty*. When any work seems to have required immense force and labour to effect it, the idea is grand' (*Enquiry*, 77). Emphasizing difficulty as a contributory factor to grandeur, Joshua Reynolds was careful to add the caveat that greatness must only *seem* 'to have required immense force and labour', not that it should descend to a particular exposition of that effort: 'An inferior artist is unwilling that any part of his industry should be lost upon the spectator. He takes as much pains to discover, as the greater artist does to conceal, the marks of his subordinate assiduity.'[98]

To combine inherently undignified labour with dignity is to achieve, however briefly, a form of generalization vibrating with alertness to the particulars from which it abstracts. Johnson agreed with Joseph Fowke that his greatest contribution to life-writing had been the notoriously difficult (and to some eyes undesirable) composition of 'trifles with dignity' (*Life*, iv. 34 n. 5)—uniting little and great, particular and

[96] William Mudford in James T. Boulton (ed.), *Johnson: The Critical Heritage* (London: Routledge & Kegan Paul, 1971), 148, 47.

[97] George Gordon, Lord Byron, *Byron's Letters and Journals*, ed. Leslie Marchand, 12 vols. (Cambridge, Mass.: The Belknap Press of Harvard University Press, 1973–82), viii. 19–20.

[98] Joshua Reynolds, *Discourses on Art* (1769–91), ed. Robert Wark (New Haven: Yale University Press, 1975), Discourse IV (1771), 59.

general in a manner that directly contradicts Aristotle's definition of propriety, as mentioned in the Introduction: 'Style is proportionate to the subject matter when neither weighty matters are treated offhand, *nor trifling matters with dignity*' (my emphasis). That combination of trifles with dignity might be applied not only to the *Lives of the Poets* but also to *The Vanity of Human Wishes*, which largely consists, like *Rasselas* and *A Journey to the Western Islands of Scotland*, of a picaresque series of biographical, enumerative, and anthropological vignettes—all of which draw attention to their incompleteness and extensibility. Johnson attempted a similar alliance of trifles with dignity in the 'Preface to Shakespeare' (*Yale*, vii. 108–9), and in his defence of petty authors via a comparison with agricultural labourers in *Rambler* 145:

It is allowed, that vocations and employments of least dignity are of the most apparent use . . . This is one of the innumerable theories which the first attempt to reduce them into practice certainly destroys. If we estimate dignity by immediate usefulness, agriculture is undoubtedly the first and noblest science; yet we see the plow driven, the clod broken, the manure spread, the seeds scattered, and the harvest reaped, by men whom those that feed upon their industry will never be persuaded to admit into the same rank with heroes, or with sages; and who, after all the confessions which truth may extort in favour of their occupation, must be content to fill up the lowest class of the commonwealth, to form the base of the pyramid of subordination, and lie buried in obscurity themselves, while they support all that is splendid, conspicuous, or exalted . . . there is another race of beings equally obscure and equally indigent, who because their usefulness is less obvious to vulgar apprehensions, live unrewarded and die unpitied, and who have been long exposed to insult without a defender, and to censure without an apologist . . .

That such authors are not to be rewarded with praise is evident, since nothing can be admired when it ceases to exist; but surely though they cannot aspire to honour, they may be exempted from ignominy, and adopted into that order of men which deserves our kindness though not our reverence. These papers of the day, the *Ephemerae* of learning, have uses more adequate to the purposes of common life than more pompous and durable volumes . . . Every size of readers requires a genius of correspondent capacity. (*Yale*, v. 8–12)

Johnson had already recommended attention to the '*Ephemerae* of learning'—'small Pamphlets', and 'single Sheets' (*Prefaces*, 51)—in his *Proposals* for the *Harleian Miscellany* (1744). The *OED* cites *Rambler* 145 as containing the earliest known example of a figurative sense of 'ephemera': 'One who or something which has a transitory existence' (sense 2). Yet it was not Johnson's intention to become the apologist of individual hacks: 'That such authors are not to be rewarded with praise is evident.' He draws a distinction between figurative and actual non-existence, between individual oblivion and collective annihilation. Although petty authors are habitually overlooked, their labours play a vital supporting role and permit 'all that is splendid, conspicuous, or exalted' in literature. Accomplished writers (such as Pope, who would not readily have acknowledged the fact) stand in the same dependent relationship towards dunces as all of us to the agricultural workers who produce our food. For this reason alone, their works as a whole 'must not be rashly doomed to annihilation', even if their separate performances justly meet with its literary equivalent, oblivion. Johnson sought recognition of the usefulness of their combined activity, rather than of the dignity of its discrete productions. That he claims it is the '*order* of men', rather than any specific author, which deserves our kindness indicates the nature of his argument: 'Laws are not made for particular cases, but for men in general' (Johnson in *Life*, iii. 25).

Collapsing from the heights of incarnate dignity to something teetering on the edge of irrelevant exemplarity, or exemplary irrelevance—a vain human wish to be greater than the sum of his fractured parts—Wolsey is pregnant with instruction to a writer seeking to moralize about the vanity of human wishes, as well as to his audience. His fall remains, however, in *general* terms, 'a triumph over the temptation to idealize; and consequently, the factual or real tends to blur into the abstract form of any figure that frustrates the idealizing impulse'. [99] One disproportion in Johnson's writing, by his own admission, resides in the difference between recommending little things in general and writing about them in particular, for he did not naturally incline towards the petty detail.[100] Hence *Rambler* 98's self-interrogating complaint, which has Addison and Steele's exemplary journalistic descent to private life and trivial things in mind (see Chapter 2), that:

it may be doubted whether you have accommodated your precepts to your description; whether you have not generally considered your readers as influenced by the tragick passions, and susceptible of pain or pleasure only from powerful agents and from great events . . . nothing can justly seem unworthy of regard, by which the pleasure of conversation may be increased, and the daily satisfactions of familiar life secured from interruption and disgust

For this reason you would not have injured your reputation, if you had sometimes descended to the minuter duties of social beings, and enforced the

---

[99] Reinert, *Regulating Confusion*, 148.
[100] John Courtenay thought that 'In the *Ramblers* the abstract too often occurs instead of the concrete;—one of Dr. Johnson's peculiarities'. *A Poetical Review of the Literary and Moral Character of the late Samuel Johnson*, 3rd edn. (1786; Los Angeles: William Andrews Clark Memorial Library, 1969), 13 n. 28.

observance of those little civilities and ceremonious delicacies, which, inconsiderable as they may appear to the man of science, and difficult as they may prove to be detailed with dignity, yet contribute to the regulation of the world. (*Yale*, iv. 160)

This observation might be applied to the disjunction between Johnson's idea of biography in *Rambler* 60 ('there has rarely passed a life of which a judicious and faithful narrative would not be useful', *Yale*, iii. 320) and his actual exercises in the genre—most of which focus on renowned subjects. *Rambler* 98 is a theoretical argument about Johnson's practical neglect of familiar life. It was a neglect for which he repeatedly rebuked himself, so that the subject appears with a peculiar frequency in his work—a conscious absence becomes a fitful presence, a habitual omission something invoked too frequently for it to be termed exclusion, yet which translates too rarely into a practical descent to low or mean things for it to be called inclusion, or conclusion. The 'half drunk' Revd George 'Telemachus' Graham may have touched on a sore point when he 'rattled away' at Johnson: 'You're a clever fellow, but you can't write an essay like Addison or verses like *The Rape of the Lock*' (*Tour*, 69).

Johnson's brand of inclusiveness was perplexed; aggrandizing peripheral subjects and characters allowed him to challenge presumptions about the proper domain of writing, yet his sympathies were fiercely divided between centre and margin, between dignified generality and the squalid multiplicity of particulars. As Reinert puts it: 'Critics argue that Johnson's skepticism about generalization expresses and amplifies his preoccupation with the texture of lived experience. His attention to particulars leads naturally to his taste for biography. If one is to convey moral instruction, it will have to be by way of the concrete scenes of real lives with their complexity of circumstance'; 'It is surely true that Johnson writes skeptically about generalization; but is it also true that that skepticism promotes a realist writing style that attends to the texture of the everyday?'[101] Reinert's answer to this question—that Johnson's suspicion of the general truths to which he is also attracted does not lead simply or directly to espousing the concrete, everyday particular—seems broadly correct. Ambivalence about the moral direction and uses of his work leads Johnson on the one hand to enlarge and on the other to diminish its remit, and that of literature in general. Sometimes he will argue, as above, that 'Every size of readers requires a genius of correspondent capacity' (*Rambler* 145, *Yale*, v. 11–12), and that every category of

[101] Reinert, *Regulating Confusion*, 36, 89.

author therefore deserves some recognition. At other times, perceiving unwarranted incursions on literary territory, he appears to have a 'design of maintaining the dignity of the empire, without attempting to enlarge its limits'.[102]

Walt Whitman's verse inclines towards an enumerative method of assembling high and low materials precisely in order 'to enlarge' the literary empire's 'limits'—he ranks, for instance, 'a leaf of grass' with 'the journey-work of the stars' and compiles inventories of manufactures and trades, of objects and occupations.[103] The technique was received by enthusiastic critics as the outcrop of a democratic spirit, a roll-call for the nation: 'equality . . . enters into Whitman's poetry, as one of its organic and organizing constituents'; it 'explains the poet's passion for bestowing an exalted lyric treatment upon everything which up to his time had been looked upon as vile and "unworthy of the Muse" '.[104] Appraising his own work, Whitman's apparent summary of the value of displaying America's 'enormous diversity' swiftly collapses into a list exceeding two hundred words.[105]

Unsympathetic commentators thought the catalogues offensively workaday, outside or beyond the peripheries of legitimate poetic endeavour, in part because there is no means of limiting potential additions to their listed items. The form is too informal. Yet those same commentators make no objections to Homer's epic catalogues. They seem, under the guise of disparaging a technique, to be protesting about the lowliness of the *things* enumerated in Whitman's lists. Content, rather than form, is at issue.[106] John Bailey took the catalogue to be reliant on 'the insatiable appetite of the uneducated for insignificant and disconnected occurrences': its 'style and language do not appear to be those of poetry at all'. Whitman's best poetry, Bailey argued, 'hardly ever indulges in the tedious catalogues or in the vulgar jargon. . . When once he is really moved he has no time to compile these auctioneering inventories of things in general.'[107] The catalogues should not, however, be glossed as an unmoved or mundane impulse to orderliness (although they have the

[102] Gibbon, *Decline and Fall*, i. 37.
[103] Walt Whitman, *Complete Poetry and Collected Prose*, ed. Justin Kaplan (New York: Viking Press, 1982), 'Song of Myself', 31.1; 'A Song for Occupations'.
[104] D. Mirsky in Francis Murphy (ed.), *Walt Whitman: A Critical Anthology* (Harmondsworth: Penguin, 1969), 248.
[105] Walt Whitman, 'Walt Whitman and his Poems', ibid. 31–2 (p. 31).
[106] See also A. D. Nuttall, 'Auerbach's *Mimesis*', *Essays in Criticism*, 54 (2004), 60–74: 'Homer is "high" because he deals with nobles and heroes fighting bravely, that is to say, because of the content, not the form' (p. 63).
[107] John Bailey, *Walt Whitman* (London: Macmillan, 1926), 61, 58.

appearance of order, in spite of Bailey's claim that they contain merely 'disconnected occurrences'). The analogous relationships elicited from and between their listed items, and the obvious potential to add to that list, are an outpouring of sympathy intended to stir up rather than to settle readers' responses. Bailey's vexed reaction might therefore be read as a measure of Whitman's success.

Whitman's catalogues resemble Johnson's idea of biography, since both speak to the bulk of human experience. We read 'Histories of the downfal of kingdoms, and revolutions of empires ... with great tranquillity', but 'the man whose faculties have been engrossed by business, and whose heart never fluttered but at the rise or fall of stocks, wonders how the attention can be seized, or the affections agitated by a tale of love'. It is by an appeal to what literary works habitually dismiss as commonplace, to incidents which 'nothing but their frequency makes considerable', that the attention of most readers is engaged and the ends of literature best achieved (*Rambler* 60, *Yale*, iii. 319). If Johnson 'may be suspected of sometimes, endeavouring to give dignity to trifles, of which he was conscious', this is because the trifling or diminutive subject paradoxically 'makes the best provision against that inattention by which known truths are suffered to lie neglected'.[108] It is the ability to startle readers into attention by renewing their interest in the commonplace for which Johnson commends mock-heroic, particularly *The Rape of the Lock*, in which 'familiar things are made new' ('Life of Pope', *Lives*, iii. 234). Addison is praised in similar terms; his humour gives 'the grace of novelty to domestick scenes and daily occurrences' ('Life of Addison', *Lives*, ii. 148). Those subjects habitually dismissed from literary works as too exiguous, tedious, or minute to merit attention acquire a peculiar value when they do appear, because of their rarity in literature and because of their recurrence in daily life.

'No man knew better than Johnson in how many nameless and numberless actions *behaviour* consists: actions which can scarcely be reduced to rule, and which come under no description' (Piozzi in *Miscellanies*, i. 161). A sense (such as Pope's) of the potential for ordering what is at the margins of literature and of life should be read in light of an awareness that something that counts must always be left out of account. The fact that it is peripheral to our consciousness may constitute its importance, so that the marginal briefly becomes central: hence Wordsworth's emphasis on the fact that 'little, nameless, unremembered

---

[108] Mudford and George Gleig in Boulton (ed.), *Johnson: The Critical Heritage*, 75, 73. Gleig is quoting (with some modification) Johnson on Swift ('Life of Swift', *Lives*, iii. 52).

acts' comprise 'that *best* portion of a good man's life'.[109] Hence, too, Johnson's advice to Boswell on the contents of his journal: 'I told Mr. Johnson that I put down all sorts of little incidents in it. "Sir," said he, "there is nothing too little for so little a creature as man. It is by studying little things that we attain the great knowledge of having as little misery and as much happiness as possible." '[110] 'Little' harbours a variety of meanings here—smallness of duration, size, and value; indignity, meanness, or want of grandeur (see Johnson's *Dictionary* entries for 'LITTLE' and 'LITTLENESS')—encapsulating in its semantic flexibility the claim that trifles combine to shape our existence: 'The main of life is ... composed of small incidents, and petty occurrences'; 'the misery of man proceeds not from any single crush of overwhelming evil, but from small vexations continually repeated' (*Rambler* 68, *Yale*, iii. 359; 'Life of Pope', *Lives*, iii. 234). In a characteristically swift manoeuvre, Johnson establishes that '*little* things' lead to '*great* knowledge'. He might have reversed the equation and argued that great things, by contrast, prompt little knowledge, especially as he is discussing a personal diary—*Rambler* 60's arguments about the uselessness of 'Histories of the downfal of kingdoms' to private life spring to mind, as well as a comment recorded by Piozzi: 'learn by this perpetual echo of even unapprehended distress, how historians magnify events ... Who sleeps the worse, for one general's ill success, or another's capitulation?' (Johnson in *Miscellanies*, i. 203–4). She was herself fond of reformulating the comparative insignificance of public to private life, in defence of her 'mere *candle-light* picture' of the Great Cham's 'latter days', passed 'among friends' at home in Streatham (*Miscellanies*, i. 310).

Acknowledging Boswell's use of 'little' in the sense of trifling or insignificant, and scenting a whiff of disingenuousness, Johnson embraces great and little in a feat of simultaneous encompassment and reduction. He pans out from Boswell's specific fear of individual pettiness to consider humanity *en masse*, yet also diminishes man himself to the status of a little 'creature' ('A general term for man' but also 'A word of contempt for a human being', senses 4 and 5 of 'CREATURE' in the *Dictionary*) for whom the study of little things is most apposite. 'These little things are great to little Man', as he observed to Hester Thrale (quoting Goldsmith's

---

[109] William Wordsworth, *The Major Works*, ed. Stephen Gill (Oxford: Oxford University Press, 1984; repr. 2000), 'Lines Written Above Tintern Abbey' (1798), l. 33 (my emphasis).

[110] *Boswell's London Journal: 1762–1763*, ed. Frederick A. Pottle (London: Heinemann, 1950), 305. 'Knowledge' became 'art' in the version of this conversation that Boswell reported in the *Life* (i. 433).

The Traveller, or a Prospect of Society (1764), l. 42; *Collected Works*, iv. 250), with reference to Boswell's journal of the Hebridean tour (*Letters*, ii. 228–9).[111]

The reward for a cumulative alertness to the word 'little' in Boswell's journal entry is its fifth and final use as another kind of diminution: that of misery. *Rasselas* gives some idea of what this attention to man's native littleness—to one person's insignificance 'in the mighty heap of human calamity', or to 'the small proportion which every man bears to the collective body of mankind' (*Rambler* 99, *Yale*, iv. 166; *Rambler* 146, *Yale*, v. 15)—might mean in practice. It guards against delusions of grandeur, and therefore also against madness: 'keep this thought always prevalent, that you are only one atom of the mass of humanity, and have neither such virtue nor vice, as that you should be singled out for supernatural favours or afflictions' (Imlac in *Rasselas*, *Yale*, xvi. 163).

---

[111] Hazlitt used the same line as a motto for his essay 'On Great and Little Things' (1822). *Complete Works*, viii. 226.

2

'Voluntary Degradation': Johnson's Prefaces and Dedications

Hester Thrale remarked that Johnson, who never dedicated his own work to anyone,[1] had contributed 'Prefaces, Dedications Introductions & c. out of Number ... for People in Distress who wanted Money Wit or advice from him', adding later that 'His Friends often prevailed on him to write Prefaces, Dedications & c. for them, but he did not love it—one would rather says he one Day give anything than that which one is used to sell' (*Thraliana*, i. 162, 185). The desire for 'advice from him' suggests that such friends often wished him to edit, revise, and amend their own efforts, but it also alludes to the morally instructive strain Johnson lent to such writing, and to a central element of his literary and private character. Regardless of whether he disliked the practice ('No man but a blockhead'—and Johnson—'ever wrote, except for money', *Life*, iii. 19), he prided himself on his abilities as a jobbing scribbler, working in generically apologetic forms for 'People in Distress'. Poverty-stricken beneficiaries included Charlotte Lennox, for whom he provided dedications to *The Female Quixote, or, The Adventures of Arabella* (1752), *Shakespear Illustrated: or the Novels and Histories, on which the Plays of Shakespear are founded, collected and translated from the Original Authors* (1753–4), *Memoirs of Maximilian de Bethune, Duke of Sully* (1755), *Philander: A Dramatic Pastoral* (1757), *The Greek Theatre of Father Brumoy* (1760), and *Henrietta* (1758); Alexander Macbean, one of his amanuenses on the *Dictionary*, for whom he wrote the preface to *A Dictionary of Ancient Geography* (1773); Thomas Maurice, a country parson, for whose *Poems and Miscellaneous Pieces* (1780) Johnson 'condescended to write the Preface'; French prisoners of war, for whose

---

[1] A fact that John Courtenay noticed: '[He] firmly scorn'd, when in a lowly state, | To flatter vice, or court the vain and great'; 'It is observable that Dr. Johnson did not prefix a dedication to any one of his various works.' *A Poetical Review*, 28 and n. 53.

relief he wrote an introduction to the *Proceedings of the Committee for Cloathing French Prisoners* (1760); and his blind lodger Anna Williams, for whom he furnished proposals and an advertisement, individual poems, and a fairy tale, *The Fountains*, as part of her *Miscellanies* (1766) (*Prefaces*, 89–116, 132–42, 189–93, 213–16).

Through voluntarily composing prefaces, advertisements, proposals, introductions, and dedications, Johnson exercised benevolence towards the humble authors he anonymously impersonated. In his prefatory writings themselves, this original, charitable act of submission reappears in the form of advising readers to bestow their own judgements with circumspection, to elevate to a position of worthiness and dignity those topics and characters seemingly beneath their regard. When Johnson talked to Boswell of 'the attention that is necessary in order to distribute our charity judiciously', he might have phrased it the other way round—and remarked on the charity that is necessary in order to distribute our attention judiciously (*Tour*, 367).

Considering 'the authour' and 'the publick' in general, Johnson expanded on what he thought introductions and conclusions required: 'There are two things which I am confident I can do very well: one is an introduction to any literary work, stating what it is to contain, and how it should be executed in the most perfect manner; the other is a conclusion, shewing from various causes why the execution has not been equal to what the authour promised to himself and to the publick' (*Life*, i. 292). In practice, these contrary emphases—theoretical perfection and imperfect execution—are, for Johnson, combined. While the audience habitually reads a preface before embarking on the work it describes, the author has usually composed it after that work is completed, and with the benefit of hindsight—so that it acts as a conclusion and as an introduction (an exception to this rule, discussed below, is the preface to a journalistic enterprise). Johnson's 'Preface to the Dictionary' not only unites the breadth of intention with the shortfall of performance, but also extracts a general moral from its particular example of aspiration and disappointment, looking outwards from the text to humanity. The dream of all-embracing inclusiveness and applicability with which the writer sets out on his collection of examples ends in a partial representation: 'When I first collected these authorities, I was desirous that every quotation should be useful to some other end than the illustration of a word'; 'Such is design, while it is yet at a distance from execution. When the time called upon me to range this accumulation of elegance and wisdom into an alphabetical series, I soon discovered that the bulk of my volumes would fright away the student, and was forced to depart from my scheme of including all that was pleasing or useful in *English literature*' (*Prose and Poetry*, 313).

The active construction 'I . . . collected' yields to the external imposition of 'time called upon me'. Johnson's beginnings tend in this way to be modified by a sense of the necessity of ending, and vice versa. The opening sentence of *Rasselas* endeavours at once to prompt and to check the reader's appetite for event: 'Ye who listen with credulity to the whispers of fancy, and pursue with eagerness the phantoms of hope; who expect that age will perform the promises of youth, and that the deficiencies of the present day will be supplied by the morrow; attend to the history of Rasselas prince of Abisinnia' (*Yale*, xvi. 7). The oracular tone seems to imply that Johnson will *not* fulfil the whispers of fancy and the phantoms of hope. But the injunction, in fact, is merely to 'attend', not least to the shape of this introductory command. 'Attend' is a word that gives equal weight to raising and to deferring fruition of the reader's expectations (reinforced by the periodic structure of the sentence). It enjoins submission, due to the implication of 'attending' or 'waiting on' the author as his fiction unfolds (sense 6 of 'To ATTEND, *v.a.*' is 'To expect'; sense 2 of 'attend, *v.n.*' is 'To stay; to delay'; sense 1 of 'To ATTEND, *v.n.*' is 'To yield attention'; senses 2 and 7 of 'To ATTEND, *v.a.*' are: 'To wait on; to accompany as an inferiour'; 'To wait on, as on a charge', Johnson's *Dictionary*).

Our anticipation that Johnson's first sentence heralds the demise of romance, or a straightforward attack on the delusions of youth, will be subject to as much revision as are Rasselas and Nekayah's naïve enthusiasms. Real accents of disapproval are located, if anywhere, in the qualifications 'with credulity' and 'with eagerness', not in the faculties of hope and imagination, which—in spite of chastening experience—remain operative and necessary throughout the book (Johnson was a closet admirer as well as a stern critic of quixotic fiction. Thomas Percy reported that 'when a boy [Johnson] was immoderately fond of reading romances of chivalry, and he retained his fondness for them through life ... Yet I have heard him attribute to these extravagant fictions that unsettled turn of mind which prevented his ever fixing in any profession'; *Life*, i. 49 and n. 2; see also iii. 2). In *Rasselas*, 'The conclusion, in which nothing is concluded' sees the travellers resolve to make their way back to the Happy Valley—where the story began—and is famously indecisive rather than axiomatic (*Yale*, xvi. 175). As Fred Parker observes, Johnson's deep-seated 'horror at finality' translates into a kind of writing which, even in its closing stages, eschews the 'possibility of conclusiveness' in favour of 'a more open-ended sense of relations and differences', and therefore of new fields of enquiry.[2]

His prefaces reveal the same stop-start motion and divided awareness of themselves as conclusions and as introductions, as obstacles or delays to readers' progress and as the removal of impediments. Typically, they favour the metaphor of a path. The opening of the 'Preliminary Discourse to the London Chronicle' (1757) notes with wry self-consciousness that 'Even those who profess to teach the Way to Happiness have multiplied our Incumbrances, and the Author of almost every Book retards his Instructions by a Preface', while the second paragraph of the 'Preface to the Dictionary' might be depicting the conventionally 'humble', often anonymous introductory author, as well as the lexicographer (in this instance the same person), as one 'doomed only to remove rubbish and clear obstructions from the paths through which Learning and Genius press forward to conquest and glory, without bestowing a smile on the humble drudge that facilitates their progress' (*Prose and Poetry*, 327, 301).

In 1775, Johnson contributed a preface to his friend Giuseppe Baretti's *Easy Phraseology for the Use of Young Ladies, who intend to learn the Colloquial Part of the Italian Language*. This preface reveals a complicated vigour and a protracted gravitas that teeter on the edge of bathos—a feeling that the slightness of the topic will barely sustain the energy with which it is recommended to our attention:

Of every learned and elegant people the language is divided into two parts: the one lax and cursory, used on slight occasions with extemporary negligence; the other rigorous and solemn, the effect of deliberate choice and grammatical accuracy. When books are multiplied and style is cultivated, the colloquial and written diction separate by degrees, till there is one language of the tongue, and another of the pen.

No language can be said to have been learned till both these parts are understood: but to reach the colloquial without the opportunities of familiar conversation, is very difficult. By reading great Authors it cannot be obtained, as books speak but the language of books; and those, who in England intend to learn Italian, are seldom within the reach of Italian conversation.

This deficience I have, by a bold experiment, endeavoured to supply, in the following Dialogues, in which I have undertaken to comprize not the gross and barbarous, but the careless and airy diction of casual talkers. Let no supercilious contemner of trifles look upon these productions with too much elevation, or indulge himself in merciless censures on the humble author, who knows already,

[2] Parker, *Scepticism and Literature*, 240, 236.

with full conviction, the levity of his subjects, and the unimportance of his personages. His design is not to refine the language of the senate or the school: it is only to teach Italian; to teach those words and phrases, which are appropriated to trifles; but of which, as life is made of trifles, there is a frequent use . . .

These are, however, not the first pages that have been compiled only for the sake of teaching words; but, as I cannot boast of having invented the method that I have taken, I will not, by voluntary degradation, place myself below other nomenclators. Let my Dialogues be compared for copiousness of language, variety of topics, and power of entertainment, with other collections of words and phrases; and of the place, which honest criticism may give me, I shall have no reason to be much ashamed. (*Prefaces*, 10–11)

In its linguistic self-consciousness, magisterial precision, and stadial overview of 'cursory', 'careless', and 'casual' terrain, Johnson's style introduces a sense of doubt into the reader's mind about whether any subject can ever fully articulate with the 'importance of debate' and 'solemnity of diction' that he would lend it ('Preface to Shakespeare', *Yale*, vii. 108). The weight of assertion and his authoritative survey of social, linguistic, and intellectual progress are counteracted by a feeling of imbalance, as Johnson displays and reflects on the compulsion of the human mind 'to supply' a 'deficience' or to fill an intellectual void, its abhorrence of meaninglessness.[3] That imbalance arises in part from the firmness of the adversatives 'however' and 'but', and the force of '*no*'—not 'little'—'reason to be much ashamed'. In his last contribution to *The Adventurer* (no. 138), again combining the sense of an ending with that of a beginning, Johnson had pondered the condition of authors 'with regard to themselves' and implicitly associated vacuity with the preface's generic rehearsal of the journey from intention to execution (*Yale*, ii. 492). A 'design' is here characterized as a distant, external prospect, its performance as an internal oscillation between imagined fertility and actual emptiness (although the qualifiers 'frequently' and 'sometimes' allow us to retain a measure of hope about the outcome): 'It frequently happens, that a design which, when considered at a distance, gave flattering hopes of facility, mocks us in the execution with unexpected difficulties; the mind which, while it considered it in the gross, imagined itself amply furnished with materials, finds sometimes an unexpected

---

[3] 'All knowledge is of itself of some value. There is nothing so minute or inconsiderable, that I would not rather know it than not' (Johnson in *Life*, ii. 357); 'Ignorance is mere privation, by which nothing can be produced: it is a vacuity in which the soul sits motionless and torpid for want of attraction; and, without knowing why, we always rejoice when we learn, and grieve when we forget' (Imlac in *Rasselas*, *Yale*, xvi. 49). See also Parker, *Scepticism and Literature*, 269–70.

barrenness and vacuity, and wonders whither all those ideas are vanished, which a little before seemed struggling for emission' (*Yale*, ii. 494).

In the Baretti preface, significance is generated by a precariously elevated linguistic register, one that perhaps serves to conceal the 'barrenness and vacuity' of Johnson's topic. He is defending the merits of a colloquial form of expression, one that markedly contrasts with the form he predominantly employs. Like the 'Preface to Shakespeare', which had pointed out that 'those who wish for distinction forsake the vulgar, when the vulgar is right', and praised Shakespeare for catching and transmitting the 'easy and familiar dialogue' of real life rather than the language of books (*Yale*, vii. 70, 68), Johnson here pits gains against losses. The advances of learning and elegance, far from unmitigated triumphs, entail the separation of writing from speaking, of polished from common life. But there is no relaxation of his style to coincide with the reference to 'lax' qualities of talking on 'slight occasions'. The author, having fixed the language of the pen at a distinct remove from everyday colloquialisms, is left in an odd position regarding his own claim to have married the two in his scripted 'Dialogues'.[4] He brushes aside the classical aspirations of 'the language of the senate' that might nevertheless be said to characterize his own declamatory style, studied diction, involved syntax, and pompous Latinisms ('supercilious contemner', 'personages', 'nomenclators'), dropping briefly into a plainer, contrasting register with the insistence that his 'design' is 'only to teach Italian . . . ', the vernacular descendant of Latin. But the two modes of expression—ancient and modern, formal and informal—feel equally compelling and at comic variance with one another, conveying a sense that the subject is being held at arm's length alongside assertions of its important proximity to life. It is as though Johnson seeks to drive a wedge between the activities of speaking and writing, at the same time as recommending a work that combines them.

The entire preface is, in fact, structured on a series of divisions—the first of which is that of its author from the man responsible for *Easy Phraseology*, reinforcing the distinction between a preface and the subsequent work to which it does and does not belong. A series of morally freighted words in the first sentence ('lax', 'cursory', 'slight', 'negligence', as against 'rigorous', 'solemn', 'deliberate', 'choice', 'accuracy') cleaves the field of observation into two camps of colloquial and written diction. It apparently endorses a stern preference for the governance of the

---

[4] On the division between spoken and written language, see also *Yale*, ix. 115–16.

latter—the effect of the same rigorous 'choice' and 'accuracy' is evident in the author's style—yet Johnson is also defending the necessity of 'familiar conversation', whose 'casual' properties might appear to resist the stringency of definition, strict principles of selection, and seriousness of purpose he is directing at them. We are encouraged to interpret the effort of thinking—and the medium in which that effort is expressed—as a force that may impose itself upon, rather than cohere with, its object. Our decision as to whether Johnson's stylistic vehicle is appropriate to his topic will depend partly on whether we side with the (reprehensibly) lofty perspective of the 'supercilious contemner of trifles', the (perhaps reprehensibly) lowly perspective of the object of thought—as embodied in 'casual talkers'—or with the defensive and apologetic figure of the author, compromised between height and lowness, between self-promotion and self-abasement. When the first-person voice makes an appearance in the third paragraph, it triggers associations with embarrassment, revealing a self-inflicted obligation to dissociate itself from the work it also seeks to defend (fostered, in this instance, by the actual dissociation of the preface-writer from the author of *Easy Phraseology*). The last word given to Baretti, the awkward, half-retracted bow of 'much ashamed', exposes the contrary postures endemic to prefaces and dedications: forms of address in which humility, soliciting the patronage of an aristocratic individual or of the general public, is most at stake.

1. HUMILITY

When Johnson defined the noun 'PREFACE' as 'Something *spoken* introductory to the main design' and the verb 'To PREFACE' as 'To *say* something introductory' (my emphases) in his *Dictionary*, he was probably thinking in terms of 'the language of the senate', or of ancient oratorical practice. In the *Ad Herennium*, the first of six canons of oratory is the exordium, whose role is to predispose the audience in favour of the speaker and his topic. The exordium might include an introduction of the subject, a direct address, or an 'insinuatio' (indirect address) in which the speaker attempts covertly and through dissimulation to create a positive impression of his character and motivation. The insinuatio is thus bound up with the relationship between orator and audience, as it promotes the speaker's good sense, good will, and good morals. It is particularly recommended 'when our cause is discreditable, that is, when the subject itself alienates the hearer from us'.[5] Colloquial Italian

---

[5] Anon., *Ad C. Herennium*, I. vii. 11; I. vi. 9.

might feasibly be viewed as such a cause (*Rambler* 168 had described the sense of being 'irresistibly alienated by low terms ... debased by vulgar mouths', *Yale*, v. 126–7), yet Johnson strives not to bypass but to heighten consciousness of his audience's potential alienation, as well as endeavouring to persuade readers of the centrality of low and trifling subjects to their own lives. Humility—the key virtue for establishing a harmony between speaker and hearer—has long been encouraged as the correct tone and posture to adopt for the performance of an exordium. Cicero stated the case early in *Of Oratory*: 'the best orators, those who can speak with the utmost ease and elegance, unless they are diffident in approaching a discourse and diffident in beginning it, seem to border on the shameless ... the better the orator the more profoundly is he frightened of the difficulty of speaking, and of the doubtful fate of a speech, and of the anticipation of an audience.'[6]

In Johnson's preface, the writer is alternately figured as a bold experimenter and as a humble supplicant, a pioneer and a drudge, above and beneath his audience; his 'shame' is a disgrace and (insofar as he displays awareness of it) a shield from disgrace. To be 'covered with shame' is to be at once exposed to and protected from ignominy—on display and concealed from the indignity of exhibition—just as a preface, especially in the hands of someone other than the author of the ensuing text, does and does not represent the work that follows.[7] Johnson combines deference with an assertion of independence during a key period in the establishment of the professional writer: a period whose antagonistic conceptions of authorship set ancients against moderns, patronage against self-determination, status against merit, genius against commercial flair, and public against private character.

As Sarah Scott announced in 1766, a preface was designed 'to make the Author's Apology'.[8] But the word 'apology' itself harbours strains of humility and defiance, vulnerability and resistance, covering the plea of 'guilty' and 'not guilty' simultaneously. Its earliest meaning, from the Greek via Latin ('apo'+'logos'), is that of a formal defence or justification—it is therefore a vehicle not only for excusing, but also

[6] Cicero, *De Oratore*, trans. E. W. Sutton and H. Rackham, 2 vols. (London: Heinemann, 1942; repr. 1959), I. xxvi. 119–20. Addison summarizes this passage in *Spectator* 213 (ii. 398-9); Steele later refers to Pliny and to the necessary fear and modesty that accompany public speaking (*Spectator* 484, iv. 216).

[7] 'Shame': '2. Fear of offence against propriety or decency, operating as a restraint on behaviour; modesty, shamefastness. 3. a. Disgrace, ignominy, loss of esteem or reputation' (*OED*).

[8] Sarah Scott, *The History of Sir George Ellison*, 2nd edn. (London: F. Noble, 1770), p. iii.

for arguing in favour of a topic, client, or project. [9] An 'apology' thus harbours antithetical impulses and might be identified as the overarching prefatory antagonym (a single word whose meanings contradict one another), suited to a mind as fundamentally combative as Johnson's.[10] His *Dictionary* worries at the distinction between the two senses of the word in terms of authorial conduct and of legalistic nicety: 'Defence; excuse. *Apology* generally signifies rather excuse than vindication, and tends rather to extenuate the fault, than prove innocence. This is, however, sometimes unregarded by writers.'

'Generally', 'rather', 'tends', and 'sometimes' themselves contain accents of apology and of hesitation. Although its use of examples always refers lexicographical definitions to literary practice, the *Dictionary* does not usually specify that particular significations or shades of meaning are regarded or unregarded 'by writers', rather than by mankind in general;[11] Johnson seems here to be highlighting a professional concern with the shiftiness of a literary apology. He was not one of those authors to disregard the fact that a preface might only 'extenuate the fault' of the ensuing work, even if he was not directly responsible for its contents. 'Harmlessness' (the third *Dictionary* definition of 'INNOCENCE') at the level of intention and execution is a recurrent anxiety in his prefaces, while Boswell observed that 'it was indifferent to [Johnson] what was the subject of the work' to which he contributed a dedication, 'provided it were innocent'. And yet, beyond this (as befits a lawyer), Boswell cast his friend in the Ciceronian mould of a rhetorically accomplished and disinterested advocate, rather than as a personally committed author, one who 'In writing Dedications for others . . . considered himself as by no means speaking his own sentiments' (*Life*, ii. 2).

[9] See Elizabeth Howells, 'Apologizing for Authority: The Rhetoric of the Prefaces of Eliza Cook, Isabelle Bird, and Hannah More', in Frederick Antczak, Cinda Coggins and Geoffrey D. Klinger (eds.), *Professing Rhetoric: Selected Papers from the 2000 Rhetoric Society of America Conference* (Mahwah, NJ: Lawrence Erlbaum Associates, 2002), 131–8.

[10] Other antagonyms include 'cleave' (to adhere and separate), 'quite' (completely and incompletely), and 'secrete' (to release or conceal). See Freud, 'On the Antithetical Meaning of Primal Words', in *Complete Psychological Works*, xi. 155–61; Empson, *Seven Types of Ambiguity*, 192–233. The contradictory meanings of 'overlook' (to attend to and to ignore) were perhaps what led Johnson to revise 'O'erlook' to 'Survey' in l. 2 of *The Vanity of Human Wishes* (for the first draft, see *Poems*, 167).

[11] See, for instance, a comment under the noun 'FOAL'—'The custom now is to use *colt* for a young horse, and *foal* for a young mare; but there was not originally any such distinction'—and under the adjective 'TRIVIAL' (sense 2): 'Light; trifling; unimportant; inconsiderable. This use is more frequent, though less just.' But see also the pointed complaint beside '*FRAISCHEUR*': 'A word foolishly innovated by Dryden.'

But Johnson voiced many of the same sentiments in his prefaces and dedications for other people as in those writings published under his own name, and he wavered in his classically informed opinion that the efficacy of an author's argument stood independent of the sincerity with which he or she espoused his or her cause. He sometimes viewed the writer as one whose task was merely 'to say all you can for your client' or topic, and the strength of whose public claims had no dependence on private motives or practice (*Life*, ii. 47).[12] At other times, surveying the whole character of the author rather than literary persona alone, he saw the inability to live up to the morals inculcated or experiences described in his or her writing as potentially harmful to its validity.[13] On several occasions, he opposed artificial imitation of the ancients to genuine expression of personal feeling, and came out strongly in favour of the latter. In the 'Life of Hammond', for instance, he noted that his subject's *Love Elegies* (1743) benefited from 'The recommendatory preface of the editor', probably Lord Chesterfield, who 'raised strong prejudices in their favour':

But of the prefacer, whoever he was, it may be reasonably suspected that he never read the poems; for he professes to value them for a very high species of excellence, and recommends them as the genuine effusions of the mind, which expresses a real passion in the language of nature. But the truth is these elegies have neither passion, nature, nor manners. Where there is fiction, there is no passion; he that describes himself as a shepherd, and his Neæra or Delia as a shepherdess, and talks of goats and lambs, feels no passion. He that courts his mistress with Roman imagery deserves to lose her; for she may with good reason suspect his sincerity. (*Lives*, ii. 314–15)[14]

---

[12] 'The writer of an epitaph should not be considered as saying nothing but what is strictly true. Allowance must be made for some degree of exaggerated praise'; 'It does not always follow . . . that a man who has written a good poem on an art has practised it. Philip Miller told me that in [John] Philips's *Cyder, a Poem* all the precepts were just, and indeed better than in books written for the purpose of instructing; yet Philips had never made cider' (Johnson in *Life*, ii. 407; Johnson in *Tour*, 54).

[13] See Savage's comments in 'Life of Thomson', *Lives*, iii. 297–8. The question whether art should be tested against life is bound up with the problem of whether or not to include an author's vices in biography, as they may unsettle the efficacy of his or her published moral precepts. Yet such information also shows that even 'learning and genius' may be 'debased', thus cautioning the reader against the same fault (Johnson in *Life*, iii. 154–5 (p. 155); iv. 396–7). On Johnson's 'polar senses of literature as self-expression and actual record on the one hand, and, on the other, of literature as rhetoric and necessary artifice', see Fussell, *Samuel Johnson and the Life of Writing*, 43–61 (p. 55).

[14] This echoes Johnson's famous complaint of Milton's *Lycidas* (1638) that it was 'not to be considered as the effusion of real passion; for passion runs not after remote allusions and obscure opinions' ('Life of Milton', *Lives*, i. 163). See also 'Life of Butler' (*Lives*, i. 213) and 'Life of Gay' (*Lives*, ii. 283).

Johnson's eighth sermon—based on the text 'Be not wise in your own conceits' (Romans 12: 16)—is directed against such insincerity, censuring 'literary pride', and 'the insolent triumphs of intellectual superiority'. Men of letters, 'necessarily advanced to degrees of knowledge above them who are dispersed among manual occupations, and the vulgar parts of life', tend 'to with-hold their attention from their own lives' and thus become vain and authoritarian (*Yale*, xiv. 95, 89, 88, 87). The 'dispersed' and 'vulgar' might here represent the horizontal axis of proliferation, dissemination, and indiscriminate multiplicity, as well as the foundation stone of hierarchical subordination, while the learned progressively ascend the vertical axis of choice, selection, and cultivation (as in the opening section of the Baretti preface). But Johnson does not allow us to divide the field in this way for long. He may have been 'a friend to subordination', his 'favourite subject' (*Life*, i. 408; ii. 13), but—as his review of Soame Jenyns's *Free Inquiry into the Nature and Origin of Evil* (1757) demonstrates—he found the idea of 'the regular subordination of beings, the scale of existence, and the chain of nature', with its implication that those '*born to poverty*' must remain without the education that would allow them 'to escape from it', repellent (*Prose and Poetry*, 354, 359).

In his eighth sermon, as in the preface to *Easy Phraseology*, Johnson rebukes the heights of intellect as illicitly removed from common life. In their capacity as teachers, the learned 'necessarily converse with those, who are their inferiours', yet they often fail to treat their charges 'with . . . dignity' (Baretti is twice described as a teacher in Johnson's preface; he was, in fact, tutor to the eldest Miss Thrale). The advance to knowledge properly entails 'submission to authority', 'modesty', and 'patience of attention'. Johnson counsels self-examination, comparison with others, and a consciousness of 'the little they possess' as the scholar's 'method of obtaining humility' in later life. Should this fail, the man of learning must be guided by the Bible, 'which will shew him the inefficacy of all other knowledge', and 'will imprint upon his mind, that he best understands the sacred writings who most carefully obeys them. Thus will humility fix a firm and lasting basis, by annihilation of all empty distinctions and petty competitions, by shewing, that "one thing only is necessary" and that "God is all in all" ' (*Yale*, xiv. 90–5).

At its most serious, as here, such a view requires the writer's voluntary abrogation of dignity not on grounds of mere advocacy (the rhetorically effective version of humility), but as a result of adhering to the scriptures: in the King James Bible, immediately preceding Johnson's text for his eighth sermon, is the injunction to 'Mind not high things, but condescend to men of low estate' (Romans 12: 16). In his sixth sermon, he follows up on this command, enjoining on writer and reader a choice of poverty, of low and mean things, that strives to imitate that of Christ:

> the life of our Lord was one continued exercise of humility. The son of God condescended to take our nature upon him, to become subject to pain, to bear, from his birth, the inconveniencies of poverty, and to wander from city to city, amidst opposition, reproach and calumny. He disdained not to converse with publicans and sinners, to minister to his own disciples, and to weep at the miseries of his own creatures. He submitted to insults and revilings, and, being led like a lamb to the slaughter, opened not his mouth. At length, having borne all the cruel treatment that malice could suggest, or power inflict, he suffered the most lingering and ignominious death.—God of his infinite mercy grant, that, by imitating his humility, we may be made partakers of his merits! (*Yale*, xvi. 73)

Many of Johnson's immediate predecessors and contemporaries circled hesitantly around the problem of how to reconcile the claims of ancient decorum with the pressing requirement to imitate such a descent, to understand the scriptures by obeying them, and to 'exercise . . . humility' in their works as well as in their lives. Singling out the text 'Unto me, who am less than the least of all saints, is this grace given, that I should preach among the Gentiles the unsearchable riches of Christ' (Ephesians 3: 8), Isaac Watts (included at Johnson's request in the *Lives of the Poets*)[15] recommended St Paul as the prime embodiment—after Christ himself—of 'this *diminishing Idea of Self*', of a 'holy Diminution or Lessening of Self', and therefore as a pattern for eighteenth-century authors (*Humility*, 3, 13).[16] Responding to such an example, a flexible vocabulary of mock-humility surfaces throughout the period, revealing on the one hand consciousness of an illicit pride that may lurk behind the show of authorial modesty, on the other hand a sense of uncertainty about how proper it was for low subjects to plead for literary attention.

---

[15] 'To the Collection of English Poets I have recommended the volume of Dr. Watts to be added. His name has been long held by me in *veneration*; and I would not willingly be reduced to tell of him, only, that he was born and died . . . My plan does not exact much; but I wish to distinguish *Watts*; a man who never wrote but for a good purpose' (*Letters*, iii. 38). See also Chapter 4.

[16] Cowper models his ideal preacher—'simple, grave, sincere; . . . in language plain'—after St Paul. *The Task* (1785), II. 399–400, in *The Poems of William Cowper*, ed. John D. Baird and Charles Ryskamp, 3 vols. (Oxford: Clarendon Press, 1980–95), ii.

Addison, one of Watts's favourite authors,[17] had established humility and modesty as behavioural and stylistic touchstones for the Christian author,[18] while Steele treated both subjects at length in numerous essays for *The Spectator*.[19] In no. 461, he has a *'humble'* fictional correspondent tell him that 'Modesty is become fashionable, and Impudence stands in need of some Wit, since you have put them both in their proper Lights' (iv. 128-9). He had already exalted a feminized, domesticated protagonist, one who located his chief sphere of action and excellence in the private realm, in *The Christian Hero* (1701), eulogizing 'that Sublime and Heroick Virtue, Meekness'.[20] In *The Tatler* and *The Spectator*, he repeatedly called for a laying aside of authorial pretensions in order to celebrate 'private Characters' and 'lower Stations', 'worthy Minds in a domestick Way of Life', or 'the Dignity of human Nature ... in all Conditions of Life' (*Tatler* 56, i. 395; *Spectator* 248, ii. 463; *Tatler* 87, ii. 48).

Donald Bond notes that 'Modesty, not only as the chief ornament in the female sex but also as a praiseworthy characteristic in men, is one of Steele's settled convictions' (*Tatler* 52, i. 368 n. 6). He might have added that, for eighteenth-century readers, it was the hallmark of his collaborator Addison's writing, perhaps even of his private behaviour. A *Tatler* sketch of the character of *'Aristaeus'*—which John Nichols and George Aitken took to represent Addison—speaks of a laudable self-adaptation to any social or intellectual capacity. Like Johnson's ideal teacher/writer, 'he frequently seems to be less knowing to be more

---

[17] Watts called him 'The most authentick Judge of fine Thoughts and Language that our Age has produced', not least because Addison's *Spectator* 405 'assures us of the Beauty and Glory of the Stile of Scripture'. Watts, *A Guide to Prayer*, 96.

[18] On Addison's 'naturall modesty', which 'breaths indeed thro all his works', see, for instance, *The Glasgow Edition of the Works and Correspondence of Adam Smith*, ed. R. H. Campbell, D. D. Raphael, and A. S. Skinner, 7 vols. (Oxford: Clarendon Press, 1976–83), iv: *Lectures on Rhetoric and Belles Lettres* (delivered 1762–3), ed. J. C. Bryce (1983), 52–63 (pp. 52–3). Johnson, quoting *Hamlet*, commended Addison's style for never straying from 'the modesty of nature', but savaged his fear about exposing *Cato* (1713) to the stage as 'the despicable cant of literary modesty' ('Life of Addison', *Lives*, ii. 148 and n. 6; 98). He observed disapprovingly that: 'Of [Addison's] habits, or external manners, nothing is so often mentioned as that timorous or sullen taciturnity, which his friends called modesty by too mild a name' ('Life of Addison', *Lives*, ii. 118).

[19] See, for instance, passages in *Spectator* 2 (i. 11–12); 20 (i. 85–8); 45 (i. 193–4); 104 (i. 432–5); 119 (i. 488–9); 154 (ii. 103–4); 206 (ii. 306–9); 274 (ii. 567–8); 350 (iii. 303–4); 354 (iii. 321–2); 484 (iv. 215–18).

[20] Richard Steele, *The Christian Hero: An Argument Proving that no Principles but those of Religion are sufficient to make a Great Man*, 2nd edn., with additions (London: for Jacob Tonson, 1701), 52–3. See also Ronald Paulson, *Breaking and Remaking: Aesthetic Practice in England, 1700–1820* (New Brunswick, NJ: Rutgers University Press, 1989), 169.

obliging, and chuses to be on a Level with others rather than oppress with the Superiority of his Genius' (*Tatler* 176, ii. 462 and n. 6).

This tendency of *choosing* to be on a level with inferiors manifests itself as a joint stylistic principle of 'voluntary degradation' on Steele and Addison's part. Both authors make a point of disregarding ostentation in order to familiarize noble characters, abstract language, and complex arguments to private life. Steele observed that he had 'no Need of Camps, Fortifications, and Fields of Battle; I don't call out for Heroes and Generals to my Assistance' (*Tatler* 18, i. 151), while Addison aspired, after Socrates, to 'have brought Philosophy out of Closets and Libraries, Schools and Colleges, to dwell in Clubs and Assemblies, at Tea-Tables, and in Coffee-Houses' (*Spectator* 10, i. 44). The novelty and mixed reception of this approach are clear from Eustace Budgell's comment that the *Spectator* had not only been celebrated but also rebuked 'for having prostituted Learning to the Embraces of the Vulgar' (*Spectator* 379, iii. 423). As early as the sixteenth number, Addison found it necessary to reassure his readers 'once for all . . . that it is not my Intention to sink the Dignity of this my Paper with Reflections upon Red-heels or Top-knots, but rather to enter into the Passions of Mankind' (*Spectator* 16, i. 70), yet the public remained unconvinced. One correspondent, 'J.C.', vetoing the project (outlined in no. 16) of a 'petty-censorship' devoted to abuses of dress, argued that instead of producing 'trifling pieces of low life', the paper should 'advance human nature'. Otherwise, it would forfeit its claim to the dignity of being bound up in the more permanent form of a book (*Spectator* 16, i. 70–1 n. 6).

Addison's invocation of a classical precedent (Socrates) in defence of his and Steele's familiarizing journalistic efforts is accompanied, in practice, by a competing consciousness of such descent as a version of the Christian *sermo humilis*, requiring 'an Incorrectness of Style, and writing in an Air of Common Speech' (Steele, *Tatler* 5, i. 51) that stoops to apply itself to the conduct and moral improvement of everyday life.[21] Both here and in *The Christian Hero*, Steele exhorted his readers to the practice of humility in chattier, less formidable language than Johnson's. He seemed thus to be anticipating the latter's eighth sermon — 'the first objection and the last to an unacceptable pastor, is, that he is proud, that he is too wise for familiarity, and will not descend to the level,

---

[21] On the *sermo humilis*, see Auerbach, *Literary Language and its Public*, 39–40. Of Christ's Sermon on the Mount, Steele remarks: 'he gives his Divine Precepts in so easy and familiar a manner, and those are so well adapted to all the rules of life and right reason, that they must needs carry throughout a self evident Authority' (*The Christian Hero*, 43).

with common understandings' (*Yale*, xiv. 93)—and indeed Johnson's
requirement that a journalist should, above all other characters, acquaint
himself 'with the lowest orders of mankind, that he may be able to
judge, what will be plain, and what will be obscure . . . He is to consider
himself not as writing to Students and Statesmen alone, but to Women,
Shopkeepers, and Artisans, who have little time to bestow upon mental
attainments, but desire, upon easy terms, to know how the world goes'
(second introductory essay to the *Universal Chronicle*, '*Of the Duty of a*
JOURNALIST' (1758), *Prefaces*, 212).

Yet Steele's predominantly sociable and secular frame of reference
entails that humility shifts from being 'the very Characteristick of
a Christian' to a public bearing or mere performance. Like Addison's attack on fashionable dress, Steele's moralizing endeavour—in
spite of its appeal to biblical example—totters on the edge of elegant trifling:

Meekness is to the Mind, what a good Mein is to the Body, without which
the best Limb and finest Complection'd Person, may be very Disagreeable; and
with it, a very Homely and Plain one, cannot be so; for a good Air, supplies
the Imperfection of Feature and Shape, by throwing a certain Beauty on the
whole, which covers the disagreeableness of the parts; it has a State and Humility
peculiar to its self above all other Virtues, like the Holy Scripture its sacred
Record, where the highest things are Express'd in the most easy terms, and
which carries throughout a condescending Explanation, and a certain meekness
of Stile.[22]

'Certain' hedges its bets as to whether it is a quantity or a quality
(a graceful measure of assumed humility, which might imply quite the
opposite; or a resolute meekness), hinting at a fundamental lack of
certainty. Steele typically styles Christian humility an 'Air' (as in *Tatler*
5, i. 51), by which he appears to mean a gesture or bearing expressive
of personal emotion. Yet the word's prominent associations (in *The
Tatler* as elsewhere) with fashion and affectation produce a strangely
uncomfortable marriage between the worldly and the unworldly, between
pride and humility.[23] It is apt that the *OED* cites Steele's as the first
recorded use of 'air' in the sense of a personally revealing gesture
and in the sense of airs and graces: 'Grand air; stylishness; "style" '

[22] Steele, *The Christian Hero*, 53–4.
[23] See Davie, *Purity of Diction*, 14; Benedict Anderson, *Imagined Communities: Reflections
on the Origin and Spread of Nationalism*, rev. edn. (London: Verso, 1991), 11–12, 22–36.
See also Michael G. Ketcham, *Transparent Designs: Reading, Performance, and Form in the
Spectator Papers* (Athens: University of Georgia Press, 1985), 17–26.

(see *OED* 'air', senses 14 d. and 16). Vocabulary with strongly moral or religious connotations acquires, in his hands, a blanched, lightly mocking sense of overstatement as it is related wholly to infractions of manners and civility: 'The *Evil* of unseasonable Visits has been complain'd of to me with much Vehemence'; 'new *Evils* arise every Day to interrupt their Conversation' (*Tatler* 89, ii. 61; *Spectator* 148, ii. 81; my emphases).

Describing himself as a 'very great Criminal' liable to the 'Vice' of 'impertinent Promisers', the Spectator concludes: 'I am left under the *Compunction* that I deserve, in so many different Places to be called a Trifler' (Steele, 448, iv. 75–6; my emphasis). The *OED* definition of 'compunction' is: '1. Pricking or stinging of the conscience or heart; regret or uneasiness of mind consequent on sin or wrong-doing; remorse, contrition. b. In mod. use, often in weakened sense, denoting a slight or passing regret for wrong-doing, or a feeling of regret for some slight offence.' *Spectator* 448 is given as the earliest known example of this 'weakened sense'; the speaker's slight regret is born itself of trifling, so that the whole episode is a study in a secularizing rather than in a Christian 'Diminution or Lessening' of the authorial self: from moral arbitration to social culpability, from great things to little, from remorse to fleeting embarrassment. Sometimes Steele will rebuke the public, rather than himself, for the cant use of moral language, but he soon falls in with the prevailing tendency when doing so. In the following example, 'pleasant' and 'pretty Rogues' belong to the same laxly tolerant category of speaking as the slang use of 'virtue' that Steele is criticizing ('virtue' here bears the restricted definition of 'not sexually promiscuous, as far as I know'):

methinks it is so very easy to be what is in the general called *Virtuous*, that it need not cost one Hour's Reflection in a Month to preserve that Appellation. It is pleasant to hear the pretty Rogues talk of *Virtue* and Vice among each other: She is the lazyest Creature in the World, but I must confess, strictly *Virtuous*: The Peevishest Hussy breathing, but as to her *Virtue* she is without blemish: She has not the least Charity for any of her Acquaintance, but I must allow rigidly *Virtuous*. (*Spectator* 390, iii. 466; my emphases)

Within such an arena, where the moral regulator is himself liable to the faults he proscribes, authorial claims to humility always harbour the potential to collapse into their opposite. On the one hand, Isaac Bickerstaff (Steele and Addison's alter ego in *The Tatler*) is the submissive Christian proponent of neglected virtue, the champion of 'Under-Characters . . . of the sociable World', who endeavours to 'raise obscure Merit' to our notice

(*Tatler* 85, ii. 40; 69, i. 477). On the other, he is the haughtily impervious neoclassical Roman Censor, remorselessly preoccupied with putting 'the whole Race of Mankind in their proper Distinctions'—with measuring, defining, cataloguing, and adjudicating the worth of his subjects—who seeks 'to extirpate from among the polite or busy Part of Mankind all such as are either prejudicial or insignificant to Society' (*Tatler* 67, i. 463; 186, iii. 10). The *OED* credits *The Tatler* with the first known figurative use of 'nonentity', 'A person or thing with no special or interesting qualities; a characterless, unimportant, or insignificant person or thing' (sense 3; see *Tatler* 118, ii. 203), and Bickerstaff's mockery of the 'Metaphorically Defunct' (*Tatler* 46, i. 331) anticipates the 'metaphorically debased' targets of *Peri Bathous*, 'many fathoms beyond Mediocrity' (Pope, *Prose*, 182). Elevating and diminishing the status of intellectually and socially inferior people, and the legitimacy of their claims on the reader's interest, Bickerstaff is presented as modest and as arrogant—as a figure who is implicated in, or as one who is personally immune to the charges he levels at society.

The Spectator's definition of his 'Province' as 'the Correction of Impudence' (Steele, no. 20, i. 85) issued in a project of national reclamation, buttressed by Addison's perception that the English were a 'naturally Modest' people, yet plainly afflicted by instances of the contrary quality (*Spectator* 407, iii. 520; see also Steele, *Spectator* 148, ii. 82). Genuine mocking and demanding letters from lowly, impertinent correspondents had earlier besieged *The Tatler*, so that Steele found it necessary to upbraid his readers for the patent falsehood of their claims to be '*my humble Servant*' (*Tatler* 78, i. 533; see also no. 164, ii. 412–13). They, in turn, testing Bickerstaff's persona against Steele's private character (especially against his sojourns in debtors' prison), often assailed *his* pretensions to honesty and modesty as incongruous and downright absurd.[24] The comically divided nature of the Tatler's character—his ironic and apparently sincere manifestations of concern for low subjects—invites such responses, as does the Spectator's combination of silent withdrawal from, and confident arbitration of, the social world (see, for instance, *Spectator* 1, i. 1–6); of disinterested judgement with commercial savvy. Surveying the landscape of journalism, Addison wrote that:

Advertisements are of great Use to the Vulgar: First of all, as they are Instruments of Ambition. A Man that is by no Means big enough for the *Gazette*, may easily

[24] See, for instance, Edward A. Bloom and Lillian D. Bloom (eds.), *Addison and Steele: The Critical Heritage* (London: Routledge, 1995), 52–8, 203–7, 217–22.

creep into the Advertisements; by which Means we often see an Apothecary in the same Paper of News with a Plenipotentiary, or a Running-Footman with an Ambassador. An Advertisement from *Pickadilly* goes down to Posterity, with an Article from Madrid; and *John Bartlett* of *Goodman's-Fields* is celebrated in the same Paper with the Emperor of *Germany*. Thus the Fable tells us, That the Wren mounted as high as the Eagle, by getting upon his Back. (*Tatler* 224, iii. 166–7)

The Tatler and *The Spectator* depended heavily on advertising and on the promotion of quack remedies, luxury goods, and public entertainments in order to keep their journals afloat (John Bartlett's 'Inventions for the Cure of Ruptures', which receive an indirect plug here, had already appeared in *The Tatler*; see iii. 166–7 n. 2 and n. 4). Addison thus implies a purely commercial explanation for what is presented, on other occasions, as an ethically driven heterogeneity. Bickerstaff and the Spectator's insinuating arts of persuasion and of self-presentation, their financially (as well as morally) prompted descent to homely, bourgeois, and female life, find an analogue in mock-humble, fictional petitions such as this one (by Steele), in which the governing journalistic persona seems to ally itself with the comically self-promoting, socially low targets of its arbitration. The motives behind a 'beseeching Air' of 'perswasive' humility come under deliberate suspicion:

The humble Petition of *Bartholomew Ladylove*, of *Round-Court* in the Parish of St. *Martins in the Fields*, in Behalf of himself and Neighbours, Sheweth,

That your Petitioners have with great Industry and Application arrived at the most exact Art of Invitation or Entreaty: That by a beseeching Air and perswasive Address, they have for many Years last past peaceably drawn in every tenth Passenger, whether they intended or not to call at their Shops, to come in and buy; and from that Softness of Behaviour, have arrived among Tradesmen at the gentle Appellation of *the Fawners*.

That there have of late set up amongst us certain Persons from *Monmouth-street* and *Long-lane*, who by the Strength of their Arms and Loudness of their Throats, draw off the Regard of all Passengers from your said Petitioners; from which Violence they are distinguished by the Name of *the Worriers*.

That while your Petitioners stand ready to receive Passengers with a submissive Bow, and repeat with a gentle Voice, *Ladies what do you want? pray look in here*, the Worriers reach out their Hands at Pistol-shot, and sieze the Customers at Arm's Length.

That while the Fawners strain and relax the Muscles of their Faces, in making Distinction between a Spinster in a coloured Scarf, and an Hand-maid in a Straw-Hat, the Worriers use the same Roughness to both, and prevail upon the Easiness of the Passengers to the Impoverishment of your Petitioners.

Your Petitioners therefore most humbly pray, that the Worriers may not be permitted to inhabit the politer Parts of the Town; and that *Round-Court* may remain a Receptacle for Buyers of a more soft Education. (*Spectator* 304, iii. 94–5)

'*Bartholomew Ladylove*' might stand as another pseudonym for Steele and Addison, 'Buyers of a more soft Education' in 'the politer Parts of the Town' for their audience. One of the immediate selling points of *The Tatler* and *The Spectator* was the journals' delicate invitation to female readers to '*look in here*', facilitated by the intermittent contributions (from no. 10 onwards) of Jenny Distaff, Isaac's half-sister, to *The Tatler*.[25] (By impersonating Jenny, Steele and Addison might be said—like Johnson—to have played 'Hercules' at the 'distaff', *Life*, iii. 242). This comic request, one of many urgent mock-pleas for intervention in both journals, practises the commercial arts of entreaty it describes; the fictional specificity of Ladylove's business demonstrates Steele's relish of multiplying and rehearsing claims on his own attention. Calling themselves 'Petitioners', Bartholomew and his fellow-tradesmen become generic as well as professional 'Fawners', performing a 'submissive Bow' in writing and in life; 'While your Petitioners stand . . .' elides the present occasion of imploring with their daily endeavours to attract notice and patronage.

The petition reflects in turn on the simultaneously 'humble' and 'gentle' journalist as a common hawker, drawing in susceptible female customers to purchase his sub-literary wares. The worriers' crime is to override those clarities of social demarcation that are the journalist's as well as the fawners' stock-in-trade. The humour of this writing arises from the play-off between a concreteness which replicates Bickerstaff the Censor's impulse to tidy promiscuous humanity into its 'proper Distinctions'—the precise, familiar, urban locations of the battle; a stringently 'exact Art of Entreaty' that mechanically bewitches 'every tenth Passenger'; the exaggeratedly clean and minutely observed division of 'a Spinster in a coloured Scarf' from 'an Hand-maid in a Straw-Hat'—and the hit-and-miss vagaries of competitive persuasion. The gap between intention and execution, as rehearsed in Johnson's prefaces, has disappeared. Until the rougher handling of the worriers interposes (perhaps an allusion to rival newspapers, of whose impertinence *The*

---

[25] Discussing his wish to attract female readers, Steele again reverts to an 'Air' of humble persuasion: 'When it is a Woman's Day, in my Works, I shall endeavour at a Stile and Air suitable to their Understanding. When I say this, I must be understood to mean, that I shall not lower but exalt the Subjects I treat upon. Discourse for their Entertainment, is not to be debased but refined' (*Spectator* 4, i. 21).

Tatler and *The Spectator* sometimes complain),[26] an unspoken sympathy between expert fawners and soft customers has made commerce—and, by implication, journalism—a charmed science.

Such overstated precision in the necessarily inexact sphere of human relations tends to uncover the arrogance of supposedly 'humble' authors and their petitioners. Swift composed four humble addresses, two humble petitions, one humble representation, two modest defences, and one modest enquiry as well as the more renowned *Modest Proposal* (1729).[27] Many of them demonstrate the hallmarks of what Empson identified as 'the humility of impertinence', or 'Ironical Humility, whose simplest gambit is to say, "I am not clever, educated, well born," or what not (as if you had a low standard to judge by), and then to imply that your standards are so high in the matter that the person you are humbling yourself before is quite out of sight'.[28]

Swift's light-hearted *Humble Petition of the Footmen in and about the City of Dublin* (1732) follows the pattern of Bartholomew Ladylove's epistle to *The Spectator*. It proposes 'humbly' to demonstrate the presumptuousness of 'certain Persons' who have been 'pretending to be genuine *Irish Footmen*'. The speaker labours, however, under the additionally risible difficulty of acknowledging that counterfeit footmen display a 'transcendent Pitch of Assurance' which allows them to pass unsuspected for the real thing; he, on the other hand, a genuine footman, has cast himself in the role of humble, unassuming petitioner. It seems that the only definitive characteristic of footmen is that same 'Assurance' which the speaker attributes to his competitors—comically

[26] See, for instance, *Spectator* 239, which promises 'a full and satisfactory Answer to all such Papers and Pamphlets as have yet appeared against the *Spectator*' (ii. 432); for the Spectator's attitude to his detractors, see no. 355 (iii. 323–5). On reactions to *The Tatler*, see, for instance, no. 164, ii. 410–13.

[27] Jonathan Swift, *The Humble Address of the Knights, Citizens and Burgesses* (1723); *The Humble Address of the Lords Spiritual and Temporal* (1724); *An Humble Address to Both Houses of Parliament* (1724); *The Humble Address of the Right Honourable the Lords Spiritual and Temporal* (1713); *The Humble Petition of the Doctor, and the Gentlemen of Ireland* (1707); *The Humble Petition of the Footmen in and about the City of Dublin* (1732); *The Humble Representation of the Clergy of the City of Dublin* (1724); *A Modest Defence of a Late Poem by an unknown Author, call'd, The Lady's Dressing-Room* (1732; probably by Swift); *A Modest Defence of Punning* (1716); *A Modest Enquiry into the Reasons of the Joy Expressed by a Certain Sett of People, upon the Spreading of a Report of her Majesty's Death* (written 1715–20; partly by Swift); *A Modest Proposal for preventing the Children of poor People in Ireland from being a Burden to their Parents or Country; and for making them beneficial to the Publick* (1729). Swift, *Prose Works*, iv. 205–10, 261–2; v. 87–92, 337–40; viii. 198–9, 183–92; x. 177–9, 119–41; xii. 109–18, 235–7.

[28] William Empson, *Some Versions of Pastoral* (1935; London: Hogarth Press, 1986), 211–12.

demonstrated by his inability to adhere to the humility his part requires (Swift, *Prose Works*, xii. 235–6). Although he wishes, like Bartholomew Ladylove, to insist on a firm division between two rival parties, his mock-humble medium compels him to blend them into one. This is an exquisite refinement on Steele's original petition. While Ladylove opposed his party of fawners to that of the worriers on the grounds that only the latter eroded social and professional distinctions, here, the speaker's own impudence, masquerading as humility, makes clarity of demarcation between pride and modesty, truth and falsehood, friend and foe, simultaneously crucial and impossible.

In quite another mood, however, Swift adopted an attitude of mock-humility in order to savage impudence run wild. The *Drapier's Letters* (1724–5), written to encourage the Irish in their opposition to William Wood's copper coinage, embody a distinctively Pauline art of literary sinking: 'Pauline' in its sense of urgency; in the speaker's self-characterization; in his reiterated, and specifically urban, Christian affiliations; in the assertive appeal to, and confident representation of, a humble collective; and in the endeavour to frame such an appeal in language comprehensible to the working man.[29] The speaker's modesty highlights the impudence of his apparent superiors, rather than his own or that of the beleaguered masses, who 'do, upon maturest Consideration, universally join, in openly declaring, protesting, addressing, petitioning against these Half-pence'. Swift descends to style himself as 'M.B.'—the representative, plain-speaking linen draper whose shop is located in the familiar cityscape of St Francis Street, Dublin, and who is 'but *one* Man, of obscure Condition' and 'inferior Calling', offering up 'very insignificant Reflections' on behalf of 'the whole Kingdom' (Swift, *Prose Works*, x. 124–9). Far from casting a sense of doubt on the Drapier's humility, his visceral assertions of vulnerability and lowliness, combined with expressions of unanimous popular disgust, lend his sense of outrage a valiant dignity. 'Having already written *Two Letters* to People of my own Level and Condition', he warned the Irish nobility in a homely, prophetic,

---

[29] 'But Paul said, I am a man which am a Jew of Tarsus, a city in Cilicia, a citizen of no mean city: and, I beseech thee, suffer me to speak unto the people. And when he had given him licence, Paul stood on the stairs, and beckoned with the hand unto the people. And when there was made a great silence, he spake unto them in the Hebrew tongue, saying, Men, brethren, and fathers, hear ye my defence which I make now unto you. (And when they heard that he spake in the Hebrew tongue to them, they kept the more silence: and he saith,) I am verily a man which am a Jew, born in Tarsus, a city in Cilicia, yet brought up in this city at the feet of Gamaliel, and taught according to the perfect manner of the law of the fathers, and was zealous toward God, as ye all are this day' (Acts 21: 39–22: 3). See also *The Task*'s 'freeman. Free by birth | *Of no mean city*' (V. 763–4; my emphasis).

tradesman's strain to bear in mind that even the worm will turn (Swift, *Prose Works*, x. 27). The weakest may be strongest, the servant may be master, and David will, perhaps, beat Goliath for a second time:

> I am very sensible, that such a Work as I have undertaken, might have worthily employed a much better Pen. But when a House is attempted to be robbed, it often happens that the weakest in the Family, runs first to stop the Door ... I was in the Case of *David*, who *could not move in the Armour of* Saul; and therefore I rather chose to attack this *uncircumcised Philistine* (*Wood* I mean) *with a Sling and a Stone*. And I may say for *Wood*'s Honour, as well as my own, that he resembles *Goliah* in many Circumstances ... *he defied the Armies of the living God*. *Goliah*'s Conditions of Combat were likewise the same with those of *Wood*: *If he prevail against us, then shall we be his Servants*. But if it happen that I *prevail* over him, I renounce the other Part of the Conditions; he shall never be a *Servant* of mine; for I do not think him fit to be trusted in any *honest* Man's Shop. (Swift, *Prose Works*, x. 48)

Grundy claims that 'Direct urging of humility is not a high priority of [Johnson's] moral writing, and he seldom depicts the practice of humility, either fictional or biographical'.[30] This way of phrasing the matter—'Direct urging'—sidesteps the generically humble and indirectly suasive persona inhabited by the prefatory or dedicating author (and Johnson's responses to such a persona),[31] the recurrent emphasis of Johnson's sermons on condescension, submission, charity, and humility,[32] the concern to recommend low characters as the proper subjects of literary attention in, say, *Rambler* 60 and 145 (*Yale*, iii. 318–23; v. 8–12), and the instinct throughout his writings to descend more or less straightforwardly to common topics. It also fails to mention the fact that it is notoriously difficult to praise or recommend humility directly without sounding as if you are (recommending) something quite different. The capacity of Johnson's writing to elevate the peripheral and lowly to a position of temporary significance lies at the heart of the problem involved in urging a similar humility on the reader; once central to our attention, the little or mean thing may cease to be humble.

John Norris acknowledged that 'exceeding little' had been 'professedly written' on his subject—humility—'which though Practical, is not the most easie of any in the World to write *well* upon'.[33] He grapples with the

---

[30] Grundy, *Samuel Johnson and the Scale of Greatness*, 2.

[31] See, for instance, Johnson, 'Life of Dryden', *Lives*, i. 359, 366.

[32] See James Gray, *Johnson's Sermons: A Study* (Oxford: Clarendon Press, 1972), 152–5.

[33] John Norris, *A Practical Treatise Concerning Humility. Design'd for the Furtherance of that Great Christian Vertue, both in the Minds and Lives of Men* (London: for S. Manship, 1707), 'To the Reader', A3, A4.

dilemma of how to praise what he calls in his subtitle a '*Great Christian Vertue*' without making an achievement of that virtue, a misapprehension that would confuse humility with self-regarding ambition. A better writer than Norris on the subject, one who had a critical influence on Johnson's thinking, was William Law. Johnson came across his *Serious Call to a Devout and Holy Life* (1728) at Oxford, 'expecting to find it a dull book . . . and perhaps to laugh at it. But I found Law quite an overmatch for me; and this was the first occasion of my thinking in earnest about religion.' Boswell remarks that 'From this time forward, religion was the predominant object of his thoughts' (*Life*, i. 68–9; the conflict suggested by 'overmatch' is equally characteristic of his thoughts about religion from this point on). A recurrent willingness to 'descend to some particulars' of the humble and quotidian elements of Christian life, thus confounding the emphases of ancient decorum, facilitates Law's comparison of our stature in the eyes of the world to our stature in the sight of God:

Thus do the impressions which we have receiv'd from living in the world enslave our minds, that we dare not attempt to be *eminent* in the sight of God, and holy Angels, for fear of being little in the eyes of the world.

From this quarter arises the greatest difficulty of humility, because it cannot subsist in any mind, but so far as it is dead to the world, and has parted with all desires of enjoying its greatness, and honours. So that in order to be truly humble, you must unlearn all those notions which you have been all your life learning from this corrupt spirit of the world.[34]

The problem with Norris calling a Christian virtue 'great', akin to the awkwardness of praising a literary work in a preface, which impugns the humility of the conventionally humble author, is that it becomes subject to the tenth definition of the word in Johnson's *Dictionary*: 'Swelling; proud.' William Dodwell thought that 'some are proud of being *humble*, and others through wrong Affection have rendered both the Notion and Practice of [humility] contemptible, and exposed it to the Ridicule of profane and witty Scoffers'.[35] In his sixth sermon, Johnson noted that 'pride is a very dangerous associate to greatness' and that 'There is another more dangerous species of pride, arising from a consciousness of virtue' (*Yale*, xiv. 71–2). John Hoole reported that Johnson thought Edmund

---

[34] William Law, *A Serious Call to a Devout and Holy Life. Adapted to the State and Condition of all Orders of Christians*, 2nd edn., corrected (London: for William Innes, 1732), 46, 310.

[35] William Dodwell, *Practical Discourses on Moral Subjects*, 2 vols. (London: for Sam. Birt, 1748–9), 'On Humility', i. 68.

Waller's 'affectation of candour or modesty was but another kind of indirect self-praise, and had its foundation in vanity' (*Miscellanies*, ii. 153).

Conceptions of the author as either rhetorically detached or personally involved, as properly concerned with high or with low subjects and styles, jostle for pre-eminence in Johnson's writing, especially when he encounters stubborn topics. Sooner or later, many of his prefaces and dedications (whether in defence of his own work or other people's) reveal a sense of having trespassed on ground unworthy of readers' attention, sometimes of compounding the fault by delaying their progress still further in saying so. This in turn prompts the reflex counter-move to self-rebuke and/or castigation of others who assume that trifles do not deserve their regard. Johnson's prefaces typically shift, then, from classical to Christian values, from denigrating to advocating the humble author and his or her subject. The sheer repetition of such concerns, and the opposing emphases that cluster around them, suggest that classical literary hierarchies—in which low topics garner little esteem and merit only cursory attention—might directly contradict the importance of such subjects to common and general life. A heightened and decorous linguistic register then seems to express a worry that reconciliation between the cultivated selections of literature and the dispersed bulk of mankind is impossible.

Johnson's style thus demonstrates the presence of one realm (life) straining to make itself heard in another (art), or a realized discrepancy between two competing realms. He frets at the possibility of reconciling contrary things—variously construed as greatness and littleness, height and lowness, significance and insignificance. Each of these pairs super-ficially represents opposite ends of a vertical moral axis, but, having been prised apart, they are usually merged in terms of the importance and recurrence of little, low, and insignificant matters to everyday life. And yet, although he observes that things 'of least dignity are of the most apparent use', and that 'Some have been so forcibly struck by this observation that they have . . . thought it reasonable to alter the common distribution of dignity' (*Rambler* 145, *Yale*, v. 8), Johnson cannot quite bring himself to redefine dignity as usefulness, or height as lowness. Such a move would collapse the basis of classical hierarchies to vest wholehearted esteem in those things and styles that, to 'the great masters of moral learning' in *Rambler* 66, are most contemptible (*Yale*, iii. 351). As in the preface to *Easy Phraseology*, Johnson typically proclaims the inevitability of subordination in literature, as in life, but enjoins charity towards those who 'form the base of the pyramid' and 'lie buried in

obscurity themselves, while they support all that is splendid, conspicuous, or exalted' (*Rambler* 145, *Yale*, v. 9). His arguments about trifles
call for adherence to ancient convention, for affirmative action, and for
equality of opportunity. Empson might say of this writing, divided as
it is between pagan and Christian influences and loyalties, that 'it gives
prominence neither to the horizontals nor to the verticals'; like the figure
of the cross, 'it is at once an indecision and a structure'. (For the Romans,
too, crossroads were 'charged with spiritual energy', watched over by
ancestral and household gods, the Lares.)[36]

In the third paragraph of the Baretti preface, there is an odd indecisiveness about the reader's capacity to feel '*too much* elevation' (how much is
too much?), as there is about the author's having 'no reason to be *much*
ashamed' at the end: to look on this writing with some degree of superiority to the topic seems appropriate, instinctive, and natural. Philosophic
diction with a pronounced generalizing implication, and remote from
common life, might locate the author in the situation of the 'contemner of
trifles' he is criticizing, pre-empting the reader's excessive elevation above
the subject by displaying his own. When Johnson writes of 'the levity of
his *subjects*, and the unimportance of his *personages*', he could be casting
Baretti as the imperious sovereign of his linguistic terrain, borrowing the
imagery of his many dedications (also drawn up for other people) to the
royal family. Yet, in the next breath, he reverses his emphasis from high
to low, invoking the language of Christian mercy for 'the humble author'
(as opposed to the 'great Authors' mentioned earlier, and without their
safety in numbers or the grandeur of capitalization)—a variation on
'your humble servant', the stock eighteenth-century conclusion to a letter or to a dedication. If the writer is shamefacedly aware of his subject's
unimportance, the reader should not be. Johnson seems incapable of
bridging the gap between his refusal voluntarily to degrade himself to
apologize for the work, and his assertion that the audience should stoop
to acknowledge its importance. His writing is populous, thick with contradictory ideas and attitudes expressed through vivified abstractions and
human types—'learned and elegant people', 'great Authors', 'casual talkers', 'supercilious contemner', 'humble author', 'subjects', 'personages',
'other nomenclators'—creating a virtual community of the learned,
chattering, and professional classes, characters that embody without ever
exchanging or modifying their particular views on the book.

[36] Empson, *Seven Types of Ambiguity*, 192; Holland, *Rubicon*, 17.

These contradictory impulses find another joint expression in the antagonym 'Let . . . ' that appears throughout Johnson's prefaces and dedications. 'Let' is the weakest kind of injunction and thus appropriate for the twin strains of supplication and exhortation that characterize such writing. It is also an internally divided word, since, as Empson noted, it means both 'allow' and 'hinder'—suggesting at one and the same time that you should and should not permit 'trifles', 'levity', and 'slight occasions' to infringe on your attention.[37] As such, 'Let . . . ' formulations conceive of the preface simultaneously as a barrier and as a gateway to the subsequent work. Gérard Genette numbers prefaces, introductions, and dedications among what he calls 'paratexts'—those aspects of a book, such as the author's name, the title, epigraph, acknowledgements, and illustrations, which 'ensure the text's presence in the world, its "reception" and consumption':

> More than a boundary or a sealed border, the paratext is, rather, a *threshold*, or . . . a 'vestibule' that offers the world at large the possibility of either stepping inside or turning back. It is an 'undefined zone' between the inside and the outside, a zone without any hard and fast boundary on either the inward side (turned toward the text) or the outward side (turned toward the world's discourse about the text), an edge, or, as Philippe Lejeune put it, 'a fringe of the printed text which in reality controls one's whole reading of the text.'[38]

Lejeune's apparent insistence on the preface's 'control' does not quite square with the tone of Johnson's writing (nor with the indeterminacy of Genette's slew of 'or's). His prefaces, countenancing a multitude of contradictory responses, are too inconclusive to prescribe a single reaction, while their attempts at control are overcast by a sense of human limitation, of divided sympathies, and of the reader's freedom to reject or to diminish the significance of the author's efforts.

2. ENLARGING TRIFLES

Hints of Johnson's alertness to his introductory genre recur throughout the Baretti preface. In a form of writing which is the first to be read, there is an appropriate concern at the level of content with coming

---

[37] Empson, *Seven Types of Ambiguity*, 192. See also Johnson's *Dictionary* definitions of the verb 'To LET', senses 1 and 18: 'To allow; to suffer; to permit'; 'To hinder; to obstruct; to oppose.'

[38] Gérard Genette, *Paratexts: Thresholds of Interpretation*, trans. Jane E. Lewin (Cambridge: Cambridge University Press, 1997), 1–2. See also Marie McLean, 'Pretexts and Paratexts: The Art of the Peripheral', *New Literary History*, 22 (1991), 273–9.

first—both in the sense of winning a literary race and of being an original writer—hence the admission that 'These are ... not the first pages that have been compiled only for the sake of teaching words' (although these *are* the first pages, after the title, that the reader will encounter). When Johnson has the author refuse in the same sentence to submit to a 'voluntary degradation', he seems to be reminding us that this is a preface, not a dedication, which he defines in the *Dictionary* as a 'servile address to a patron'. *Rambler* 208 (the last issue) combines aspects of a conclusion with those of an introduction when it refuses to 'degrade' the paper's 'dignity' by subjecting it to 'the meanness of a dedication' (*Yale*, v. 317). It seems appropriate that the author is spoken of throughout the preface in the third person, since he is an intermediate figure, hovering between Johnson and Baretti. Yet this is also one of the proudest of Johnson's introductions, and thus seems a good fit for the notoriously sensitive, arrogant, and hot-tempered Baretti, of whom Hester Thrale wrote that: 'his Character is easily seen, & his Soul above Disguise. Haughty & Insolent and breathing defiance against all Mankind; while his Powers of Mind exceed most people's, and his Powers of Purse are so slight that they leave him dependent on all,—Baretti is forever in the State of a Stream dam'd up—if he could once get loose—he would bear down all before him' (*Thraliana*, i. 43).

This stark opposition of powers of the mind to those of the purse lays bare the financial exigencies of authorship behind the decorous repartee in the Thrales' drawing room; it also calls Savage's extreme defiance to mind. Baretti is at once approachable ('easily seen', 'above Disguise') and distant ('Haughty & Insolent', 'his Powers of Mind exceed most people's'). As a character sketch, Thrale's writing has the appeal of a stagy caricature not far removed from the 'supercilious contemner of trifles' in Johnson's preface. It is a shock after all this to discover that *Easy Phraseology* (originally composed for the young 'Queeney' or 'Hetty' Thrale) consists for the most part of tedious and clumsily executed dialogues between two horses, a sheet of paper and a pen, a dog and a cat, a hammer and an anvil, and so on, and that it was—if Boswell is to be believed—its trifling eccentricity that led Johnson to his famous dismissal of Sterne: 'I censured some ludicrous fantastick dialogues between two coach-horses, and other such stuff, which Baretti had lately published. He joined with me, and said, "Nothing odd will do long. 'Tristram Shandy' did not last" ' (*Life*, ii. 449).

Only one dialogue—no. 44, '*Between two Idlers at a Coffee-House*', in which the newspapers, weather, pretty women in the park, and gambling come up for discussion—seems to approximate the work as Johnson conceived of it in his preface (although it is scarcely appropriate to the young female readers described in the title).[39] Perhaps Johnson did not read *Easy Phraseology* until after it had been published (if at all), and supplied a generic defence of the uses of slighter topics to social intercourse and therefore to literary endeavour. He does not even bother to tell us why young ladies might want to speak Italian (possible motives include the opera, or Grand Tourism), instead homing in on the low category or *'Colloquial Part'* of any language. *Easy Phraseology* is mentioned amongst the contents of his library at his death, but he styles it throughout his preface 'Dialogues'—perhaps suggesting awareness merely of the form, not of the precise title or contents.[40] Boswell was disconcerted to hear of Richard Rolt's *New Dictionary of Trade and Commerce* (1756), to which Johnson contributed a preface, that he 'never saw the man and never read the book. The booksellers wanted a Preface to a Dictionary of Trade and Commerce. I knew very well what such a Dictionary should be, and I wrote a Preface accordingly' (*Life*, i. 359).

As in his comments on the requirements of introductions and conclusions (*Life*, i. 292), Johnson here implies that a preface-writer need only know what the contents of the ensuing work '*should* be', rather than what it is, in order to fulfil the remit of his task—perhaps because human nature will always fail to measure up to the grandeur of its initial conceptions. This has certain consequences for the style in which his prefaces and dedications are written. It suits Johnson's talents to defend in general terms the category of subject or intellectual province to which a book belongs (or seems to Johnson that it ought to belong). It frees him from the constraints of immersion in, or direct responsibility for, the work that follows. It allows him to couch his arguments in mournfully abstract form, to recast variations on the same serio-comic oscillation between human hopes and human disappointments, between intention and execution. Yet the fact that many of his prefaces and dedications are written in defence of transparently low subjects—the game of draughts, newspapers, pamphlets, trade, and conversation—creates a perceptible discrepancy between style and topic that prevents the writing

[39] Giuseppe Baretti, *Easy Phraseology, for the Use of Young Ladies, who intend to learn the Colloquial Part of the Italian Language* (London: for G. Robinson and T. Cadell, 1775), 267–70 (p. 267).

[40] J. D. Fleeman (ed.), *The Sale Catalogue of Johnson's Library: A Facsimile Edition* (Victoria English Literary Studies, 1975), lot 189, p. 31. Piozzi says that Johnson also contributed 'the 'pretty Italian verses' at the end of Baretti's *Easy Phraseology* (p. 424), thus providing the first and last sections of the book (*Miscellanies*, i. 194).

from becoming impervious. Whether or not he had read *Easy Phraseology*, there is a sharp contrast between the acerbic nobility of Johnson's defence of trifles on Baretti's behalf, and the genuinely colloquial style in which the author himself then dedicates his work to Miss Thrale:

I have told it you, my dear Hetty, that some day or other you would have my Dialogues in print; and here at last they are, every one of them. Are'n't you delighted at it, and quite impatient to give them a second perusal? . . . Nor are you to fear neither, that by any blotting or mutilation I may have curtailed or taken away any essential part of their primitive nonsense, as I can give you my word and honour, that I have on the contrary encreased rather than diminished the dose of it in most of them, being well apprised by several months observation and experience, that nothing goes so quick to your heart and fastens upon your imagination so well, as stark nonsense, and that you give it the preference not only over mathematicks and philosophy, but even over eating unripe cherries and sucking milk and water through a straw.[41]

Baretti here provides a different, biographically specific, and slighter motive for publication than Johnson's preface does. He is also recalling a position of employment as Hetty's resident tutor, which fleshes out the sense of frustrated dependence captured in Hester Thrale's sketch. The heterogeneous public of Johnson's preface collapses into the single child with a fondness for 'stark nonsense', wholly alien to the 'supercilious contemner of trifles' who might 'look upon these productions with too much elevation'. Johnson thus deflects the obtrusive elevation of his own style onto a putative adult observer who would side too readily with the writer's consciousness of his subject's deficiency—and in agreeing with him actually contradict him. But why does he write 'look upon' rather than 'look down upon'? As if to say that to 'look upon' something (the humble author, his lowly subject) need not entail looking down on it? The *OED* definitions of 'look on' and 'look upon' ('look', senses 18 a. and 24 a.)—'To pay regard to; to hold in esteem; to respect'; 'To pay regard to; *esp.* to regard favourably, hold in esteem'—similarly imply a subordination of the observer to the object of his or her attention, as if the act of recognizing inferiority should transform itself into one of elective, charitable elevation. 'Regard' in this instance entails respecting as well as mere seeing, a voluntary humbling of the self in order to acknowledge the superiority of another, or to attend to something conventionally thought unworthy. Pride is thus often conceived as inattention, humility

---

[41] Baretti, *Easy Phraseology*, 'Dedication', pp. v–ix.

as attention: 'nothing promotes Pride so much as want of Consideration in the Person tainted with it.'[42]

Johnson's anonymous dedication to the Earl of Rochford of William Payne's *Introduction to the Game of Draughts* (1756) reconciles the potential disparity between a trifling work and a socially or intellectually superior onlooker by proposing a form of equality between the skills celebrated in the patron and those exemplified in the author—namely, 'Caution, Foresight, and Circumspection':

My LORD,
When I take the Liberty of addressing to Your Lordship *A Treatise on the Game of* DRAUGHTS, I easily foresee that I shall be in danger of suffering Ridicule on one Part, while I am gaining Honour on the other, and that many who may envy me the Distinction of approaching You, will deride the Present I presume to offer.

Had I considered this little Volume as having no Purpose beyond that of teaching a Game, I should indeed have left it to take its Fate without a Patron. Triflers may find or make any Thing a Trifle; but since it is the great Characteristic of a wise Man to see Events in their Causes, to obviate Consequences, and ascertain Contingencies, your Lordship will think nothing a Trifle by which the Mind is inured to Caution, Foresight, and Circumspection. The same Skill, and often the same Degree of Skill, is exerted in great and little Things, and your Lordship may sometimes exercise, at a harmless Game, those Abilities which have been so happily employed in the Service of your Country. (*Prefaces*, 150)

Once again, he divides the field into sets of contrary possibilities—on the one hand, ridicule and derision of the work; on the other, honour and distinction for the writer—before smudging the borders of that division. Like Steele and Swift's mock-humble supplicants, but without their satirical edge, Johnson insists on a firmness of demarcation that he proceeds to override. The capitalized pairing of 'LORD' and 'DRAUGHTS' raises the question of whether they are opposites or equals, a possibility lightly worn in the preface ('draughts are unworthy of my Lord, yet my Lord will have the social clout and intellectual nous to discern that this is not really the case'). The accents of charitable solicitude—akin to the attempt to curtail 'merciless censures' of the 'humble author' in the Baretti preface—surface in the description of 'this little Volume', potentially 'left to take its Fate without a Patron'. The solicitous diminutive at once downplays and asserts a seriousness of purpose which deserves a better fate than abandonment (little things *can* have value); it resembles the

---

[42] Francis Astrey, *Humility Recommended. In a Sermon Preach'd before the Right Honourable the Lord Mayor and the Court of Aldermen in the Cathedral Church of St. Paul* (London: for Henry Clements, 1716), 21.

paternal tenderness of Chaucer's release of *Troilus and Criseyde* (*c.* early 1380s) from his protection: 'Go, litel bok, go, litel myn tragedye.'[43] Rather than persistently flagging up the disjunction between a great man and a minor subject, work, or author, this dedication re-orientates itself as a defence of *any* subject as great to the great-minded and as trifling to the small-minded—it shifts between the first and second paragraphs from excuse to advocacy. But this is advocacy of a kind that leaves its evaluative terms in uncertain territory. Johnson finally dignifies the book rather than the writer (already honoured in the very act of approaching the Earl of Rochford), elevating the work's nobility of intention to match its dedicatee's powers of perception and thus confounding the distinction between great man and little subject.

This dedication, with its emphasis on the noble intellect's ability to raise a trifle to something of significance, resembles a point in Johnson's 'Life of Francis Drake'—published in the *Gentleman's Magazine* (1740–1)—at which he celebrates the capacity of the apparently trifling incident to harbour or to promote future greatness, thus overcoming its superficial meaninglessness, degradation, or unworthiness. This prognosis of significance appears at the beginning of Drake's career. The description of his exemplary conduct as 'the most successful Introduction to greater Enterprizes' might also apply to the commercial or intellectual outcomes of the lowly genre of literary introductions such as prefaces (encouraging the reader to proceed sympathetically to the ensuing work) or dedications (prompting the financial and social endorsement of a wealthy patron):

how few Opportunities soever he might have in this Part of his Life for the Exercise of his Courage, he gave so many Proofs of his Diligence and Fidelity, that his Master dying unmarried left him his little Vessel in reward of his Service; a Circumstance that deserves to be remembered, not only as it may illustrate the private Character of this brave Man, but as it may hint to all those who may hereafter propose his Conduct for their Imitation, That Virtue is the surest Foundation both of Reputation and Fortune, and that the first Step to Greatness is to be honest.

If it were not improper to dwell longer on an Incident at the first View so inconsiderable, it might be added, That it deserves the Reflection of those, who, when they are engaged in Affairs not adequate to their Abilities, pass them over with a contemptuous Neglect, and while they amuse themselves with chimerical Schemes, and Plans of future Undertakings, suffer every Opportunity of smaller Advantage to slip away as unworthy their Regard. They may learn

---

[43] Geoffrey Chaucer, *The Riverside Chaucer*, ed. Larry D. Benson, 3rd edn. (Oxford: Oxford University Press, 1987; repr. 1992), *Troilus and Criseyde*, V. 1786.

from the Example of *Drake*, that Diligence in Employments of less Consequence is the most successful Introduction to greater Enterprizes. (*Early Biographical Writings*, 37)

Solidity, tangibility, vigour, and progress underpin this simultaneously mobile and grounded exposition of exercise, foundations, the first step, and the material evidence of a 'little Vessel'. We are solicited to attend to an apparently 'inconsiderable' incident because Drake himself became successful by not despising low employment. We imitate him by heeding the biographer who sees in this incident something morally instructive, and Johnson thus combines a series of descents: Drake's to service, the biographer's to relating it, ours to heeding to the moral of this attention. Those tempted to skip the lesson of the story are precisely the ones who ought to profit from it. But the biographer is not entirely confident that he *should* prolong our regard for this lowly episode. He rehearses the second and third of his trenchant, axiomatic truths ('That it deserves the Reflection . . . '; 'that Diligence in Employments of less Consequence . . . ') within the auspices of a hesitant, paraliptic introduction to his second paragraph ('If it were not improper to dwell longer . . . '). Extending the duration as well as enlarging the bulk of a trifle, he acknowledges that, at least on one view, he should not be lending this transaction the importance he also insists that it demonstrates. Johnson here strongly recommends what he formally rejects as improper. The trifle is at one and the same time relegated to the margins and elevated to the centre of his interest.

It is possible to see in this early journalistic rather than book-length biography a form of self-admonition: Johnson, by now in his early thirties and having set out to London in hopes of making an impression on the stage, had been reduced to hack work to order, an employment below what he had set out to achieve but to the pursuit of which he is indirectly urging himself.[44] The voice of this passage might be inward-looking—expressing the hopes of a man who had schemed for a better, grander literary fate than this—as well as outward-looking, facing a public which tended to overlook not only the seemingly insignificant incident, but also the anonymous author who described it. Drake's successful pursuit of greatness via little and mean employments may have provided a limited model for Johnson's own. As Dustin Griffin observes of the *Rambler* essays on the subject of patronage, Johnson 'writes out of the very uncertainties and dependencies that he warns

---

[44] See, for instance, James Clifford, *Young Sam Johnson* (New York: McGraw-Hill, 1955), especially 265–309.

against'.[45] The pregnant trifle or aspiring hack may herald imminent defeat, rather than the resounding success of a Drake.

In the *Dictionary*, 'To TRIFLE' (sense 4) is 'To *be* of no importance' (as in a '*trifling* debt'), and a 'TRIFLE' is 'A thing of no moment', but 'To TRIFLE' is given a further, separate sense, 'To *make* of no importance' (first and third emphases mine). Although Johnson describes this last sense as 'Not in use', in fact it dominates his perception of what determines the status of a trifle, as in his dedication of Payne's *Introduction to the Game of Draughts*: 'Triflers may find or make any Thing a Trifle.' Something becomes unimportant by virtue of the onlooker's attitude towards the object she or he spurns, rather than by virtue of that object's inherently low status ('to an editor nothing is a trifle by which his authour is obscured', 'Preface to Shakespeare', *Yale*, vii. 104). The relationship between a particular Johnsonian dedication and the 'servile' form of dedications in general might be said to approximate the relationship between literary citations and the definitions of certain words in the *Dictionary*. Quotations, in exemplifying the titular sense, may contradict it, just as the generic servility of the dedicating author can, in practice, turn into a defence of his endeavour. Although Johnson defines the adjective 'INCONSIDERABLE' as 'Unworthy of notice; unimportant', two of his authors tell a different story: 'The most *inconsiderable* of creatures may at some time or other come to revenge itself on the greatest' (L'Estrange); 'Let no sin appear small or *inconsiderable* by which an almighty God is offended, and eternal salvation endangered' (John Rogers).

Only a fool, in that case, would remain satisfied with the titular definition; seemingly unimportant things are worthy of careful attention and pregnant with future instruction: 'we may neglect the most deserving objects' (Johnson in *Tour*, 367). According to the *OED*, from at least 1640 'inconsiderable' could mean 'Inconsiderate; thoughtless' as well as 'Not to be considered; unworthy of consideration; beneath notice' (senses 3 and 2), a re-orientation highlighting the shortcomings of the observer rather than those of the object of his or her inattention which Johnson well expresses. His citation from John Denham seems to hover between both meanings: 'No, I am an *inconsiderable* fellow, and know nothing.' The *Dictionary*'s definition of 'INCONSIDERABLE', read alongside its contrary exemplifications, represents 'one of the innumerable theories which the first attempt to reduce them into practice certainly destroys' (*Rambler* 145,

[45] Dustin Griffin, *Literary Patronage in England, 1650–1800* (Cambridge: Cambridge University Press, 1996), 224.

Yale, v. 8). An apparently neutral definition of 'To PREPONDERATE' ('To outweigh; to overpower by weight', sense 1), once illustrated, similarly amplifies into a moral the scientific fact of an '*inconsiderable* weight' (my emphasis) sometimes possessing greater efficacy than more substantial 'magnitudes', thus translating the small-scale lexicographical endeavour itself into something of wider ethical applicability. It also calls to mind the judicious imbalances in Johnson's own style, and the effect they have of generating significance: 'An inconsiderable weight, by distance from the centre of the balance, will *preponderate* greater magnitudes' (John Glanville); 'The trivialllest thing, when a passion is cast into the scale with it, *preponderates* substantial blessings' (Richard Allestree).

Perhaps influenced by the inherently combative activities of outweighing and overpowering, Johnson makes 'PREPONDERATE' shoulder an implication beyond the apparent remit of the word he is defining. The first illustration repeats the fabular lesson provided by L'Estrange under 'INCONSIDERABLE' (small things may triumph over much greater ones), so harbours implications beyond its scientific context. The second—which might stand as a plot summary of *Othello*—extends the same lesson still further, to the realm of human passions that threaten to unseat our reason by their metaphoric rather than by their literal weight.[46] The apparently trifling thing again dominates the more substantial one, but the effect is not neutral or commendable; it is to be lamented and held in check, as the title of Allestree's *Government of the Tongue* (1674), from which this citation comes, implies. *Dictionary* exemplifications of the preponderating or superior power of the small, inconsiderable thing might be viewed as instances of the lexicographer's or of the editor's claims to distinction and to ridicule, as laid out in the prefaces to Shakespeare and to the *Dictionary*: his focus on minutiae. Literary and moral authorities endorse the claim that trifles are important not only to language, but to life (although they differ in their interpretations of whether this is a good or a bad thing), while the titular definitions of such words present an opposing, conventional assumption of their insignificance. The dynamic process of weighing up many words in the *Dictionary* thus replicates locally the movement of a preface—such as that to the *Dictionary* itself—from intention to execution, from insignificance to significance (and sometimes back again).

Such a process also reveals a modulation from classical to Judaeo-Christian values, since equally implicit in these exchanges between great

---

[46] See also Johnson, *Thoughts on the late Transactions respecting Falkland's Islands* (1771), *Yale*, x. 365–6.

and little, high and low, considerable and inconsiderable, is a series of biblical emphases which underpins Johnson's (as well as M. B. Drapier's) renovation of lowly subjects: 'he bringeth down to the grave, and bringeth up. The LORD maketh poor, and maketh rich: he bringeth low, and lifteth up. He raiseth the poor out of the dust, and lifteth up the beggar from the dunghill, to set them among princes, and to make them inherit the throne of glory'; 'The LORD lifteth up the meek: he casteth the wicked down to the ground'; 'Blessed are the meek: for they shall inherit the earth'; 'But he that is greatest among you shall be your servant. And whosoever shall exalt himself shall be abased; and he that shall humble himself shall be exalted' (1 Samuel 2: 6–8; Psalm 147: 6; Matthew 5: 5, 23: 11–12).

The *Dictionary* is packed with such reversals of fortune and of expectation, often brought about by reference to biblical precedent. Sense 1 of 'BEGGAR' ('One who lives upon alms; one who has nothing but what is given him'), citing 1 Samuel 2: 8, suggests a future change of state: 'He raiseth up the poor out of the dust, and lifteth up the *beggar* from the dunghill, to set them among princes.' Sense 4 of the adverb 'LOW' ('In a state of subjection'), as exemplified by Spenser, does the same thing: 'How comes it that, having been once so *low* brought, and thoroughly subjected, they afterwards lifted up themselves so strongly again.' The third sense of the adjective 'MEAN' ('Contemptible; despicable') is supported by quotation from *Cyder* (1708), in which John Philips's proud negation of English pusillanimity in the face of Roman persecution naturalizes St Paul's description of himself, through litotes, as 'a citizen of no mean city' (Acts 21: 39): 'The Roman legions, and great Cæsar found | Our fathers no *mean* foes.' Similarly, the adverb 'CONTEMPTIBLY' ('Meanly; in a manner deserving contempt') collides with a solitary litotes from Milton: 'Know'st thou not | Their language, and their ways? They also know, | And reason not *contemptibly*.' The third sense of the adjective 'LITTLE' ('Of small dignity, power, or importance') is supported by a quotation from 1 Samuel 15: 17 that associates great rewards with a conscious littleness, thereby at once agreeing with and contradicting the terms of its definition: 'When thou wast *little* in thine own sight, wast thou not made the head of the tribes.'

By contrast, sense 2 of the adjective 'CONTEMPTIBLE', 'Despised, scorned; neglected', resembles L'Estrange's fabular re-orientation of worth from great things to little: 'There is not so *contemptible* a plant or animal that does not confound the most enlarged understanding' (Locke). Just as 'inconsiderable' can point to someone habitually inconsiderate as well as to something beneath our notice, so 'contemptible' can indicate someone who is habitually contemptuous, as well as something that meets with our scorn: sense 3 of 'CONTEMPTIBLE' in the *Dictionary* is 'Scornful; apt to despise' ('no proper use', according to Johnson—but then neither is the sense of 'To TRIFLE' which he usually employs). Sense 2 of the noun 'LITTLE' ('A small part; a small proportion') misquotes Ecclesiasticus 19: 1 in order to make a similar point to that expressed by the illustrations under 'INCONSIDERABLE'. Things that seem unworthy of attention may prove to be our downfall: 'He that despiseth little things, shall perish by *little* and *little*'[47] (Johnson complicates matters by the extra ambiguity as to what the unitalicized 'little' means—will the inconsiderate onlooker be destroyed by precisely those things to which he fails to pay heed, or by something equally trifling, or by painfully little degrees, as a punishment for his inattention?). This last sense of 'LITTLE' is given seven citations in all, two of which emphasize that little things combine to form greater and more significant masses (such as a dictionary, or 'collections of words and phrases' like Baretti's *Easy Phraseology*, *Prefaces*, 11): 'The poor remnant of human seed which remained in their mountains, peopled their country again slowly, by *little* and *little*' (Bacon); 'By freeing the precipitated matter from the rest by filtration, and diligently grinding the white precipitate with water, the mercury will *little* by *little* be gathered into drops' (Robert Boyle).

The process of accumulation means that 'inconsiderable' things, far from being the opposite of 'considerable' ones, will eventually merge into them (with desirable and undesirable results). Sense 4 of 'CONSIDERABLE' ('More than a little. It has a middle signification between little and great') is supported by Gilbert Burnet in terms similar to Bacon and Boyle's illustrations of 'LITTLE', again prompting thoughts of lexicographical collections: 'Those earthy particles, when they came to be collected, would constitute a body of a very *considerable* thickness and solidity.' Yet Johnson also suggests that this apparent significance may be unwarranted; mere quantity is no guarantee of quality, and numerous particulars do not necessarily add up to splendid generality. 'CONSIDERABLENESS' ('Importance; dignity; moment; value; desert; a claim to notice') is, like 'To PREPONDERATE', checked in its aspirations by Allestree's *Government of the Tongue*: 'Their most slight and trivial occurrences, by being theirs,

---

[47] The original reads 'he that contemneth small things, shall fall by little and little', recalling the 'contemner of trifles' in the Baretti preface. See also: 'The wisdom of the humble shall exalt his head, and shall make him sit in the midst of great men'; 'The bee is small among flying things but her fruit hath the chiefest sweetness'; 'Many tyrants have sat on the throne, and he whom no man would think on, hath worn the crown' (Ecclesiasticus 11: 1, 3, 5).

they think to acquire a *considerableness*.' The 'Preface to the Dictionary', like the 'Preface to Shakespeare', is equally uncertain about the value of accumulation, and questions whether its own endeavours amount to mere proliferation rather than to cultivation. Readers may upbraid such multiplicity—itself defended in prolix terms here—as needlessly self-generated replication:[48]

There is more danger of censure from the multiplicity than paucity of examples; authorities will sometimes seem to have been accumulated without necessity or use, and perhaps some will be found which might, without loss, have been omitted. But a work of this kind is not hastily to be charged with superfluities: those quotations, which to careless or unskilful perusers appear only to repeat the same sense, will often exhibit, to a more accurate examiner, diversities of signification, or, at least, afford different shades of the same meaning . . . every quotation contributes something to the stability or enlargement of the language. (*Prose and Poetry*, 315)

'Stability' (or 'Fixedness; not fluidity', sense 2 of the word in the *Dictionary*) and 'enlargement' (or 'Encrease; augmentation; farther extension', sense 1 of the word in the *Dictionary*) might be construed as mutually exclusive aims for a lexicographer. Those who wish to see the language firmly entrenched by Dr Johnson will not welcome his contributions to its expansion. The preface here demonstrates the value, however, of attending to 'diversities' in its own style: 'necessity *or* use', 'careless *or* unskilful', 'diversities of signification *or* . . . different shades of meaning', and 'stability *or* enlargement', as pairs of alternatives, might appear to be merely restating the same point. But they subtly account for contradictory motives in author and in reader, and Johnson's multiplicity squares with the number of years he has spent on his endeavour, as well as with the number of reactions he attempts to cover. 'Necessity' implies either authorial 'compulsion' or 'indispensableness' to the reader (parts of senses 1 and 2 in the *Dictionary*), while 'use' suggests customary linguistic 'Usage' and habitual 'Practice' as well as the reader's 'Need', 'Advantage', and 'Convenience'—in other words, a neutral register of the language as it is spoken, or a tailoring of that language to more specific requirements ('USE', noun, parts of senses 3–7 in the *Dictionary*). 'Careless' summons up a host of moral failings—'Without care; without solicitude; unconcerned; negligent; inattentive; heedless; regardless; thoughtless; neglectful; unheeding; unthinking; unmindful' (sense 1, *Dictionary*)—while 'unskilful' implies mere clumsiness or ignorance:

[48] See Edinger, *Samuel Johnson and Detailed Representation*, 13–26.

'Wanting art; wanting knowledge' (*Dictionary*). A necessarily limited 'stability' *and* 'enlargement' of vision as well as of language are the hoped-for outcomes of such a style, which reinforces its general precepts by appealing to a plurality of examples and attitudes, but the 'danger' is always that multiplicity will unsettle the grandeur of generality, just as literary exemplifications of certain words challenge the validity of their abstract, defining terms.

Johnson's 'Preface to Shakespeare' defends its author's style on terms akin to the preface to *Easy Phraseology*. Shakespeare is lauded for reproducing the 'easy and familiar dialogue' of real life (*Yale*, vii. 68)—and real life, as the Baretti preface notes, consists largely of trifles. These are not, however, the same kinds of rarefied trifles as those in which the editor deals, which may be unhelpfully remote from common experience (*Yale*, vii. 107–8), nor the cheap verbal effects for which Johnson criticizes his subject:

> A quibble is to Shakespeare, what luminous vapours are to the traveller; he follows it at all adventures, it is sure to lead him out of his way, and sure to engulf him in the mire. It has some malignant power over his mind, and its fascinations are irresistible. Whatever be the dignity or profundity of his disquisition, whether he be enlarging knowledge or exalting affection, whether he be amusing attention with incidents, or enchaining it in suspense, let but a quibble spring up before him, and he leaves his work unfinished. A quibble is the golden apple for which he will always turn aside from his career, or stoop from his elevation. A quibble, poor and barren as it is, gave him such delight, that he was content to purchase it, by the sacrifice of reason, propriety and truth. A quibble was to him the fatal Cleopatra for which he lost the world, and was content to lose it. ('Preface to Shakespeare', *Yale*, vii. 74)

Johnson pluralizes and thus disperses the solidity of a little thing; mere vapours approximate the editor's 'evanescent atoms' or 'evanescent truth' (*Yale*, vii. 107) and differ from concrete particulars in that they cannot be captured or purchased, representing sound without substance (the *Dictionary* defines a 'QUIBBLE' as 'A low conceit depending on the sound of words; a pun'). They also imply a 'Mental fume; vain imagination; fancy unreal' (sense 4 of the noun 'VAPOUR' in the *Dictionary*). Yet the insistent anaphora of 'A quibble', and the extended illustration of its attractions, contribute to a feeling that Johnson is, in spite of his censures, drawn to his subject: the critical framework acts as a shield for the editor's own fascinated pursuit of little things. As in his other defences of trifling subjects, Johnson follows a horizontal and a vertical line of enquiry: breadth and height in 'enlarging' and 'exalting', height and depth in 'dignity' and 'profundity' (the two potential meanings of 'bathos' in Longinus, *On the Sublime*, II. 1. In the first number of *The Idler*, Johnson wrote that he might 'descend into profoundness, or tower into sublimity', *Yale*, ii. 5). The proliferation and layered restatement of what a quibble does, has, and is makes the object of Shakespeare's distraction the more elusive and less specific, the more vigorously it is sought.

The 'let . . . ' formulation again implies '*don't* let yourself be distracted by trifles' *en route* to greatness: the sense of ancient grandeur slipping away from Shakespeare is reinforced by Johnson's classicizing frame of reference. 'Spring up before him' makes the repeated 'quibble' sound like Cadmus' dragon's teeth, sown to yield an instantaneous human army (Piozzi wrote of Johnson that 'his notions rose up like the dragon's teeth sowed by Cadmus all ready clothed, and in bright armour too, fit for immediate battle', *Miscellanies*, i. 285). The 'golden apple' is one of three, provided by Aphrodite, which prevent Atalanta from winning a race against her suitor Melanion and thus cement their union. But it might also refer to the golden apple that Eris, goddess of discord and chaos, introduced to Peleus and Thetis' wedding, thereby eventually provoking the Trojan War. In either case, the apple provides a link between amorous stooping and self-abasement in the pursuit of wordplay, which may have suggested the association of Cleopatra with the quibbling objects of Shakespeare's interest. In *Antony and Cleopatra* itself, hero and heroine invoke ruinous vapours and clouds shortly before their deaths (associating them with mockery, theatrical display, and visual trickery), so that Johnson's allusive critique merges playwright into protagonist as well as editor into author, each individual character's claim to greatness and to immortality potentially compromised by his or her association with trifles.[49] The subtitle of Dryden's blank-verse, quibble-free rewrite of *Antony and Cleopatra*—*All for Love, or The World Well Lost* (1678)—might provide another source for 'he lost the world, and was content to lose it' (Johnson remarked of this play that: 'It is by universal consent accounted the work in which [Dryden] has admitted the fewest improprieties of style or character', 'Life of Dryden', *Lives*, i. 361). But whenever Johnson writes about 'vapours' or *ignis fatuus* in connection with being led astray, or with falling from an elevation, he has a specific, Christian blank-verse precedent in mind—one that changes how we interpret the 'malignant power' and the 'golden apple'

---

[49] William Shakespeare, *The Complete Works: Compact Edition*, ed. Stanley Wells, Gary Taylor, John Jowett, and William Montgomery (Oxford: Oxford University Press, 1994; repr. 1995), *The Tragedy of Antony and Cleopatra*, IV. xv. 2–8; v. ii. 204–9.

of this passage. (He later commented of Milton's own fondness for puns, or 'play on words, in which he delights too often', that they 'scarcely deserve the attention of a critick', 'Life of Milton', *Lives*, i. 188.) Book IX of *Paradise Lost* (1667), in which Satan brings about the doom of mankind, is pervaded by the devil's 'midnight vapour' and 'mazy', serpentine 'folds', as well as by the 'exhilarating vapour' of 'that fallacious fruit'—the apple for which we all lost the world. The 'fatal Cleopatra' is also Eve.[50]

3. PERPETUATING EPHEMERA

Many of Johnson's publications might be classified as introductory: the prefaces to Shakespeare and to the *Dictionary*; the prologues, prefaces, and dedications he contributed to other peoples' works; and his *Prefaces Biographical and Critical, to the Works of the English Poets*. The generic designation of *Prefaces* rather than of *Lives* affects the status and function of the last work, now published independently of the authors' poems for which it was designed to lay the groundwork. Individually, each 'Life' or 'Preface' might be said to combine elements of 'an introduction to any literary work, stating what it is to contain, and how it should be executed in the most perfect manner' with elements of 'a conclusion, shewing from various causes why the execution has not been equal to what the authour promised to himself and to the publick'. Johnson broaches Gay's *Fables* (1726–38), for instance, with a survey of the genre, of the author's departure from its requirements, and of his local felicities of style ('Life of Gay', *Lives*, ii. 283). In a spurt of diminution, he first referred to his biographical and critical undertaking as 'little Lives, and little Prefaces, to a little edition of the English Poets' (*Letters*, iii. 20), although he initially conceived of 'this minute kind of History' in the even more contracted shape of 'Advertisement[s] ... containing a few dates and a general character', as he noted in his own 'Advertisement' to the third edition of the *Prefaces*: 'The Booksellers having determined to publish a Body of English Poetry I was persuaded to promise them a Preface to the Works of each Author; an undertaking, as it was then presented to my mind, not very extensive or difficult' (*Lives*, i, pp. xxv–xxvi).

Whether it was the booksellers or Johnson himself who thus 'presented' the edition 'to my mind', he might not have seen this enterprise as particularly 'extensive or difficult' because it appeared to be a mere

---

[50] John Milton, *Paradise Lost*, ed. Alastair Fowler (London: Longman, 1968; repr. 1990), IX. 159, 161, 1046–7.

variation on his lifelong practice of contributing anonymous copy or introductions to other people's work. The generalizing tendency in his own writing may partly have come about as a result of having spent much of his career composing or editing in someone else's name; in this respect, he was schooled in the art of retreating from self-identification. (It was not until he reached his late thirties, with the publication of his *Plan of a Dictionary of the English Language* (1747) that he put the name 'Samuel Johnson' to his own work.) He writes in the 'Preface to Shakespeare' that 'These observations are to be considered not as unexceptionably constant, but as containing general and predominant truth' (*Yale*, vii. 70), and his lifelong defence of trifles is overwhelmingly generic—as if to say 'trifles are worth heeding' rather than 'this particular trifle is important'. Later in the 'Preface to Shakespeare', the editor's endeavour is itself subjected to a general view, according to which its local truths may come to seem irrelevant rather than admirable (*Yale*, vii. 107–8).

A disjunction between the dignity of Johnson's generalizing style and the indignity of its specific object comes across with particular force in his prefaces to journalistic enterprises, in which a concern for permanence, weight, and for the comprehension of posterity seems at odds with the perishable class of dailies (and the transient interests to which they cater) that he is recommending. In such prefaces, he is writing for remuneration rather than voluntarily. He tends to open with a survey of the realm of print, of its proliferation and its casualties. More solicitous than satirical in tone, and defending the province of harmless amusement, these writings convey a sense of sympathetic fellowship with—as well as a vantage point on—the journalist's plight. Johnson's address 'TO THE PUBLIC', prefacing the *Literary Magazine* (1756), highlights the difference between introducing newspapers and magazines (generic compendia of trifles) and composing prefaces to literary works, whose mere physical form as books lays greater claim to survival than the hack's ephemeral productions. The necessity for the journalist to 'dwell upon . . . trifles' bespeaks more investment of time in the enterprise than readers are expected to bestow on it:

In a paper designed for general perusal, it will be necessary to dwell most upon things of general Entertainment. The elegant trifles of literature, the wild strains of fancy, the pleasing amusements of harmless wit, shall therefore be considered as necessary to our Collection. Nor shall we omit researches into antiquity, explanations of coins or inscriptions, disquisitions on converted history, conjectures on doubtful geography, or any other [of] those petty works upon which learned ingenuity is sometimes employed.

To these accounts of temporary transactions and fugitive performances, we shall add some dissertations on things more permanent and stable. (*Prefaces*, 130)

There is no direct appeal to, or characterization of the audience in this piece; the author's mind is fixed on the distinction and possible reconciliation between transient fads and permanent things. Amongst those activities he classes as 'temporary' are 'researches into antiquity' and 'disquisitions on converted history', which, despite their illumination of the past, are not expected to survive. Johnson's endeavour to prolong our attention to, and to heighten the status of, 'elegant trifles' is gravely comic. He promises to collect and to pin down evanescent and exiguous materials. Yet 'wild *strains* of fancy' seem to buck against the propriety and stability of a journalistic catalogue; will an 'account' of 'temporary transactions' seek to ensure that their interest is 'more permanent and stable'? Four years before this preface was written, Johnson had called a halt to his own twice-weekly paper, *The Rambler*, a work signally devoid of fashion, news, or up-to-the-minute controversies, which failed to become popular until it was re-issued in book form (*Life*, i. 208). He later complained that Steele's periodical essays were 'too thin . . . being mere Observations on Life and Manners without a sufficiency of solid Learning acquired from Books, they have the flavour, like the light French Wines you hear so often commended; but having no Body, they cannot keep' (*Thraliana*, i. 172).

Johnson called his own *Rambler* 'pure wine', and Boswell followed suit: 'Addison's style, like a light wine, pleases every body from the first. Johnson's, like a liquor of more body, seems too strong at first, but, by degrees, is highly relished' (*Life*, i. 210 n. 1; i. 224). It might seem to be the essence of all journalism that it does not 'keep'. Yet if Johnson's writing habitually eschews finality, this also entails the pursuit of longevity—of ideas, languages, institutions, and writing—and he always seems eager to 'confer duration' on journalism by casting it as 'diurnal historiograph[y]' or 'diminutive history' (*Idler* 4, *Yale*, ii. 15; *Rambler* 145, *Yale*, v. 11; *Idler* 1, *Yale*, ii. 5). In the last number of *The Rambler*, he was pleased to acknowledge that he had not contributed to the survival of unworthy, inherently transient particulars, instead perpetuating the applicability of matters of eternal, general significance (matters which include the public's ceaseless hunger for such particulars): 'I have seen the meteors of fashion rise and fall, without any attempt to add a moment to their duration. I have never complied with temporary curiosity, nor enabled my readers to discuss the topick of the day' (*Yale*, v. 316).

The fact that the *Tatler* and *Spectator* essays ceased to be applicable to posterity, Johnson implied in the 'Life of Addison', was due to 'Their usefulness to the age in which they were written'. Thanks to the overwhelming success of their admonitions on dress, conversation, and social conduct, manners changed, and their familiar style and precisely targeted attempts at reform came to seem clumsy and outdated: 'Addison is now despised' (*Lives*, ii. 93, 146). He thought their style could become too conversational (and therefore not a durable medium), their subjects too low—while also seeming in his defences of trifles, his intermittent self-rebukes in *The Rambler*, and occasionally in his sermons to have wished that all writers (himself included) would imitate their example ('Life of Addison', *Lives*, ii. 147–9). Since Mr Rambler deals in 'the general misery of man in this state of being' (*Life*, i. 213), however, there is no permanent cure for the maladies he describes—and the writing will never cease to apply to the human condition (although, by the same token, it also risks being useless). Johnson's shadowy journalistic persona lacks the garrulous specificity of Bickerstaff's self-characterization, the level of detail invested in Mr Spectator's description of his withdrawal from the world (see, for instance, *Spectator* 1, i. 1–6), and the fictional circle of friends and acquaintants that surrounds both speakers.

If Addison hoped, after Socrates, to 'have brought Philosophy out of Closets and Libraries, Schools and Colleges, to dwell in Clubs and Assemblies, at Tea-Tables, and in Coffee-Houses' (*Spectator* 10, i. 44), Boswell thought that the Rambler 'delighted to express familiar thoughts in philosophical language; being in this the reverse of Socrates, who, it was said, reduced philosophy to the simplicity of common life' (*Life*, i. 217–18). Putting it this way makes it sound as if Johnson set out confidently to reverse Addison and Steele's emphases, to abstract himself from the realities of 'common life', although Boswell quickly counters that impression by quoting Johnson's remark in his concluding paper: 'I have familiarized the terms of philosophy by applying them to popular ideas' (*Rambler* 208, *Yale*, v. 319; *Life*, i. 218). But he often felt deficient as a journalist for having paid scant heed to the social ceremonies so often discussed by his predecessors: 'as much of life must be passed in affairs considerable only by their frequent occurrence, and much of the pleasure which our condition allows, must be produced by giving elegance to trifles, it is necessary to learn how to become little without becoming mean, to maintain the necessary intercourse of civility, and fill up the vacuities of actions by agreeable appearances' (*Rambler* 152, *Yale*, v. 44;

see also Richardson's *Rambler* 97, *Yale*, iv. 153–9, on the usefulness of *The Spectator*).

As was noted in Chapter 1, Johnson reprimanded himself in *Rambler* 98, via a mock-correspondent, Eutropius, for his failure to descend (unlike Addison and Steele) to the 'minuter duties of social beings', to 'little civilities and ceremonious delicacies' (*Yale*, iv. 160–1), although this did not presage any change in his journal's style or subject matter. No. 98 is, typically, a general defence of the importance of such duties, rather than a focus on their practical or contemporary applicability. And Johnson's journalistic mastery of common life is of a different order from Addison and Steele's. *The Rambler*'s domestic portraits of young women, in particular, combine a vivid, comic alertness to the charms of fashion with an authorial desire for permanence. Thus an impatient Rhodoclia, inveterately attached to news but imprisoned in rustic 'ignorance and obscurity', begs the Rambler for up-to-date information about 'the entertainments of the town': 'I can read, I can talk, I can think of nothing else' (*Rambler* 62, *Yale*, iii. 333–4). Recalling the overweening precision of Steele and Swift's mock-humble petitioners, she boasts that she is 'so well versed in the history of the gay world, that I can relate, with great punctuality, the lives of all the last race of wits and beauties; can enumerate, with exact chronology, the whole succession of celebrated singers, musicians, tragedians, comedians, and harlequins; can tell to the last twenty years all the changes of fashions' (*Yale*, iii. 332).

Rhodoclia is a peculiarly youthful relic of those audiences whose tastes had been formed by *The Tatler*. Her mother, the elderly communicator of titbits who condemns the present age's 'fopperies and trifles' as inferior to those of her youth, might have been one of Steele's original readers. What Rhodoclia's objection perpetuates is our sense of the eternal, transgenerational attractions of ephemeral things, rather than the character or value of any particular trifle currently in vogue: her interest in fashion is out of date, as she knows only its recent 'history' and is 'a complete antiquary with respect to head-dresses' (*Yale*, iii. 332–3).

Johnson wrote in his 'Life of Butler' that: 'Such manners as depend upon standing relations and general passions are co-extended with the race of man; but those modifications of life and peculiarities of practice which are the progeny of error and perverseness, or at best of some accidental influence or transient persuasion, must perish with their parents' (*Lives*, i. 214). The contest between Rhodoclia and her mother—a one-time participant in the sociable world who, in old age, prohibits her daughter's access to the town—perhaps reveals a sense of

Mr Rambler himself as Isaac Bickerstaff's 'progeny' (Johnson was born in 1709, the year of *The Tatler*'s inception), and of rivalry between the two journalists: but the son appears to be playing the role of severe and old-fashioned parent. As in *Rambler* 98, Johnson leaves his correspondent's request for comment on the intimate workings of present-day social life unanswered. No. 84 again humorously stages the difference between *The Tatler* and *The Rambler*, between youth and seniority, transience and permanence, the attractions of social life and the abiding wisdom of respect. The 16-year-old Myrtylla, another rustic teenager bankrupted by an urban sophisticate, pants for 'assemblies and routs' and sneers at 'the antiquated part of the world' with its talk of 'unreserved obedience' to 'parents' (*Yale*, iv. 80–1). In a further essay, Properantia claims, tongue in cheek, to experience 'great pleasure in listening to the conversation of learned men, especially when they discourse of things which I do not understand', before urging Mr Rambler to help her 'run from ball to ball, and from drum to drum' (no. 107, *Yale*, iv. 205, 207). Like Rhodoclia's complaint, Myrtylla and Properantia's petulant wish to break free of tiresome, moralizing authority is a lighter version of Eutropius' concern that Johnson's weighty journal seemed to be omitting the properly slight contents of a twice-weekly, short production. Through the use of such fictional correspondents, in which he rehearses conversations with himself, Johnson seems conscious that their objections may be justified, while he also suggests that the appetite for gossip and fashion sits awkwardly with the solemnity of his usual subjects:

Among the various censures, which the unavoidable comparison of my perfor-mances with those of my predecessors has produced, there is none more general than that of uniformity. Many of my readers remark the want of those changes of colours, which formerly fed the attention with unexhausted novelty, and of that intermixture of subjects, or alternation of manner, by which other writers relieved weariness, and awakened expectation.

I have, indeed, hitherto avoided the practice of uniting gay and solemn subjects in the same paper, because it seems absurd for an author to counteract himself, to press at once with equal force upon both parts of the intellectual balance, or give medicines, which, like the double poison of Dryden, destroy the force of one another. (*Rambler* 107, *Yale*, iv. 204–5)

By casting such censures as 'general', Johnson points out that they are nothing new. There is 'such an uniformity in the state of man' (*Rambler* 60, *Yale*, iii. 320) that, in setting out to disagree with him, those readers who thirst for novelty—and not for generality—have unwittingly concurred with Mr Rambler by proving their common, eternal nature (and hence, in turn, the irrelevance of news). But Johnson seems frequently to be 'counteracting' himself in his writing, to be giving equal weight and consideration to both sides of a question, such as whether or not to introduce novelty into his journal, or how to combine temporary transactions with relevance to posterity. In 'An Account of this Undertaking'—prefixing the *Harleian Miscellany*—he weighed up the possibility of transforming evanescence into longevity, the little into the great:

It has been for a long Time, a very just Complaint, among the Learned, that a Multitude of valuable Productions, published in small Pamphlets, or in single Sheets, are in a short Time, too often by Accidents, or Negligence, destroyed, and intirely lost; and that those Authors, whose Reverence for the Public has hindered them from swelling their Works with Repetitions, or encumbering them with Superfluities, and who, therefore, deserve the Praise and Gratitude of Posterity, are forgotten, for the very Reason for which they might expect to be remembered. It has been long lamented, that the Duration of the Monuments of Genius and Study, as well as of Wealth and Power, depends in no small Measure on their Bulk; and that Volumes, considerable only for their Size, are handed down from one Age to another, when compendious Treatises, of far greater Importance, are suffered to perish, as the compactest Bodies sink into the Water, while those, of which the Extension bears a greater Proportion to the Weight, float upon the Surface.

This Observation hath been so often confirmed by Experience, that, in the Neighbouring Nation, the common Appellation of small Performances is derived from this unfortunate Circumstance; a *flying Sheet*, or a *fugitive Piece*, are the Terms by which they are distinguished, and distinguished with too great Propriety, as they are subject, after having amused Mankind for a While, to take their Flight, and disappear for ever.

What are the Losses which the learned have already sustained, by having Neglected to fix those Fugitives in some certain Residence, it is not easy to say; but there is no Doubt that many valuable Observations have been repeated, because they were not preserved; and that, therefore, the Progress of Knowledge has been retarded ... The obvious Method of preventing these Losses, of preserving to every Man the Reputation he has merited by long Assiduity, is to unite these scattered Pieces into Volumes, that those, which are too small to preserve themselves, may be secured by their Combination with others; to consolidate these Atoms of Learning into Systems, to collect these disunited Rays, that their Light and their Fire may become perceptible.

Of encouraging this useful Design, the Studious and Inquisitive have now an Opportunity, which, perhaps, was never offered them before, and which, if it should now be lost, there is not any Probability that they will ever recover. They may now conceive themselves in Possession of the Lake into which all those Rivulets of Science have for many Years been flowing; but which, unless its Waters are turned into proper Channels, will soon burst its Banks, or be dispersed in imperceptible Exhalations. (*Prefaces*, 50–1)

As a defence of minor authors, this initially appears to be whimsical and implausibly portentous. The purported nobility of their motives ('Reverence for the Public has hindered them from swelling their Works') verges on ridicule—and few people can expect to be remembered on the sole ground of not having written much. The punning references (including the litotes of 'no small Measure . . . ') to size and duration, weight and lightness, as well as to the mixed elements of air and water, recall *Peri Bathous*. These productions, like Pope's targets, are equally capable of sinking and of flying.[51] Yet such accents of satire combine with expressions of tender concern for rescuing, or at least for prolonging the survival of sinking 'Bodies' of exiguous writing, and the concern that 'the Progress of Knowledge has been retarded' is a serious one here, as in other prefaces. Like the 'Preface to the Dictionary', Johnson's 'Account' seems to be weighing up quantity against quality, pondering whether 'Volumes' and 'Size' are tantamount to significance: whether 'compendious', yet lighter and more concise productions are not metaphorically 'greater' than their bulky siblings.

In spite of the dignified plenitude of his own style, and the scope of his subsequent literary endeavours, Johnson was always drawn to the literary arts of condensing, compressing, diminishing, contracting, and reducing.[52] Moving from dispersal to collection and back again to dispersal, the fusion of atomic particulars into consolidated systems anticipates the lexicographical and editorial enterprises of his later life, while the 'imperceptible Exhalations' into which these pieces will evaporate, without the aid of a benefactor, resemble the editor's 'evanescent atoms', and the 'invisible circumstances' which are the life-blood of biography (*Rambler* 60, *Yale*, iii. 321). The 'Combination' of 'those, which are too small to preserve themselves' into stronger unions has prominently social as well as scientific and literary implications. Johnson employs the word

---

[51] See also 'A dissertation on the art of flying' in *Rasselas*: 'to swim is to fly in a grosser fluid, and to fly is to swim in a subtler' (*Yale*, xvi. 22, 24–5).

[52] Johnson foresaw text-messaging: 'I love anecdotes. I fancy mankind may come in time to write all aphoristically, except in narrative; grow weary of preparation and connexion and illustration and all those arts by which a big book is made' (*Tour*, 22). Here, perhaps, is another reason for Austen's love of Johnson: 'Ladies who read those enormous great stupid thick Quarto Volumes . . . must be acquainted with everything in the World.—I detest a Quarto.—Capt. Pasley's Book is too good for their Society. They will not understand a Man who condenses his Thoughts into an Octavo.' To Cassandra Austen (9 Feb. 1813), *Letters*, 206.

'small', rather than the potentially more affectionate 'little', to refer to these pieces throughout his introduction, in spite of the fact that his language becomes overtly protective ('Neglected', 'too small to preserve themselves'), as well as gravely judicial and comically overstated in its prosecutions ('to fix these Fugitives in some certain Residence' implies 'arrest the pamphlets!'). The owlish coexistence of paternal fondness with mock-heroic distance, of pathos with bathos, characterizes much of Johnson's short work (whose own survival was in doubt) in this period.

In his 'Preliminary Discourse to the London Chronicle', Johnson found himself in the process of creating, as well as of defending, fugitive tracts and trifling repositories, uniting theory with practice:

It has been always lamented, that of the little Time allotted to Man, much must be spent upon Superfluities. Every Prospect has its Obstructions, which we must break to enlarge our View: Every Step of our Progress finds Impediments, which, however eager to go forward, we must stop to remove. Even those who profess to teach the Way to Happiness have multiplied our Incumbrances, and the Author of almost every Book retards his Instructions by a Preface.

The Writers of the *Chronicle* hope to be easily forgiven, though they should not be free from an Infection that has seized the whole Fraternity; and, instead of falling immediately to their Subjects, should detain the Reader for a Time with an Account of the Importance of their Design, the Extent of their Plan, and the Accuracy of the Method which they intend to prosecute. Such Premonitions, though not always necessary when the Reader has the Book complete in his Hand, and may find by his own Eyes whatever can be found in it, yet may be more easily allowed to Works published gradually in successive Parts; of which the Scheme can only be so far known as the Author shall think fit to discover it . . . We shall repress that Elation of Malignity, which wantons in the Cruelties of Criticism, and not only murders Reputation, but murders it by Torture. Whenever we feel ourselves ignorant, we shall, at least, be modest. Our Intention is not to preoccupy Judgment by Praise or Censure, but to gratify Curiosity by early Intelligence, and to tell rather what our Authors have attempted, than what they have performed . . . Many Facts are known and forgotten; many Observations are made and suppressed; and Entertainment and Instruction are frequently lost, for Want of a Repository in which they may be conveniently preserved.

No Man can modestly promise what he cannot ascertain. We hope for the Praise of Knowledge and Discernment, but we claim only that of Diligence and Candour. (*Prose and Poetry*, 327, 329)

In a newspaper or magazine, as Johnson is aware, the preface-writer stands on the same threshold with regard to the text as the reader; there is no certain conclusion to his enterprise. He faces a profusion of trifles, and a sense of the infinity of news. When he writes of works published in successive parts that 'the Scheme can only be so far known as the Author shall think fit to discover it', the word 'discover' is poised between 'To shew; to disclose' and 'To find out'; between the author's superior knowledge and a lack of certainty that parallels the reader's (senses 1 and 3 of 'To DISCOVER' in Johnson's *Dictionary*). Unlike the Spectator, a notoriously lax promiser, Johnson is very careful about how he words his journalistic agreements with the public (see, for instance, *Idler* 1, in which readers 'will hope to be gratified' by what follows; 'I make no contract, nor incur any obligation'; the author 'excludes no style, he prohibits no subject', *Yale*, ii. 5). Delaying the word 'Preface' until the end of his first paragraph, Johnson casts his own writing as a superfluous delay. It is an obstacle to the continuation of the paper, as well as a clearing of the path. As the first issue of a journal, the 'Preliminary Discourse' is formally incorporated (unlike the preface to a book) into the enterprise it is prefacing, rather than existing apart from or subordinate to it. The word 'Repository' shows that Johnson is thinking of a 'magazine' in its etymological sense, as a storehouse (in this case, of minutiae and exiguous particulars).[53] The 'Preliminary Discourse' begins by casting itself as a trifling obstacle and ends by defending the journal as the proper home for such trifles—it thus displays the knowledge that it is contained by the enterprise on which it also has a vantage point. A marked distaste for 'Elation of Malignity' and for 'the Cruelties of Criticism', alongside the promise 'to tell rather what our Authors have attempted, than what they have performed', sounds as if it heralds further prefaces along the lines of this one, or as if the whole task of a newspaper—representing the vulnerable sub-literary fraternity of journalists—is to serve as a sympathetic vehicle for meritorious *intentions*, rather than as a satiric prose *Dunciad*, rehearsing the lamentable failure of their executions.[54]

4. PATRONAGE

It seems appropriate that the last work Johnson prepared for the press was a dedication to George III of Charles Burney's *Account of the Musical*

---

[53] 'MAGAZINE': '1. A storehouse, commonly an arsenal or armoury, or repository of provisions'; '2. Of late this word has signified a miscellaneous pamphlet, from a periodical miscellany named the *Gentleman's Magazine*, by *Edward Cave*' (*Dictionary*).

[54] See also *Rambler* 145: 'the common interest of learning requires that her sons should cease from intestine hostilities, and instead of sacrificing each other to malice and contempt, endeavour to avert persecution from the meanest of their fraternity' (*Yale*, v. 12).

Performances in Westminster-Abbey ... In Commemoration of Handel
(1784), in which he counselled the king—much as he had advised himself
in *The Rambler*—to attend to common amusements:

Greatness of mind is never more willingly acknowledged, nor more sincerely
reverenced, than when it descends into the regions of general life, and by
countenancing common pursuits, or partaking common amusements, shews
that it borrows nothing from distance or formality.

By the notice which Your Majesty has been pleased to bestow upon the
celebration of HANDEL's memory, You have condescended to add Your voice to
public praise, and give Your sanction to musical emulation.

The delight which Music affords seems to be one of the first attainments of
rational nature: wherever there is humanity, there is modulated sound. The mind
set free from the resistless tyranny of painful want, employs its first leisure upon
some savage melody. Thus in those lands of unprovided wretchedness, which
Your Majesty's encouragement of naval investigation has brought lately to the
knowledge of the polished world, though all things else were wanted, every nation
had its Music; an art of which the rudiments accompany the commencements,
and the refinements adorn the completion of civility, in which the inhabitants of
the earth seek their first refuge from evil, and, perhaps, may find at last the most
elegant of their pleasures.

But that this pleasure may be truly elegant, science and nature must assist
each other; a quick sensibility of Melody and Harmony, is not always originally
bestowed, and those who are born with this susceptibility of modulated sounds,
are often ignorant of its principles, and must therefore be in a great degree
delighted by chance; but when Your Majesty is pleased to be present at Musical
performances, the artists may congratulate themselves upon the attention of a
judge in whom all requisites concur, who hears them not merely with instinctive
emotion, but with rational approbation, and whose praise of HANDEL is not the
effusion of credulity, but the emanation of Science. (*Prefaces*, 32–3)

It is unclear whether the first paragraph constitutes description or
exhortation, or the two combined (George III has already descended
to notice Handel, but this invites him to extend his participation of
common praise and enjoyment). The voluntary acknowledgement of
regal greatness turns out to depend on the king's abrogation of superiority. Greatness is a quality not fully recognized until it stoops to
intellectual and social inferiority or littleness. Yet Johnson's opening
sentence is so abstract in expression at the same time as practical in its
exhortation that his own 'modulated sound' is simultaneously unconvinced and earnest—it maintains, in spatial and temporal terms, a
studious 'distance' from the realities of 'common amusements' at the
same time as enjoining proximity to them. (This resembles the injunction

to attend to the importance of colloquial language in the preface to *Easy Phraseology*, and Johnson's predominant refusal to do just that in his own linguistic register). Its 'formality' is thus either faintly comic, or half-incredulous that the informal action it recommends will ever be carried out.

Johnson continually emphasizes the heightening effects of mental operations and 'rational nature', as opposed to instinctive, emotional reactions—the latter must be improved, regulated, and educated, as nations proceed from barbarity to politeness. Two progressions run in parallel: that of an individual mind and that of a mighty collective. The inward and upward development in the first sentence from 'willingly' to 'sincerely' and from 'acknowledged' to 'reverenced' reflects a larger overall advance—from rude ignorance to civilization—that the king himself is capable of furthering across the globe. Prepositions shore up the move from 'recommended' to 'dignified', and from 'attention' to 'patronage'—both involve vertical relationships, looking down from a position of superiority and up from a position of inferiority (the act of condescension invoked in the second paragraph is simultaneously a descent on the king's part, and an elevation on the part of the subject). The second paragraph—indeed, the whole piece—is full of discreet varieties of display ('acknowledged', 'countenancing', 'shews', 'notice', 'brought lately to the knowledge', 'sensibility', 'attention'). It wants to draw attention to the potential courtliness rather than to the degradation of paying heed to common subjects, and to be seen to have done so.

Beneath the elegant suavity of Johnson's style, however, something more disquieting is at work; certain forces in the writing act against incipient triumphalism. The ascent from 'resistless tyranny' and 'painful want' to polished ease feels disconcertingly hasty. '*Some* savage melody' sounds urbane, detached, and throwaway, but is immediately checked by the harsh abstraction of 'unprovided wretchedness'. This is so stark in its failure to be specific that it paradoxically calls for provision—at least of the reader's attention, and by extension of the monarch's largesse—to the incarnated version of what it describes. Combining decorous, hands-off generality with an urgent awareness of reality, it is the proper form in which to address your ruler. Such alternation between luxury and misery is comparable to the way in which *A Journey to the Western Islands of Scotland* switches from naked 'rudeness' to polished 'elegance' and back again (see, for instance, *Yale*, ix. 40–50, 59–73), or in which the 'Preface to the Dictionary' shifts between images of verbal profusion (as befits a lexicographer, surveying the fertility of his domain) and a desert of incapacity, solitude, and grief (as befits a lonely drudge, whose execution has not matched up to the breadth of his original conception).[55]

The conclusion of the third paragraph almost completes the sense with the 'completion of civility', so that the sentence has an atmosphere of victory—displayed by the pronounced balance as well as by the crescendo. Yet there is a mismatch at the end of this sentence: the epoch-leaping progression from 'first refuge from evil' to 'most elegant of their pleasures' leaves barbarity nudging up against refinement as a form of coexistence rather than something that has been left behind. Empson's seventh type of ambiguity describes the feeling which arises from this apposition of contrarieties—the sense of hurtling up and down a scale, or of extreme opposites entailing a interdependence: 'In so far, in short, as you know that two things are opposites, you know a relation which connects them'; 'two opposed judgments are being held together and allowed to reconcile themselves, to stake out different territories, to find their own level, in the mind.'[56] The 'relation which connects' a ruler with his subjects is expressed through the use of prepositions, and in the vertical link between a condescending patron and a populace struggling to ascend. If Johnson ever quite reaches a state of reconciliation, the king is its focus. As one paradoxically 'superior to the rest of the same kind' (sense 2 of 'MONARCH' in the *Dictionary*), George III is called upon to embody two extremes: he is a safeguard for the system of hierarchical subordination, but he might also practise an exemplary descent towards his fellow human beings. The figure 'in whom all requisites concur', he acts as a concentrated embodiment of opposites whose reward for the inspiration of music is the exhalation of approval ('not the effusion of credulity, but the emanation of Science').

Had Johnson published this dedication in his own name, the concluding reference to 'patronage' (*Prefaces*, 33) would have drawn his

---

[55] 'I found our speech copious without order, and energetick without rules: wherever I turned my view, there was perplexity to be disentangled, and confusion to be regulated; choice was to be made out of boundless variety'; 'the exuberance of signification'; '[I] was forced to ... reduce my transcripts very often to clusters of words, in which scarcely any meaning is retained; thus to the weariness of copying, I was condemned to add the vexation of expunging. Some passages I have yet spared, which may relieve the labour of verbal searches, and intersperse with verdure and flowers the dusty desarts of barren philology'; 'I then contracted my design'; 'this gloom of solitude' (Johnson, *Prose and Poetry*, 301, 312, 313, 317, 323).

[56] Empson, *Seven Types of Ambiguity*, 196, 218.

contemporaries' attention. He had himself, notoriously, accepted this king's pension, in spite of his contemptuous definition of a 'PATRON' in the *Dictionary* as (in part) 'Commonly a wretch who supports with insolence, and is paid with flattery' (sense 1), his bitter rebuke to Chester-field ('Is not a Patron, My Lord, one who looks with unconcern on a Man struggling for Life in the water and when he has reached ground encumbers him with help', *Letters*, i. 96), and his inclusion of the word 'Patron' among the revised list of ills assailing scholarly life in *The Vanity of Human Wishes* (l. 160).[57] Over the past thirty years, however, critics have noted that traditional interpretations of the two-fingered salute to Chesterfield—as heralding the demise of aristocratic sponsorship and of authorial dependence—represent a fundamental misprision of the nature of Johnson's complaint. He was not thereby declining the offer of a would-be patron, but reprimanding Chesterfield for having failed to make good his promise of support, to play by the rules of the game.[58] Thomas Gordon baldly outlined those rules in terms more critical of the author than of his patron; the former tries to combat his hunger by force-feeding the latter with insincere encomia. The restraint and courtliness of a dedication are here exploded in a burst of straight talking, characterized by taking rather than by begging leave to proceed:

YOUR Lordship and I are not at all acquainted, I therefore take Leave to be very familiar with you, and to desire you to be my Patron, because you do not know me nor I you: Nor can this Manner of Address seem strange to your Lordship, whilst it is warranted by such numerous Precedents . . . no Lord of low Fortune must expect an humble Admirer amongst us Wits and Writers, unless he bargain with us at a set Price, and give us so much a piece for every good Quality he has Occasion for . . . For my self, when I see a long Drift of Excellencies and Talents cramm'd down a Nobleman's Throat, who has no Relish of them, or Right to them, I am not at all surpriz'd, because I am sure it is not meant as an Encomium upon *his Honour*, but meerly as a Declaration of the Author's Wants, and a heavy Complaint of Nakedness and Hunger.[59]

This is notably lacking in any sympathy for 'the Author's Wants', unlike Johnson's habitually grave and sympathetic presentations of the writer's hunger, poverty, and shabbiness (as in the *Life of Savage*). Although

---

[57] 'Toil, Envy, Want, the Patron, and the Jail': 'Patron' originally read 'Garret', but was altered around 1755, shortly after Johnson had written his letter to Chesterfield (see *Poems*, 211n.).

[58] See Griffin, *Literary Patronage in England*, 220–45, and Lawrence Lipking, *Samuel Johnson: The Life of an Author* (Cambridge, Mass.: Harvard University Press, 1998), 11–16.

[59] [Thomas Gordon], *A Dedication to a Great Man, Concerning Dedications* (London: for James Roberts, 1718), 3–5.

he prided himself on the notion that 'No man ... who ever lived by literature, has lived more independently than I have done', and claimed to regard booksellers as the real 'patrons of literature' (*Life*, i. 443, 305), Johnson was himself a lifelong 'participant in the traditional patronage system'[60]—first, as a client of Lichfield benefactors such as Gilbert Walmesley,[61] later as a supporter of impoverished authors, including those for whom he wrote prefaces and dedications—and became less critical of it as he grew older.[62] The relation between aristocratic patron and dedicating client is ideally, for Johnson, one of mutual kindness and profit, not necessarily marked by impervious hauteur on the one hand and servile flattery on the other. In fact, the call to dedicate his or her work may enable a writer to attain decency, grace, elegance, or nobility.

Hazen and Griffin have noted the recurrence of the morally loaded word 'condescension' and its cognates in Johnson's dedications; Hazen calls it his 'favorite'.[63] Lipking sees condescension in the letter to Chesterfield as conveying the 'deeply competitive view of human relations' embedded in Johnson's rebuke. He reminds us that 'condescend', like 'patronize', 'did not yet imply the arrogance now associated with those words', but it nevertheless 'suggests a constant struggle' between superiors and inferiors, at the same time as enjoining their proximity.[64] As a form of 'voluntary submission to equality with inferiors' (part of the definition of 'CONDESCENSION' in the *Dictionary*), the patron's stooping is a positive counterpart to the negative associations of a writer's 'voluntary degradation' in the preface to Baretti's *Easy Phraseology*. (The *voluntary* conferral and reception of benefits, another recurrent element of Johnson's dedications, is central to the real possibility of a happy union held out by the patron–client relationship: it resurfaces in the desirability of the king's greatness being 'willingly acknowledged' in the dedication to Burney's *Account of the Musical Performances*).[65] The positive and negative ramifications of 'condescension' in the period (see Chapter 4) indicate, in broader terms, an unease about the merits of

[60] Griffin, *Literary Patronage in England*, 221.

[61] See Clifford, *Young Sam Johnson*, 87, 159–64; W. Jackson Bate, *Samuel Johnson* (London: Chatto & Windus, 1978), 45–58; Boswell, *Life*, i. 81, 102.

[62] See Gae Holladay and O. M. Brack, Jr., 'Johnson as Patron', in Paul Korshin and Robert R. Allen (eds.), *Greene Centennial Studies: Essays Presented to Donald Greene in the Centennial Year of the University of Southern California* (Charlottesville: University of Virginia Press, 1984), 172–99.

[63] Johnson, *Prefaces*, 61. For examples of its use, see pp. 3, 29, 32, 62, 66, 101, 154.

[64] Lipking, *Samuel Johnson*, 18.

[65] On the language of 'benefits' in Johnson's dedications, see Griffin, *Literary Patronage in England*, 273–4.

the patron's sinking to attend to the lowly author—and, in turn, of
the author's descent to his subject—at the same time as promising that
a superior observer's attention will elevate the writer and his book to
a position of worthiness, thus rescuing all three participants from the
imputation of degeneracy. As Griffin puts it: 'In the context of patronage,
"condescension" affirms a social order of hierarchy and subordination,
in which the patron stands higher than the author but, in ideal circumstances, descends to a kind of "equality." Such happy condescension,
furthermore, has the effect of *raising* the author and his book.'[66]
   Johnson thus praises the king for praising Handel, the subject of
Burney's work: the efforts of the monarch and those of the author are
seen as jointly descending to heighten a lowly subject (the writer being,
in this case, also a subject). The king, as head of church and state, can
inflect a domino-like series of judicious condescensions down the whole
line of social and intellectual subordination. Similarly, in Johnson's
dedication to the queen of another of Charles Burney's works, the *History
of Music* (1776), the reciprocal obligations and pleasures arising from
condescension (the monarch's to her author, and the author's to his
subject) will validate the object of study and the status of the writer, as
well as reinforcing—as newly manifested to her people—the superiority
of the patron: 'The condescension with which your Majesty has been
pleased to permit your name to stand before the following History, may
justly reconcile the author to his favourite study, and convince him, that
whatever may be said by the professors of severer wisdom, the hours
which he has bestowed upon Music have been neither dishonourably,
nor unprofitably spent' (*Prefaces*, 29). Like a formal eighteenth-century
dance, characterized by elaborate courtly gestures of mutual deference
and regard, parallel forms of charitable descent are at work here: the
queen, by bountifully deigning to attend to Burney in turn vindicates *his*
deigning to study music (seen as a low profession in the period). Her
elevation of the humble author has a trickle-down effect whereby several
trifles (book/author/study/topic), each construed as a lesser and smaller
object of attention than the last, are simultaneously dignified—as if the
queen has permitted them to rise from a kneeling position.
   Johnson's introduction to Baretti's *Guide through the Royal Academy*
(1781) is, like the preface he contributed to the same author's *Easy
Phraseology*, concerned to supply a 'deficience'. The audience, standing

---

[66] Ibid. 273.

on the brink of the work, is in a similar position to the visitor, physically
hesitating on the threshold of the Academy:

> To those, whom either vagrant curiosity, or desire of instruction, brings into the
> Apartments of the Royal Academy, not to know the design, the history, and the
> names of the various Models that stand before them, is a great abatement of
> pleasure, and hindrance of improvement. He who enters, not knowing what to
> expect, gazes a while about him, a stranger among strangers, and goes out not
> knowing what he has seen. The subsequent lists of the Casts in the Academy,
> with some kind of explanation to each, may therefore be useful to those that love
> the Arts and desire not to love them blindly. I am able to estimate better the
> deficiency of that kind of knowledge in others, by the difficulty I met in obtaining
> that information which I am now desirous to afford.[67]

The periodic structure and breathy punctuation of this opening sentence leave readers uncertain, until a relatively late stage, of where they
are and thus enact (like many of the prefaces) the route from ignorance
to knowledge. Johnson then reduces his group from 'those' to the more
vulnerable figure of an individual. As in other prefaces, he describes and
promises to remove a barrier (the 'hindrance of improvement'), and
reveals an abhorrence of vacuity. The 'vagrant curiosity' that he first
identifies as a trigger for visiting the Royal Academy recalls the situation
of the reader at the outset of *Rasselas*, uncertain whether that curiosity,
'one of the permanent and certain characteristicks of a vigorous intellect', will be satisfied or upbraided (*Rambler* 103, *Yale*, iv. 184). Direction
follows indirection, as the 'desire of instruction' appears to be a more
rational, targeted motive than the first ('curiosity' stands to 'instruction'
as 'pleasure' to 'improvement'), but both prompts are construed as the
possessors of their human agents, as if the targets of this writing have
no control over their feelings or actions ('*To* those, *whom* either vagrant
curiosity, or desire of instruction *brings into*').

Here, the inquisitive but uninformed and timorous observer begins to
sound as if he is morally lost or homeless, divorced from his own life,
incapable of governing his desires, or of recognizing his experiences: 'not
to know the design . . . not knowing what to expect . . . not knowing what
he has seen.' Specifying your 'design', the expectations with which you
set out on your work, the knowledge of what you have 'seen' in the course

---

[67] Hazen identifies and quotes the first two sentences as Johnson's (*Prefaces*, 11–12);
Arthur Sherbo cites the rest of the introductory paragraph as it appears here and suggests,
I think rightly, that it should be attributed to Johnson. 'Some Observations on Johnson's
Prefaces and Dedications', in John H. Middendorf (ed.), *English Writers of the Eighteenth
Century* (New York: Columbia University Press, 1971), 122–42 (p. 123).

of its execution, the bulk of mankind or the individual to whom you are speaking, and the 'history' of your genre and subject, are the backbones of a Johnsonian preface. They come very close here to approximating the human condition and the journey of life: 'how frequent soever may be the examples of existence without thought, it is certainly a state not much to be desired'; 'It is the part of every inhabitant of the earth to partake the pains and pleasures of his fellow beings; and, as in a road through a country desart and uniform, the traveller languishes for want of amusement; so the passage of life will be tedious and irksome to him who does not beguile it by diversified ideas' (*Idler* 24, *Yale*, ii. 77).

The title of *Guide through* (rather than *to*) *the Royal Academy* accordingly promises intimate companionship: a step-by-step, hand-in-hand accompaniment across new terrain that will no longer abandon readers and spectators to the vacuum of their want of knowledge, which the author sets out to combat on the basis of his own experience. There is something superabundantly bereft about the condition of a visitor moving alone amongst, and beholding a spectacle of, strangers—even if they are inanimate. The passage reaches beyond the immediate auspices of a preface (offering to fill a literary gap) to describe a condition of intellectual vagrancy and emptiness as one of utter isolation in the midst of a community. In promising to redress such a condition, Johnson seeks to re-introduce the solitary reader at home, and the curious rambler abroad, to the fold of humanity: 'In travelling even thus almost without light thro' naked solitude, when there is a guide whose conduct may be trusted, a mind not naturally too much disposed to fear, may preserve some degree of cheerfulness; but what must be the solicitude of him who should be wandering, among the craggs and hollows, benighted, ignorant, and alone?' (*Yale*, ix. 77).

3

Diminishing Returns: *A Journey to the Western Islands of Scotland*

Johnson crops up frequently in the course of John Barrell's argument that literary landscapes exhibit a more socially inclusive, and hence less intellectually cohesive or commanding prospect over the course of the eighteenth century. The purported 'loss' of a topographically and figuratively 'general view' duly accounts for the titles of *The Rambler* and *The Idler*: these are 'identities which, as they pretend to legitimize the claim to a comprehensive view, avow that, by these means, it cannot be attained'.[1] But Johnson never thought it practicable, desirable, or indeed permissible for a human being to attain an entirely general or comprehensive view: 'pride grasps at the whole' (Sermon 8, *Yale*, xiv. 91). This has more to do with his sense of mankind's native frailties than it has to do with Barrell's vision of the historically conditioned, progressively inclusive ways in which literature might look at the world. In *Idler* 37, one of the few occasions on which he allows himself to speculate what might be seen, '*If* the extent of the human view could comprehend the whole frame of the universe', Johnson immediately subordinates such a view to that of a higher one—governed, as he says, by what 'I believe'. For this humanly impossible, universal survey would reveal 'that Providence has given that in greatest plenty, which the condition of life makes of greatest use; and that nothing is penuriously imparted or placed far from the reach of man, of which a more liberal distribution, or more easy acquisition would increase *real* and *rational* felicity' (*Idler* 37, *Yale*, ii. 115; my emphasis). In the first two lines of *The Vanity of Human Wishes*, even the personified Observation's 'extensive View' abides by the geographical parameters 'from *China* to *Peru*'. In 1753, Johnson made a point about the disadvantages of intellectual progress during a period apparently 'so little given to specialisation':[2]

---

[1] Barrell, *English Literature in History*, 41–2.   [2] Rogers, *Grub Street*, 185.

At our first sally into the intellectual world, we all march together along one strait and open road; but as we proceed further, and wider prospects open to our view, every eye fixes upon a different scene; we divide into various paths, and, as we move forward, are still at a greater distance from each other. As a question becomes more complicated and involved, and extends to a greater number of relations, disagreement of opinion will always be multiplied, not because we are irrational, but because we are finite beings, furnished with different kinds of knowledge, exerting different degrees of attention, one discovering consequences which escape another, none taking in the whole concatenation of causes and effects, and most comprehending but a very small part; each comparing what he observes with a different criterion, and each referring it to a different purpose. (*Adventurer* 107, *Yale*, ii. 441)

He handles with care the shop-worn metaphor of life or knowledge as a journey (a care that has implications for the title of his *Journey to the Western Islands of Scotland*).[3] The passage's initial 'At' serves to make time and place happily coincide in momentary stasis as 'we all march *together*', while the two introductory phrases of the opening sentence ('At our first sally into the intellectual world', 'we all march together upon one strait and open road') are evenly matched, with fourteen syllables apiece. But the three phrases following the first semicolon are comparatively ill matched and incremental (at seven, ten, and thirteen syllables), displaying the claim that wider prospects entail division. The gains of increasingly lengthy phrases are weighed against the fact that those phrases are lopsided with respect to each other: 'our faculties are unequal', as Johnson goes on to point out (*Yale*, ii. 444). The synecdochic figure of 'every eye', suddenly contracting the scope of 'our view', heralds a statement that 'we divide'. And 'as we move forward', we 'are still at a greater distance from each other'. The latter phrase has a stop-start feel to it. 'Still' implies a pause in the journey, at the same time as it describes perpetual motion. It maintains distance between individuals as a constant attendant of progress, while 'greater' increases that distance—although the degree of increase is left unclear, anticipating the 'different degrees' mentioned in the next sentence.

This syntactic imitation or enactment of fracturing perspectives encourages readers to notice Johnson's 'concatenation' of phrases and of clauses with 'causes', as in the tripartite subdivision, via semicolons, of the first sentence. The paragraph builds bridges between topic and

---

[3] On the metaphor of the journey and its moral implications in Johnson's writing, see Thomas Curley, *Samuel Johnson and the Age of Travel* (Athens: University of Georgia Press, 1976), 113–46.

style, at the same time as arguing that a parting of ways is inevitable. Such an arena is one in which it has become obvious that 'Those who have attempted much, have seldom failed to perform more than those who never deviate from the common roads of action', and that 'A commentary must arise from the fortuitous discoveries of many men, in devious walks of literature' (*Adventurer* 99, *Yale*, ii. 435; Johnson to Thomas Warton on his edition of Shakespeare, *Letters*, i. 162). But it is also one in which the primary meanings of 'To DEVIATE' and 'DEVIOUS' in the *Dictionary* ('To wander from the right or common way'; 'Out of the common track') are overcast by the threat of abandonment or of isolation, and by a sense—bound up with images of moral deviance from *Paradise Lost*—of having taken the wrong turn ('To go astray; to err; to sin; to offend', sense 2 of 'To DEVIATE'; 'Erring; going astray from rectitude', sense 3 of 'DEVIOUS'). It is only 'When conviction is present, and temptation out of sight' that 'we do not easily conceive how any reasonable being can deviate from his true interest' (*Idler* 27, *Yale*, ii. 85).

Johnson described William Collins as possessing a mind in one respect akin to Shakespeare's, 'somewhat obstructed in its progress by deviation in quest of mistaken beauties': a phrase which, like the association of quibbles with Cleopatra, conjures up the poet straying from rectitude in order to chase errant women as well as misguided literary effects; Collins, like Johnson, was 'a literary adventurer' (*Lives*, iii. 338, 335).[4] Thomas Warton himself wrote in morally freighted terms of being '*betrayed* into minute researches', producing 'many trifling discoveries, and intricate discussions of insignificant circumstances'.[5] And Cowper created the same ambivalence in his Miltonic, doubly qualified noun, 'devious course uncertain'[6]—employed to capture that divergence from original intent which Johnson portrays as a labyrinthine process of direction and indirection, of losing and finding, in his 'Introduction' to the *Harleian Miscellany* and in the 'Preface to the Dictionary': 'the Mind once let loose to Enquiry, and suffered to operate without Restraint, necessarily deviates into peculiar Opinions, and wanders in new Tracks, where she is indeed sometimes lost in a Labyrinth, from which, tho' she cannot return, and scarce knows how to proceed; yet, sometimes, makes useful Discoveries, or finds out nearer Paths to Knowledge'; 'the

---

[4] The first quotation is from a section of the 'Life of Collins' that Johnson originally published in 1763, two years before the 'Preface to Shakespeare' (see *Lives*, iii. 337 n. 2).

[5] Thomas Warton, *The Life of Sir Thomas Pope* (London: T. Davies, 1772), 'Preface', p. [iii], my emphasis.

[6] Cowper, *The Task*, iii. 3.

mind, afraid of greatness, and disdainful of littleness, hastily withdraws herself from painful searches, and passes with scornful rapidity over tasks not adequate to her powers, sometimes too secure for caution, and again too anxious for vigorous effort; sometimes idle in a plain path, and sometimes distracted in labyrinths, and dissipated by different intentions' (*Prefaces*, 54–5; *Prose and Poetry*, 319).

In both extracts, the writing gradually peters out, having burst free of constraints only to gain the modest prize of an intermittent, comparative usefulness, or to dissipate mental energies in splintered intentions. Being 'suffered to operate' is a hamstrung form of agency. The bewildered mind, a female personification in both passages, itself displays allusive fragments of learning, reminiscent not only of Theseus physically 'distracted' in the devious labyrinth but also of Eurydice ('she cannot return') trapped in the underworld. A specific form of restraint is in operation here—one imposed by the limits of our own perception. No one is capable of 'taking in the whole concatenation of causes and effects'. Yet in our disagreement and limitation, in our fear of greatness and disdain for littleness, we have something in common. All human things are little and diverse. But, as that littleness and diversity is a universal human condition, the fact of our division, multiplicity, and particularity beneath an all-seeing God is also the basis of our unity—the consideration of which leads to Johnson's closing remarks in *Adventurer* 107 that:

we see a little, very little; and what is beyond we only can conjecture. If we enquire of those who have gone before us, we receive small satisfaction; some have travelled life without observation, and some willingly mislead us. The only thought, therefore, on which we can repose with comfort, is that which presents to us the care of Providence, whose eye takes in the whole of things, and under whose direction all involuntary errors will terminate in happiness. (*Yale*, ii. 445)

He shows a related concern for direction, for travelling through life, for those who have gone before him, and for termination in the opening section of *Rambler* 2, whose second paragraph concludes on the word 'truth':

That the mind of man is never satisfied with the objects immediately before it, but is always breaking away from the present moment, and losing itself in schemes of future felicity; and that we forget the proper use of the time now in our power, to provide for the enjoyment of that which, perhaps, may never be granted us, has been frequently remarked; and as this practice is a commodious subject of raillery to the gay, and of declamation to the serious, it has been ridiculed with all the pleasantry of wit, and exaggerated with all the amplifications of rhetoric.

... It affords such opportunities of triumphant exultation, to exemplify the uncertainty of the human state, to rouse mortals from their dream, and inform them of the silent celerity of time, that we may believe authors willing rather to transmit than examine so advantageous a principle, and more inclined to pursue a track so smooth and so flowery, than attentively to consider whether it leads to truth. (*Yale*, iii. 9–10)

Here, a protracted series of decorated nouns 'leads to' and finally proffers a naked, unadorned 'truth' which is the goal of the sentence: a syntactic microcosm both of life as a journey and of Johnson's dogged endeavour to arrive at a morally invigorating, not at a lethargically pretty form of writing. The same thing happens in the 'Preface to Shakespeare', which also repeats the desire of *Adventurer* 107 for 'repose' on secure ground: 'The irregular combinations of fanciful invention may delight a-while, by that novelty of which the common satiety of life sends us all in quest; but the pleasures of sudden wonder are soon exhausted, and the mind can only repose on the stability of truth' (*Yale*, vii. 61–2). The structure of the final sentence quoted from *Rambler* 2 indulges the ideas it seeks to check—but with which it is in wry authorial sympathy—dawdling *en route* ('so smooth and so flowery') at the same time as regarding its end. Piozzi recalled that Johnson, a rambler in life as in prose, 'loved indeed the very act of travelling'; to her, he described one letter written during the Highland tour as 'the story of me and my little ramble' (*Miscellanies*, i. 263; *Letters*, ii. 98). He may have complained about 'how few books' there were 'of which one ever can possibly arrive at the *last* page', but the three he immediately singled out as works that their readers 'wished longer' are all journeys: *Don Quixote* (1605), *Robinson Crusoe* (1719), and *The Pilgrim's Progress* (1678–84); 'After Homer's Iliad, Mr. Johnson confessed that the work of Cervantes was the greatest in the world' (Johnson and Piozzi in *Miscellanies*, i. 332–3).

In the first paragraph of *Rambler* 2, the passive voice and a foregrounding of subordinate over main clause perform several tasks. They create an authoritative statement by virtue of issuing from an impersonal source. They foster a sense of man's generic helplessness (more acted on than active) that belies the authority of such a statement. And they promote a feeling of suspense about the direction of Johnson's comments, prior to a bathetic denouement. The author's potential superiority to the scene he describes, and to the writers that have gone before him, is complicated by the periodic syntax. The two opening, dependent clauses make us wait until 'has been frequently remarked' for the completion of their sense. This delay encourages us to race ahead, to 'forget the proper use of the time now in our power' and to discover what is to come, only to meet with disappointment. We arrive at a destination which underlines the familiarity of the terrain through which we have been travelling—a feeling akin to Johnson's experience in Scotland, where his anticipation of surprise was itself to meet with a surprise: 'This image of magnificence raised our expectation'; 'We came thither too late to see what we expected, a people of peculiar appearance, and a system of antiquated life'; 'The use of travelling is to regulate imagination by reality, and instead of thinking how things may be, to see them as they are' (*Yale*, ix. 48, 57; *Letters*, ii. 78). By the time he approaches Iona, Johnson upbraids Boswell for talking 'As if we were going to a *terra incognita*', when all that they are about to see 'is so well known' (*Tour*, 308).

In *Rambler* 2, this disappointment at reverting to the contracted domain of a well-rehearsed truth is a salutary lesson in itself, a check to readers' impatience and desire for novelty. Yet the wonder afforded by the very triteness of Johnson's topic, by the sudden recognition of seemingly unknown territory, resembles the effect of *The Rape of the Lock*—in which 'we feel all the appetite of curiosity for that from which we have a thousand times turned fastidiously away' ('Life of Pope', *Lives*, iii. 234). An ethic of attentiveness is written into the syntax of Johnson's prose, which creates an appetite for what we might otherwise have dismissed, combined with a stylistic version of Adam Smith's law of 'diminishing returns': 'As capitals increase in any country, the profits which can be made by employing them necessarily diminish.'[7] The proliferation of knowledge and expenditure of intellectual labour beyond a certain point yield ever-decreasing opportunities for the profit of originality, as authors are compelled to follow well-worn paths, although that thirst for originality is itself misguided: 'men more frequently require to be reminded than informed' (*Rambler* 2, *Yale*, iii. 14; see also *Idler* 3, *Yale*, ii. 10). Hazlitt may have complained that *The Rambler* 'does not set us thinking for the first time' (*Complete Works*, vi. 100), but it does set us thinking about why second or second-hand thoughts could be useful.

We might expect a more pointed comment on human nature than the studied neutrality Johnson offers (something along the lines of 'this is a terrible state of affairs', or 'man is a weak creature'). But Mr Rambler is implicated in the charges he is levelling at humanity in general—and at authors in particular—so he does well to hold back here. In remarking on the fact of his assertion having been previously

---

[7] Adam Smith, *An Inquiry into the Nature and Causes of the Wealth of Nations* (1776), in Smith, *Works*, ii. 352.

and 'frequently remarked', however, he unobtrusively demonstrates that 'the mind of man' can do something other than lose itself in 'schemes of future felicity'. While we have been driving onwards, thereby proving the truth of the essay's initial claim, he has been considering the past. Dynamically propulsive and retrogressive, active and passive, projected backwards and forwards in time, space, and syntax, such passages in *The Rambler* resemble the intricate pursuit of a horizontal and of a vertical line of enquiry, 'an indecision and a structure' (in Empson's phrase), throughout Johnson's prefaces and dedications. Here, the horizontal axis emerges via the periodic, idling, and questing sentence whose destination is truth; while the vertical axis, upon which little things may be translated into great ones (and vice versa), appears in the diminuendo/crescendo formulation: 'ridiculed with all the pleasantry of wit, and exaggerated with all the amplifications of rhetoric.'

In his *Journey to the Western Islands of Scotland*, Johnson is repeatedly preoccupied by what it means to 'see a little, very little', as opposed to 'the whole of things' (or as close as human beings can get to the whole of things), and by whether or not they are incompatible goals. Freud, writing on jokes, argued that little things might be employed as one 'sub-species of indirect representation ... which performs the task of giving full expression to a whole characteristic by means of a tiny detail'.[8] That same act of bringing a peripheral, latent, or habitually overlooked element into the foreground, thereby illuminating a bigger picture, may be performed in the service of serious ends. A good example occurs early in Johnson's *Journey* (published in the same year as his preface to Baretti's *Easy Phraseology*):

Their windows do not move upon hinges, but are pushed up and drawn down in grooves, yet they are seldom accommodated with weights and pullies. He that would have his window open must hold it with his hand, unless what may be sometimes found among good contrivers, there be a nail which he may stick into a hole, to keep it from falling ... a stranger may be sometimes forgiven, if he allows himself to wish for fresher air.

These diminutive observations seem to take away something from the dignity of writing, and therefore are never communicated but with hesitation, and a little fear of abasement and contempt. But it must be remembered, that life consists not of a series of illustrious actions, or elegant enjoyments; the greater part of our time passes in compliance with necessities, in the performance of daily duties, in the removal of small inconveniencies, in the procurement of petty pleasures; and we are well or ill at ease, as the main stream of life glides on smoothly, or

[8] Freud, *Complete Psychological Works*, viii. 80.

is ruffled by small obstacles and frequent interruption. The true state of every nation is the state of common life. (*Yale*, ix. 22)

The conduct of this passage reverses the progression from ascent to descent and from the exterior to the interior of Scottish houses, as outlined in the previous paragraph of the *Journey* ('the entrance into them is very often by a flight of steps, which reaches up to the second story, the floor which is level with the ground being entered only by stairs descending within the house', *Yale*, ix. 21), so that it has the feeling of a breath of fresh air in more ways than one. Having stooped to report a first-hand experience of domestic shortcomings (albeit in the third person), he then sounds as if he is writing himself upwards and outwards to a daunting occasion, slowly gaining in certainty, conviction, and breadth. Moving away from the window itself to the category of 'diminutive observations' into which discussion of such matters falls, he hesitates before communicating his hesitation. '*Seem* to take away *something*' is a doubly bashful circumlocution that registers the difficulty of ascertaining quite how far literary propriety might be affronted by the introduction of private, homely concerns.

'A *little* fear' is equally ambiguous concerning the purchase of minutiae on greatness, of the trivial on the dignified. The phrase could 'denote not the degree but the species of our sentiments' (*Idler* 50, *Yale*, ii. 158). It might therefore be read as a petty rather than as a negligible fear (a quality, not a quantity), which would make that fear itself the object of contempt—to be countered with a stern injunction: '*But* it *must* be remembered . . .' In the 'Life of Browne', published almost twenty years earlier, Johnson's 'little fear' had also arisen in terms of a worry about affronting decorum: 'he has many "verba ardentia," forcible expressions, which he would never have found, but by venturing to the utmost verge of propriety; and flights which would never have been reached, but by one who had very little fear of the shame of falling' (*Early Biographical Writings*, 467). Here, a potentially disastrous willingness to sink beneath himself is also proof positive of Browne's literary elevation: as in *Rasselas*, there are no flights without the risk of crash landings (*Yale*, xvi. 22–8).

In the *Journey* excerpt, the passive voice facilitates an authoritative generalization—a decisive overcoming of doubt—whereas Boswell's first-person defence of his '*innumerable detached particulars*' in the 'Advertisement' to the first edition of the *Life* is a less assured vindication of minutiae (*Life*, i. 6). Johnson's 'diminutive observations' and their compatriots ('little', 'small', 'petty', and 'common') court and finally dismiss synonymity with senses 3 and 4 of 'DIMINUTION' in his *Dictionary*: 'Discredit; loss of dignity; degradation'; 'Deprivation of dignity; injury of reputation.' 'A little fear' might accordingly be read as a mark of timidity, or as an allusion to those 'false' but compelling 'measures of excellence and dignity' (*Rambler* 60, *Yale*, iii. 320) which associate the little with a feeling of 'abasement'—on the part of the author, who has stooped too low—and of 'contempt'—on the part of the reader, disgusted at the spectacle of puerility.

Hazlitt reveals a curious variation on this response when he writes of Johnson's style that 'He condescends to the familiar till we are ashamed of our interest in it: he expands the little till it looks big ... We can no more distinguish the most familiar objects in his descriptions of them, than we can a well-known face under a huge painted mask' (*Complete Works*, vi. 102). While Johnson fears a diminution of his own writing when he stoops to window-frames, Hazlitt objects to the grandiose and inflated terms in which such stooping is elaborated: 'His subjects are familiar, but the author is always upon stilts' (*Complete Works*, vi. 101). It is the consistently overblown nature of Johnson's seeming descent to trifles, the importance he would lend them through pompous magnification into a general statement, that makes a reader (not the author) feel ashamed. The spectacle of such a forced alliance between great and little things, in which everything is made to appear on one plane of importance—rather than a more discriminating medium that might allow the low particular to speak, as it were, for itself—produces discomfort: 'The fault of Dr. Johnson's style is, that it reduces all things to the same artificial and unmeaning level' (*Complete Works*, vi. 101–2). Yet the fact that Hazlitt is so aware of the discrepancy between Johnson's high style and its little object (a discrepancy that is equally obvious in the preface to Baretti's *Easy Phraseology*), and that he cannot decide in the course of four sentences whether the effect of such a style is to 'expand' or to 'reduce' its object, means that the uniformly elevating or diminishing process he describes has not succeeded in creating a uniform effect; or, at least, that its effect is less decisive or conclusive than Hazlitt would have us believe. That Johnson, in Hazlitt's ambiguous term, 'condescends' does not tell us whether he is heightening or abasing his topic: the virtuous and Christian sense of the word would imply an elevation of mean objects, while the pagan sense of condescending to, or of patronizing the lowly, would imply their further diminution (both possibilities seem to be compassed in 'expands the little' and 'reduces all things').

In fact, the point at which Johnson's *Journey* comes closest to realizing Hazlitt's image of a familiar face expanded into a huge mask is self-consciously 'artificial' and amusingly smug: 'The ladies have as much beauty here as in other places, but bloom and softness are not to be expected among the lower classes ... To expand the human face to its full perfection, it seems necessary that the mind should co-operate by placidness of content, or consciousness of superiority' (*Yale*, ix. 83–4). In other words, the fullest beauty—where internal attributes and external nature magically combine—requires an expansive smirk. ('To SMERK' is beautifully defined in the *Dictionary* as 'To smile wantonly', implying a profligacy of conduct as well as 'the wantonness of abundance', or a perkily indiscriminate facial expression. *Idler* 37, *Yale*, ii. 115.) And this picture of smugness calls for an answering smile on the face of a reader, not least because 'full perfection' is humanly impossible. Johnson usually trounced anyone displaying such 'placidness of content, or consciousness of superiority': '[he] did not like any one who said they were happy, or who said any one else was so. "It is all *cant* (he would cry), the dog knows he is miserable all the time ... If your sister-in-law is really the contented being she professes herself Sir (said he), her life gives the lie to every research of humanity; for she is happy without health, without beauty, without money, and without understanding" ' (*Miscellanies*, i. 334–5; see also Johnson in *Life*, iii. 241: 'He said, "nobody was content." ').

Another way of appraising passages such as that on window-frames might be to view them as evidence of Johnson's attempt to rationalize, without resolving, an 'instinctive self-division'. Confronted by the rival claims of particularity and generalization on his attention, he brings this self-division to the surface of his writing. Like Coleridge, in this respect at least, Johnson strives 'to correct into oneness the apparently incorrigible plurality continually re-discovered in the sharpness of his senses; while ... in the teeth of his commitment to universality and oneness, diversity and particularity continue to exert their interest—so that, in practice, the unity ... is typically submerged by the protracted exhibition of the contradictory elements he is meant to be bringing together'.[9]

The *Journey* extract weighs a prevailing assessment of the little particular as inherently undignified—and hence properly shut out from the remit of literature—against comprehensiveness of vision and of feeling. Johnson's dignified, impersonal tone implies that only small-mindedness (the 'vulgar apprehensions' of *Rambler* 145, *Yale*, v. 10)

[9] Perry, *Coleridge*, 60, 22.

equates the diminutive with the insignificant; greatness stoops to elevate it to significance. Thus vulgarity or narrowness is no longer imputed so much to potential authorial failing as to a reader's potential lack of discernment, although the tone is not remotely bitter or derisive. A series of variants on 'little' introduces an assertive simple sentence concerned with what is 'true'; plural 'diminutive observations' ascend to the level of a maxim: 'The true state of every nation is the state of common life.' Yet Johnson's generalization evidently necessitates further 'diminutive observations' in order to maintain its status; it is a theory whose own 'true state' makes no sense until translated into a practical descent to the realities of common life. As particulars ascend to generalizations, generalizations must be reduced to particulars: 'The manners of a people are not to be found in the schools of learning, or the palaces of greatness'; 'The great mass of nations is neither rich nor gay: they whose aggregate constitutes the people, are found in the streets, and the villages, in the shops and farms; and from them collectively considered, must the measure of general prosperity be taken' (*Yale*, ix. 22). Martin Wechselblatt discerns at such moments in Johnson's prose 'a shuttling movement between an authority without application and a world of application without authority'.[10] So 'The true state of every nation is the state of common life' quite properly remains buffeted by the preceding inventory of mellifluously phrased, yet persistent little disruptions to its apparently serene and timeless finality: 'necessities . . . daily duties . . . small inconveniencies . . . petty pleasures . . . small obstacles . . . frequent interruption'.

Boswell, on the other hand, thought his friend's 'diminutive observations' ill judged and unrepresentative: 'Here unluckily the windows had no pulleys; and Dr. Johnson, who was constantly eager for fresh air, had much struggling to get one of them kept open. Thus he had a notion impressed upon him, that this wretched defect was general in Scotland; in consequence of which he has erroneously enlarged upon it in his *Journey*. I regretted that he did not allow me to read over his book before it was printed' (*Tour*, 79 n. 9). A different influence is lent to empirical detail in this footnote. Boswell's 'unluckily' and 'impressed' (that is, having the immediate force of a sense impression) foster an atmosphere in which the minute and chance irritations of life, those rufflings of the surface on which our happiness repeatedly founders, seem insufficient prompts to

---

[10] Martin Wechselblatt, 'Finding Mr. Boswell: Rhetorical Authority and National Identity in Johnson's *Journey to the Western Islands of Scotland*', *ELH* 60 (1993), 117–48 (p. 133).

larger truths. In fact, they are distractions from it. The gloss of Johnson's 'diminutive observations' as 'erroneously enlarged' (a gloss which anticipates Hazlitt) indicates that one accidental deficiency has been unjustly inflated into a national failing. Johnson's usually commendable drive towards generalizing on the basis of his 'insatiable appetite for accurate particulars' is, in this instance, found wanting in applicability.[11]

To support his point, Boswell might have quoted *Adventurer* 107 on synecdochic human views: 'Where, then, is the wonder, that they, who see only a small part, should judge erroneously of the whole?' (*Yale*, ii. 441). While Johnson employs variations on the diminutive and particular sense impression as groundwork for wider conclusions about national progress or stagnation (retreating from first-person assertion to the passive voice), Boswell dismantles those conclusions by placing renewed emphasis on their small and personal beginnings. Johnson's carefully qualified and demure third-person constructions ('*He that would have* his window open . . .'; '*a stranger may* be *sometimes* forgiven, *if* he allows himself to wish for *fresher* air'), which place him at some distance from his original experience, boil down to eccentricity and impatience: 'Dr. Johnson, who was *constantly eager* for *fresh* air . . .' The passage, as is often the case in Boswell's *Tour*, operates as if it were Johnson's *Journey* in reverse gear: by placing an emphasis on its source's private character, the biographer steps in to unsettle the authority of the writing.

Taken together, these extracts from Johnson and Boswell reveal the potential for co-operation and for discordance between a dignified, axiomatic truth and the low particular(s) or individual source from which such truths derive. In the *Journey* passage, a local experience is translated into a general statement. Yet it is a statement retaining the possibility that local experience may work with or against any abstract formulation, inviting Boswell to object to the course of the argument. Johnson's generalizations do not always amount to unequivocal rules. They often hold their doors ajar in order to engage a reader's disagreement, perhaps even to facilitate his own escape from habitually gloomy prognoses of the human condition. Hence his recurrent use of words and phrases such as 'the greater part', 'the bulk of mankind', 'sometimes', 'frequently', 'often', and 'perhaps' to disrupt otherwise unexceptionable claims or perfect symmetries, and to preserve a sense of chance in writing—as in the world beyond it. *Adventurer* 138, for instance, presents the author's struggle with vacuity in less than universally applicable terms: 'It *frequently* happens,

---

[11] Robert Voitle, *Samuel Johnson the Moralist* (Cambridge, Mass.: Harvard University Press, 1961), 176.

that a design ... mocks us in the execution'; 'the mind ... finds *sometimes* an unexpected barrenness' (*Yale*, ii. 494; my emphases). In the 'Life of Cowley', those 'accidents' leading to the comically overstated plight of becoming 'irrecoverably a poet' are said to be '*sometimes* remembered, and *perhaps sometimes* forgotten' (*Lives*, i. 2; my emphases). 'Irrecoverably', which exaggerates Cowley's own description of how he came to be a poet ('immediately'), masks a serious point: Johnson never forgot his own journalistic background or the Grub Street fraternity as instructive counter-examples to what was, in cases such as Cowley's, only a seemingly involuntary vocation. For Johnson, as for Savage, the decision to pursue a life of writing derived from 'the utmost Miseries of Want', not from a leisurely whim dressed up as compulsion: 'He was therefore obliged to seek some other Means of Support, and having no Profession, became, by Necessity, an Author' (*Lives*, i. 2 n. 4; *Savage*, 12).

Something that is 'GENERAL', according to the *Dictionary*, focuses on 'the main, without insisting on particulars' (part of sense 1), but the seventh sense of the adjective 'GENERAL' is careful to note that it means 'Extensive, though not universal' (like Observation's 'extensive View' in *The Vanity of Human Wishes*). 'GENERALLY' is at once 'In general; without specification or exception' and 'Extensively, though not universally' (senses 1 and 2); 'GENERALNESS' is 'Wide extent, though short of universality; frequency; commonness.' The *Dictionary*'s eighth sense of the adjective 'GENERAL' is 'Common; usual', creating a union between the low particular and its broad applicability to mankind. Such a conjunction redeems Scottish window-frames from the charge of mere irrelevance: a descent from the 'GENERAL' to the 'Common' in the *Dictionary* stands in a chiastic relationship to the ascent from a 'diminutive' particular to the universalizing 'every nation' in the *Journey*. Generalization must, more or less openly, acknowledge indebtedness to the empirical realities on which it builds.[12]

For if 'GENERALNESS' is also 'commonness', it should vibrate with, while not 'insisting on' the specific indignities of 'common life' (in the wording of the *Journey* extract) from which it is also meant to refrain. 'GENERALITY' is, in the *Dictionary*, 'the quality of *including* species or particulars', or 'the common mass' (parts of senses 1 and 2; my emphasis),

---

[12] On the interplay between abstraction and concreteness in Johnson, see, for instance, Curley, *Samuel Johnson and the Age of Travel*, 114–15; T. S. Eliot, 'Johnson as Critic and Poet', in *On Poetry and Poets* (London: Faber and Faber, 1957; repr. 1990), 162–92 (p. 179); Thomas Kaminski, 'Some Alien Qualities of Samuel Johnson's Art', in Jonathan Clark and Howard Erskine-Hill (eds.), *Samuel Johnson in Historical Context* (Basingstoke: Palgrave, 2002), 222–38 (especially pp. 224–5); Wimsatt, *Prose Style*, 52–62.

while the adjective 'GENERAL' means '*Comprehending* many species or individuals' (part of sense 1; my emphasis), raising the possibility of a teeming alertness to real life within the summary comment, rather than the uniform abstraction that might seem to result from defining the 'GENERAL' as a lack of insistence on specifics: 'Great thoughts are always general, and consist in positions not limited by exceptions, and in descriptions not descending to minuteness' ('Life of Cowley', *Lives*, i. 21). Considering the figure of Wolsey, Chapter 1 discussed the combination of generality with an inclusive or allusive consciousness of the particulars from which it stems. Another example might be cited here: 'misery's darkest caverns' in Johnson's late poem 'On the Death of Dr. Robert Levet' (l. 17). This general figure remains alert to the physical 'caverns' in which misery is sheltered, and as they are 'known' at first hand by the 'Obscurely wise' doctor, who is in turn known to Johnson (ll. 17, 10). The phrase 'Obscurely wise' compliments Levet's personal acquaintance with obscurity, his ability 'to peep into neglected corners' and 'calamities unseen' (*Idler* 3 and 4, *Yale*, ii. 10, 13), at the same time as tactfully alluding to his deficiencies in other kinds of wisdom. (Savage is similarly described as 'skulking in obscure Parts of the Town, of which he was no Stranger to the remotest Corners', *Savage*, 104.) By casting its periphrastic formulation as a *container* of human beings, with whom Johnson's subject was intimate, 'misery's darkest caverns' draws attention to the population within it (as does 'hope's delusive mine' in l. 1 of the same poem): empty and full, it is dispassionate and compassionate at the same time.

Boswell habitually cast Johnson as a paternal figure of moral authority, and had mechanisms in reserve to escape from the pressures that this characterization induced. His recurrent, apparently self-abasing claim that Johnson's was too great an intellect to stoop to the petty affairs of everyday life, or to spheres beyond London, conceals a suspicion of his friend's native disproportion and a possessiveness about minutiae. 'I love little peculiar circumstances', as he writes in Scotland, a fact which perhaps led Johnson—who liked to laugh 'at his friends in trifles'—to name one of the Highland rocks Inch Boswell, 'with a strange appearance of triumph' (*Tour*, 315, 322). The sage himself, Boswell concluded, was incapable of handling insignificant subjects without aggrandizing them. Goldsmith, warning Johnson off fable, thought the same: 'if you were to make little fishes talk, they would talk like WHALES' (*Life*, ii. 231). Early in the *Tour*, Boswell openly questions Johnson's ability to descend to Scottish life: 'I doubted [i.e. suspected] that he would not be willing to come down from his elevated state of philosophical dignity; from

a superiority of wisdom among the wise and of learning among the
learned; and from flashing his wit upon minds brilliant enough to reflect
it' (*Tour*, 4). Another observation seems to wish that Johnson had never
heeded such trifles as the window-frame, whether or not they were truly
defective or representative:

> To apply his great mind to minute particulars is wrong. It is like taking an
> immense balance, such as you see on a quay for weighing cargoes of ships, to
> weigh a guinea. I knew I had neat little scales which would do better. That his
> attention to everything in his way, and his uncommon desire to be always in the
> right, would make him weigh if he knew of the particulars; and therefore it was
> right for me to weigh them and let him have them only in effect. (*Tour*, 110–11)[13]

Although 'great' and 'little' are mutually reliant, comparative terms,
Johnson's circle tended to locate his intellectual character firmly in the
realm of heroism, identifying his talent as a withdrawal from petty
specifics to the grandeur of generality. Piozzi may have thought, by
comparing Johnson's mind to an elephant's trunk, that she was praising
his attention to minutiae as well as to great matters, but Boswell wrote
that: 'Mr. Johnson has much of the *nil admirari* in smaller concerns
... Besides, so great a mind as his cannot be moved by inferior objects.
An elephant does not run and skip like lesser animals' (*Miscellanies*, i.
287; *Tour*, 81). When Hazlitt considered the moments at which Johnson's
writing became playful or light-hearted, he also thought of an elephant's
awkward gaiety—specifically, of Milton's 'unwieldy elephant', who 'To
make them mirth used all his might, and wreathed | His lithe proboscis'.[14]
Boswell and Fanny Burney, amongst others, might happily have applied
this elephantine portrait of Milton to Johnson himself: 'He sometimes
descends to the elegant, but his element is the great. He can occasionally
invest himself with grace; but his natural port is gigantick loftiness' ('Life
of Milton', *Lives*, i. 177).[15] And yet, as Howard Erskine-Hill remarks, 'the
category of the little', as invoked in the *Journey*, 'is no less general than the
category of the great'—both are amenable to morally directed oscillations
between importance and insignificance.[16] Part of the effective deployment
of 'diminutive observations' involves playing on an assumption that the
little or local sense impression lies, by virtue of its peripheral standing,

---

[13] See also Fanny Burney in Page (ed.), *Dr Johnson: Interviews and Recollections*, 52.
[14] Milton, *Paradise Lost*, IV. 345–7. Hazlitt misquotes the line as: 'The elephant | To
make them sport wreath'd his proboscis lithe' (*Complete Works*, vi. 101).
[15] See also Christopher Ricks, *Milton's Grand Style* (1963; Oxford: Clarendon Press, 1978;
repr. 1985), 22–77.
[16] Erskine-Hill, 'Johnson and the Petty Particular', 40.

outside or beneath more ostentatiously persuasive, great, or noble topics, which in turn permits it to assume a temporary centrality.

Watts faced a parallel dilemma to Johnson's in his *Journey*, and executed a similar balancing act, when he included realistic vignettes of 'little Tyrants in their own little Dominions' in *Humility Represented in the Character of St. Paul*:

> I almost reprove my self here and suspect my Friends will reprove me for introducing such low Scenes of Life, and such trivial Occurrences into a grave Discourse. I have put the Matter into the Balances as well as I can, and weighed the Case, and the Result is this. General and distant Declamations seldom strike the Conscience with such Conviction as particular Representations do; and since this Iniquity [domestic tyranny] often betrays itself in these trivial Instances, it is better perhaps to set them forth in their full and proper Light than that the Guilty should never feel a Reproof, who by the very Nature of their Distemper are unwilling to see or learn their own Folly, unless 'tis set in a glaring View. (*Humility*, 49 and 52n.)

Like Johnson, Watts proceeds with caution: the adverbs 'almost', 'seldom', 'often', and 'perhaps', nervously admitting the possibility of exceptions, finally yield to 'never'. Watts's near self-reproach stems from an abashed sense of having sunk to the depths of literary inappropriateness. Yet the shock or 'glaring View' of something 'low', 'trivial', and 'particular' in the context of a 'grave' and 'General' religious tract should bring guilty readers up short, compensating for his own loss of face. In a tract on humility, the author fittingly practises the resignation of dignity he preaches. Watts's repudiation of unwavering gravity serves as an apt reprimand to those who tyrannize their domestic kingdoms. This hesitant footnote indicates that Johnson was not alone in his concern about the literary impropriety and ethical centrality of attending to mean 'Occurrences', nor in his concern about creating their written 'Representations'. It serves morally to endorse the vigorous practical criticism the *Journey* exercises in its encounters with low and trivial things, and sets Johnson's recurrent defensiveness about stooping to petty particulars in the context of Christian humility as well as that of classical decorum. The author's fear of seeming little must be 'weighed' against the universal influence of little subjects on common life.

1. THE CATEGORY OF THE DIMINUTIVE

'[W]e are finite beings', Johnson reminds us in *Adventurer* 107 (*Yale*, ii. 441), and, as Henry Brooke wrote in 1735, 'properly speaking, whatever is finite, in respect of what is finite, is not really little; whereas, on the other hand, in respect of infinity, all things finite are equally diminutive'.[17] What Brooke means is that the humanly 'little' might, according to our dispersed and limited estimations, appear insignificant at one time and at another not so. It is a mobile, complex word whose objects cannot be given permanently marginal status by other, comparably diminutive, earthly creatures. Another scale of measurement, one infinitely beyond the human, will have to determine what is absolutely little—if that can be determined at all. Burke revealed only half the range of our attitudes to little things when (investigating beauty as a 'quality in bodies, acting mechanically upon the human mind by the intervention of the senses') he wrote that:

The most obvious point that presents itself to us in examining any object, is its extent or quantity. And what degree of extent prevails in bodies, that are held beautiful, may be gathered from the usual manner of expression concerning it. I am told that in most languages, the objects of love are spoken of under diminutive epithets. It is so in all the languages of which I have any knowledge . . . diminutives were commonly added by the Greeks to the names of persons with whom they conversed on terms of friendship and familiarity. Though the Romans were a people of less quick and delicate feelings, yet they naturally slid into the lessening termination upon the same occasions. Anciently in the English language the diminishing *ling* was added to the names of persons and things that were the objects of love. Some we retain still, as darling, (or little dear) and a few others. But to this day in ordinary conversation, it is usual to add the endearing name of *little* to every thing we love; the French and Italians make use of these affectionate diminutives even more than we. In the animal creation, out of our own species, it is the small we are inclined to be fond of; little birds, and some of the smaller kinds of beasts. A great beautiful thing, is a manner of expression scarcely ever used; but that of a great ugly thing, is very common. There is a wide difference between admiration and love . . . we submit to what we admire, but we love what submits to us; in one case we are forced, in the other we are flattered into compliance. (*Enquiry*, 112–13)

The difficulty with this account—as Burke realizes elsewhere in the *Enquiry*—is that, like Watts's domestic tyrants, we do not only 'love what submits to us': littleness and familiarity also breed 'contempt', a reaction Johnson fears when his *Journey* descends to window-frames.[18]

---

[17]   Henry Brooke, *Universal Beauty: A Philosophical Poem, in Six Books* (1735), IV. 205n., in *The Poetical Works of Henry Brooke, Esq.*, ed., rev., and corrected by Miss Brooke, 4 vols., 3rd edn. (Dublin: for the editor, 1792), ii.

[18]   'Dogs are . . . the most social, affectionate, and amiable animals of the whole brute creation; but love approaches much nearer to contempt than is commonly imagined; and

It may be true, as Adam Smith observes, that 'Diminutives and such-like are the terms in which we speak of objects we love', but (as the throwaway 'such-like' indicates) those same objects may attract diminutive epithets because we 'esteem [them] of less capacity and worth than ourselves; and to these we never express ourselves in the superlative degree'.[19] (Hence Goldsmith's dislike of Johnson's contracting his name to 'Goldy', a habit he interpreted as contemptuous.)[20] Ivy Compton-Burnett, whose characters frequently reformulate the Johnsonian view that 'little things . . . are more important than big ones, because they make up life', constructs entire scenes around the prickly, depreciative insinuations or wheedling attempts at *rapprochement* harboured in diminutive constructions:

'It is a very nice little room,' said Blanche, sitting down and looking round. 'How do you like the little paper? Don't you think it is just the thing? It is the one the boys have in their study.'

'Yes, dear, is it? Yes, it would be nice for that,' said Matty, following her sister's eyes. 'Just the thing, as you say. For this room in my house, and for a little, odd room in yours. It is the suitable choice.'

'Don't you like it in this room, dear?' said Blanche, evidently accustomed to answering her sister's meaning rather than her words.

'Yes, yes, I do. It is best to realise that we are in a little room, and not in a big one any longer. Best to leap the gulf and have a paper like the one in the boys' study.'

'And then those funny, little, country shoes! Dear Blanche, still full of her quaint, little, old touches! . . . And then her own little, charitable ways, a mixture of daughter and sister and lady bountiful! So full of affection and kindness and yet with her own little sharpness, just our old Blanche! . . . Poor Miss Griffin, you were the target. You might have been a little dark slave or a wee beastie in a trap, from the way she spoke.'[21]

accordingly, though we caress dogs, we borrow from them an appellation of the most despicable kind, when we employ terms of reproach; and this appellation is the common mark of the last vileness and contempt in every language' (Burke, *Enquiry*, 67). Yet the sense of 'dog' in this period is, as Empson notes, not invariably contemptuous. See *The Structure of Complex Words*, 168–74. Burke's later attempts to pin down the association between smallness and beauty reach a pitch of absurdity: 'should a man be found not above two or three feet high, supposing such a person to have all the parts of his body of a delicacy suitable to such a size, and otherwise endued with the common qualities of other beautiful bodies, I am pretty well convinced that a person of such stature might be considered as beautiful; might be the object of love; might give us very pleasing ideas' (*Enquiry*, 157).

[19] Smith, *Works*, iv. 131.

[20] See Boswell, *Life*, ii. 258; *Tour*, 297; Page (ed.), *Dr Johnson: Interviews and Recollections*, 28, 44, 60.

[21] Ivy Compton-Burnett, *A Family and a Fortune* (1939; Harmondsworth: Penguin, 1983), 48, 42, 58–9.

As such instances make plain, Burke's 'endearing name of *little*', like his 'diminishing' suffix '*ling*', is as prone to depress its targets from a conjectured elevation or proximity to our regard as it is to distinguish the objects of love. The *OED* notes that 'The personal designations in *-ling* are now always used in a contemptuous or unfavourable sense (though this implication was not fully established before the 17th c.)', and that 'in this use it is still a living formative': examples include 'bardling', 'courtling', 'earthling', 'fopling', 'godling', 'kingling', 'lordling', 'pope-ling', 'princeling', 'starveling', 'vainling', and 'witling' ('-ling, *suffix*', senses 1 and 2). And our affection does not necessarily increase as the span of an object diminishes: many people dislike insects enough to be scared of them and despise them enough to squash them. T. S. Eliot saw Pope, a miniaturizing genius, as 'the great master of hatred'.[22] But the possibility that acts of diminution might spring from a sense of loathing or of revulsion is one that Peter Ackroyd, like Burke, overlooks: 'The English affection for miniatures has a long history. It may be that those who live upon a small island take a delight in small things'; 'The obsession with the miniature continued well into the eighteenth century'; 'A liking for the miniature has become something of a national speciality'; 'the landscape of Lilliput is too well known to require further rehearsal.'[23] The landscape of Lilliput may be well known, yet Swift miniaturizes in a surprisingly unaffectionate way. His little creatures are bellicose, petty, and vindictive, not the seven dwarfs summoned up by Burke's 'diminishing *ling*'.

Joseph Boruslawski, a Polish dwarf who published his *Memoirs* in 1788, noted that people were 'wont to look upon beings of my stature as upon abortive half-grown individuals, kept far beneath other men, both in body and mind'. He received 'no other education but such as was analogous to my size', and an early benefactress 'looked upon me as a being merely physical, without morality, on whom [she] might try experiments of every kind'.[24] Walter de la Mare's tiny 'Miss M' recalls one reaction to her stature: 'He raised himself in his chair, his spectacles still fixed on me; as if some foul insect had erected its blunt head at him'; 'he turned his face away to conceal the aversion that had suddenly overwhelmed him at sight of me' — yet she, too, detests beetles.[25] The *OED*'s third sense of the

[22] T. S. Eliot, 'Andrew Marvell', in *Selected Prose*, 161–71 (p. 162).

[23] Ackroyd, *Albion*, 274, 276–7.

[24] Joseph Boruslawski, *Memoirs of the Celebrated Dwarf, Joseph Boruslawski: a Polish Gentleman; Containing a Faithful and Curious Account of his Birth, Education, Marriage, Travels and Voyages; Written by Himself*, trans. Mr Des Carrieres (London: [n.p.], 1788), 3, 155, 33.

[25] Walter de la Mare, *Memoirs of a Midget* (Harmondsworth: Penguin, 1955), 197–8.

adjective 'little' balances its caritative against its pejorative affiliations: 'Used to convey an implication of endearment or depreciation.' Johnson combined these hybrid impulses when (in affectionate derision of 'your shyness, & slyness', perhaps burlesquing 'Your Highness') he christened 'little' Fanny Burney a 'toadling'. Burney composed her dramatic skit *The Witlings* during the period in which Johnson was furiously embracing her as a 'darling' and a 'toadling'—while urging her to dethrone the established female wits—and may have taken a hint for the title from him.[26]

Burke's emphasis on the 'extent' and 'degree of extent' to which something is 'little' or 'great' raises the question of how we categorize an object as one or the other. Douglas, writing about dirt, argues that 'holiness is exemplified by completeness. Holiness requires that individuals shall conform to the class to which they belong. And holiness requires that different classes shall not be confused . . . Those species are unclean which are imperfect members of their class, or whose class itself confounds the general scheme of the world.'[27] Yet people do not tend to regard category membership as a clear-cut issue, but as a matter of Burke's ambiguously modified 'degree of extent'. Members of a given species are not simply dunces or non-dunces, birds or non-birds, but dunces and birds up to a point, or even the two combined: 'a monster of a fowl, | Something betwixt a Heideggre and owl' (*Dunciad*, I. 289–90).

George Lakoff, proposing that 'the fact of hierarchical ranking' is 'indisputable', argues that robins are perceived as more typical of birds than are chickens, and chickens as more typical of birds than are penguins (which, according to Douglas, might to some cultures seem anomalous 'because they swim and dive as well as they fly, or in some other way they are not fully bird-like'[28]), although all are birds to some degree: 'Logicians have, by and large, engaged in the convenient fiction that sentences of natural languages (at least declarative sentences) are either true or false or, at worst, lack a truth value, or have a third value often interpreted as "nonsense". And most contemporary linguists . . . have largely shared this fiction, primarily for lack of a sensible alternative.' Yet 'natural language concepts have vague boundaries and fuzzy edges and . . ., consequently, natural language sentences will very often be neither

[26] She remarked that 'nobody else' called her 'little Burney'. Burney, *Dr Johnson & Fanny Burney*, 57, 51. For Burney as Johnson's 'darling', and on his urging her to take on the Bluestockings, see, for instance, ibid. 35, 52, 58. Burney had completed *The Witlings* by May 1779. It remained unpublished due to fears of the public identifying her characters and their leader, Lady Smatter, with Elizabeth Montagu and her entourage.

[27] Douglas, *Purity and Danger*, 55.   [28] Ibid. 56–7.

true, nor false, nor nonsensical, but rather true to a certain extent and
false to a certain extent, true in certain respects and false in other respects'.
Hence the possibility that: 'Fuzziness can be studied seriously'; 'when
such an approach is taken, all sorts of interesting questions arise.'[29]

The fruitful hesitancy of Johnson's 'diminutive observations' bears
out Lakoff's claim that 'vague boundaries and fuzzy edges' need not
resolve themselves into wholehearted truths or falsehoods, exclusions
or inclusions, sense or nonsense. The window-frames passage implies
two conditions: first, a set of ordered relations, inherited from ancient
criticism, between style and subject; second, a contravention of that set of
ordered relations—as Johnson put it elsewhere in his *Journey*, 'a breach
of the common order of things' (*Yale*, ix. 109)—created by pairing a
low and particular subject with a dignified and general style. Bearing all
this in mind, it seems a carefully deliberated choice that he concluded
his travels on the word 'little': 'Novelty and ignorance must always be
reciprocal, and I cannot but be conscious that my thoughts on national
manners, are the thoughts of one who has seen but little' (*Yale*, ix. 164).
The fact that he has 'seen' rather than, say, narrated 'but little' of his
surroundings returns the reader to those frequently undignified points
in the *Journey* at which Johnson has been confronted by the evidence
of his senses—as in Skye, when 'flattering' expectations of refinement
drop into a flattening reality, a floor that has been 'softened' not by 'all
the arts of southern elegance', but by drizzle: 'after a very liberal supper,
when I was conducted to my chamber, I found an elegant bed of Indian
cotton, spread with fine sheets. The accommodation was flattering; I
undressed myself, and felt my feet in the mire. The bed stood upon the
bare earth, which a long course of rain had softened to a puddle' (*Yale*,
ix. 68, 100–1; see also *Tour*, 312). It is not only the case, then, that 'the
story has gained but little' by the end of the *Journey*, but also that its
author has experienced 'but little' through his own eyes: 'he *looked* even
on the smaller parts of life with minute attention, and remembered such
passages as escape cursory and common observers' (Johnson and Piozzi
in *Miscellanies*, i. 225; my emphases).

The *Journey*'s closing 'little' might be associated with the merely
'contemptible'—the last word of the *Life of Savage*, whose final paragraph
was added by Johnson some time after he had finished the rest of the
work; a fact suggestive in itself of mixed feelings about how contemptible
or praiseworthy his friend's life really was (*Savage*, 140 and n. 103). Or

[29] George Lakoff, 'Hedges: A Study in Meaning Criteria and the Logic of Fuzzy Concepts',
Journal of Philosophical Logic, 2 (1973), 458–508 (pp. 460, 458).

it might summon up the 'little wit and little virtue' Johnson discerns in Congreve's verse, in the concluding sentences of his 'Life' (*Lives*, ii. 234). The last sentence of the 'Life of Stepney' reads: 'But there is in the whole little either of the grace of wit, or the vigour of nature' (*Lives*, i. 311). The 'Life of Denham' begins with the assertion that 'very little is known' of Johnson's subject, and winds down with the phrase that Denham 'left much to do'; similarly, in the final paragraph of the 'Life of Otway', of whom, at the outset, Johnson tells us that 'little is known', he finds 'little to commend' in his subject's longest late work (*Lives*, i. 70, 83; i. 241, 247). Lord Roscommon, in the final sentence of his 'Life' (first published in 1748), is said to have 'improved taste if he did not enlarge knowledge' (*Lives*, i. 239–40). George Lyttelton's poems have, in the final analysis, 'nothing to be despised, and little to be admired'; his 'little performances' are 'sometimes spritely and sometimes insipid' (*Lives*, iii. 456). The last sentence of the 'Life of Mallet' decides that his works convey 'little information' and give 'no great pleasure' (*Lives*, iii. 410). 'Of the little that appears' in Parnell's work, we are told near the end of his 'Life', 'still less is his own'; by contrast, the last sentence of the 'Life of Swift' conjectures that 'perhaps no writer can easily be found that has borrowed so little, or that in all his excellences and all his defects has so well maintained his claim to be considered as original' (*Lives*, ii. 54; iii. 66). Like the periodic syntax leading to 'has been frequently remarked' in *Rambler* 2, these last two instances of 'little' act as a way of determining authorial originality or novelty, something Johnson felt was lacking in his remarks on Scotland—less alien a place and therefore more reduced in its investigative scope than he had imagined.

The diminutive has long served as a compendium semantic category for things that blur, smudge, contradict, or otherwise confuse accepted classifications. As such, it may (like dirt, mess, or wickedness) seem to be a catch-all for whatever is ejected from our given schemes of categorization, and therefore tricky to keep in view in its own right.[30] Perry's assessment of 'muddle' holds as true of 'little': 'the connotations of the word are more intricate than mere disapproval, and this greater complexity stems from a sense that sorts of disorder or irresolution might have their own interest and value.'[31] Some recent work in linguistics has described as pervasive the range of contradictory meanings associated

[30] See Mary Midgley, *Wickedness: A Philosophical Essay* (London: Routledge, 1984; repr. 1997), 6; David Trotter, *Cooking with Mud: The Idea of Mess in Nineteenth-Century Art and Fiction* (Oxford: Oxford University Press, 2000), 57.

[31] Perry, *Coleridge*, 8.

with the little. Arising from semantic and pragmatic contexts involving private and domestic life, women, and children, the diminutive can indicate affection ('sweet little child') or vexation ('you little so-and-so'—and worse), playfulness, attenuation, or approximation (to weaken or minimize the force of an entire utterance). In some languages, the diminutive form signals intensification or deictic precision. Attached to words in Mexican Spanish meaning 'now' or 'here', it comes to mean 'exactly now' or 'exactly here'. In Japanese it marks up the centre or prototype of a social category, while in Chinese it gestures towards the socially marginal.[32]

This dual function of challenging and endorsing the status quo means that diminutives can elicit distinctions of degree within category membership, or suggest that some criterion for category membership is lacking. Intensifying or weakening the utterance it qualifies, when the little word or construction appears as an approximative, or as a 'semantic hedge' (in Daniel Jurafsky's phrase),[33] it serves to redirect our attention from what we habitually assume to be of central importance towards what we habitually assume to be of marginal importance. An example of this occurs when Johnson rejects 'Hyperbole' and ancient 'Sallies of Excellence' in favour of modest, charitable behaviour and unassuming chit-chat: 'Heroick Virtues ... are the bon Mots of Life, they seldom appear & are therefore when they do appear—much talked of; but Life is made up of little Things, & that Character is best which does little, but continued Acts of Beneficence; as that Conversation is the best which consists in little, but elegant & pleasing Thoughts; expressed in easy, natural and pleasing Terms' (*Thraliana*, i. 183).

'Little', like 'a little fear' (which might refer to a quality or to a quantity) in the *Journey* passage on window-frames, has two possible applications here. 'That Character is best which does little, but continued Acts of Beneficence' and 'that Conversation is best which consists in little, but elegant & pleasing Thoughts' might refer to the scale or to the frequency of those acts and thoughts (that is, the best character/conversation might consist of little *and* continued/elegant acts/thoughts, or of little *other than* continued/elegant acts/thoughts). The ambiguity of this 'little' recalls a

---

[32] Examples are taken from Daniel Jurafsky, 'Universal Tendencies in the Semantics of the Diminutive', *Language: Journal of the Linguistic Society of America*, 72 (1996), 533–78, to which my discussion of the little is indebted. I am grateful to Sylvia Adamson for bringing this article to my attention. See also Pamela Munro, 'Diminutive Syntax', in William Shipley (ed.), *In Honor of Mary Haas: From the Haas Festival Conference on Native American Linguistics* (Berlin: Mouton de Gruyter, 1988), 539–55.

[33] Jurafsky, 'Universal Tendencies', 549.

sentence from *Rambler* 60 on 'private life', which is said to derive 'its comforts and its wretchedness from the right or wrong management of things *which nothing but their frequency makes considerable*' (*Yale*, iii. 319; my emphasis). Little acts of kindness cease to be inconsiderable if life consists of little else, just as the pleasing turn given to a little thought will compensate for its diminutive stature. An appeal to the common particular is paradoxically able to register distinction and uniqueness, restoring to view some individual detail lost in the broad strokes of classification (literary or otherwise), and hence acquires importance. T. S. Eliot recognizes this when he has Eeldrop and Appleplex—both of whom are 'endeavoring to escape not the commonplace, respectable or even the domestic, but the too well pigeonholed, too taken-for-granted, too highly systematized areas'—encounter a 'fat Spaniard' who 'belonged to a type' and 'could easily be classified in any town of provincial Spain'. As Eeldrop summarizes the Spaniard's effect on him, however: 'under the circumstances—when we had been discussing marriage, and he suddenly leaned forward and exclaimed: "I was married once myself"—we were able to detach him from his classification and regard him for a moment as an unique being, a soul, however insignificant, with a history of its own, once for all. It is these moments which we prize, and which alone are revealing.'[34]

Little things, then, are able to displace types and to evade typecasting; they may question the established grounds for inclusion in or for exclusion from a literary or social group by making prominent category members less central, and peripheral category members more central. They may confront one relevant structure by another, apparently less relevant structure, one that is less subject to control (because dismissed or habitually overlooked). The diminutive can operate as something straight and comic, praised and deprecated, elevated and subordinated within a given order of things whose orientation it may question, unsettle, or alter—sometimes only to restore it. In one mood or literary mode, it is (as Freud argued) a joke category invoked in contrast to a dominant category of the great, sublime, or dignified. Empson noted the 'casualness and inclusiveness' of *The Beggar's Opera* (1728) and its attitude to low life, while Hazlitt thought Crabbe's minute poetry written in a wholly different spirit: 'He exhibits the smallest circumstance of the smallest things … the very costume of meanness; the nonessentials of every trifling incident'; in other words, 'just the contrary view of human life

---

[34] Eliot, *Eeldrop and Appleplex*, 2–3.

to that which Gay has done in his Beggar's Opera'.[35] The process set in train by introducing little and low subjects may take the form of a descent or of an ascent. In one sense, Johnson's 'diminutive observations' on window-frames assault a classical scale of values and of propriety by directing our attention downwards, making it discover in private, daily life merits usually ascribed to things of great, heroic worth. This descent or condescension involves a humbling of the authorial self and so may be dismissed as mere puerility. On the other hand, such a movement may be cast as an ascent in the sense that it attributes to writer and reader a power akin to the mock-heroic poet's, to elevate the quotidian, and to make 'familiar things . . . new' ('Life of Pope', *Lives*, iii. 234).

The *Journey*'s handling of its 'diminutive observations' suggests a potentially strained relation between the fullness of life and the elegant selections of writing; if 'life consists not of a series of illustrious actions' (and 'what should books teach but the art of *living*?', Johnson in *Miscellanies*, i. 324), neither should a useful literature: 'in the esteem of uncorrupted reason, what is of most use is of most value' (*Rambler* 60, *Yale*, iii. 320–1). Yet *Rambler* 4 warns that it is 'not a sufficient vindication . . . of a narrative, that the train of events is agreeable to observation and experience'. Some criteria of choice must be introduced to modern fiction, for instance, whose 'authors are at liberty, tho' not to invent, yet *to select* objects' (*Yale*, iii. 22; my emphasis). In the *Journey*, however, Johnson writes that life does not consist of 'elegant enjoyments', *hence* the justification for emphasizing something little and mean (*Yale*, ix. 22). It seems as if he is consciously spurning one thing that can militate against the charge of impropriety: the claim that his diminutive observations are choice. But the deficient window-frame is, after all, a low (and therefore representative) detail selected for its familiarity, not a rare jewel culled for its exquisiteness. The book also concludes that Johnson has seen neither a representative nor an elegant selection of the 'national manners' he set out to see, and the *Journey* is informed throughout by allusions to what has been necessarily omitted: 'We came thither too late to see what we expected' (*Yale*, ix. 164, 57).

2. ELEGANCE

Johnson's admission that life does not consist of 'elegant enjoyments' implies that it is—unsurprisingly—difficult to identify or to prescribe

---

[35] Empson, *Some Versions of Pastoral*, 195; Hazlitt, *Lectures on the English Poets* (1818): V: 'On Thomson and Cowper', in *Complete Works*, v. 97–8.

the components of 'human felicity, which is made up of many ingredients, each of which may be shewn to be very insignificant' (Johnson in *Life*, i. 440). The use of the word 'elegance' in his *Dictionary* definition of 'RHETORICK' ('The act of speaking not merely with propriety, but with art and elegance', sense 1), and its etymological implications—as a principle of judicious selection—have already been noted in the Introduction and in Chapter 1. Patricia Ingham remarks on Johnson's habitual recourse to 'elegance' and its cognates in his literary criticism, in order to praise 'accuracy in respect of precision of thought and expression'.[36] In this context, the word describes anything that is pinned down, fitting, logically coherent, or exact: 'The beauty of propriety not of greatness', as it is first defined in the fourth and revised edition of the *Dictionary* (1773). In the *Journey*, however, Johnson sees accuracy as a necessary precursor to, rather than as a permanent aspect of elegance, casting it as one stage in a progressively civilizing ascent: 'By degrees one age improves upon another. Exactness is first obtained, and afterwards elegance' (*Yale*, ix. 115). Here, he is focusing on the brand of linguistic and belletristic improvement which leads him to conclude of Dryden (in a re-envisioning of classical precedent for a new Augustan era) that: 'What was said of Rome, adorned by Augustus, may be applied by an easy metaphor to English poetry embellished by Dryden, "lateritiam invenit, marmoream reliquit," he found it brick, and he left it marble' ('Life of Dryden', *Lives*, i. 469). And of Inverness he writes that: 'The soldiers seem to have incorporated afterwards with the inhabitants, and to have peopled the place with an English race; for the language of this town has been long considered as peculiarly elegant' (*Yale*, ix. 27; the necessarily physical sense of 'incorporated' is, by contrast, peculiarly inelegant).

Since little things habitually blur or raise doubts about accepted classifications, they have a relationship with imprecision (and therefore with the serious business of human happiness, which Johnson tends to describe in vague terms) that sits uncertainly with the selective and precise requirements of literary elegance. But it is also a laudable mark of social progress—and therefore of happiness and of elegance in a broader sense—to have the leisure and surplus attention to bestow on minutiae. Throughout his *Journey*, Johnson carefully observed whether the Scots themselves paid sufficient heed to little things, and employed his findings to measure their advance towards civilized society. Writing to Hester Thrale of their domestic habits, he remarked that Scotland was 'a Nation

[36] Patricia Ingham, 'Dr. Johnson's "Elegance" ', *Review of English Studies*, NS 19 (1968), 271–8 (p. 271).

just rising from barbarity, long contented with necessaries, now somewhat studious of convenience, but not yet arrived at delicate discriminations' (*Letters*, ii. 96). As he phrased it in a rhetorical climax or 'gradatio' at the beginning of his dedication to the king of Reynolds's *Discourses* (1778): 'The regular progress of cultivated life is from Necessaries to Accommodations, from Accommodations to Ornaments' (*Prefaces*, 197). He might have been recalling *Idler* 63: 'The natural progress of the works of men is from rudeness to convenience, from convenience to elegance, and from elegance to nicety' (*Yale*, ii. 196). Yet this move from 'necessaries' to 'ornaments', from 'rudeness' to 'nicety', could also be seen as a form of enervation—of social 'retrogradation' as well as of social 'gradatio'—expressing a fear that the English citizen, weakened as well as polished by 'all the arts of southern elegance', may have 'improved his delicacy more than his manhood' (*Yale*, ix. 51, 68, 55).[37] Hence Johnson's wish to appear sturdy, as well as refined—two of many contradictory impulses in the *Journey*: 'he soon produced more provision than men not luxurious require', 'but a very nice man would not be pampered' (*Yale*, ix. 149; *Letters*, ii. 95).

As in the opening lines of Book I of Cowper's *Task*, ornaments and nicety may indicate a civilized nation, but such a nation also lacks the primitive vigour that characterized our ancestors. For 'civilization', as John Stuart Mill notes, is 'a word of double meaning'. On the one hand, it denotes, in a 'general' sense, a country 'more improved; more eminent in the best characteristics of Man and Society; farther advanced in the road to perfection'. On the other, and in a 'particular' sense, 'it stands for that kind of improvement only, which distinguishes a wealthy and powerful nation from savages or barbarians. It is in this sense that we may speak of the vices or the miseries of civilization; and that the question has been seriously propounded, whether civilization is on the whole a good or evil?'[38] Johnson seems to have a similar distinction in mind when he writes of 'civilized nations' in *Idler* 37 that: 'Nature makes us poor only when we want necessaries, but custom gives the name of poverty to the want of superfluities' (*Yale*, ii. 116).

Although, in his letter to Thrale, Johnson conceived of the Scots in private life as 'just rising from barbarity . . . but not yet arrived at delicate discriminations', in fact, as Wechselblatt notes, Scotland turned out to

---

[37] See Eric Griffiths, 'Dryden's Past', *Proceedings of the British Academy*, 84 (1992), 113–49 (pp. 120–41).

[38] John Stuart Mill, 'Civilization' (1836), in *The Collected Works of John Stuart Mill*, ed. John M. Robson et al. 32 vols. (Toronto: University of Toronto Press, 1963–91), xviii. 119.

affront Johnson's progressive English model of refinement. Like Smith and Hume, Johnson's *Journey* 'subscribes to the so-called *four stages* theory of national development', according to which 'emergent societies depart from a rudimentary level of hunting and gathering, pass through pastoral and agricultural phases, to . . . arrive at commercial activity, the stage at which trade makes possible an intellectual intercourse that results in the flowering of the liberal arts. Because in Scotland the liberal arts have developed without the aid of commerce Johnson cannot reconcile Scotland's national identity with the model governing England's.'[39] The passage to which Wechselblatt refers is one in which Johnson's hesitant double negative is itself the mark of a cultivated sensibility—one which is in two minds about whether its own refinement is a good or a bad thing, at the same time as it is in two minds about how far advanced Scotland truly is. He is compelled to prise apart the notion of linguistic, stylistic, intellectual, or literary elegance from that of a more basic social elegance, because the Scots have seemingly arrived at one form of 'delicate discriminations' without first attaining the other: 'I know not whether it be not peculiar to the Scots to have attained the liberal, without the manual arts, to have excelled in ornamental knowledge, and to have wanted not only the elegancies, but the conveniencies of common life' (*Yale*, ix. 28; see also *Tour*, 210).

It is a paradox of eighteenth-century refinement that little things are held to be at once valuable and worthless: though nothing in themselves, it is a mark of sophistication to be able to make much of them. Yet to make too much of them is to become vain, petty, and intellectually narrow, as ridicule of the scientific virtuoso throughout the eighteenth century attests: 'it is, methinks, the Mark of a little Genius to be wholly conversant among Insects, Reptiles, Animalcules, and those trifling Rarities that furnish out the Apartment of a Virtuoso'; 'as several of our Modern Virtuoso's manage it, their Speculations do not so much tend to open and enlarge the Mind, as to contract and fix it upon Trifles' (*Tatler* 216 and 236, iii. 132, 219). Henry Fielding wrote in 1746 that 'the Generality of Mankind are apt to entertain a low and contemptible Opinion of [*Virtuosi*], as an useless Sett of People'.[40] The first sense of the word 'elegant' in the *OED* raises a related suspicion about how desirable a quality it might be: 'Tastefully ornate in attire; sometimes in unfavourable sense: Dainty, foppish.' Truth is not synonymous with

---

[39] Wechselblatt, 'Finding Mr. Boswell', 128.
[40] *The Criticism of Henry Fielding*, ed. Ioan Williams (London: Routledge & Kegan Paul, 1970), 125.

elegance, especially when Johnson comes to consider 'elegant learning' in Scotland: '[Boethius'] history is written with elegance and vigour, but his fabulousness and credulity are justly blamed'; 'The first race of scholars, in the fifteenth century, and some time after, were, for the most part, learning to speak, rather than to think, and were therefore more studious of elegance than of truth.' But nor is rudeness: 'Honesty is not greater where elegance is less' (*Yale*, ix. 14–15, 42).

Applied to literary works, 'elegant' may describe something that has fallen short of what a reader expected (like the restricted domain of a truth that 'has been frequently remarked' in *Rambler* 2, or the 'but little' that Johnson has seen in his *Journey*), as well as something that deserves praise, as the *OED* observes: '4. a. Of composition, literary style, etc.; also of words or phrases: Characterized by grace and refinement; "pleasing by minuter beauties" ' (the quotation is from Johnson's *Dictionary*). This definition of the elegant, the *OED* notes, was 'Formerly used somewhat vaguely as a term of praise for literary style'. From the eighteenth century onwards, however, 'it has tended more and more to exclude any notion of intensity or grandeur, and, when applied to compositions in which these qualities might be looked for, has a depreciatory sense'. Like the association of little things with a domestic setting, this kind of elegance is sociable, tempered, and comforting—qualities to which Johnson often refers when describing an 'elegance of conversation' or of company in Scotland (*Yale*, ix. 26; see also, for instance, *Yale*, ix. 21, 59, 68). Again like the diminutive, elegance may be 'Used to convey an implication of endearment or depreciation' (*OED*, 'little', sense 3). The Scottish milieu turned out to be less foreign than Johnson had anticipated, its intermittently elegant resemblances to English life a disappointment after the savage 'intensity or grandeur' he had been led to anticipate. For elegance characterizes a tamed and cultivated scene, rather than a sublime or rugged landscape. According to Jean Hagstrum, Johnson first conceived of beauty as a single quality 'which could either *soothe* or *strike*, which was either *elegant* or *grand*'. She argues that later, following the appearance of Burke's *Enquiry*, he began to sharpen into an antithesis the distinction between two kinds of beauty: the 'awfully vast' and the 'elegantly little', the 'sublime' (or 'grand') and the merely 'beautiful' (or 'elegant').[41] And if we link Imlac's 'elegantly little' (*Rasselas*, *Yale*, xvi. 42) to Ingham's perception that elegance is, for Johnson, a form of precision,

[41] Jean H. Hagstrum, *Samuel Johnson's Literary Criticism* (Minneapolis: University of Minnesota Press, 1952), 130–1.

he would seem to agree with Burke that 'A clear idea is therefore another name for a little idea' (*Enquiry*, 63).

As his conclusion to the *Journey* suggests, Johnson found numerous varieties of this 'little idea' in Scotland—varieties of elegance in the sense of 'Anything that pleases by its nicety' (the new, secondary meaning of 'ELEGANCE' in the 1773 *Dictionary*). Some of the *OED* definitions of 'elegant' help to expand on what he meant by the word: '3. Of modes of life, dwellings and their appointments, etc.: Characterized by refined luxury'; '4. b. Of a speaker or author: Characterized by refinement and polish of style'; '6. b. Refined in manners and habits (formerly also, in feeling)'; '7. Of pursuits, studies (formerly also, of sentiments): Graceful, polite, appropriate to persons of refinement and cultivated taste.' Johnson's tone changes according to whether he is surprised by the rudeness, or by the elegance of his surroundings. He often endeavours to capture through his own 'refinement and polish of style' the absence of 'refined luxury' in a domestic setting, and the shock this presents to an English traveller and writer 'of refinement and cultivated taste': 'I know not how it is, but I cannot bear low life. And I find others, who have as good a right as I to be disgusted, bear it better, by having mixed with different sorts of men. You would think that I have mixed pretty well, too' (Johnson in *Tour*, 293). But on other occasions, when, accustomed to lowering his expectations, he finds them suddenly overturned, the 'surprise' of dark barbarity yielding to enlightened civility is 'delightful': 'Our reception exceeded our expectations. We found nothing but civility, elegance, and plenty . . . The general air of festivity, which predominated in this place, so far remote from all those regions which the mind has been used to contemplate as the mansions of pleasure, struck the imagination with a delightful surprise, analogous to that which is felt at an unexpected emersion from darkness into light' (*Yale*, ix. 59).

The England in which Johnson's parents grew up has been appealingly described as 'a time when we learned to live peaceably in brick houses, to grow flower bulbs in pots, to dine off blue-and-white china dishes, to drink tea, chocolate and coffee, to take toast and marmalade at breakfast and to read the newspapers'.[42] Things were not quite so comfortable in the Highlands their son visited over half a century later. Johnson trained a keen eye on the peculiar combination of 'exotic luxury' and 'antiquated life' that he discovered in the trappings of Scottish domesticity, commenting minutely in the course of three pages on the

---

[42] Jonathan Keates, *Purcell: A Biography* (London: Chatto & Windus, 1995), 201.

ingredients of a Highland breakfast, dinner, tea, and supper; on whisky, baking, kitchen gardens, cutlery, plates, and table linen; on honey, conserves, marmalade, cheese, milk, eggs, sugar, and potatoes — 'not of the mealy, but the viscous kind' (*Yale*, ix. 55–7). He politely negotiates the difficulty inherent in capturing for his English readers a transitional state between barbarity and civilization, as well as the fitful improvements already made to what he comically represents as a barren, treeless landscape (see, for instance, pp. 9–11, 21, 30, 35, 60, 70). To seek out such details about table manners may seem trifling as a form of anthropological enquiry, and Johnson was not averse to making jokes about eating habits at the expense of the Scots, as in his notorious definition of 'OATS' in the *Dictionary*: 'A grain, which in England is generally given to horses, but in Scotland supports the people.' However, Elias's comments on the use of forks suggest the representative power of such minor innovations: 'What we take entirely for granted, because we have been adapted and conditioned to this social standard from earliest childhood, had first to be slowly and laboriously acquired and developed by society as a whole. This applies to such a small and seemingly insignificant thing as a fork.'[43] In other words, 'The true state of every nation is the state of common life.'

And yet, at the outset of his *Journey*, Johnson is seeking romance — the thrill afforded by 'ruins of ancient magnificence' rather than a humdrum, present-day reality — and his writing has a feel of the novelistic about it (*Yale*, ix. 5). He and Boswell come across as passive, helpless *ingénus*, procured 'lodgings' by 'some invisible friend', drawn 'out of our way' by the 'magnetism' of Lord Monboddo's 'conversation', 'being conducted wherever there was any thing which I desired to see, and entertained at once with the novelty of the place, and the kindness of communication'. Combining a 'sense of danger' and 'heated' imaginations with a 'delight in rarity', their 'curiosity pants for savage virtues and barbarous grandeur' (*Yale*, ix. 5, 12, 13, 19, 25, 58). Even at the late stage of his visit to Auchinleck, Boswell's ancestral pile, Johnson is 'less delighted with the elegance of the modern mansion, than with the sullen dignity of the old castle' (*Yale*, ix. 161). Earlier in the *Journey*, he flirts with the idea that he is himself a 'ROMANCER', or 'A liar; a forger of tales', as the *Dictionary* unflinchingly defines the word — someone remarkably like James 'Ossian' Macpherson, in fact, prone to encourage the 'easy reception' of 'an improbable fiction' (*Yale*, ix. 117–19):

---

[43]   Elias, *The Civilizing Process*, 55.

As the day advanced towards noon, we entered a narrow valley not very flowery, but sufficiently verdant ... I sat down on a bank, such as a writer of romance might have delighted to feign. I had indeed no trees to whisper over my head, but a clear rivulet streamed at my feet. The day was calm, the air soft, and all was rudeness, silence, and solitude. Before me, and on either side, were high hills, which by hindering the eye from ranging, forced the mind to find entertainment for itself. Whether I spent the hour well I know not; for here I first conceived the thought of this narration. (*Yale*, ix. 40)

'Rudeness' has, in this instance, gentle connotations of the 'calm' and the 'soft', of 'silence' and 'solitude'. In spite of the absence of shelter, the setting appears to offer a positively comforting type of primitivism, resembling the associations of pastoral with 'stillness', 'tranquillity', and 'childhood' that Johnson describes in *Rambler* 36 (*Yale*, iii. 196–7). None of the definitions of 'RUDENESS' in the *Dictionary* accounts for its soothing effects here: in fact, it is interpreted as, amongst other things, 'Violence; boisterousness' and 'Storminess; rigour' (senses 4 and 5). Yet Johnson never thinks for long of silent isolation as a happy or desirable state: 'The great business of his life (he said) was to escape from himself; this disposition he considered as the disease of his mind, which nothing cured but company' (Reynolds reporting Johnson in *Life*, i. 144–5; see also *Tour*, 261). To be actively hindered from ranging, so that the mind is forced to find entertainment for itself, sounds uncomfortably close to the plight of those imprisoned in another 'narrow valley' or 'seat of tranquillity', blessed with 'solitary walks' and opportunities for 'silent meditation': the Happy Valley of *Rasselas* (*Yale*, xvi. 12). And Johnson soon becomes uneasy: 'the imaginations excited by the view of an unknown and untravelled wilderness are not such as arise in the artificial solitude of parks and gardens'; 'Whoever had been in the place where I then sat, unprovided with provisions and ignorant of the country, might, at least before the roads were made, have wandered among the rocks, till he perished with hardship, before he could have found either food or shelter' (*Yale*, ix. 40–1).[44]

Johnson comically restaged this solitary, pastoral vision in a long letter to Hester Thrale, written in 1773. Here, he imagines Thrale in turn imagining that the lofty sage's darting, penetrative view spans the rugged

---

[44] The putative traveller of earlier times, who might 'have wandered among the rocks, till he perished with hardship', recalls Johnson's letter to Chesterfield, on the perils of trusting a guide whose support is offered only when it comes too late: 'The Shepherd in Virgil grew at last acquainted with Love, and found him a Native of the Rocks. Is not a Patron, My Lord, one who looks with unconcern on a Man struggling for Life in the water and when he has reached ground encumbers him with help' (*Letters*, i. 96).

scene in all its greatness and its littleness, compassing the 'awfully vast' and the 'elegantly little'. But Johnson's tone is one of piquant mock-gravity about the distinction between his surroundings and those of a hermit philosopher. Where the *Journey* re-envisages Scottish reality as pastoral romance, his letter translates its pastoral romance into reality. He makes no mention of the fact that he first conceived of his *Journey* in this location (although he does say that he made notes, and later tells Thrale, 'I keep a book of remarks', *Letters*, ii. 95). The comparatively fertile scene is made to seem barren in its terrain, and in the effects it produces on Johnson, by comparison with the rewards of elegant conversation:

we came to a small glen, so they call a valley, which compared with other places appeared rich and fertile ... I sat down to make notes on a green bank, with a small stream running at my feet, in the midst of savage solitude, with Mountains before me, and on either hand covered with heath. I looked round me, and wondered that I was not more affected, but the mind is not at all times equally ready to be put in motion. If my Mistress, and Master, and Queeny had been there we should have produced some reflections among us either poetical or philosophical, for though *Solitude* be the *nurse of woe*, conversation is often the parent of remarks and discoveries ...

You are perhaps imagining that I am withdrawn from the gay and the busy world into regions of peace and pastoral felicity, and am enjoying the reliques of the golden age; that I am surveying Nature's magnificence from a mountain, or remarking her minuter beauties on the flowery bank of a winding rivulet, that I am invigorating myself in the sunshine, or delighting my imagination with being hidden from the invasion of human evils and human passions, in the darkness of a Thicket, that I am busy in gathering shells and pebbles on the Shore, or contemplative on a rock, from which I look upon the water and consider how many waves are rolling between me and Streatham.

The use of travelling is to regulate imagination by reality, and instead of thinking how things may be, to see them as they are ... I shall only see other rocks, and a wider circuit of barren desolation. Of streams we have here a sufficient number, but they murmur not upon pebbles but upon rocks; of flowers, if Chloris herself were here, I could present her only with the bloom of Heath. (*Letters*, ii. 73, 78–9)

Austen certainly recognized undercurrents of fearful distaste and of comedy in the 'writer of romance' passage, since the thirteenth letter of 'Love and Freindship' (written 1790) shoves Johnson's treeless Scottish landscape into overt, weed-strewn parody—with the pointed addition of 'A Grove of full-grown Elms'. She also seems to be aware of the fact that Johnson remains near a road and in company, in spite of his fictional indulgence of a time 'before the roads were made', and his equally hypothetical isolation in a purportedly 'untravelled wilderness' through which he and Boswell are accompanied by local guides (the effect is not dissimilar to televised, documentary-style travelogues, in which we are encouraged to believe that the presenter who speaks to the camera is struggling alone through an untamed landscape). Johnson's contrived solitude at this point in his *Journey*, itself reminiscent of Gothic, sublime, and sentimental romance's heightened terrors of abandonment, may have prompted Austen's comic response in the first place:

we left Macdonald Hall, & having walked about a mile & a half we sate down by the side of a clear limpid stream to refresh our exhausted limbs. The place was suited to meditation—. A Grove of full-grown Elms sheltered us from the East—. A Bed of full-grown Nettles from the West—. Before us ran the murmuring brook & behind us ran the turn-pike road. We were in a mood for contemplation & in a Disposition to enjoy so beautifull a spot. A mutual Silence which had for some time reigned between us, was at length broke by my exclaiming—'What a lovely Scene! Alas why are not Edward & Augustus here to enjoy its Beauties with us?' (Austen, *Works*, vi. 97; see also p. 459n.)

The original of this passage is the only one in which Johnson invokes a 'writer of romance', rather than 'The fictions of the Gothick romances', or 'the fictions of romantick chivalry' to which he refers elsewhere in the *Journey* (*Yale*, ix. 77, 155). His allusion to a specific kind of author—one concerned not with reality, but with feigning—introduces a question about his own literary identity. He conceives his first thought of what we are now reading in a geographical location poised between truth and fiction, between the empirical evidence of his senses ('sufficiently verdant . . . no trees') and the tempered or 'terrifick representations' into which that evidence might be translated (*Letters*, ii. 66). He simultaneously reflects, as in the 'Life of Pope', on the rude origins of a polished text (see below), just as the *Journey* on a larger scale considers the rude origins of English civility. At this point, he seems still to be toying with what kind of 'narration' his will turn out to be. As the *Journey* proceeds, the heightened expectations of romance or of novelistic language sometimes co-operate with reality, and sometimes collide with it:

The fictions of the Gothick romances were not so remote from credibility as they are now thought. In the full prevalence of the feudal institution, when violence desolated the world, and every baron lived in a fortress, forests and castles were regularly succeeded by each other, and the adventurer might very suddenly pass from the gloom of woods, or the ruggedness of moors, to seats of plenty, gaiety, and magnificence. Whatever is imaged in the wildest tale, if giants, dragons, and enchantment be excepted, would be felt by him, who, wandering in the mountains without a guide, or upon the sea without a pilot, should be carried amidst his terror and uncertainty, to the hospitality and elegance of Raasay or Dunvegan. (*Yale*, ix. 77)

Here, Johnson finds an element of his appetite for fictional adventure—bar the old chivalric trappings of 'giants, dragons, and enchantment'—suddenly realized, alongside a fairy-tale ending in the relief of discovering up-to-date 'hospitality and elegance'. In this passage, 'terrour without danger' is 'a voluntary agitation of the mind that is permitted no longer than it pleases' (*Yale*, ix. 20). The juxtaposition of 'fortress, forests and castles' with modern ease—the latter a prompt to feeling 'agreeably disappointed' (*Tour*, 316)—resembles Catherine Morland's loss of 'The visions of romance' in *Northanger Abbey* (1818), when a 'precious manuscript', concealed in an ancient chest, turns out to be the heartbreakingly prosaic 'inventory of linen, in coarse and modern characters' (among other equally tedious items). Catherine is shamed chiefly by her supposition that 'a manuscript of many generations back could have remained undiscovered in a room such as that, so modern, so habitable!' (Austen, *Works*, v. 199, 169, 172–3). In *Rambler* 4, Johnson had seemed almost as regretful about dissolving 'the visions of romance' in favour of regulating 'the imagination by reality'. There, he precluded the eighteenth-century novel, which exhibits 'life in its true state', from 'the machines and expedients of the heroic romance' and from building castles in the air; it 'can neither employ giants to snatch away a lady from the nuptial rites, nor knights to bring her back from captivity; it can neither bewilder its personages in desarts, nor lodge them in imaginary castles' (*Yale*, iii. 19).

Faced with the prospect of the Highlands, however, 'life in its true state' could strike him as not so far away from 'the heroic romance' as he had thought; sometimes, in Scotland, 'fictions begin to operate as realities' (Imlac in *Rasselas*, *Yale*, xvi. 152): 'These castles afford another evidence that the fictions of romantick chivalry had for their basis the real manners of the feudal times, when every lord of a seignory lived in his hold lawless and unaccountable, with all the licentiousness and insolence of uncontested superiority and unprincipled power' (*Yale*, ix. 155). Johnson may have heated his imagination by such architectural evidence, at the same time as satisfying his desire for empirical data. But the intensity of his conjectured feudal despotism hints at why he worried about the perils of indulging in imaginary acts. The fictions of romantic chivalry, as they

reproduce the *real* manners of ancient times, may seem historically faithful, but they are faithful to a 'lawless', 'unaccountable', and rightly over-
thrown social system. To yield even through reading to 'the full prevalence
of the feudal institution, when violence desolated the world'—phrasing
that recalls the 'dangerous prevalence of imagination' and the 'despotick'
'reign of fancy' in *Rasselas*—is to give way to something morally 'unprincipled': 'This, Sir, is one of the dangers of solitude', and therefore of
romance (Imlac, *Yale*, xvi. 150, 152–3). It encourages a slavish dependence, captivity, and abrogation of responsibility in its young, susceptible
audience; hence Johnson's opinion that reading such works had prevented
him from ever settling on a profession (*Life*, i. 49 and n. 2).

In this context, the sublime tyranny of romance—which isolates its
reader as well as its hero or heroine from the rest of humanity—seems
alien to the milder, companionable charms of modern elegance, yet they
are yoked together by the assertion that: 'Whatever is imaged in the
wildest tale ... would be felt by him, who, wandering in the mountains
without a guide, or upon the sea without a pilot, should be carried amidst
his terror and uncertainty, to the hospitality and elegance of Raasay or
Dunvegan.' The implication is either that romance necessarily combines
feudal terrors with the surprise discovery of hospitable elegance, or
that despotic romance should be compelled to yield, as in *Northanger
Abbey*, to the comforts of modern society. Johnson's narrative repeatedly
indulges in sweeping fictional hypotheses of abandonment and of fear,
hypotheses that conclude in the same way as the astronomer's madness
in *Rasselas*—by reference to 'but little', or to a smaller-scale reality:
'ease and elegance, and ... conversation took possession of his heart';
'he found his thoughts grow brighter by their company; the clouds
of solicitude vanished by degrees'; 'He began gradually to delight in
sublunary pleasures' (*Yale*, xvi. 160).

Of Inch Kenneth, Johnson writes that:

Romance does not often exhibit a scene that strikes the imagination more than
this little desert in these depths of western obscurity, occupied not by a gross
herdsman, or amphibious fisherman, but by a gentleman and two ladies, of high
birth, polished manners and elegant conversation, who, in a habitation raised
not very far above the ground, but furnished with unexpected neatness and
convenience, practised all the kindness of hospitality, and refinement of courtesy.
(*Yale*, ix. 142–3)

Appositional genitives seem here to act as stylistic improvements
on the second of the two nouns they join to one another, although
they also risk a luxurious redundancy in so doing: is 'refinement of

courtesy' a refinement of courtesy itself, or merely the refinement that belongs to courtesy? By singling out refinement as a possible ingredient of courtesy, Johnson also suggests that one can exist without the other. This interpretation is encouraged by his remark that, in spite of their 'narrowness of life', 'Civility seems part of the national character of the Highlanders'; here, 'true hospitality' may be 'a plain but plentiful table' (*Yale*, ix. 29–30; *Tour*, 366). Just as courtesy is not necessarily refinement (and vice versa), hospitality is not always kind, nor kindness always hospitable. At an Edinburgh inn, Johnson threw out of the window some lemonade insolently sweetened by the waiter's 'greasy fingers', and he was angered by the sincerely kind offer made to him (in Loch Buy) of 'cold sheep-head' for breakfast (*Tour*, 11, 345).

Johnson's ascending, civilizing triplet of 'high birth, polished manners and elegant conversation', of the kind which feeds into Austen's description of Emma in the opening sentence of her novel as 'handsome, clever, and rich' (*Works*, iv. 5), gives the writing a pronounced sense of arrival: not only of Boswell and Johnson at their destination, but also of its inhabitants at a state of leisured ease, beyond what their English visitors had anticipated. The figurative elevation of 'high birth' acts as a civilizing influence on a location whose 'depths' are 'raised not very far above the ground': a naturally brutish and socially demeaning geography has been improved by its surprisingly genteel owners. The courtliness of this description resembles a passage in the 'Life of Shenstone', in which Johnson imitates, through stylistic ornamentation, the poet's horticultural elevation of his 'little domain' to 'a place', like Inch Kenneth, 'to be visited by travellers' (*Lives*, iii. 350). As Fred Parker notes, 'Johnson's dignifying style mimics Shenstone's gardening activities in raising a "little domain" into something considerable, something of significance.'[45] The effect here is more obviously comic than in the passage on Inch Kenneth, since Johnson's dignifying style yields suddenly to the plainly phrased assertion that Shenstone 'valued what he valued merely for its looks' (*Lives*, iii. 352). Johnson seems instinctively suspicious of poets' gardens—a suspicion that is bound up with his dislike of retirement, of 'silence and retreat' (see his remarks on Pope's grotto, 'Life of Pope', *Lives*, iii. 134–5).

The Inch Kenneth excerpt, then, like the passage on 'Raasay or Dunvegan', plays on the fact that to write romance in the eighteenth century is to write in an inherently outmoded form, one which is

---

[45] Parker, *Scepticism and Literature*, 269.

structured on 'a delightful contrariety of images' (*Yale*, ix. 66).[46] It marries the threat of primitive barbarity with exquisitely cultivated feelings.[47] Parodic romances push this odd combination to its logical extremities. The effect is alternately to translate a heightened fiction into a low reality, and a degraded reality into an exaggerated fiction. Thus Arabella, heroine of Lennox's *Female Quixote*, whose mind has been as 'disorder'd' by tempestuous chivalric exploits as that of her male predecessor, mistakes a dishevelled prostitute for a 'Lovely Unknown', whom she implores for 'the History of your Misfortunes', and an ineffectual fop for a demented would-be rapist.[48] Hence, too, a ludicrous episode in Austen's 'Jack & Alice' (written c.1787–90), in which the quivering sensibilities of the female characters allow them to overlook the fact that the victim with whom they are ardently, abstractedly sympathizing is, more 'apparently' to us than to them, caught by the leg in a man-trap: 'A lovely young Woman lying apparently in great pain beneath a Citron-tree, was an object too interesting not to attract their notice ... "You seem fair Nymph to be labouring under some misfortune which we shall be happy to releive if you will inform us what it is. Will you kindly favour us with your Life & adventures?" ' (*Works*, vi. 20).[49] The courteous and barbaric, emotional and physical extremes of romance seem, in this respect, an appropriate form in which to cast Johnson's experience of Scotland: a country that has somehow arrived at the heights of elegant learning and of polite conversation without attaining basic domestic 'conveniencies' (*Yale*, ix. 28). So it is, perhaps, unsurprising that chivalric romance should often turn out to be synonymous with Scottish reality.

Boswell wrote that, 'like the ancient Greeks and Romans, [Johnson] allowed himself to look upon all nations but his own as barbarians'—as gross herdsmen and amphibious fishermen, for instance (*Tour*, 9). And Thomas R. Preston notes that 'cultural development in the Highlands is related in Johnson's mind to the larger question of "barbarous" and "civilized" states in general, a question the Augustans tended to treat in terms of standard beliefs about heroic Greece ... The hortatory sociological analysis of the *Journey* is informed with allusions to Homeric matter

---

[46] See Auerbach, *Mimesis*, 134–7.

[47] See Northrop Frye, *The Secular Scripture: A Study of the Structure of Romance* (Cambridge, Mass.: Harvard University Press, 1976), 161–77.

[48] Charlotte Lennox, *The Female Quixote, or, The Adventures of Arabella*, ed. Margaret Dalziel, introd. Margaret Anne Doody (Oxford: Oxford University Press, 1989), 301, 335–6, 298–301.

[49] Austen was reading *The Female Quixote* for at least the second time in 1807, as she tells Cassandra on 7 January (*Jane Austen's Letters*, 116).

and its traditional interpretation.'[50] Hence the intermittent references to Odysseus in the *Journey* (see, for instance, the complimentary comparison of 'Raasay' to 'Phaeacia', *Yale*, ix. 66). The ancients appear by turns as markers of civilization and of barbarity. The Scots are sometimes cast as Greeks or as Romans, at other times as the objects of Roman cultivation—and therefore against the English, hoping to recover the foundations of their own civility: 'Men are softened by intercourse mutually profitable, and instructed by comparing their own notions with those of others. Thus Caesar found the maritime parts of Britain made less barbarous by their commerce with the Gauls'; 'Like the Greeks in their unpolished state, described by Thucydides, the Highlanders, till lately, went always armed, and carried their weapons to visits, and to church'; 'the Highlanders were unwilling to lay aside their plaid, which yet to an unprejudiced spectator must appear an incommodious and cumbersome dress ... The Romans always laid aside the gown when they had any thing to do. It was a dress so unsuitable to war, that the same word which signified a gown signified peace' (*Yale*, ix. 43–4, 45, 52).

But the distinction between 'rudeness' and 'elegance' provides the most common ground for comparisons between Scotland and England in the *Journey*. The 'RUDE', defined (in part) as 'inelegant' in the *Dictionary* (sense 6), may stand for the opposite of stylistic precision, as well as for the opposite of social graces: 'RUDELY' is 'Without exactness' (part of sense 2), while 'RUDE' is 'Rough; savage; coarse of manners; uncivil; brutal' (sense 1). Inexactness governs Johnson's self-reproach for having left Iona with 'rude measures of the buildings, such as I cannot much trust myself, inaccurately taken, and obscurely noted' (*Yale*, ix. 149). This opposition later surfaces in his 'Life of Pope', where he quotes from variant manuscript versions of *The Iliad* in order to reveal how his subject's mind developed 'from the rudeness of its first conceptions to the elegance of its last' (*Lives*, iii. 125–6). Elegance implies not only a precision arrived at by labouring over lines and phrases, but also (in view of the etymology of the word) Pope's refined ability to choose between several things. Rude, naked necessity implies the absence or diminution of that choice, in life as in writing: 'I sent for fresh hay, with which we made beds to ourselves, each in a room equally miserable. As Wolfe said in his letter from Quebec, we had "choice of difficulties." Mr. Johnson made things better by comparison ... he said we were better than if we

<hr />

[50] Thomas R. Preston, 'Homeric Allusion in *A Journey to the Western Islands of Scotland*', *Eighteenth-Century Studies*, 5 (1972), 545–58 (p. 546).

had been upon the hill'; 'As we were to catch the first favourable breath, we spent the night not very elegantly, nor pleasantly in the vessel' (*Tour*, 112; *Yale*, ix. 137). Here, by adding 'nor pleasantly' to 'not very elegantly', Johnson seems to be underlining the elective aspect of elegance; he and Boswell had no other option than to spend the night thus. It was an inelegant experience because it was involuntary. For the 'elegant' is already 'pleasant', but part of the reason for its being so is that it involves doing something 'at ease and *by choice*' (*Yale*, ix. 40; my emphasis).

3. THE RHETORIC OF DIMINUTION: LITOTES

Deriving from the Greek word 'litos', meaning plain, small, or meagre, litotes (also known as leptotes) is a variety of meiosis that might have been created to express the movements of a divided mind—perhaps especially of one that is divided about the value of elegance. Understated and emphatic, demure and assertive, it has long been associated with a refined show of modesty, or recommended in order to soften the impression of arrogant superiority. Like the diminutive form to which it is etymologically related, litotes may serve to weaken or to strengthen what it describes, or to strengthen a topic under the guise of weakening it. In the *Journey*, it frequently works to reinforce or to counter an expectation of rudeness or of elegance, by summoning up the English standard from which Scottish reality deviates or with which it unexpectedly concurs. It is therefore centrally concerned with eliciting differences and affiliations between the two countries, between the traveller and the scene he experiences: 'He said he would not wish to be disgusted in the Highlands, for that would be to lose the power of distinguishing, and a man might then lie down in the middle of them. He wished only to conceal his disgust' (Boswell reporting Johnson in *Tour*, 307–8).

Burke's comments on the distinction, when writing, between creating resemblances and creating differences help to define Johnson's litotes as a form of mediation that is neither affirmation nor negation: it is a means of occupying 'the middle' without losing 'the power of distinguishing'. The fact that this passage from Burke's *Enquiry* itself creates a series of distinctions rather than a series of resemblances, while simultaneously expressing a preference for the latter, reveals a writer in two minds even about the value of being in two minds:

When two distinct objects are unlike to each other, it is only what we expect; things are in their common way; and therefore they make no impression on the imagination: but when two distinct objects have a resemblance, we are struck, we attend to them, and we are pleased. The mind of man has naturally a far greater alacrity and satisfaction in tracing resemblances than in searching for differences; because by making resemblances we produce *new images*, we unite, we create, we enlarge our stock; but in making distinctions we offer no food at all to the imagination; the task itself is more severe and irksome; and what pleasure we derive from it is something of a negative and indirect nature. (*Enquiry*, 17–18)

Yet Burke is often prone to indulge in the pleasures of the 'negative and indirect' figure that is litotes, especially the phrase 'no small . . .' (See, for instance, 'a degree of delight, and that no small one', 'not an unmixed delight, but blended with no small uneasiness', 'no small terror', 'no small sublimity', 'no small violence', *Enquiry*, 45–6, 58, 66–7.) He seems, in practice, to experience as much delight in tracing the distinction between two superficially proximate objects or activities as in describing their affinities with one another. Johnson himself sought pleasure in the distinction between Scotland and England, and was disappointed to find it in many ways resembling the country he had left. His fondness for litotes in the *Journey* might appear to spring from a lexicographer's habit of defining things by their contraries (sense 2 of the adjective 'LITTLE' in the *Dictionary* is 'Not great', for instance), but his tendency to judge according to at least two viewpoints is a lifelong characteristic: the *Life of Savage*, which pre-dates the *Dictionary*, shows an even greater frequency of litotes than his *Journey*.

Throughout that *Journey*, litotes is an imprecise measure of exactness, if (as Ingham argues) exactness is one aspect of what Johnson takes elegance to mean. In St Andrews, for instance, litotes conveys the idea of a physical threshold between exterior and interior, while it also acts as a semantic hedge between elegance and inelegance: 'The chapel of the alienated college is yet standing, a fabrick *not inelegant* of external structure; but I was always, by some civil excuse, hindred from entering it' (*Yale*, ix. 7; my emphasis). Here, litotes registers a hesitant judgement due to Johnson's inability to enter indoors; he is therefore equally unable to enter into an unqualified assertion of 'elegance'. Aptly enough, 'some civil excuse'—which is itself a kind of elegance—is the barrier to such an assertion, so that 'not inelegant' appears to be compassing the Scotsman's polite fudges as well as the building's uncertain appearance. Civil uncertainty governs double negatives of the same kind in the *Journey* and in Johnson's letters from Scotland, expressing the middle ground between elegance and inelegance that characterizes his surroundings: 'a young woman *not inelegant* either in mien or dress'; 'a hut, that is, a house of only one floor, but with windows and chimney, and *not inelegantly* furnished'; 'The churches of the two convents are both standing, though unroofed. They were built of unhewn stone, but solid, and *not inelegant*'; 'The Highland Girl made tea, and looked and talked *not inelegantly*'; 'Raarsa himself is a man [of] *no inelegant* appearance, and of manners uncommonly refined' (*Yale*, ix. 37, 121, 149; *Letters*, ii. 72, 82; my emphases). The effect is much more decisive when he bluntly refutes any evidence of civility. Litotes compasses inelegant domesticity in an elegant style that will not descend to recite all of its disgusting attributes. Here, the gap between English traveller and Scottish reality is heightened: 'Of the provisions the negative catalogue was very copious. Here was no meat, no milk, no bread, no eggs, no wine ... Other circumstances of *no elegant* recital concurred to disgust us' (*Yale*, ix. 48; my emphasis).

Litotes would not work in statements such as 'the sea was not blue', for which there is no obvious contrary quality. Yet the degree to which, say, St Paul's 'no mean city', cited in Chapter 2, implies a grand, a very grand, or a reasonably well-appointed metropolis is hard to determine. By affirming something through negating its opposite, litotes leaves the nature of that affirmation, and of the speaker's commitment to it, unclear. A categorical indeterminacy continues to hover about the thing being described, as if the speaker is better acquainted with what she or he is denying than with what she or he is asserting. Litotes and ten other figures (including antithesis, irony, paradox, and paralipsis) are related to the rhetorical topic of invention called opposites, of which there are four types: contraries, relatives, privatives, and contradictories.[51] Litotes based on the first three categories is often indeterminate. Although immediately contradictory qualities (life/death, for example) may appear to have no species between them—so that one or the other is necessarily asserted—mediate contraries produce a broad range of options between two things. Thus relative forms of litotes (such as 'no few' and 'not many'), or privatives ('not hate', say, which could mean love, like, dislike, or indifference), may also be indecisive and non-committal.

Quentin Skinner writes that, among Quintilian's *figurae sententiarum*, meiosis is 'especially susceptible of being applied in a contemptuous or reproachful way': a point that was further emphasized by Tudor

---

[51] See Elizabeth McCutcheon, 'Denying the Contrary: More's Use of Litotes in the *Utopia*', *Moreana: Bulletin Thomas More*, 8 (1971), 107–21 (pp. 116–17). My overview of litotes is indebted to this article. See also Claudia Caffi, 'Litote', *Journal of Pragmatics*, 13 (1989), 903–12.

rhetoricians. George Puttenham sees meiosis as tending to abase or to diminish a topic through spite, resulting in contempt for the speaker's adversary. Skinner also observes that, for Henry Peacham, although litotes is perceived as creating the impression of modesty, it can be deployed 'with malice and arrogance'.[52] The anonymous author of *The Whores Rhetorick* (1683)—had his aged speaker not determined to leave unnamed 'the Tropes and Figures' in whose deployment she is instructing her eager charge—might have numbered litotes among the devices that characterize 'the art' of speaking in 'insinuating words', 'ambiguous expressions', and 'synonymous terms', in order 'to equivocate, vary and double, according to your fancy and the present circumstances: all which do extreamly enhaunce the value of your words; and add a particular gallantry to your discourse'.[53] In the early eighteenth century, the slipperiness of litotes continues to have associations with an insinuating, gossipy malice, as well as with refinement and with elegance—at least for Martinus Scriblerus, who elicits a class distinction when he observes that: 'The *Periphrasis* or *Circumlocution* is the peculiar Talent of *Country Farmers*, ... the *Litotes* or Diminution of *Ladies*, *Whisperers* and *Backbiters*' (*Peri Bathous*, Pope, *Prose*, 203). Sniping, catty, backbiting diminution comes across in Richardus Aristarchus' view of Dulness as 'a Goddess of *no small* power and authority amongst men' from whom Cibber, newly minted anti-hero of the 1743 *Dunciad*, claims direct lineage ('RICHARDUS ARISTARCHUS OF THE HERO OF THE POEM', *Dunciad*, 264; my emphasis). Ten years earlier, John Stirling had viewed litotes more neutrally, as a form of 'Lessening' that is simultaneously an expansion and an emphasis: '*Litotes* does more Sense than Words include, | And often by two Negatives has stood.'[54]

By repeatedly describing Scotland as 'not inelegant', Johnson employs a construction to which, as Elizabeth McCutcheon notes, classical writers and Thomas More were especially partial, and which Stirling notices—a negative followed by the negative form of an adjective. Like More's recurrent use of litotes in *Utopia* (1516), a use which McCutcheon describes as 'a paradigm of the structure and method of the book as a whole, echoing, often in the briefest of syntactical units, the larger, paradoxical and double vision which will discover the best state of the

[52] Quentin Skinner, *Reason and Rhetoric in the Philosophy of Hobbes* (Cambridge: Cambridge University Press, 1996), 209–10.
[53] Anon., *The Whores Rhetorick (1683): A Facsimile Reproduction*, introd. James R. Irvine and G. Jack Gravlee (Delmar, NY: Scholars' Facsimiles and Reprints, 1979), 36, 39, 42–3.
[54] John Stirling, *A System of Rhetoric* (1733), ed. R. C. Alston (Menston: Scolar Press, 1968), 2.

commonwealth in an island called Noplace',[55] this economical figure comes in Johnson to stand for the double vision of his entire *Journey*: for its assertions and for its denials of progress, elegance, and refinement, and for the advantages and disadvantages of such qualities. Small things, 'but little' as they may be, are the best place to look for evidence of a progressive refinement (or of its absence), as elegance is itself to be located in a precise attention to minutiae—although, as was previously noted, Johnson is also unsure about how desirable such an attention might be.

It is therefore an index of the reader's own refinement to be able to notice shades and degrees of meaning such as those conveyed through litotes. In the *Journey*, the figure implies a quality of determinedly hesitant, minutely enquiring, and intellectually rigorous perception that endeavours to arrive at the truth, but is equally conscious that it may have to conclude in uncertainty (in which case, to express its findings in a more overt or decisive form than that of litotes would be to exaggerate, or to produce a fiction). This quality was, Johnson felt, lacking in many of the Scots he met: 'He that travels in the Highlands may easily saturate his soul with intelligence, if he will acquiesce in the first account. The Highlander gives to every question an answer so prompt and peremptory, that skepticism itself is dared into silence, and the mind sinks before the bold reporter in unresisting credulity'; 'They have inquired and considered little, and do not always feel their own ignorance'; 'A Scotchman must be a very sturdy moralist, who does not love Scotland better than truth: he will always love it better than inquiry; and if falsehood flatters his vanity, will not be very diligent to detect it' (*Yale*, ix. 51, 117, 119; see also *Tour*, 335−6).

For Johnson, the inherently doubtful form of litotes had a close association with scruples. He was 'afraid of scruples' and, in Scotland, proclaimed himself 'no friend to scruples', although he also criticized the Scots for being 'not very scrupulous adherents to truth' (*Letters*, ii. 295; Johnson in *Tour*, 41; *Journey*, 117). But to be wholly without scruples is impossible and undesirable, even if the morally opprobrious quality of being 'unscrupulous' is not in Johnson's *Dictionary* (according to the *OED*, it does not come into use until the early nineteenth century). The fact that he expressed his own suspicion of scruples so scrupulously—through the figure of litotes, and as 'no friend' to them, rather than stating less equivocally that he was their 'enemy'—suggests that his *Dictionary* definition of the noun 'SCRUPLE' might also stand as a

---

[55] McCutcheon, 'Denying the Contrary', 108–10.

definition of litotes itself: 'Doubt; difficulty of determination; perplexity: generally about minute things.' Those who are 'exceedingly scrupulous', he argued, 'and find their scrupulosity invincible', are unfit for the world. But he did not number himself among such people: 'I have thought of retiring, and have talked of it to a friend, but I find my vocation is rather to active life' (Johnson in *Tour*, 41–2). The relationship of litotes to what is inherently and necessarily 'doubtful' or perplexing in 'active life' comes across when Johnson considers Savage's murder of James Sinclair, 'an Event, of which it is not yet determined, whether it ought to be mentioned as a Crime or a Calamity': 'The Nature of the Act for which he had been tried was in itself *doubtful*; of the Evidences which appeared against him, the Character of the Man was *not unexceptionable*' (*Savage*, 30, 40; my emphases).

Litotes can be scrupulously indecisive about the use of being scrupulous—like Burke's comments on negatives, it then has the effect of seeming doubtful about the value of doubt, an effect which makes something serious of the joke 'I used to be indecisive, but now I'm not so sure'. In the *Life of Savage*, Johnson perpetuates his scrupulous uncertainty about scrupulousness: 'It cannot but be imagined, that such Representations of his Faults must make great Numbers less sensible of his Distress; many who had only an Opportunity to hear one Part, made *no Scruple* to propagate the Account which they received'; 'This was a Distinction to which [he] made *no Scruple* of asserting that his Birth, his Misfortunes, and his Genius gave him a fairer Title, than could be pleaded by him on whom it was conferred' (*Savage*, 68, 103; my emphases). The one-sided 'Account' of Savage's 'Faults', propagated by those who 'made no Scruple' about its authenticity, is placed in a contrasting relationship to Johnson's scrupulously authentic, and therefore double-minded *Account of the Life of Mr. Richard Savage*. The second occurrence of 'no Scruple' instead refers to Savage's claims on royal patronage and on public favour. The phrasing here allows us to agree with Johnson that, on the one hand, Savage's birth, misfortunes, and genius *did* entitle him to notice and support; on the other, that it might better have served his interests to have been more circumspect. Because Johnson thinks it unequivocally true that Savage was robbed of one title, to which he had a perfectly just claim, at birth, he is also in two minds about the prudence or imprudence of Savage's seizing 'the Title of *Volunteer Laureat*' (*Savage*, 79).

Nearly fifty years after Johnson's *Journey* was published, Charles Lamb complained about a Scottish resistance to indirect, fuzzy, or uncertain language—about the native exaggeration of doubtful into unequivocal evidence—a complaint that chimes with the *Journey*'s description of the Highlander as one who 'gives to every question an answer so prompt and peremptory, that skepticism itself is dared into silence'. It is against this tendency that Johnson could be said to have deployed his sceptical use of litotes. The 'metaphor' in Lamb's essay is Johnson himself, if we take him to be 'a suspected person in an enemy's country': 'You cannot hover with [a Scotsman] upon the confines of truth, or wander in the maze of a probable argument. He always keeps the path. You cannot make excursions with him—for he sets you right'; 'He cannot compromise, or understand middle actions'; 'He stops a metaphor like a suspected person in an enemy's country'; 'Above all, you must beware of indirect expressions before a Caledonian.'[56] Lamb's 'indirect expressions' might include litotes as it appears in the *Journey*, a figure borne of a dubiously antithetical cast of mind that fluctuates between the romantic and the empirical, the straight path and the devious excursion, between elegant progress and barbaric rudeness. The figure permits Johnson to hover on the confines of truth, to wander in the labyrinthine, Miltonic mazes of doubt and probability, and, especially, to compass a range of 'middle actions' and of intermediate states in Scotland.

McCutcheon remarks that More's 'denied negations' comment 'pointedly, on aspects of life elsewhere'; his 'general and ironic "awareness of a contradiction between the two worlds" . . . is made much more precise by way of litotic contrasts'.[57] Yet litotes, as she proceeds to note, is also an imprecise tool, residing in Johnson's *Journey* as in More's *Utopia* between the foreign and the native. A particularly tricky form of ambivalence emerges from the psychological oddity of negating a negation in passages such as this one about Inch Kenneth: 'It was *not without* some mournful emotion that we contemplated the ruins of religious structures, and the monuments of the dead' (*Yale*, ix. 144; my emphasis). Why does Johnson not assert that he felt 'some mournful emotion', a feeling that is already indeterminate? Partly, perhaps, because of his scrupulous aversion to such spectacles (Boswell writes of Johnson's 'horror at dead men's bones', *Tour*, 319); partly because 'mournful emotion' is itself hard to articulate, and sticks in the throat; and partly because this scene is a 'proper prelude' to the 'ruins of Iona', where every man's 'piety' ought to 'grow warmer'. Even there, however, Johnson's piety remains unfocused and curiously reluctant, and he resorts to virtually the same double

---

[56] Charles Lamb, 'Imperfect Sympathies' (1821), in *Selected Prose*, ed. Adam Phillips (Harmondsworth: Penguin, 1985), 115.
[57] McCutcheon, 'Denying the Contrary', 114.

negative as in the passage on Inch Kenneth, 'nor . . . without', as well as to the same experience of 'some emotion': 'We now left those illustrious ruins, by which Mr. Boswell was much affected, nor would I willingly be thought to have looked upon them without some emotion' (*Yale*, ix. 144, 148, 153). By imagining how he looks to a reader (a conjecture encouraged, perhaps, by Boswell's excitement: 'the seeing of Mr. Samuel Johnson at Icolmkill [Iona] was what I had often imaged as a very venerable scene', *Tour*, 331), he removes himself still further from his original experience of looking on the ruins, and therefore saps his narration of its immediacy. But at the same time, he suggests a perturbing recalcitrance in the face of such a scene, a recalcitrance that serves to heighten our impression of a strong feeling of *some* kind.

Since litotes as a rhetorical and literary technique may intensify a statement, so that, as John Smith points out, '*sometimes a word is put down with a sign of negation, when as much is signified as if we had spoken affirmatively; if not more*',[58] Johnson's recurrent phrase 'not inelegant' may be either stronger or weaker than 'elegant'. How we interpret this depends on the context—on whether he has English or Scottish standards in mind, for instance—but we are always called upon to hesitate about the degree to which a particular example of litotes is tempering, and to what extent it is emphasizing, its topic. Better still, we should attempt to hold two apparently contradictory effects in our minds at the same time. Each instance of litotes therefore brings the author into closer contact with the reader, who tries to replicate, as best she or he can, the original mental and judicial processes that produced the need for this trope in the first place.

4. A SCOTTISH SAVAGE

As Puttenham remarked, litotes is a '*Sensable*' figure that should '*alter and affect the minde by alteration of sense*'.[59] The advocacy of ancient rhetoric is implied here, so it is not surprising that the *Life of Savage*, the most legalistic of all Johnson's biographies—both in the sense of its

[58] John Smith, *The Mystery of Rhetorick Unveil'd. Wherein above 130 of the Tropes and Figures are severally derived from the Greek into English; together with lively Definitions, and Variety of Latin, English, Scriptural Examples, pertinent to each of them apart. Eminently delightful and profitable for young Scholars, and others of all sorts, enabling them to discern and imitate the Elegancy in any Author they read, & c.* (London: for George Eversden, 1683), 'Litotes' ('The Index').

[59] George Puttenham, *The Arte of English Poesie*, ed. George Doidge Willcock and Alice Walker (Cambridge: Cambridge University Press, 1936; repr. 1970) 178.

descriptions of divorce proceedings, murder, trials, debts, and prisons, and in the sense of its painfully judicious weighings-up of one form of evidence against another—should also be the work in which he calls most often on litotes. Johnson employs the figure to alter and to affect our minds about Savage, a slippery character 'of complicated Virtue' whose friendship was '*no* very *certain* possession' (*Savage*, 40, 45; my emphases). Yet it is also true that the alternatives he asks us to consider stem from Johnson's trusting reactions to his friend in the first place. Boswell was not swayed by Savage's claims to nobility:

Johnson's partiality for Savage made him entertain *no doubt* of his story, however extraordinary and improbable. It never occurred to him to question his being the son of the Countess of Macclesfield, of whose unrelenting barbarity he so loudly complained, and the particulars of which are related in so strong and affecting a manner in Johnson's life of him ... I have received such information and remarks, as joined to my own inquiries, will, I think, render it at least somewhat *doubtful*. (*Life*, i. 169–70; my emphases)

So litotes makes us conscious of a specifically directed authorial intelligence, 'perpetually on the wing, excursive, vigorous, and diligent, eager to pursue knowledge, and attentive to retain it' ('Life of Pope', *Lives*, iii. 216): an intelligence that begins by asserting in the subtitle of Savage's *Life* that he is indeed '*Son of the Earl Rivers*'. Stanislaus Joyce noted 'the significance of ... unregarded trifles, delicately weighed, in assaying states of mind', and 'states of mind', as expressed through litotes, hover between the writer, his subject, and the reader.[60] The figure reminds us of certain ongoing divisions in Johnson's thinking, of his moral and literary sympathies and choices (hence, too, of his elegance)—as well as of his intermittent refusal or inability to make such choices. Litotes can therefore operate as a form of free indirect style, signalling an uncertainty in Johnson's mind as well as one in his subject's: 'What was intended, and whither they were to go, *Savage* could not conjecture, and was *not willing* to enquire' (*Savage*, 14; second emphasis mine).

The fact that Johnson repeatedly employs litotes in the *Life of Savage* as well as in his *Journey* is in many ways appropriate. For Savage—'a Man whose Writings entitle him to an eminent Rank in the Classes of Learning, and whose Misfortunes claim a Degree of Compassion, *not always* due to the unhappy' (*Savage*, 4; my emphasis)—shares some key qualities with Scotland: the tragic loss of 'a legal Claim to Honour and to

---

[60] Stanislaus Joyce, *My Brother's Keeper* (1958), ed. Richard Ellmann, introd. T. S. Eliot (London: Faber and Faber, 1982), 137.

Riches', and therefore of autonomy (*Savage*, 6); a peculiar combination of extreme refinement with extreme coarseness, of the noblest conduct with the depths of vagrant destitution; and a romantic history that, seemingly unknown to Johnson in spite of his and Savage's famous invectives 'against the minister' when 'brimful of patriotism' in St James's Square (*Life*, i. 164), had first been brought to light by the Jacobite rebellion. (Before the rising broke out in September 1715, Savage had composed at least two pieces of doggerel, *An Ironical Panegyrick on his Pretended Majesty G*—and *The Pretender*. He was arrested in November on the charge of possessing a treasonable pamphlet and used the occasion to name himself for the first time as Rivers's natural, disinherited son. *The Wanderer: A Vision* (1729), with its references to 'Rebellion's Council, and Rebellion's Fall', shows a continuing self-identification with the exiled Stuart claimant.)[61]

As in the *Journey*, in the *Life of Savage* Johnson negotiates his subject's contradictory qualities through indirectly persuasive means from the first paragraph onwards:

IT has been observed in all Ages, that the Advantages of Nature or of Fortune have contributed very little to the Promotion of Happiness; and that those whom the Splendor of their Rank, or the Extent of their Capacity, have placed upon the Summits of human Life, have *not often* given any just Occasion to Envy in those who look up to them from a lower Station . . .

That Affluence and Power, Advantages extrinsic and adventitious, and therefore easily separable from those by whom they are possessed, should very often flatter the Mind with Expectation of Felicity which they cannot give, raises *no Astonishment*; but it seems rational to hope, that intellectual Greatness should produce better Effects, that Minds qualified for great Attainments should first endeavour their own Benefit, and that they who are most able to teach others the Way to Happiness, should with most Certainty follow it themselves. (*Savage*, 3; my emphases)

'IT has been observed in all Ages . . .', by virtue of its familiarity, could itself be classed as a 'diminutive observation'. But Johnson had already implied a *personal* observation of this truth in the advertisement to his *Life*, warning any possible competitors that it was 'not credible' that they could 'obtain the same Materials' as Savage's close friend (quoted in *Savage*, 'Introduction', p. xi and n. 2). The effect of this opening resembles the bathetic contractions of scope afforded by ending the

---

[61] See Clarence Tracy, *The Artificial Bastard: A Biography of Richard Savage* (Toronto: University of Toronto Press in co-operation with the University of Saskatchewan, 1953), 29–32, 102.

Journey on the fragmentary or depreciatory 'but little', by closing the
Life of Savage itself on the word 'contemptible', or by directing *Rambler*
2 towards a 'truth' which turns out to be smaller than a syntax of
rising 'Expectation' has led us to hope. If the well-known fact with
which Johnson begins his *Life* 'raises no Astonishment', however, it has
nevertheless raised something—the expectation of that astonishment. A
residue of the public's appetite for great events is left in the text, in spite
of its being officially negated, and the remainder of this sentence then
turns its attention to recovering some optimism and anticipation of what
is to come: 'but it seems rational to hope . . .'

The author of *Ad Herennium*, in common with many English Tudor
rhetoricians, recommends the use of litotes—which he calls 'Deminutio',
or 'Understatement'—as one means to establish a speaker's modesty.
This possibility is in evidence when Johnson suggests of the novel, in
Rambler 4, that 'This kind of writing may be termed *not improperly* the
comedy of romance' (*Yale*, iii. 19; my emphasis). Litotes is also, for this
reason, useful to a rhetorical defence:

Understatement occurs when we say that by nature, fortune, or diligence, we
or our clients possess some exceptional advantage, and, in order to avoid the
impression of arrogant display, we moderate and soften the statement of it, as
follows: 'This, men of the jury, I have the right to say—that by labour and
diligence I have contrived to be no laggard in the mastery of military science.' If
the speaker had here said 'be the best' he might have spoken the truth, but would
have seemed arrogant. He has now said quite enough both to avoid envy and to
secure praise . . . This, then, is the precaution we shall take in setting forth the
exceptional advantages which we or our clients enjoy. For things of this sort, if
you handle them indiscreetly, in life provoke jealousy and in a speech antipathy.
Therefore just as by circumspection we escape jealousy in life, so by prudence we
avoid antipathy in speaking.[62]

Peacham, drawing on this passage, described litotes thus:

Lyptote, when more is understoode then is sayd, . . . thus, he setteth not a little
by his Sonne, that is, hee loueth his Sonne dearlye, he is not the wysest man in
the worlde, and I am sorrye for it, meaning that he is no wyser then a foole, I
will not be unmindfull of your matters, that is, I will always haue them in mind
or wel remember them, they were matters of no smal accoumpte, that is, they
were matters of great weight and importāce. Act. Apost. 12. There was not a little
ado: We use this fygure in extenuating our owne cunning deedes and praises, to
auoyde the suspeicion of arrogancy and boasting, thus, we are not so unskilful of
matters, that we be ignoraunt in this cause, what is to be done, or not to be done,

[62] *Ad C. Herennium*, iv. xxxviii. 50.

likewyse, I haue not bene a Niggard of my Pursse, amonge suche as had neede: I haue not eaten my meate all alone: I was not the laste in the Fyelde to fyght against the Ennemyes of my Country: I was not esteemed the worste with the King and the Noble men, nowe if he shoulde haue sayde, I haue bene liberall of my purse among poore men, I haue spent my meate amonge good fellows, I was the first in the field to fyght for my countrey, I was best esteemed with the King & noble men, he should have bene thought arrogant in his sayinge, although he had sayde truelye, yet is there [enough] sayd to get prayse.[63]

This summary, up to the point of the citation from the Bible (Acts 12: 18), might stand as a miniature narrative, or as a compressed Machiavellian curriculum in self-advancement via litotes. The move from a superficially complimentary third person to the insinuating first person suggests a courtier whispering in the ear of the next-but-one-in-line: 'the son and heir is indeed dear to his fond father, but that son (or his father) is, in fact, a fool; I will promote your interests; you can trust me.' And what Peacham says about litotes at the end of his account is itself not strictly true: the potentially deceptive element of the trope is that we may *assume* that to say 'I was not the last in the field' means 'I was the first in the field'—but it could, in fact, mean 'I was the second to last', or indeed anywhere else on the scale other than at the very bottom. Falstaff's shifty answer to Harry's question, 'What, fought you with them all?', springs to mind: 'All? I know not what you call all, but if I fought not with fifty of them, I am a bunch of radish. If there were not two- or three-and-fifty upon poor old Jack, then am I no two-legged creature.'[64]

Peacham's emphasis on how litotes may extenuate cunning deeds, or deflect suspicion away from the speaker (a potential and cynical interpretation of how Johnson manages to extenuate Savage's misdemeanours, and to cover his own tracks), is not as immediately obvious in Puttenham's account of litotes, or 'the *Moderator*'. This name suggests the figure's appropriateness to conceive of Scotland, as Johnson does, in terms of even its best-educated sons' 'mediocrity of knowledge, between learning and ignorance, *not inadequate* to the purposes of common life', or to his conjectures of an earlier period of Scottish history that 'The inhabitants were for a long time perhaps *not unhappy*; but their content was a muddy mixture of pride and ignorance' (*Yale*, ix. 160, 89; my emphases). For litotes is itself a 'muddy mixture', or a 'mediocrity' of assertion ('MEDIOCRITY' is defined as 'Small degree;

---

[63] Henry Peacham, *The Garden of Eloquence* (1577), ed. R. C. Alston (Menston: Scolar Press, 1971), Hii–Hiii.
[64] William Shakespeare, *The Complete Works, I Henry IV*, ii. v. 185–9.

middle rate; middle state' and as 'Moderation; temperance' in Johnson's
Dictionary):

As by the former figure [Emphasis] we vse to enforce our sence, so by another we
temper our sence with wordes of such moderation, as in appearaunce it abateth it
but not in deede, and is by the figure *Liptote*, which therefore I call the *Moderator*,
and becomes vs many times better to speake in that sort quallified, than if we
spake it by more forcible termes, and neuerthelesse is equipolent in sence, thus.

> *I know you hate me not, nor wish me any ill.*

Meaning in deede that he loued him very well and dearely, and yet the wordes
doe not expresse so much, though they purport so much. Or if you would say,
I am not ignorant, for I know well inough. Such a man is no foole, meaning in
deede that he is a very wise man.[65]

This seems more affectionate and straightforward than Peacham,
although it similarly implies that a wise man will make use of litotes
in order to praise someone else's good qualities (and by extension his
own). But again, like Peacham, Puttenham simplifies and exaggerates
the trope's potential. 'You hate me not' does not necessarily translate as
'you love me very well'; 'No foole' does not necessarily mean, 'in deede',
'a very wise man'. This is merely the strongest possible opposition of
surface to hidden meaning that litotes is capable of sustaining. But the
figure also covers a whole range of possibilities between the two poles of
love and hate, between wisdom and ignorance.

The love/hate opposition in Puttenham suggests that litotes may be
associated with friendship on the one hand, and with biography on the
other, as well as with the distinction between the two. In *Idler* 84, Johnson
asserted, in terms as strongly opposed to one another as Puttenham's,
that: 'He that writes the life of another is either his friend or his enemy,
and wishes either to exalt his praise or aggravate his infamy' (*Yale*, ii.
263). Yet in practice, litotes allows him to mediate judiciously between
the two extremes of friendship and enmity, between praise and blame,
as Savage oscillated from one to the other through life. Johnson often
does so via legalistic language: 'when he was pardoned and released he
found the Number of his Friends *not lessened*'; 'He was accused likewise
of living in an Appearance of Friendship with some whom he satirised,
and of making use of the Confidence which he gained by a seeming
Kindness to discover Failings and expose them; it must be confessed, that
[his] Esteem was *no* very *certain* Possession, and that he would lampoon

---

[65] Puttenham, *English Poesie*, 184.

at one Time those whom he had praised at another'; 'he had *not often* a Friend long, without obliging him to become a Stranger'; 'His Story, though in Reality *not less* melancholy, was less affecting, because it was no longer new; it therefore procured him *no new* Friends' (*Savage*, 40, 45, 60, 68; my emphases).

Litotes can help to assimilate an eccentric, singular character into the broader ethical community. By referring Savage's conduct to that of others in the same circumstances, Johnson implicitly answers readers' objections that his subject's 'Peculiarity of ... Character', by virtue of its strangeness, cannot apply to their own: 'that the Anger of Mr. *Savage* should be kept alive is *not strange*, because he felt every Day the Consequences of the Quarrel, but it might reasonably have been hoped, that Lord *Tyrconnel* might have relented, and at length have forgot those Provocations, which, however they might have once inflamed him, had not in Reality much hurt him' (*Savage*, 112, 69; second emphasis mine). The reasonable hope Johnson conjures up here recalls the second paragraph of his *Life* ('but it seems rational to hope ...'), and again it gives the impression of a mind counterbalancing aspiration and reason against real life and irrationality, involving the reader in the process of expecting great things and of judging lesser ones.

For Johnson, as for the author of *Ad Herennium*, litotes is also a way of measuring his subject's prudence, and of displaying his own; it shows a responsible variety of affection: 'Under such a Tutor' as Steele, Savage 'was *not likely* to learn Prudence or Frugality'; 'It is *not* indeed *unlikely*' that he 'might by his Imprudence have exposed himself to the Malice of a Tale-bearer'; Savage 'thought, with more Prudence than was often exerted by him, ... that the Propriety of his Observation would be *no Security* against the Censures which the Unseasonableness of it might draw upon him' (pp. 15, 16, 95; my emphases). Litotes in the *Life of Savage* frequently turns on the words 'likely' or 'unlikely'. In the context of pondering dubious evidence, hypothetical situations, or questionable aspects of Savage's conduct, it has seriously considered results for the defence or for the prosecution of his character more often than it has the comic, sly, or satirical associations elicited by Renaissance rhetoricians and by Scriblerus: 'It was therefore *not likely* that she [Savage's putative mother] would be wicked without Temptation'; 'if in so low a State he obtained Distinction and Rewards, it is *not likely* that they were gained but by Genius and Industry'; 'it is *not likely*, that in his earliest Years he received Admonitions with more Calmness [than in later life]' (*Savage*, 6, 8, 61; my emphases).

Like paralipsis, litotes is a figure of brinkmanship, permitting the author to display two competing moods and forms of evaluation at one and the same time: the elegant and the inelegant, the excluded and the included, the high and the low, the friendly and the inimical. McCutcheon rightly associates paralipsis (deriving from the Greek 'para', or 'side', and 'leipein', 'to leave')[66] with litotes: 'Understated instead of hyperbolic, [litotes] often seems to turn attention away from itself, like its cousin, paralipsis, which emphasizes something by pretending to ignore it, and it can disarm potential opponents and avoid controversy; yet it emphasizes whatever it touches.'[67] John Smith defined paralipsis as *'overpassing; it is a kind of an Ironie; and is when you say you pass by a thing, which yet with a certain elegancy you touch at full'*.[68] It allows Johnson to bestow praise on and to defend Savage's writings in the very act of saying he will not do so, showing a simultaneously inclusive and exclusive, critical and biographical sensibility that would come to fruition over thirty years later in the *Prefaces Biographical and Critical*:

But my Province is rather to give the History of Mr. *Savage*'s Performances, than to display their Beauties, or to obviate the Criticisms, which they have occasioned, and therefore I shall not dwell upon the particular Passages which deserve Applause: I shall neither show the Excellence of his Descriptions, nor expatiate on the terrific Portrait of *Suicide*, nor point out the artful Touches, by which he has distinguished the intellectual Features of the Rebels, who suffer Death in his last Canto. (*Savage*, 54–5)

These remarks are accompanied by more than a hundred lines of quotation, in the footnotes, from those passages in *The Wanderer* that Johnson is at once discussing and refusing to discuss.

Litotes and paralipsis are especially apt, and not necessarily ironic, figures for alluding to vacuities in the life of a man whose last known words were *'I have something to say to you, Sir, . . . 'Tis gone'* (*Savage*, 135). In the first half of the *Life*, Johnson (writing anonymously) tends to enter in his own person only for the express purpose of telling us about things he does *not* know, rather than about those that he does know (in which case he expresses himself through the passive voice). Such moments show us the strength of his desire for knowledge, and

[66] See 'Occultatio', in *Ad C. Herennium* iv. xxvii. 37; 'preteritio', in Peacham, *Garden of Eloquence*, Siiv; '*Paralepsis*, or the Passager', in Puttenham, *English Poesie*, 232; '*Paraleipsis* cries; I leav't behind; | I let it pass: tho' you the Whole may find', in Stirling, *A System of Rhetoric*, 7.
[67] McCutcheon, 'Denying the Contrary', 112.
[68] Smith, *Mystery of Rhetorick Unveil'd*, 'Paralipsis' ('The Index').

express the gap left by Savage's death that means further information will never be forthcoming. Like litotes, paralipsis also facilitates speculative judgements that must, finally, be left in the realms of uncertainty: 'What was the Success or Merit of this Performance I know not'; 'I know not whether he gained by his Performance any other Advantage than the Increase of his Reputation'; 'By whom this atrocious Calumny had been transmitted to the Queen, whether she that invented, had the Front to relate it; whether she found any one weak enough to credit it, or corrupt enough to concur with her in her hateful Design, I know not'; 'I know not whether he ever had, for three Months together, a settled Habitation, in which he could claim a Right of Residence' (*Savage*, 12, 30, 37, 52).

In what was originally intended to be the final paragraph of his biography (see *Savage*, 140 n. 103), Johnson turned his attention to a leisured reader who might be tempted to feel superior to Savage's life or to Savage's writing. The improprieties of his friend's conduct, as previously rehearsed through litotes, are now re-envisioned (again through litotes) in terms of the impropriety of such a reaction: 'Those are *no proper* Judges of his Conduct who have slumber'd away their Time on the Down of Plenty, nor will a wise Man easily presume to say, "Had I been in *Savage*'s Condition, I should have lived, or written, better than *Savage*" ' (*Savage*, 140; first emphasis mine). Readers may well arrive at such a conclusion, but the use of litotes is designed to ensure that the process of travelling to such a destination will not be 'easily', unreflectively, or swiftly accomplished. The figure displays and invites its audience to participate in stubbornly 'equipolent' impulses (in Puttenham's word), impulses that also account for Johnson having produced two different endings to the *Life* of a man whose 'Equity' was 'natural', and who was 'equally distinguished by his Virtues and Vices' (*Savage*, 19, 135).

In another biographical memoir, Stanislaus Joyce wrote of his brother James that:

In early youth, [he] had been in love, like all romantic poets, with vast conceptions, and had believed in the supreme importance of the world of ideas. His gods were Blake and Dante. But then the minute life of the earth claimed him, and he seems to regard with a kind of compassion his youth deluded by ideals that exacted all his service, 'the big words that make us so unhappy', as he called them . . .
    The faculty of ardent belief in the absolute is like the poet's gift. It does not come by fasting or praying or consuming midnight oil, but it hallmarks the man who possesses it. It hallmarked my brother even when he deliberately chose for his subject the commonplace person and the everyday incident, the things that are

despised. All his work is permeated by a kind of litotes which is the antithesis of romanticism; it might be considered the distinguishing characteristic of modern writing which signifies much more than it says.[69]

It is not the distinguishing characteristic of modern writing alone that it can signify much more than it says, and Stanislaus Joyce here expresses a truth about Johnson—a negatively capable figure who is himself often distorted into the 'antithesis of romanticism', but who sought, like James Joyce, to convert 'the bread of everyday life' into 'something that has a permanent artistic value of its own'.[70] Litotes may be constitutionally opposed to overstatement, yet Johnson's recurrent descent to 'the things that are despised' remains touched by his endeavour to arrive at 'the absolute': he was simultaneously drawn to 'vast conceptions' and to 'the minute life of the earth', and, most of all, to the possibility that they might be reconciled.

[69] Joyce, *My Brother's Keeper*, 53–4.
[70] James Joyce, ibid. 116.

4
Stooping to Conquer: Johnsonian Biography

Perhaps you think me stooping
I'm not ashamed of that
Christ—stooped until He touched the Grave—

Do those at Sacrament
Commemorate Dishonor
Or love annealed of love
Until it bend as low as Death
Redignified, above?[1]

Emily Dickinson's 'Perhaps . . .' might seem to issue from someone caught in the awkward, possibly habitual, posture of a bodily stoop; or, by extension, in an act of figurative self-abasement to an object beneath the speaker's or the onlooker's regard. Sense 2. c of the verb 'stoop' in the *OED* is: 'To condescend *to* one's inferiors or *to* some position or action below one's rightful dignity'; sense 2. d is: 'To lower or degrade oneself morally; to descend *to* something unworthy.' But it could also be that the speaker is kneeling or bowing, physically or figuratively, to a higher authority (see sense 2. a of the verb 'stoop' in the *OED*). The poem suggests the interdependence of both conditions: by charitably descending to their inferiors, human beings in turn subordinate themselves to a divinity that elected to become mortal. The poem moves from suggesting that the speaker might indeed, in stooping, be doing something unworthy, to a defence of stooping as a worthy attitude. Kneeling will be annealed. Spurred by the possible imputation of feeling 'ashamed', Dickinson makes her persona's descent take on the accents of defiance, transforming the low into the high in a manner that might be described as 'proud humility', the phrase with which Hazlitt characterized Wordsworth's

[1] Emily Dickinson, *The Complete Poems*, ed. Thomas H. Johnson (London: Faber and Faber, 1970; repr. 1982), no. 833 (*c.*1864).

'levelling' Muse.[2] 'And whosoever shall exalt himself shall be abased; and he that shall humble himself shall be exalted' (Matthew 23: 12).

Dickinson's is a positive defence of the 'voluntary degradation' Johnson mentioned in his preface to Baretti's *Easy Phraseology* (*Prefaces*, 11). For the speaker's stoop is revealed as a humble re-enactment of Christ's descent to be incarnated in human flesh—to 'bend as low as Death'—a consummate abrogation of superiority thereafter commemorated in the Eucharist. 'Stooping' implies a range of public attitudes and of private virtues, as well as of compromising situations poised between the two, depending on whether the context is the Christian virtue of humbling the self, or the classical spectacle of outright degradation. Initially preoccupied by appearances, Dickinson's speaker turns outwards and upwards, finally refusing, like Johnson, to plead guilty to the charges of 'abasement' and 'contempt'. So the poem's second line is self-corrective. Here, it becomes a 'Dishonor' to be ashamed of what is, from one perspective, the dishonourable act of stooping—one which will, in fact, be 'Redignified, above'. It is not entirely clear whether 'that' is the object of the stoop—the thing to which the speaker bends his or her attention—or the act of stooping. It seems to be a deictic, pointing either to the humble object of the persona's charitable aid or to the performance of self-humiliation itself. The dash and consequent pause after 'Christ' perhaps acknowledges that the fact that divinity sank so far beneath itself is a stumbling block to human comprehension. Or perhaps it represents a deferential gap between the merely human act of stooping, and a divine submission to mortality.

A reader in 1749 would not have thought it odd or contradictory, at least not in the same way a modern one might, to find a character as zestfully intimate with low life as Tom Jones commended in the final sentence of Fielding's novel for his 'Condescension' to those below him: 'as there are not to be found a worthier Man and Woman, than this fond Couple, so neither can any be imagined more happy . . . such is their Condescension, their Indulgence, and their Beneficence to those below them, that there is not a Neighbour, a Tenant, or a Servant, who doth not most gratefully bless the Day when Mr. *Jones* was married to his *Sophia*' (*Tom Jones*, ii. 981–2). In Johnson's *Dictionary*, 'To CONDESCEND' is 'To depart from the privileges of superiority by a voluntary submission; to

---

[2] 'His Muse . . . is a levelling one. It proceeds on a principle of equality, and strives to reduce all things to the same standard. It is distinguished by a proud humility. It relies upon its own resources, and disdains external show and relief.' Hazlitt, *The Spirit of the Age, or, Contemporary Portraits* (1825), 'Mr. Wordsworth', in *Complete Works*, xi. 87.

sink willingly to equal terms with inferiours; to sooth by familiarity'. By the mid-nineteenth century, as today, the word implies a habitual reluctance or inability to do just that: 'Mr. Mulliner was an object of great awe to all of us. He seemed never to have forgotten his condescension in coming to live at Cranford. Miss Jenkyns, at times, had stood forth as the undaunted champion of her sex, and spoken to him on terms of equality; but even Miss Jenkyns could get no higher.'[3]

Johnson's ideal of condescension—a laudable resignation of superiority to familiarity—springs from a sense of the word still vivid in his lifetime, and particularly evident in the works of Isaac Watts, of Christ's incarnation as God's unsurpassable act of condescension to mankind, an inexplicable yet paradoxically imitable act of self-abasement (seen from another perspective as shockingly degrading) to the little. Its human form must therefore be humbly self-explanatory, deposing itself from the summits of intellectual abstraction, as humanity is infinitely below a deity who stoops to take on humble flesh. Hence the frequency with which Johnson applies the word to, or enjoins the quality on, scholars and teachers—as, for instance, in *Rambler* 137:

> To lessen that disdain with which scholars are inclined to look on the common business of the world, and the unwillingness with which they condescend to learn what is not to be found in any system of philosophy, it may be necessary to consider that though admiration is excited by abstruse researches and remote discoveries, yet pleasure is not given, nor affection conciliated, but by softer accomplishments, and qualities more easily communicable to those about us . . . No degree of knowledge attainable by man is able to set him above the want of hourly assistance, or to extinguish the desire of fond endearments, and tender officiousness . . . Kindness is preserved by a constant reciprocation of benefits or interchange of pleasures; but such benefits only can be bestowed, as others are capable to receive, and such pleasures only imparted, as others are qualified to enjoy.

> By this descent from the pinacles of art no honour will be lost; for the condescensions of learning are always overpaid by gratitude. An elevated genius employed in little things, appears, to use the simile of Longinus, like the sun in his evening declination, he remits his splendor but retains his magnitude, and pleases more, though he dazzles less. (*Yale*, iv. 363–4)

Here, Johnson associates a charitable, social, and intellectual form of descent with a classical image of 'declination', harmonizing via his own simile that of a pagan author with a Christian age. The reference to *Peri Hupsous* (IX. 13), which summons up *Peri Bathous*, elicits a virtuous

---

[3] Gaskell, *Cranford*, 75.

rather than a Popean or satirical art of sinking. Because this essay is counselling proximity between 'elevated genius' and 'little things', however, it also seems to go against Longinian precepts: 'One ought not in elevated passages to have recourse to what is sordid and contemptible' (*On the Sublime*, XLIII. 5). The classically improper action Johnson is recommending shows an overarching preference for a Christian scale of values, one that subordinates ancient critical maxims to his own moral allegiances, and which therefore might itself be read as evidence of Longinus' 'declination'.

Johnson's *Dictionary* definition of 'To CONDESCEND' is nevertheless structured on a fundamental inequality that renders the nature of the word perplexing. How is it possible to exist on 'equal terms' with people who simultaneously remain 'inferiors'? He suggests that condescension should be understood as an active, mobile virtue, not as a quality that divides the high from the low, nor as one that serves to enforce any regimented scale of being. As Johnson writes of the desirability for the learned to 'trifle agreeably': 'any action or posture long continued, will distort and disfigure the limbs' (*Rambler* 173, *Yale*, v. 153, 150). Condescension is therefore a process of ceaseless reappraisal: sinking and elevating, advancing and retreating, it aims to unite two socially or intellectually unequal parties on a friendly footing (however temporarily). Hence the aptness of one obsolete sense of the verb 'condescend', 'To come to an agreement' (*OED*, sense 8), something already implicit in the addition of the mutual prefix 'con-' to 'descend'.

Condescension describes a process of the divine becoming visible, carnated, and human. The fact that it came to be seen as a vice rather than as a virtue, indicating pride rather than humility, is due to some gradual, far-reaching alterations in social and literary sensibilities. Among these might be singled out the slow decline of patronage—the classical precursor to Christian condescension, which explains why 'patronizing' has the same pejorative sense as 'condescending' today. It seems curious, at first glance, that the *OED* gives no negative definitions of the verb 'condescend' or of the noun 'condescension', other than the classically inflected meanings '(In bad sense) To lower oneself; stoop' ('condescend', sense 2. c) and 'The action of descending or stooping to things unworthy' ('condescension', sense 2), both of which are described as obsolete. All the other definitions point to virtuous forms of affable descent, of resolution, or of harmonizing two discordant parties: 'Voluntary abnegation for the nonce of the privileges of a superior; affability to one's inferiors, with

courteous disregard of difference of rank or position; condescending-
ness'; 'Gracious, considerate, or submissive deference shown to another;
complaisance'; 'The action or fact of acceding or consenting; concession'
('condescension', senses 1, 3, 4); 'To come down voluntarily'; 'To give
one's consent, to accede or agree *to* (a proposal, request, measure, etc.);
to acquiesce'; 'To settle or fix upon a particular point' ('condescend',
senses I, II, III).

It is only the *OED*'s definition of the participial adjective 'condescending' that captures the negative associations of the word, but even these
are mixed up with its positive ones—because to act in what we now call
a 'condescending' manner is seen as the badge of false 'condescension'.
By distinguishing the adjective from the verb and noun, the *OED* also
distinguishes virtue from vice, humility from pride, and preserves intact
the gesture or quality of true condescension: 'That condescends; characterized by, or showing, condescension. *Now*, usually, Making a show,
or assuming the air, of condescension; patronizing' ('condescending',
sense 1). The dictionary does not pay the same compliment to the verb
'patronize', which permanently courts the bad sense of 'condescending',
of merely 'assuming the air' of genuine descent: 'To assume the air of a
patron towards'; 'to treat with a manner or air of condescending notice'
('patronize', senses 1 and 3).

Translated into wholly secular terms, condescension becomes an
elaborate pretence of resigning authority. It stems not from man's native
sense of inferiority to an incarnated God, but from a sense of personal
superiority to anyone who seems lower than oneself on the social,
material, or intellectual scale. The relationship between condescension
and overweening pride does not occlude the possibility of a virtuous,
Christian, and humble equivalent until the twentieth century, although
the word's negative potential is clear in the pompous humility of Austen's
Mr Collins, and in the insulting patronage of Lady Catherine de Bourgh
in *Pride and Prejudice*. Mr Collins tells Elizabeth that he is marrying on
'the particular advice and recommendation of the very noble lady whom I
have the honour of calling patroness. Twice has she condescended to give
me her opinion (unasked too!) on this subject.' He later tempts her with
the promise of Lady Catherine's all-encompassing 'condescension . . . I
doubt not but you will be honoured with some portion of her notice', then
rejoices in 'The power of displaying the grandeur of his patroness to his
wondering visitors, and of letting them see her civility towards himself and
his wife . . . that an opportunity of doing it should be given so soon, was
such an instance of Lady Catherine's condescension as he knew not how

to admire enough.' In practice, however, 'Elizabeth found that nothing was beneath this great Lady's attention, which could furnish her with an occasion of dictating to others' (Austen, *Works*, ii. 105, 160, 157, 163).

The *Rambler* twice associates condescension with insolence and impertinence, albeit—on the first occasion—condescension of a different sort from Lady Catherine's, concerned as Johnson is here with the illicit arrogation of mental superiority, which assumes that it is virtuously descending to mental inferiority: 'There is no kind of impertinence more justly censurable, than his who is always labouring to level thoughts to intellects higher than his own' (*Rambler* 173, *Yale*, v. 154). He remarks similarly in the *Life* that: 'There is nothing more likely to betray a man into absurdity than *condescension;* when he seems to suppose his understanding too powerful for his company' (*Life*, iv. 3). But the second example from *The Rambler* is recognizably on Lady Catherine's turf, a figurative sense of superiority manifesting itself in physical elevation: 'my old friend receiving me with all the insolence of condescension at the top of the stairs, conducted me to a back room, where he told me he always breakfasted when he had not great company' (*Rambler* 200, *Yale*, v. 278–9).

In Johnson's lifetime, the pejorative sense of condescension usually implies the opposite, however, of the consciousness of station that belongs to haughty patronage. And this negative implication, which squares with the *OED*'s bad senses of 'condescend' and 'condescension', derives from antiquity. It disapprovingly signals the impropriety of stooping or grovelling to unworthy things: what Goldsmith describes as 'the meanest degree of condescension' (*Life of Richard Nash*, *Collected Works*, iii. 380). It thus locates the undesirable element of condescension not in an excessively superior person, but in the superlatively low objects of a regard that makes its possessor himself contemptible to behold. When *The Tatler* states that '*Familiarity*' will '*turn . . . into Contempt*' (no. 221, i. 175), the meaning is not the same as that implied when we now say 'familiarity breeds contempt'. For Steele does not think that any man will become contemptuous of those with whom he is on familiar terms, but that a gentleman's familiarity with subordinates breeds the contempt of onlookers, by confounding the necessary distinction between two classes: 'Servile Complaisance shall degrade a Man from his Honour and Quality, and Haughtiness be yet more debased' (*Tatler* 180, ii. 481). It was only 'sometimes' that Pope, for instance, 'condescended to be jocular with servants or inferiors', or that Dryden 'condescended to be somewhat familiar' in his writing ('Life of Pope', *Lives*, iii. 202; 'Life of Addison',

Lives, ii. 146). Aware of the risk in so doing, Hester Thrale wrote of Johnson that 'no Man ever had the power of Complimenting with a better Grace; for he always contrived to raise the Person he commended without lowering himself' — 'lowering himself' being understood here to mean a sullying degradation of which he would rightly feel ashamed (*Thraliana*, i. 186). Boswell was less confident of Johnson's ability in this regard, partly because he was even less confident about how desirable it might be:

I regretted that Mr. Johnson did not practise the art of accommodating himself to different sorts of people . . . But Mr. Johnson's forcible spirit and impetuosity of manner may be said to spare neither sex nor age. I have seen even Mrs. Thrale stunned. But I have often maintained that it is better so. Pliability of address I take to be inconsistent with that majestic power which he has, and which produces such noble effects. A bar of iron nor a lofty oak will not bend like a supple willow, or like many plants between those. What though he presses down feeble beings in his course? They get up again like stalks of ripe grass. (*Tour*, 257)

Johnson's *Dictionary* definitions of the adjective 'FAMILIAR' undergo what might verge on an imperceptible transition in life, from 'Affable; not formal; easy in conversation' to 'Too nearly acquainted' (senses 2 and 8). The progressive gradations of descent in his definition of 'To CONDESCEND' are potential degradations, or at least social slippages from the distance that properly separates a high public character from his inferiors. This feeling of having stooped too low ('to descend beneath' or 'infinitely below' oneself in *Peri Bathous*, Pope, *Prose*, 175, 177) is compat- ible in one sense with the origins of Christian condescension—that is, to describe God's voluntary diminution to human form. Yet to refer that unsurpassable self-abasement to our own descent to lesser people or to lowly subjects is at best presumptuous, which might help to explain how interpretations of this quality, action, or posture move from humility to pride—or, better, how the performance of humility might turn out to conceal pride. In *Tom Jones*, a lordly condescension to 'little People' is directly associated with 'extreme Servility' towards social superiors: '[it is] the nature of such Persons as Mrs. *Wilkins*, to insult and tyrannize over little People. This being indeed the Means which they use to recompense to themselves their extreme Servility and Condescension to their Superi- ors; for nothing can be more reasonable, than that Slaves and Flatterers should exact the same Taxes on all below them, which they themselves pay to all above them' (*Tom Jones*, i. 47–8). William Law apprehended this possibility in 1726:

It does no good to a proud heart to stoop to some low service for deprived people. Nay, there is something in it that may gratify pride, for perhaps our own greatness is never seen to more advantage than when we stoop to those who are so far below us. The lower the people are to whom we stoop, the better they show the height of our own state. So there is nothing difficult in these condescensions; they are not contradictions to pride.

The truest trial of humility is our behavior towards our equals, and those who are our superiors or inferiors in only a small degree. It is no sign of humility for a private gentleman to pay a profound reverence and show great submission to a king, nor is it any sign of humility for the same person to condescend to great familiarity with a poor person dependent upon charity. For he may act upon the same principle in both cases. It does not hurt him to show great submission to a king, because he has no thoughts of being equal to a king, and for the same reason it does not hurt him to condescend to poor people, because he never imagines that they will think themselves his equal. So it is the great inequality of condition that makes it as easy for people to condescend to those who are a great way below them as to be submissive and yielding to those who are vastly above them.[4]

It is the perceived and therefore possible exaggeration of a gap between the very high and the very low that prompts Law's desire for a more efficacious arena, one of familiar and proximate human relationships, in which to put our charity and humility to the test. François Rigolot has recently discussed Erasmus' humanist revival of the theological notion of 'condescension'—'katabasis' or 'condescendentia'—as the ability to 'descend' and 'meet the other' (the Jew, the Muslim, and the heretic, for example) on his or her own ground. He associates this fabular aptitude for stooping to low life or to unworthy subjects with a series of vernacular literary works. Examples of such flagrant stooping that bear directly on Johnson's literary criticism include Rochester's paradoxical encomium 'Upon Nothing' (1680), a poem that Johnson admired ('Life of Rochester', *Lives*, i. 224–5), and Rabelais's *Gargantua and Pantagruel* (1532–52), both of which unabashedly celebrate discordance, heightening rather than foreclosing the distinction between an ornamental, copious style and its vacuous, sordid, or redundant object. Rigolot argues that, during the Wars of Religion, the French ideal of lavish condescension yields to a programme of limited toleration.[5]

This chronology seems to tally with the habitual dislike for extravagant descent in Law and in Johnson, as well as in later authors. When Austen

[4] William Law, *A Practical Treatise upon Christian Perfection* (1726), repr. (in part) in David Lyle Jeffrey (ed.), *English Spirituality in the Age of Wesley* (Grand Rapids, Mich.: William B. Eerdmans, 1987), 133.
[5] François Rigolot, 'Tolérance et condescendance dans la littérature française du XVIe siècle', *Bibliothèque d'humanisme et renaissance*, 62 (2000), 25–47.

writes in *Mansfield Park* (1814) that 'Edmund had descended from that moral elevation which he had maintained before, and they [Maria and Tom Bertram] were both as much the happier as the better for the descent', she is describing an abrogation of moral responsibility he will come to regret: that of permitting the theatricals (*Works*, iv. 158). Johnson's peers viewed riotously self-conscious displays of condescension as embarrassingly inconsistent with Christian humility on the one hand, and with Roman decorum on the other. The hyperbolic religious-cum-amorous language of utter self-abasement before a supremely disdainful, tyrannical love object—a form of linguistic and dramatic excess which persisted into the eighteenth century and found its way into the Gothic, chivalric, and sentimental romance—is held up to ridicule in Lennox's *Female Quixote*, a novel to which Johnson contributed the dedication. And Goldsmith, as Northrop Frye recognizes, is equally indebted to such outmoded protestations of ardent servility in *She Stoops to Conquer: or, The Mistakes of a Night* (1773), a work gracefully dedicated to Johnson's condescending interest (*Collected Works*, v. 101).[6]

Goldsmith's title draws on the many comic, secularized versions of Christian condescension that exist in the eighteenth century—worldly reworkings of God's victorious self-abasement which often summon up the religious or classically incriminating associations of elective poverty. Kate Hardcastle, by 'stooping to conquer', wins Marlow. Like the uncertainly directed 'that' in Dickinson's poem, Goldsmith's title obscures the object of her stoop, translating the action in itself into one of conquering rather than one of disgrace or of mere capitulation. It is not that 'Kate stoops to Marlow', but that 'she stoops *in order to* conquer', or even that 'she stoops to the act of conquering an unworthy object'—Marlow seems to be a paltry, half-baked sort of prize—which perhaps ought to make us feel slightly uncomfortable. *She Stoops to Conquer* rests on the quixotic potential of collapsing apparent modesty into impudence, and, conversely, apparent pride into humility. The bashful Marlow mistakenly assumes that his host's abode is an inn; he is capable of assurance only in the company of servant-girls, with whom he becomes 'impudent enough of all conscience', while in front of 'women of reputation' he is 'an ideot' and 'a trembler'. So the imperious Kate Hardcastle descends to disguise herself as a servant, in order to win her man (Goldsmith, *Collected Works*, v. 129, 131–42, 168–74, 183–6, 210–13).

---

[6] Frye, *The Secular Scripture*, 75–6. See also Auerbach, *Mimesis*, 140–1.

The *OED* dates the participial adjective 'condescending'—in the good sense of being characterized by true descent, rather than by the empty show of it—back to Watts in 1707 ('condescending', sense 1), and gives 1727 for the first recorded use of a pejorative sense of the participial adjective 'patronizing' ('That patronizes, esp. with an air of superiority; ostentatiously condescending or superior'; see also the verb 'patronize', sense 3). Since both words are closely involved in the definitions of one another, there are grounds for arguing that this period is the last to counterbalance, at least with such precisely divided sympathies, the laudable and the despicable aspects of self-abasement—either in donor or in recipient. Patronage (in its classical incarnations) is structured on the donor's impervious preservation of self-worth as he graciously and temporarily descends to the objects of his attention. But Christian condescension reverses the positions of patron and client. It asks us to lay aside our dignity in the name of humility and charity towards people who may or may not merit such elevation; it is not for us to question them too closely, since an authority above our own must determine the truly deserving. Fielding's Allworthy (a Bunyanesque name which flags up the distinction between his own character and the people to whom he descends) sums it up well when he says: 'I fear I have shewn Kindness in my Life to the Unworthy more than once. But Charity doth not adopt the Vices of its Objects' (*Tom Jones*, ii. 877).

Eighteenth-century authors and critics found the question whether literature adopted the vices of its objects harder to answer. Pope remarked that 'Dr. Swift was a great reader and admirer of Rabelais'; hence, perhaps, his literary descent to ordure, scabrous poverty, and disease.[7] While *The Rape of the Lock* ornaments, elevates, and beautifies its little objects, Swift's mock-heroic strain might be said to depress his low material still further, to exaggerate our consciousness of the 'Dung' from which 'gaudy Tulips' spring. (Belinda's comb decorously unites great and small, 'The Tortoise ... and Elephant', 'the speckled and the white' [*Rape of the Lock*, I. 135–6], but Celia's comb is 'A Paste of Composition rare, | Sweat, Dandriff, Powder, Lead and Hair'.)[8] Readers of Johnson's 'Life of Swift' have rightly concluded that it is full of contradictory impulses. Yet it might be seen as a mark of compatible elements in the Dean's character that his 'delight in revolving ideas from which almost every other mind shrinks with disgust', the culpable emphasis of his poetry on 'disease, deformity, and filth', also manifested itself in his praiseworthy, charitable attention

---

[7] Pope in Spence, *Observations*, i. 55.
[8] Swift, 'The Lady's Dressing Room' (1730), ll. 23–4, 144, in *Poems*, ii.

to objects many other minds would have shrunk from contemplating, let alone descended to assist ('Life of Swift', *Lives*, iii. 62–4).

Whatever Law may say about the comparative ease with which people stoop to the extremely indigent (and he is talking in relative terms about different degrees of humility), there is a clear distinction to be drawn between ostentatiously degraded, Rabelaisian verse, which may remain—in Johnson's analysis—beneath critical attention ('Life of Swift', *Lives*, iii. 66), and a charitable elevation of the lowliest people, which deserves to be recommended to the reader. Hence Johnson's careful note that Swift's 'depravity' was intellectual, not moral ('Life of Swift', *Lives*, iii. 62). A vicious literary tendency to focus on worthless subjects should be set against a virtuous gravitation towards habitually disregarded people, although both might feasibly derive from the same human source. In as strongly ethical a writer as Johnson, the struggle between these two competing scales of evaluation—between the writing and the life, between greatness and goodness—is often audible.

The unremittingly contested act of stooping to low particulars is especially apt to Johnson, Goldsmith, and Boswell's arts of biography. Cast by some as a sordid or ludicrous saturation in trivia, the commemoration of mean detail becomes in their hands an act of homage to the humanly insignificant—although not without its comic or bathetic potential. *The Idler*'s view of 'domestic degradation', according to which 'we all sink to the common level' on private occasions (*Idler* 51, *Yale*, ii. 160, 159), here co-operates with a biographer's version of Law's perceived 'holiness of common life, this religious use of every thing that we have' (a sanctification that, in Law's words, requires the author to 'descend to some particulars').[9] This can result in some novel reappraisals of character—reappraisals that the chiastic proverb 'Home is where the great are small, and the small are great' economically expresses: 'eminent men are least eminent at home' (*Idler* 51, *Yale*, ii. 158).

Johnson's biographical co-worker in the art of delicate, morally selective condescension to common life and to trivial things was Goldsmith. After his death, Johnson singled out for praise his friend's 'art of being minute without tediousness' ('Life of Parnell', *Lives*, ii. 49). Goldsmith's *Life of Richard Nash*—his subject was better known as 'Beau'—to which Boswell alludes at the end of his dedication of the *Life of Johnson*, met with the complaint that it alighted on 'A trivial subject' in recording the petty transactions of the Master of Ceremonies at Bath and, anticipating

---

[9] Law, *A Serious Call*, 46, 139.

a strain of critical disregard which dogs Goldsmith to this day, that it copied Johnson's *Life of Savage* (*Life*, i. 3–4 and n. 2; Goldsmith, *Collected Works*, iii. 282–3). Goldsmith certainly takes his cue from Johnson's defence of private life, arguing along similar lines to *Idler* 84 and *Rambler* 60 that 'the heart of a man is better known by his private than public actions'—which leads him to 'take a view of *Nash* in domestick life'—and suggesting the usefulness of contracting his literary scope: 'whether the heroe or the clown be the subject of the memoir, it is only man that appears with all his native minuteness about him, for nothing very great was ever yet formed from the little materials of humanity . . . the generality of mankind find the most real improvement from relations which are levelled to the general surface of life'. But he also invites the reader to compare him- or herself with author and with subject in a more direct, familiar way than that of Johnson's habitually impersonal biographical voice: 'I attempt the character of one, who was just such a man as probably you or I may be'; 'They who know the town, cannot be unacquainted with such a character as I describe' (*Collected Works*, iii. 390, 290, 291, 294).

In Nash, Goldsmith encountered an ideal biographical subject, embracing great and little, as he himself acknowledged. For Nash was a trifler *and* a ruler, the self-styled and voluntarily acknowledged monarch of a Lilliputian province—'*the little king of a little people*'—regulating with inflexible authority the minutiae of social life. 'In this particular', Goldsmith says, 'perhaps no Biographer has been so happy as I. They who are for a delineation of men and manners may find some satisfaction that way, and those who delight in adventures of Kings and Queens, may perhaps find their hopes satisfied in another' (*Collected Works*, iii. 289, 292). The combination of high with low, of powerful ruler with minute kingdom, permits a form of moral calibration that relies on scale. Nash's mock-monarchy alternately gains and loses in stature by comparison with actual kings. The levelling tendencies of biography are put to sophisticated use here. Real monarchs are depressed to a 'native minuteness' when we are told that 'our titular King' Nash 'began . . . to reign without a rival, and like other kings had his mistresses, flatterers, enemies and calumniators'; that the 'magistrates of the city' paid 'the same respect to his fictitious royalty, that is generally extorted by real power'; and that 'in order to proceed in every thing like a king, he was now resolved to give his subjects a law', one which Goldsmith subsequently describes as 'stupid'. Compared to historians' claims that the deaths of rulers prompt national grief, which Goldsmith dismisses as 'ludicrous', the recipients of Nash's charity 'followed their old benefactor to his grave, shedding unfeigned tears' (*Collected Works*, iii. 352, 307, 310, 303, 304, 366).

On the other hand, Nash's kingdom from youth to old age is a toy-town; Goldsmith calls it a 'nursery', Nash 'a minion of fortune' prone to 'childish impertinence' (*Collected Works*, iii. 304, 313). This realm of the little—the word appears in almost every paragraph of the first few pages, often more than once—can accommodate solicitous and contemptuous accents, pathos and bathos, depending on Goldsmith's perspective (*Collected Works*, iii. 288–95). Occasionally, the two strains are indistinguishable. He tends to shrink his protagonists rather than to censure them, so that they remain beneath the dignity of reason and the age of responsibility. Instead of railing against their licentiousness, Goldsmith makes Restoration playboys sound harmlessly silly, their rapacious appetites directed towards peculiar foodstuffs: 'In that age, a fellow of high humour would drink no wine, but what was strained though his mistresses smock. He would eat a pair of her shoes tossed up in a fricasee. He would swallow tallow-candles instead of toasted cheese, and even run naked about the town' (*Collected Works*, iii. 297). By the time we reach the end of this list, the potential salaciousness of 'naked' has already been sapped by an overwhelming childishness. Mistresses do no more than provide the ingredients.

Nash 'performed the most trifling things with decorum'. His 'attention to . . . little circumstances', in which he is at one with his biographer, earns praise for its ceremonious regulation of everyday life. What finally redeems Nash from being a mere peacock is his own tenderness towards socially inferior people, his capacity for pity, and for charity. Thus the biographer's claim to attention and to ridicule—the ability to make much of little, a 'solemnity . . . assumed in adjusting trifles'—is also his subject's. After all, 'we talk at best of trifles' (*Collected Works*, iii. 321, 295, 333, 288, 301).

1. THE *LIVES OF THE POETS*

In 1775, Johnson repeated to Boswell the common argument that 'poetry . . . can have no value, unless when exquisite in its kind' (*Life*, ii. 351–2)—a surprising view in light of his subsequent failure to exert complete control over which authors were to be included in his *Prefaces Biographical and Critical*:

I was somewhat disappointed in finding that the edition of the English Poets, for which he was to write Prefaces and Lives, was not an undertaking directed by him: but that he was to furnish a Preface and Life to any Poet the booksellers pleased. I asked him if he would do this to any dunce's works, if they should ask him. JOHNSON. 'Yes, Sir; and *say* he was a dunce.' My friend seemed now not much to relish talking of this edition. (*Life*, iii. 137)

Boswell's disappointment is partly a reflex dislike of tradesmen dictating their terms to the Great and pensioned Cham; but it also implies that anyone not discriminating enough to choose their biographical subjects might be unable to distinguish the important characters from the duncies of English letters. Yet Johnson's mind often turned naturally to the most prolific codifier of literary impropriety. Boswell and Frances Reynolds, on separate occasions, heard him recite the conclusion of *The Dunciad*:

Johnson ... repeated to us, in his forcible melodious manner, the concluding lines of the Dunciad. While he was talking loudly in praise of those lines, one of the company ventured to say, 'Too fine for such a poem:—a poem on what?' JOHNSON, (with a disdainful look,) 'Why, on *dunces*. It was worth while being a dunce then. Ah, Sir, hadst *thou* lived in those days! It is not worth while being a dunce now, when there are no wits.' (*Life*, ii. 84; see also *Miscellanies*, ii. 254)

Life imitates art in this passage—Johnson, rehearsing a poem on dunces, is interrupted by one (Boswell himself, in fact; see *Life*, ii. 84 n. 3, and app. B, ii. 486)—the local social intrusion complementing the large-scale literary irruption that is the subject of the poem's climax. His maliciously elegiac tone ('Ah, Sir, hadst *thou* lived in those days') suggests an ambiguity in his own response to *The Dunciad*, for it might be argued that it *was* in a peculiar sense worthwhile to be commemorated in a poem in which the stature of dullness is overwhelming, its triumph conclusive, and its otherwise forgettable practitioners distinguished by name. As Johnson's circle was fond of repeating, and as Pope himself realized, the duncies would never have been immortalized without their detractor's assistance:[10]

Of the Persons *it was judg'd proper to give some account: for since it is only in this monument that they must expect to survive, (and here survive they will, as long as the English tongue shall remain such as it was in the reigns of Queen* ANNE *and King* GEORGE) *it seem'd but humanity to bestow a word or two upon each, just to tell what he was, what he writ, when he liv'd, or when he dy'd.* ('ADVERTISEMENT' to the *Dunciad Variorum*, 8)

---

[10] 'Pope perpetuates Names in the Dunciad wch never could have lived till now without his help ... much to the Delight of us Dabblers in Literary History; who unless he had told us *himself*, could never have believed that such Nonsense had been capable of paining such a Mind.' *Thraliana*, ii. 944.

This limited biographical design—notwithstanding its studiously casual 'when he liv'd, *or* when he dy'd' (rather than 'when he liv'd, *and* when he dy'd'), and the proximity of *'what'* rather than *'who* he was' to the creaturely designations of *Peri Bathous*—anticipates Johnson's initial plan for the *Lives of the Poets*: 'My purpose was only to have allotted to every Poet an Advertisement . . . containing a few dates and a general character' ('Advertisement to the Third Edition', *Lives*, i, p. xxvi). Yet where *The Dunciad* pays sarcastic lip service to 'humanity' as a motive for commemorating those writers it seeks to commit to perpetual darkness, Johnson attempts in some cases, such as Blackmore's, a charitable and straight-faced reconstruction of Pope's targets. At least one commentator recognized that the *Lives of the Poets* and *The Dunciad*, whose subjects overlapped, were two sides of the same coin. John Scott, complaining about the presence of bad authors in the *Lives*, wondered why the collection had not embraced the whole gamut of poetasters:

The title of Poet has been often bestowed on those who little deserved it. The name of English Classicks was surely ill merited, either by the Wits of Charles's days, that 'mob of gentlemen who wrote with ease,' or by the heroes of the Dunciad; their compositions were mostly trifling, and frequently immoral, and consequently unworthy of preservation. But in an Edition of poetry, where some of these are to be found, we rather wonder at not finding the others; where Rochester and Roscommon, Sprat, Hallifax, Stepney, and Duke, were received, why Carew, and Sedley, and Hopkins, were refused, one is puzzled to guess; and when Pomfret and Yalden are preferred to Eusden and Duck, it is not easy to account for the preference.[11]

Johnson managed to lend a wry gravity to the discussion of artistic no-hopers in his own potential *Dunciad*, or negative catalogue of those writers who (as he himself tells us) dare not even aspire to the name of poets and who nevertheless appear in his *Lives*. In *Rambler* 106, he wondered 'by what infatuation or caprice' the 'Granvilles, Montagues, Stepneys, and Sheffields' of the literary world 'could be raised to notice' (he downsized this phrase, which constructs a Popean threshold of aesthetic murkiness, from 'rose to reputation'), claiming in another line which resembles Pope's attitude to his dunces that 'most are forgotten, because they never deserved to be remembered' (*Yale*, iv. 201 and n.). George Granville, Charles Montague, George Stepney, and John Sheffield all went on to figure in the *Lives of the Poets*. But because Johnson did not decide on their inclusion, the sense in which they are 'raised to notice',

---

[11] John Scott, 'On Goldsmith's Deserted Village' (1785), in G. S. Rousseau (ed.), *Goldsmith: The Critical Heritage* (London.: Routledge & Kegan Paul, 1974), 93.

or in which his own attention sinks to their level, is more sober than the mercurial prompts of 'infatuation or caprice' might suggest. Granville's 'little pieces' and 'trifles', we are told, have already received 'sufficient' praise; the 'beauties' of Montague's poetry have long since 'withered'; Stepney, who Johnson irritably notes 'apparently professed himself a poet', alights on the occasional 'happy line'; Sheffield, the 'maker of little stanzas', is 'feebly laborious, and at best but pretty': 'His verses are often insipid . . . he had the perspicuity and elegance of an historian, but not the fire and fancy of a poet' ('Life of Granville', *Lives*, ii. 294–5; 'Life of Halifax' [Montague], *Lives*, ii. 47; 'Life of Stepney', *Lives*, i. 311; 'Life of Sheffield', *Lives*, ii. 175, 177).

Critics such as Marilyn Butler and Janine Barchas, who remark on his taxonomic thinking or on his resolute selectivity, seem to forget that it was not Johnson but the commissioning booksellers who largely determined his subjects.[12] Thomas Campbell reported Johnson's comment that, in the *Dictionary*, 'my business was not to *make* words but to explain them'.[13] Of the *Lives*, he might have argued that his business was not to make poets but to explain them: hence his reply to Boswell that, if asked to write the 'Life' of a dunce, he would do so, 'and *say* he was a dunce'—not a poet. That he registered some of the booksellers' oversights is obvious from one comment (in the first edition of the *Lives*), about Granville's Popean *Essay on Unnatural Flights in Poetry* (1701). Here, he seems to be continuing to negotiate the content of the ensuing volumes: 'His poetical precepts are accompanied with agreeable and instructive notes which ought not to have been omitted in this edition' (*Lives*, ii. 295 and n. 6). Of Christopher Pitt he similarly remarks that: 'he gave us a complete English *Æneid*, which I am sorry not to see joined in the late publication with his other poems' (*Lives*, iii. 278–9). Pitt's *Aeneid* was duly admitted, six years after Johnson's death, to the 1790 edition (*Lives*, iii. 279 n. 1). Less than two weeks before he died, Johnson was planning to revise the 'Life of Waller' (*Miscellanies*, ii. 153).

The reason for at least one author's absence from the *Lives* was not a principle of canonical exclusion, but the same commercial rivalry that brought the collection into being: Goldsmith, whose biography Johnson intended to write, was omitted because a bookseller who declined to

---

[12] Butler, 'Oxford's Eighteenth-Century Versions', 141; *Romantics, Rebels and Reactionaries*, 57. Janine Barchas writes that 'Samuel Johnson's catalogue of the English language in the *Dictionary*', as well as 'his canon-building *Lives of the Poets*', are 'inventories that reflect taxonomic presuppositions'. Janine Barchas, *Graphic Design, Print Culture, and the Eighteenth-Century Novel* (Cambridge: Cambridge University Press, 2003), 186.

[13] Page (ed.), *Dr Johnson: Interviews and Recollections*, 87.

come in on the project also refused to resign copyright of his works (*Life*, iii. 100 n. 1; 'Life of Pomfret', *Lives*, i. 301 n. 1). John Scott, lamenting Goldsmith's failure to appear in the *Lives*, at least directed his complaint at the right people, conjecturing that: 'The managers of this celebrated Edition, as their work approached the present period, seem to have been more fastidious in their choice, and have omitted Writers who would have done their collection no discredit.'[14] And even if Johnson had wished to exercise a more authoritative influence on the choice of biographical subjects in his *Lives*, or on the works to be appended to them, it is unlikely that he would have succeeded. He strongly disapproved of Rochester's lewd verses, but persuaded the booksellers only 'to castrate', not to excise, them; Prior's 'amorous ditties', which Johnson 'despised', were also included (*Life*, iii. 191; ii. 78).

Some contemporary readers were well aware of those areas in which Johnson had managed to exert control, and of the challenges he presented to public opinion. The poets enlisted at his suggestion (two of whom are particularly disparaged by Scott) were Richard Blackmore, John Pomfret, Isaac Watts, and Thomas Yalden—and apparently James Thomson, whom Johnson told Boswell in 1777 he had urged the booksellers 'to insert', although this seems not to have been recognized by audiences at the time (*Lives*, ii. 235 n. 1; i. 301 n. 1; iii. 302 n. 1; ii. 297 n. 1; *Letters*, iii. 20, 38). After Johnson's death, Courtenay imagined that his enemies would sing: 'Low lies the man, who scarce deigns Gray to praise, | But from the tomb calls Blackmore's sleeping lays; | A passport grants to Pomfret's dismal chimes, | To Yalden's hymns, and Watts's holy rimes.'[15] Thomson, the fifth member of this group, was a Scottish poet, which—considered alongside the presence of his fellow Scot David Mallet, and of the Irish writers Denham, Roscommon, Swift, and Parnell, whom Goldsmith would have joined were it not for the copyright issue—further complicates the sense in which we can understand the *Lives* as an *English* canon. Johnson and the booksellers seem to have understood by 'English poets' no more rigid a definition than poets (real or professed) of the British Isles who wrote in the English language.

Robert Potter, far from thinking that the *Lives* served to immortalize great writers, was astonished at Johnson's perverse 'revival' of second-rate verse, his 'commendation of Blackmore', and of 'the feeble efforts

---

[14] Scott, 'On Goldsmith's Deserted Village', Rousseau (ed.), *Goldsmith: The Critical Heritage*, 93.
[15] Courtenay, *A Poetical Review*, 1–2.

of Yalden's lyre', particularly in the context of his 'censure of Pope'.[16] (Courtenay thought Johnson's 'unaccountable prejudice against Swift' derived from his equally unaccountable sympathy for Blackmore, who had attacked *A Tale of a Tub.*)[17] Potter would have agreed with the wildly pugnacious Scottish pamphleteer James Thomson Callender that Johnson's *Lives* 'attempted to prove, that they who please many, have *no* merit' (he is drawing on the final remark of the 'Life of Pomfret': 'he who pleases many must have some species of merit', *Lives*, i. 302).[18] And both men thought that, in practice, the *Lives* showed that those who had no merit—such as Pomfret—pleased Johnson alone:

As the Poems of Pomfret, Yalden, and Watts, and the Creation of Blackmore, were inserted in this collection by the recommendation of the Biographer, we may from thence form some judgement of his taste. He, who does not dislike Pomfret, may approve Yalden; he, who finds pleasure in Blackmore, may be enraptured by Watts. But this sagacious and penetrating Critic has the peculiar felicity of discovering that Blackmore 'finds the art of uniting ornament with strength, and ease with closeness. This, he tells us is a skill which Pope might have condescended to learn from him, when he needed it so much in his Moral Essays' ... Further instances of this Critic's want of taste I leave to the observation of others.[19]

In the end, however, it seems fitting that the *Lives* span a wide range of the poets' fraternity, since the presence of unaccomplished authors within the collection writes large Johnson's principled defence of including 'the minute details of daily life' in biography (*Rambler* 60, *Yale*, iii. 321). Representatives of the lower echelons of literature are made to exert pressure on the higher. Blackmore, for instance, is especially apt to evaluate Pope's failings, since he stars in *Peri Bathous* and *The Dunciad* as the embodiment of bad writing, while John Philips, low burlesque imitator of *Paradise Lost*, facilitates discussion of the shortcomings of Milton's sublime mode (*Lives*, ii. 239; i. 316–17). Without such co-operation between high and low forces, it would be hard to estimate what makes great or good poets any greater or better than others.

[16] Robert Potter, *An Inquiry into some Passages in Dr. Johnson's Lives of the Poets: Particularly his Observations on Lyric Poetry, and the Odes of Gray* (London: for J. Dodsley, 1783), 11 n. 12.
[17] Courtenay, *A Poetical Review*, 3 n. 3.
[18] [James Thomson Callender], *Deformities of Dr Samuel Johnson*, 2nd edn. (1782; Berkeley and Los Angeles: University of California, 1971), 11.
[19] Potter, *Inquiry*, 10–11. On Johnson's peculiar taste in the *Lives*, see also [Callender], *Deformities*, 24–7.

Surveying the completed *Lives*, Boswell was delighted to conclude that they afforded 'such principles and illustrations of criticism, as, if digested and arranged in one system, by some modern Aristotle or Longinus, might form a code upon that subject, such as no other nation can shew' (*Life*, iv. 35–6). The reference to Longinus is telling. In the 'Life of Prior', immediately after quoting Longinus on Euripides' tendency to force himself 'into grandeur by violence of effort' (*On the Sublime*, XV. 3–4), Johnson comments that: 'Whatever Prior obtains above mediocrity seems the effort of struggle and of toil' (*Lives*, ii. 208–9 and n. 1; he also cites *Peri Hupsous* in the 'Life of Dryden', *Lives*, i. 412 and n. 4). Here, he has in mind both Longinus' standards for sublimity, and Scriblerus' ironic recommendations of mediocrity in *Peri Bathous* (Pope, *Prose*, 174). But while aesthetic mediocrity may incur Johnson's censure, ethical mediocrity often summons his praise. The division between the two meanings of the word comes across in the *Dictionary*. Sense 1 of 'MEDIOCRITY', 'Small degree; middle rate; middle state', is supported with quotations from Bacon and Dryden on 'a *mediocrity* of success' and 'the *mediocrity* of wit'; while sense 2, 'Moderation; temperance', is applied in the citations to bodily appetites and to religious tolerance, although this secondary meaning of 'MEDIOCRITY' is also said to be 'Obsolete'.

Longinus had asked at the beginning of chapter II of *Peri Hupsous* whether there might be 'an art of … profundity', or of 'bathous' (intellectual depth), later cautioning that 'all who aim at grandeur, in trying to avoid the charge of being feeble and arid, fall somehow into this fault [tumidity], pinning their faith to the maxim that "to miss a high aim is to fail without shame" ' and 'as likely as not producing the opposite to the effect intended' (*On the Sublime*, II. 1–4). Longinus did not make any connection between mental profundity and the shame of falling beneath a target of sublimity. It was Pope, taking his cue from the paradoxical law of aspiration's gravity in *Peri Hupsous*, who first gave the word 'bathos' its current sense of 'Ludicrous descent from the elevated to the commonplace in writing or speech; anticlimax' (*OED*, 'bathos', sense 2). But Pope also told Spence that *Peri Bathous*, 'though written in so ludicrous a way, may be very well worth reading seriously as an art of rhetoric'.[20] The *Lives of the Poets*, which incorporate some of the same authors as those ridiculed in the *Bathous*, offer one such reading—both in the sense of interpreting Scriblerus' advice as if it were given to a reader straight, and in the sense of

---

[20] Spence, *Observations*, i. 57.

seriously and overtly endorsing Pope's implied opposition to such advice. Sometimes the echo of Pope's satirical emphasis is clear: Ambrose Philips (who repeatedly appears in *Peri Bathous*; Pope, *Prose*, 177–8, 185, 186, 191, 194, 195, 199) is described as 'fall[ing] below' Pindar's 'sublimity' (*Lives*, iii. 324–5). Consider, too, the compatibility of Scriblerus on amplification and Johnson on metaphysical poetry:

above all, preserve a laudable *Prolixity*; presenting the Whole and every Side at once of the Image to view. For Choice and Distinction are not only a Curb to the Spirit, and limit the Descriptive Faculty, but also lessen the Book, which is frequently of the worst consequence of all to our Author ... WE may define *Amplification* to be making the most of a *Thought*; it is the spinning Wheel of the *Bathos*, which draws out and spreads it in the finest Thread. (*Prose*, 183–5)

The fault of Cowley, and perhaps of all the writers of the metaphysical race, is that of pursuing his thoughts to their last ramifications, by which he loses the grandeur of generality, for of the greatest things the parts are little; what is little can be but pretty, and by claiming dignity becomes ridiculous. Thus all the power of description is destroyed by a scrupulous enumeration; and the force of metaphors is lost when the mind by the mention of particulars is turned more upon the original than the secondary sense, more upon that from which the illustration is drawn than that to which it is applied. (*Lives*, i. 45)

In the language of satirical inversion, Scriblerus' 'laudable' translates directly into Johnson's 'The fault of'. Although the passages exhibit different emphases, both are concerned with the dissipation of literary strength—'the Descriptive Faculty' in Pope, 'the power of description' in Johnson. Pope's recommended '*Prolixity*' resurfaces in the use of 'tediousness' as a measure of disapproval throughout Johnson's *Lives*; that of the aesthetically mediocre Prior states that it is 'the most fatal of all faults' (*Lives*, ii. 206). And Pope's diminishing, busy figure of 'the spinning Wheel of the *Bathos*' reappears in Johnson's demonstration that 'of the greatest things the parts are little; what is little can be but pretty, and by claiming dignity becomes ridiculous'. This rhetorical inversion of the climax or 'gradatio' of the ancients, whereby the last word of a phrase is carried over to the next in an ascending rather than (as here) in a descending scale of importance, enacts the anticlimax of the writing it disparages. In so doing, it makes us admire the ingenuity of its conjunction in style with its subject matter. The excessive pursuit of trifles, for which Johnson censures Shakespeare as prime offender, is a breach of literary propriety that this passage as well as the 'Preface to Shakespeare' decorously assimilates even as it disparages such licentiousness. A drive simultaneously to reject and to accommodate the improper is also at the heart of Pope's muddier enterprise. *Peri Bathous*, structured on a wilful misprision of the Longinian 'sublime', celebrates an obscurity or ambiguity of language that it is also the intention of the work to repudiate, in favour of clarity and of common sense.

A perceived tendency to promote the exotic, strange, and unknown, while denigrating the proximate, familiar, and useful, was the butt of much Scriblerian satire. Chapter IV of *Peri Bathous* accordingly turns its nose up at 'Corn, Flowers, Fruits, Animals, and Things for the meer Use of Man', which 'are of mean price, and so common as not to be greatly esteem'd by the Curious: It being certain, that any thing, of which we know the true Use, cannot be Invaluable: Which affords a Solution, why *common Sense* hath either been totally depis'd, or held in small Repute, by the greatest modern Cricks and Authors' (*Prose*, 175). 'Invaluable', made even trickier to pin down by the double negative, is pivotal, as it means both 'priceless' and 'worthless'. Pope might seem to be insisting that the useful is indeed not without value—in fact, it is truly precious. However, 'Invaluable' has an extra sense, particularly apposite here: it describes an object we are incapable of valuing (see *OED* 'invaluable', sense 1). Scriblerus' 'certain' conclusion that we *are* capable of rating, valuing, categorizing, and so on—a certainty that is the foundation stone of his various taxonomic enterprises—dissolves into the multiple obscurities of a word whose value we are unequal to determining.

2. PALTRY CIRCUMSTANCES

In the face of such hesitation about the value of things 'of mean price', one thing we can be sure of is that 'the natural tendency of all things is downwards' (Johnson in *Tour*, 123). And in biography, a policy of authorial descent, of undignified stooping, restriction, and voluntary confinement, may therefore be desirable. Bolingbroke, who contributed to the development of life-writing as a genre distinct from history, claimed that 'the improvement of real knowledge must be made by contraction, and not by amplification'.[21] In his 'Life of Plutarch' (1683), Dryden—who, according to the *OED*, here introduced the word 'biography' to the English language—gave the preference to '*Biographia*,

[21] Henry St John, Lord Bolingbroke, *Essays Addressed to Mr. Pope*, 'Essay the Second', in *The Works of the late Right Honourable Henry St. John, Lord Viscount Bolingbroke*, ed. David Mallet, 5 vols. (London: for the editor, 1754), iv. 9.

or the History of particular Mens Lives' over history and annals, because 'the examples of vertue are of more vigor, when they are thus contracted into individuals'. It is precisely the *contraction* of virtue into particular examples, which makes 'this kind of writing . . . in dignity inferiour to *History* and *Annalls*' and restricts the author to a 'confin'd . . . action' and 'narrow compass', that increases 'the perfection of the Work, and the benefit arising from it'. Both are 'more absolute in *Biography* than in History'.[22] Johnson, who frequently protested against the incursions of unlicensed imagination, found the limitations of biography congenial and sought to restrict still further its proper domain. He wished to arrest the impulse (his own included) to distort individual lives into depictions of heroism or of saintliness, seeking instead to bring out the latent similarities in human nature.

In the 'Life of Pope', the last of his *Prefaces Biographical and Critical* to be completed, Johnson encountered a character who, like *The Rambler*'s ideal biographer, excelled in the 'art of doing little things with grace' ('Life of Milton', *Lives*, i. 163). Pope, he notes, 'examined lines and words with minute and punctilious observation, and retouched every part with indefatigable diligence, till he had left nothing to be forgiven' (*Lives*, iii. 221). But 'nothing to be forgiven' also introduces a different form of evaluation: that of Pope's moral character, of his goodness, not of his greatness. A perceived 'minute and punctilious observation' of poetic correctness is brought to bear on Pope's scrupulous enumeration of his enemies in *Peri Bathous* and in *The Dunciad*. His detailed public disavowal of any interest in trifling matters or in petty authors only points to a disproportionate private concern for exactly those things (since 'no man thinks much of that which he despises', *Lives*, iii. 211), a concern which Johnson bears in mind when discussing his domestic behaviour:

In all his intercourse with mankind he had great delight in artifice, and endeavoured to attain all his purposes by indirect and unsuspected methods. 'He hardly drank tea without a stratagem.' If at the house of his friends he wanted any accommodation he was not willing to ask for it in plain terms, but would mention it remotely as something convenient; though, when it was procured, he soon made it appear for whose sake it had been recommended . . . He practised his arts on such small occasions that Lady Bolingbroke used to say, in a French phrase, that 'he plaid the politician about cabbages and turnips.' (*Lives*, iii. 200)

---

[22] John Dryden, 'Life of Plutarch', in *The Works of John Dryden*, ed. Edward Niles Hooker, H. T. Swedenberg, Jr., and Alan Roper, 20 vols. (Berkeley and Los Angeles: University of California Press, 1956–2000), xvii. 273–4.

A disapproving note ('he was not willing . . . he soon made it appear') sounds through this summary of the mock-heroic poet's childish cunning about minutiae, even if Boswell thought the description equally applicable to Johnson (*Life*, iii. 324). The 'Life of Pope' follows its subject's lead to investigate 'What mighty Contests rise from trivial Things' (*Rape of the Lock*, I. 2), employing homely objects as prompts to broad reflections and lending them a representative significance beyond the trifling. According to the *OED*, Scots English developed in the mid-eighteenth century a sense of 'condescending' as 'Particularizing; going into details' (1755), indicating a minute focus appropriate to a flourishing school of empirical enquiry (*OED*, 'condescending', sense 3), but the definition of the verb 'condescend' as 'To come to particulars' (*OED*, sense 13) dates back at least to Chaucer. Johnson employs the word to criticize a lack of authorial discrimination in *Rambler* 60, an essay that repeatedly underscores the importance to life-writing of 'domestick privacies'. We learn nothing applicable to 'private life' from narratives that 'never *descend* below the consultation of senates'; yet most biographers, 'If now and then they *condescend* to inform the world of particular facts, . . . are not always so happy as to select the most important' (*Yale*, iii. 319–22; my emphases). It was a charge levelled at Johnson himself, especially at his 'Life of Pope'—notable, in Boswell's phrase, for its 'minute selection of characteristical circumstances' (*Life*, i. 256). Potter accused Johnson of a degrading condescension to unworthy trifles:

We are also sorry to see the masculine spirit of Dr. Johnson descending to . . . 'anile garrulity.' In reading the life of any eminent person we wish to be informed of the qualities which gave him the superiority over other men: when we are poorly put off with paltry circumstances, which are common to him with common men, we receive neither instruction nor pleasure. We know that the greatest men are subject to the infirmities of human nature equally with the meanest; why then are these infirmities recorded? Can it be of any importance to us to be told how many pair of stockings the author of the Essay on Man wore?[23]

Potter's sense of propriety was affronted by what he viewed as a needless reminder that superior intellects share in the common frailties of humanity, let alone by the fact that this metaphorically 'eminent person' was physically dwarfed by lesser mortals. Callender also questioned 'What "truth, moral or political", is promoted by telling us, that, when Thomson came to London, *his first want was a pair of shoes*; that Pope "wore a kind of fur doublet, under a shirt of very coarse warm linen,

---

[23] Potter, *Inquiry*, 4.

with fine sleeves" ' (see 'Life of Thomson', *Lives*, iii. 283; 'Life of Pope',
Lives, iii. 197; the quotation 'truth, moral or political' comes from the
'Life of Gray', *Lives*, iii. 438): 'Had Dr Johnson been Pope's apothecary,
we would certainly have heard of the frequency of his pulse, the colour
of his water, and the quantity of his stools' (to which the only sensible
reply is: well, yes, one would hope so). He dismissed Johnson's attention
to 'petty peculiarities' as an exhibition of 'tiresome and disgusting trifles,
which make his narrative seem ridiculous'.[24] Since Johnson singled out
for praise Pope's handling in *The Rape of the Lock* of a subject 'below
the common incidents of common life' (*Lives*, iii. 234), he was unlikely
to baulk at Potter's accusation that his *Life* of the poet included qualities
'common to him with common men'. Indeed, this was the chief strength
of biography as a genre: 'Men thus equal in themselves will appear equal
in honest and impartial biography; and those whom fortune or nature
place at the greatest distance may afford instruction to each other' (*Idler*
84, *Yale*, ii. 263). It was Pope's affected scorn both for the rabble and
for the great world that drew Johnson's censure, and a wish to reduce
his subject's claims to singularity: 'How could he despise those whom
he lived by pleasing, and on whose approbation his esteem of himself
was superstructed? Why should he hate those to whose favour he owed
his honour and his ease?'; 'His levity and his sullenness were only in his
letters; he passed through common life, sometimes vexed and sometimes
pleased, with the natural emotions of common men' (*Lives*, iii. 210).

Throughout the *Lives*, whenever the word 'common' appears, it tends
(as in the previous quotation) to do so twice in the same sentence,
thereby acting to unite the low particular with the high generalization,
and implying that petty details must be included in biography because
they speak to and potentially instruct everyone. In this respect, Johnson
is practising the descent of elevated learning to little things that he
recommended via a Longinian simile in *Rambler* 137. For 'common'
has two strands of meaning in Johnson: the merely low and quotidian
('Vulgar; mean; not distinguished by any excellence; often seen; easy to
be had; of little value; not rare; not scarce', *Dictionary*, 'COMMON', sense
3), and the universal ('Publick; general; serving the use of all', *Dictionary*,
'COMMON', sense 4). Accents of blame or praise, of descent or ascent,
are developed in Johnson's 'common' as it proceeds through repetition
towards the first or towards the second of these senses. The first citation

---

[24] [Callender], *Deformities*, 40.

under 'ploce' in the *OED* identifies it as follows: 'by an Emphasis, a word is either in praise or disgrace reiterated or repeated' (Angel Day, 1586).

Johnson's ploce can thus serve either to diminish the unique into the run-of-the-mill, or to elevate the commonplace to something worth-while.[25] If the seemingly praiseworthy becomes ordinary, the movement is a descent, as in the 'Life of Thomson': 'He was taught the *common* rudi-ments of learning . . . ; but was not considered by his master as superior to *common* boys' (*Lives*, iii. 282; my emphases). If the seemingly ordinary becomes praiseworthy, the movement is an ascent, as in the 'Life of Gray': 'I rejoice to concur with the *common* reader; for by the *common* sense of readers uncorrupted with literary prejudices . . . must be finally decided all claim to poetical honours' (*Lives*, iii. 441; my emphases). In Johnson's view, the central task and benefit of biography was, in fact, a form of ploce: life-writing reduces apparent singularity to the level of everyday experience, and it raises an individual into someone representative of, and edifying to, the bulk of humanity.

Unsurprisingly, Potter calls readers' attention to Pope as author of the grandiose *Essay on Man* (1733–4), that '*general Map* of MAN' which neglects the 'finer nerves and vessels, the conformations and uses of which will for ever escape our observation' (*Essay on Man*, 'THE DESIGN', 7–8), rather than to Pope as originator of *The Dunciad*, *Peri Bathous*, or *The Rape of the Lock*, publications that richly and variously compromise authorial dignity by focusing on the low, the small, and the particular. In biography, the sense in which *Peri Bathous* and *The Dunciad* compromise Pope's dignity becomes still more complicated, as Johnson investigates the secret solicitousness behind Pope's public show of contempt for his subject matter. On the other hand, it was *An Essay on Man* that Johnson described (in another passage to which Callender violently objected)[26] as affording 'an egregious instance of the predominance of genius, the dazzling splendour of imagery, and the seductive powers of eloquence. Never were penury of knowledge and vulgarity of sentiment so happily disguised. The reader feels his mind full, though he learns nothing' (*Lives*, iii. 243). The word 'happily' is itself happily poised between Pope's delight in concealing his intellectual vacuity, and the reader's in failing to perceive it. There is a resemblance between the way in which *An Essay on Man*, in Johnson's appraisal, covers its tracks, and the procedures of conventional biography, which 'endeavours to hide the man that [it] may produce a hero' (*Idler* 84, *Yale*, ii. 262). Pope himself 'either wilfully

---

[25] I am indebted to Sarah Howe for bringing Johnson's use of this figure to my attention.

[26] [Callender], *Deformities*, 41–2.

disguises his own character' in letters, 'or invests himself with temporary qualities'; 'it may be discovered that, when he thinks himself concealed, he indulges the common vanity of common men, and triumphs in those distinctions which he had affected to despise' (*Lives*, iii. 212; 150).

Johnson, by contrast, might be said to establish legitimate interest in the 'paltry circumstances' of a mock-heroic writer whose literary tastes and adjustments of value were partly determined by his size. After all, Pope's first authorial endeavour (at the age of 14) had been to translate Book I of Statius' *Thebaid*, on account of his admiration for the plucky, diminutive warrior Tydeus, whose 'little Body lodg'd a mighty Mind' (*Iliad*, V. 999). In Pope's *Guardian* 92 (1713) on the Club of Little Men, the president tells us that 'He has entertained so great a Respect for *Statius*, on the Score of that Line, | *Major in exiguo regnabat corpore virtus*, | that he once designed to translate the whole *Thebaid* for the sake of little *Tydeus*' (Pope, *Prose*, 53).[27] Tydeus' combination of heroic valour with 'the very *Bathos* of the human Body' (*Peri Bathous*, Pope, *Prose*, 200) must have given Pope—who, 'after his stoop had taken effect', was 'no more than four and a half feet high'[28]—some encouragement in his aspiration to match the stature of the ancients.

References to clothing serve a special purpose in Johnson's biographies—especially in that of Pope, who 'was not able to ... undress himself' either physically or metaphorically (*Lives*, iii. 197).[29] Eighteenth-century life-writers frequently employed the metaphor of undressing a subject in defence of their transition from public to private view. William Mason, whom Boswell cited as a major influence on his *Life of Johnson* (*Life*, i. 29), justified the prominence of Gray's hitherto unpublished letters in his memoir of the poet by taking issue with the 'scrupulously delicate' argument that it was 'incumbent on every well-bred soul never to appear but in full dress'.[30] Earlier still, Roger North (acknowledging the possible conflict between public and private spheres) was delighted to picture his accomplished brother Sir Dudley, 'Merchant, Sheriff, Alderman, Commissioner, & *c.* at home with us, a private Person, divested of all his Mantlings; and we may converse freely with him in his Family, and

---

[27] On Pope and Statius, see also Carolyn Williams, *Pope, Homer, and Manliness: Some Aspects of Eighteenth-Century Classical Learning* (London: Routledge, 1993), 61–2.

[28] Maynard Mack, *Alexander Pope: A Life* (New Haven: Yale University Press, in association with W. W. Norton, 1985), 98.

[29] On Johnson's treatment of clothing in biography, see John A. Dussinger, 'Style and Intention in the *Life of Savage*', *ELH* 37 (1970), 564–80.

[30] Thomas Gray and William Mason, *The Poems of Mr Gray. To which are prefixed Memoirs of his Life and Writings by W. Mason, M.A.* (York: J. Todd, 1775), 4n.

by himself, without clashing at all against any Concern of the Public. And possibly, in this Capacity, I may shew the best Side of his Character'.[31] This tender portrayal of domestic intimacies is careless enough of the public offices that might prompt readers' interest in Dudley North to wind them up with '& c.' It dwells on the removal of 'Mantlings' rather than of 'Mantles', the diminutive signalling our entrance to a private and fraternal sphere. Johnson celebrates a similar diminution when he writes of 'those soft intervals of unbended amusement, in which a man shrinks to his natural dimensions, and throws aside the ornaments or disguises, which he feels in privacy to be useless incumbrances, and to lose all effect when they become familiar' (*Rambler* 68, *Yale*, iii. 360).

In the 'Life of Pope', Johnson's interest in minutiae is informed by tactful and solicitous negotiations with his subject's diminutive size, and with its attendant trials. Pope was, the 'Life' informs us, 'extremely sensible of cold', and (in Johnson's words to Hester Thrale), 'as nothing is little to him who feels it with great sensibility', it was of no little importance to the conduct of his life, or to the precarious composure of which his stylistic equilibrium was born, 'that he wore a kind of fur doublet, under a shirt of very coarse warm linen, with fine sleeves' (*Letters*, i. 207; *Lives*, iii. 197). Even in his handling of these materials, Johnson shows an interest in combining the 'very coarse' with the 'fine', the common with the distinguished. When he writes of Pope that 'His stature was so low that, to bring him to a level with common tables, it was necessary to raise his seat', the comment sheds light on the poet's desire for a literary 'stature' above and beyond the 'common' level (*Lives*, iii. 196). Conversely, once we discover that Pope was so physically weak as 'to stand in perpetual need of female attendance', the flat, conventional metaphoric sense of 'standing in need' suddenly becomes physically vivid: 'His legs were so slender that he enlarged their bulk with three pair of stockings, which were drawn on and off by the maid' (*Lives*, iii. 197).

A similar effect occurs when Johnson notes that 'His hair had fallen almost all away, and he used to dine sometimes with Lord Oxford, privately, in a velvet cap'. The 'velvet cap', covering Pope's near-naked scalp, diminishes an expected comment on the location or residence in which he and Lord Oxford are privately dining to a Tom Thumb scale of clothes (*Lives*, iii. 198). Writing about the end of the poet's life,

---

[31] Roger North, *The Life of the Honourable Sir Dudley North: Commissioner of the Customs, and afterwards of the Treasury to His Majesty King Charles the Second. And of the Honourable and Reverend Dr. John North, Master of Trinity College in Cambridge, and Greek Professor* (London: for the editor, 1744), 194.

and considering Martha Blount's dwindling affections, Johnson remarks that 'if he had suffered his heart to be alienated from her, he could have found nothing that might fill her place: he could only have shrunk within himself; it was too late to transfer his confidence or fondness'—a comment which also happens to anticipate the sad end of Johnson's relationship with Hester Thrale (*Lives*, iii. 190; *Letters*, iv. 338, 343–4). As 'a man', Pope 'shrinks to his natural dimensions'; dimensions that were, to begin with, naturally small. He contracts himself into an ever-decreasing circle of 'fondness'; he is also diminished in the physically suggestive sense of shrinking as shrivelling, and in the sense of metaphorically shrinking from the fear of utter abandonment (see 'To SHRINK', senses 1–4, *Dictionary*; Pope is quoted twice). Robert Folkenflik well observes of this passage that: 'The horror of further shrinkage within that already shrunken body is not dwelt upon, but we are given in full the contraction of human scope as Pope moves towards his death.'

Johnson's references to Pope's clothing—which so affronted Pot-ter—have implications for other spheres of his subject's experience, since 'The indulgence and accommodation which his sickness required had taught him all the unpleasing and unsocial qualities of a valetudinary man. He expected that every thing should give way to his ease or humour, as a child whose parents will not hear her cry has an unresisted dominion in the nursery' (*Lives*, iii. 198). An irksome routine has ramifications beyond the domestic, and may account for Pope's petulant sensitivity to criticism:

He had another fault, easily incident to those who suffering much pain think themselves entitled to whatever pleasures they can snatch. He was indulgent to his appetite: he loved meat highly seasoned and of strong taste, and, at the intervals of the table, amused himself with biscuits and dry conserves. If he sat down to a variety of dishes he would oppress his stomach with repletion, and though he seemed angry when a dram was offered him, did not forbear to drink it. (*Lives*, iii. 199)

Pace Potter's objections to such passages—'Achilles and Thersites eat, and drank, and slept; in these things the Hero was not distinguished from the Buffoon: are we made the wiser or the better by being informed that the Translator of Homer stewed his Lampreys in a silver saucepan?'[33]—it seems fitting that Pope's death, in another bathetic and pathetic contrac-tion of scope that he might himself have relished, 'was imputed by some of his friends to a silver saucepan, in which it was his delight to heat

---

[32] Folkenflik, *Samuel Johnson, Biographer*, 54.   [33] Potter, *Inquiry*, 4.

potted lampreys'. While Potter makes it sound as if the fact that a hero ate
and drank might be his Achilles' heel, Johnson deduces from the rumour
about Pope's eating habits a general observation that: 'The death of great
men is not always proportioned to the lustre of their lives. Hannibal, says
Juvenal, did not perish by a javelin or a sword; the slaughters of Cannæ
were revenged by a ring' (*Lives*, iii. 200). That 'lustre' borrows some of
its tragicomic sheen from the silver saucepan that may or may not have
occasioned Pope's demise. Like Boswell's 'spoils' (concealing the indignity of Johnson's orange peels), 'lustre' has a faint martial glimmering
of antiquity, as well as a low material shine, an appropriate combination
to describe the close of a mock-heroic poet's life. In *The Iliad* itself,
Pope sometimes confronted anomalies when describing simple matters
of food and drink. One note excuses the line 'Before great Ajax plac'd the
mighty Chine' in terms of palates unvanquished by potted lampreys:

This is one of those Passages that will naturally fall under the Ridicule of a true
modern Critick. But what *Agamemnon* here bestows on *Ajax* was in former Times
a great Mark of Respect and Honour: Not only as it was customary to distinguish
the Quality of their Guests by the Largeness of the Portions assigned them at their
Tables, but as this Part of the Victim peculiarly belong'd to the King himself. It
is worth remarking on this Occasion, that the Simplicity of those Times allowed
the eating of no other Flesh but Beef, Mutton, or Kid. This is the Food of the
Heroes of *Homer* (*The Iliad*, VII. 387 n.).

And 'THESE are the . . . Characteristicks of the *Bathos*' (Pope, *Prose*,
181). As Pope consumes his delight, Johnson's 'Life' swallows its pride. To
introduce details about eating, as well as remarks on clothing, might be
thought culpably low and puerile. Yet, as a universally necessary activity,
eating affords a lesson to each and every reader. Thomas Tyers recalled
Johnson applying such a lesson to his own life, by observing in conversation and 'perhaps to remind himself', that Pope and Addison 'ate and
drank too much, and thus shortened their days' (*Miscellanies*, ii. 336).
Many of Johnson's subjects seem to have been killed by the violence of
their appetites. The starving Otway died horribly, 'in a manner', Johnson
says, 'which I am unwilling to mention': 'by swallowing, after a long fast,
a piece of bread which charity had supplied. He went out, as is reported,
almost naked, in the rage of hunger, and, finding a gentleman in a
neighbouring coffee-house, asked him for a shilling. The gentleman gave
him a guinea, and Otway going away bought a roll, and was choaked with
the first mouthful' ('Life of Otway', *Lives*, i. 247). Savage, too, 'suffered
the utmost Extremities of Poverty, and often fasted so long, that he was
seized with Faintness, and had lost his Appetite, not being able to bear

the smell of Meat, 'till the Action of his Stomach was restored by a Cordial' (*Savage*, 120). Edmund Smith expired on swallowing a taste of 'his own medicine', having eaten and drunk to excess and insisted on a violent purge 'to ease himself by evacuation' ('Life of Smith', *Lives*, ii. 17–18). Elijah Fenton, notorious for his indolence, would (so a maid reported) 'lie a-bed, and be fed with a spoon' ('Life of Fenton', *Lives*, ii. 262).

Writing for bread is perfectly understandable, but hungering for praise can be as fatal as a penchant for expensive fish. Charles Montague (Lord Halifax), one of four poets who, according to *Rambler* 106, 'never deserved to be remembered', was, in Pope's luxurious, debauched phrase, 'Fed with soft Dedication all day long' (*Arbuthnot*, l. 233). This 'Dedication', especially in Johnson's pluralized rendition—'fed with soft dedications'—conflates the servility of authors inscribing their works to a patron and the sycophantic pliancy of a catamite, tempting his master with edible dainties. Stuffed with encomia, Montague fittingly died of an 'inflammation' ('Life of Halifax', *Lives*, ii. 47 and n. 1; ii. 46). Incidentally, Pope's depiction of him in the *Epistle to Dr. Arbuthnot* might have triggered the portrayal of Wolsey's 'full-blown Dignity', 'Pride', 'glitt'ring Plate', and 'Wealth', pregnant with imminent disaster. It may also have inspired Johnson's 'Sycophant . . . fed by Pride', in the same poem (*The Vanity of Human Wishes*, ll. 99, 113, 114, 122, 56). Montague, or 'Bufo', 'Proud, as Apollo on his forked hill | Sate full-blown . . . puff'd by ev'ry quill' (*Arbuthnot*, ll. 231–2).

Johnson often plays on the tenth sense of 'GREAT' in his *Dictionary*—'Swelling, proud'—depicting literary pre-eminence in bloated, Swiftian terms akin to the description of a victim of trapped wind, or of 'tympany', in his review of Soame Jenyns ('To swell a man with a tympany is as good sport as to blow a frog', *Prose and Poetry*, 365). Of Pope, he writes: 'It is evident that his own importance swells often in his mind' (*Lives*, iii. 211). Under the definition of 'TYMPANY' in the *Dictionary* ('A kind of obstructed flatulence that swells the body like a drum'), the first five of six citations are figurative. The physical sense (from Arbuthnot, which appears last) is subordinated to the rich moral potential of the word to express inflated hope, tyranny, affectation, and pride.

In *An Essay concerning the Nature of Aliments* (1731), Arbuthnot had defended the importance of trifling circumstances to medical diagnosis, cautioning that '*The Reader must not be surpriz'd to find the most common and ordinary Facts taken notice of . . . many important Consequences*

may be drawn from the Observation of the most common Things.'[34]
Johnson went on to outline the significance to ethical diagnosis of such
common, ordinary, or 'evanescent' facts (*Rambler* 60, *Yale*, iii. 323) — a
word Arbuthnot glosses as 'vanishing, or growing extremely small'.[35]
Here is proof of what Donald Davie noted with regard to Berkeley and
his age: 'the discrimination which we make between the scientific and
the moral was unnecessary and positively unwanted'.[36] Longinus had
commented in *Peri Hupsous* that: 'Tumours are bad things whether
in books or bodies, those empty inflations, void of sincerity' (*On the
Sublime*, III. 4). 'Empty; vain' and 'puffy' authors, 'big without substance
or reality' ('FLATULENT', sense 2, *Dictionary*), are prone to drop back to
the ground once relieved of their windy effusions or blasts of pride, as
Johnson's citation from Dryden underlines: 'How many of these *flatulent*
writers have sunk in their reputation, after seven or eight editions of
their works.'

   Recording an instance of his own self-indulgence, Johnson made a
brisk transition from a leg of mutton to broader speculations about the
nature of unhappiness: 'At my aunt Ford's I eat so much of a boiled leg
of mutton, that she used to talk of it. My mother, who had lived in a
narrow sphere, and was then affected by little things, told me seriously
that it would hardly ever be forgotten. Her mind, I think, was afterwards
much enlarged, or greater evils wore out the cares of less' (*Yale*, i. 20).
Johnson noted of such 'little memorials' that they soothed his 'mind'
(*Yale*, i. 14). One sense in which they did so lay in the recognition of
his ability to be 'seriously' affected by a leg of mutton. But the sense in
which he *was* affected differed from that of the 'narrow sphere' of his
mother's sad fluster. Following Fielding's rule of thumb, that you should
not introduce a 'merely common incident ... for its own sake, but for
some observations and reflections naturally resulting from it', the mutton
acquires importance as a result of its prompt to general formulations.[37]
Johnson wrote in the 'Life of Ambrose Philips' that 'little things are not
valued but when they are done by those who can do greater' (*Lives*, iii.

[34] John Arbuthnot, *An Essay concerning the Nature of Aliments, and the Choice of Them,
according to the different Constitutions of Human Bodies. In which the different Effects,
Advantages and Disadvantages of Animal and Vegetable Diet are Explain'd* (London: for J.
Tonson, 1731), p. v.

[35] Ibid., p. xxi.

[36] Donald A. Davie, 'Berkeley's Style in *Siris*', *Cambridge Journal*, 4 (1950–1), 427–33
(p. 433).

[37] Henry Fielding, 'Preface' to *The Journal of a Voyage to Lisbon* (1755), in *The Criticism
of Henry Fielding*, 144.

324), and it is as if the mention of 'little things' in his diary acts as a turning point, provoking thoughts about comparatively 'greater evils' and a subsequently 'enlarged' mind.

Pondering the significance of Pope's great trifle, his grotto, Johnson observed that:

It may be frequently remarked of the studious and speculative that they are proud of trifles, and that their amusements seem frivolous and childish; whether it be that men conscious of great reputation think themselves above the reach of censure, and safe in the admission of negligent indulgences, or that mankind expect from elevated genius an uniformity of greatness, and watch its degradation with malicious wonder; like him who having followed with his eye an eagle into the clouds, should lament that she ever descended to a perch. (*Lives*, iii. 135)

As in his comments on the heroic or unheroic 'lustre' of Pope's potentially lethal saucepan, Johnson here summons up the martial and antique associations of his subject's descent to trifles. References to the triumphant stooping of the 'Eagle, sacred Bird of Heav'n' abound in Pope's translations of Homer: 'So the strong Eagle from his airy Height | Who marks the Swan's or Crane's embody'd Flight, | Stoops down impetuous, while they light for Food, | And stooping, darkens with his Wings the Flood' (*Iliad*, VIII. 297; XV. 836–9); 'The bird of *Jove* | Fierce from his mountain-eyrie downward drove; | Each fav'rite fowl he pounc'd with deathful sway'; 'But whilst with grief and rage my bosom burn'd, | Sudden the tyrant of the skies return'd: | Perch'd on the battlements he thus began, | (In form an eagle, but in voice a man.)' (*Odyssey*, XIX. 629–31, 637–40). The eagle's surprise attack on his helpless prey, which is in its turn grubbing for food, suggests Pope's pursuit of the hungry dunces—his 'fav'rite fowl', or foul favourites—as well as the unexpected swoop from literary heights that is represented by his gardening activities (in a letter to Swift, Pope depicts himself as 'falling upon' bad writers, *Correspondence*, ii. 481). *The Odyssey*'s 'Perch'd' describes the eagle's descent to a human realm, an image reworked in Johnson's 'Life' as the domestic degradation of a king of poets. And the next line might also be rephrased, in terms of Johnson's reading of Pope at this point, as: 'In verse an eagle, but in life a man'. For his biographical method in the 'Life of Pope', at least when he considers his subject's moral or domestic character, is always to 'fetch th'aerial Eagle to the ground' (Pope, *Essay on Man*, III. 222).

There are implicit parallels between Pope's descent to his grotto and the biographer's inherently undignified task when confronted with such details. To present your subject's humiliation of himself, in pursuit of private gratification, involves your own, for the public's benefit. But the lofty diction and syntax of this passage reveal a decorous art of sinking especially apt to discuss the author of *Peri Bathous*. Its careful excisions of authorial self promote a series of passively anchored generalizations—anchored in the best sense that they never lose sight of the petty realities from which they abstract. For the argument is balanced on a delicate uncertainty, hovering between descent *from* something—'The act of passing from a higher place'—and descent *to* the 'Lowest place' (*Dictionary*, 'DESCENT', part of sense 1, sense 4), or degradation. Readers, Johnson suggests, may think authors are as uniformly sublime in all aspects of their lives as they appear to be in their writings, for which they forget that there is only a little human source. That source can, in fact, become so little—in writing or in life—as to verge on contradicting the greatness of its literary productions. The *Dictionary*'s second definition of 'GENIUS' is 'A man endowed with superiour faculties', but such superiority is immediately challenged by the mock-heroic coupling of 'little' with 'prodigious' in a citation from Addison: 'There is no little writer of Pindarick who is not mentioned as a prodigious *genius*.' The conjunction serves to bring sublimity down to earth, restoring the would-be eagle to his perch. In the 'Life of Pope', 'malicious wonder' similarly calibrates the full range of expansive and mean, admiring and contemptuous, telescopic and microscopic responses to poetic genius; and again, it might serve to sum up Pope's attitude to his dunces.

'Be not too hasty', Imlac tells Rasselas, 'to trust, or to admire, the teachers of morality: they discourse like angels, but they live like men' (*Yale*, xvi. 74). The half-formulated question of this passage in Pope's 'Life'—to do with the tricky distinction between descent and degradation, and therefore also to do with the good and bad varieties of condescension—is not quite answered. An initial observation on the pride of the studious in their trifling pursuits remains largely unelaborated. Johnson adds to it, first, the remark that great minds may think themselves safe in such pastimes; secondly, that the public loves to detect the reduction of elevated claims into trifling practice. He remains cautious, at this point, about the purchase of Pope's domestic condescension on his moral and authorial character. Only by comparison with a lesser poet can his littleness be fully assessed; and it is in this context that Johnson finally prefers a Christian art of sinking to that of *Peri Bathous*.

3. CORRECTIVE READINGS: POPE AND BLACKMORE, MILTON
AND WATTS

Of the five poets whose inclusion in the *Lives* was requested by Johnson, Blackmore was by far the most vilified in his own lifetime. Richard C. Boys writes that he 'has the doubtful distinction of being attacked by more illustrious pens than any minor poet in English literary history before or since'.[38] None of those pens was more illustrious or more malicious than Pope's. Considering the verdict of *Rambler* 145 on minor or ephemeral writers—'That such authors are not to be rewarded with praise is evident' (*Yale*, v. 11)—the 'Life of Blackmore' has an odd fondness for the word 'praise' (it appears, in various forms, twelve times, not always in Blackmore's favour. See *Lives*, ii. 239, 241, 242, 243, 244, 249, 253). Johnson remarked of Milton that 'he had the usual concomitant of great abilities, a lofty and steady confidence in himself, perhaps not without some contempt of others; for scarcely any man ever wrote so much and praised so few. Of his praise he was very frugal, as he set its value high; and considered his mention of a name as a security against the waste of time and a certain preservative from oblivion' (*Lives*, i. 94).

Johnson seems personally familiar with 'the usual concomitant of great abilities', yet his disapproving suspicion of Milton's 'contempt of others', as well as his sense that—in the case of the dunces—to be preserved 'from oblivion' might only entail perpetual infamy, feeds into his solicitous treatment of Blackmore. He believed it was 'peculiar to' Blackmore 'that his first publick work was an heroick poem' (*Lives*, ii. 237), and this observation could easily have led to comic conclusions. In the 'Life of Milton', there is said to be 'merriment' in seeing the contrast between 'great promises' and 'small performance' (*Lives*, i. 98). James Beattie wrote in similar vein that 'Extreme absurdity is particularly entertaining ... where the author seriously meant to do his best', classifying 'a vast disproportion between the intention and execution, between the seriousness of the author and the insignificance of the work' as one of the kinds of 'Risible incongruity' in ludicrous composition.[39] Yet that discrepancy between intention and execution was something Johnson lamented in himself, and whose exposition in prefaces (such as the *Prefaces Biographical and Critical*) he considered to be one of his

---

[38] Richard C. Boys, *Contributions in Modern Philology*, 13: *Sir Richard Blackmore and the Wits: A Study of "Commendatory Verses on the Author of the Two Arthurs and the Satyr against Wit"* (1700) (Michigan: University of Michigan Press, 1949), 36.

[39] James Beattie, *Essays* (Edinburgh: for William Creech, 1776), 'An Essay on Laughter, and Ludicrous Composition', 642.

particular gifts (*Life*, i. 292). In Blackmore's own 'Preface' to *King Arthur* (1697), which Johnson mistakes for the 'Preface' to his first epic work, *Prince Arthur* (1695), the author states modestly but ill-advisedly that he '*had been long a stranger to the Muses. I had read but little* Poetry *throughout my whole Life, and in fifteen years before, I had not, as I can remember, wrote a hundred Lines in Verse, excepting a Copy of Latine Verses in honour of a Friend's book.*'[40] Johnson reproduces a shorter version of this sentence in his 'Life', silently reducing '*honour*' to '*praise*' (*Lives*, ii. 237 and n. 3).

This is likely to have been the result of carelessness, but Johnson's distinction between the two words in other contexts suggests why 'praise' might have seemed, instinctively, the more appropriate. The *Dictionary* defines 'To HONOUR' as 'To dignify; to raise to greatness' (sense 2); 'To PRAISE' as 'To commend; to applaud; to celebrate' (sense 1)—not necessarily resulting in an elevation either to dignity or to greatness. The modification to Blackmore's 'Preface' implies that Johnson considered it beyond his subject's poetic capacities to honour a literary work by his verse: 'he who thus praises will confer no honour' ('Life of Milton', *Lives*, i. 164). And the transition from one word to the other shows how acute a critic of Johnson Hester Thrale was, when she wrote in anticipation of the 'Life of Blackmore' that he might rescue his subject from the malevolent old wits solely in order to 'do him the *honour* to devour him yourself—as a lion is said to take a great bull now and then from the wolves which had fallen upon him in the desert, and gravely eat him up for his own dinner'.[41] Boswell reports Johnson's remark that 'the cricks had done too much honour to Sir Richard Blackmore, by writing so much against him' (*Life*, ii. 107). Of *Prince Arthur* as a literary performance, Johnson comments only on its surprising popularity, and on the fact that Dennis's consequent attack was 'more tedious and disgusting than the work which he condemns' (*Lives*, ii. 238).

This is not to deny Blackmore the honour he merits when Johnson takes leave of the bulk of his poetry. Like Milton and like Johnson, both of whom were 'degraded' to the 'honest and useful employment' of 'a schoolmaster', Blackmore was 'compelled' by 'indigence' to 'teach a school; an humiliation with which ... his enemies did not forget to reproach him, when he became conspicuous enough to excite malevolence: and let it be remembered for his honour that to have been once a

---

[40] Sir Richard Blackmore, *King Arthur: An Heroick Poem in Twelve Books* (London: for Awnsham and John Churchil[l] and Jacob Tonson, 1697), 'Preface', p. v.

[41] Piozzi and Johnson, *Letters to and from the late Samuel Johnson*, ii. 122 (my emphasis).

school-master is the only reproach which all the perspicacity of malice, animated by wit, has ever fixed upon his private life' ('Life of Milton', *Lives*, i. 98; *Life*, i. 96–100; 'Life of Blackmore', *Lives*, ii. 235–6). While he reduces the '*honour*' of Blackmore's writing, here Johnson restores 'honour' to Blackmore's life. And his capacity to do good in his subsequent profession as a doctor was materially damaged by his lambasting in *The Dunciad*, an injury which Johnson duly addresses in corporeal terms: 'Contempt is a kind of gangrene, which if it seizes one part of a character corrupts all the rest by degrees. Blackmore, being despised as a poet, was in time neglected as a physician' (*Lives*, ii. 250).

Earmarked in *The Dunciad* as the loudest of the braying fools, Blackmore 'sings so loudly, and . . . sings so long' (II. 268). Johnson adapts a line from *An Essay on Man* in order to redress this unwelcome distinction, by referring Pope's words to Blackmore's private conduct: 'It is remarked by Pope that what "raises the hero often sinks the man." Of Blackmore it may be said that as the poet sinks, the man rises; the animadversions of Dennis, insolent and contemptuous as they were, raised in him no implacable resentment: he and his critick were afterwards friends' (*Lives*, ii. 239). The whole couplet from Pope is relevant: 'In each how guilt and greatness equal ran, | And all that rais'd the Hero, sunk the Man' (*Essay on Man*, IV. 293–4).[42] 'And *all* that rais'd the Hero, sunk the Man' reads more emphatically than Johnson's version of the line. Typically, he reduces an unexceptionable statement to one of mere frequency. Yet even so, it cannot be strictly true to say of Blackmore that his morals improved in strict proportion to the decline of his poetry—except in the sense that his reactions to criticism were instructively courteous. What is being described is the progress of Johnson's response to his subject. A survey of Blackmore's life increasingly discovers 'more of the dignity of virtue than the vivacity of wit' (Johnson in *Miscellanies*, i. 257), repudiating Pope's assertion that 'each *Ill Author* is as bad a *Friend*' (*Essay on Criticism*, l. 521). Steele, citing the 'Preface' to *Prince Arthur*, wrote that: 'Sir *Richard Blackmore* says, with as much good Sense as Virtue, *It is a mighty Dishonour and Shame to employ excellent Faculties and abundance of Wit, to humour and please Men in their Vices and Follies. The great Enemy of Mankind, notwithstanding his Wit and Angelick Faculties, is the most odious Being in the whole Creation*' (*Spectator* 6, i. 29 and n. 2).

---

[42] A slightly different version of the couplet appears in a cancelled 'Character' from *An Essay on Man*, reprinted in volume vi of the Twickenham edition of Pope's poems: 'One equal course how Guilt and Greatness ran, | And all that rais'd the Hero sunk the Man' (ll. 3–4).

But Steele omits Blackmore's intervening sentence—'*Such a one is more hateful, as an* ill Man, *than valuable, as a* good Poet'—a sentence which might be read as an invitation to turn Pope's words in the *Essay on Criticism* against their author.[43]

Johnson's allusion to *An Essay on Man* indeed turns against the great and guilty satirist, underlining the fact that, while Pope may have left 'nothing to be forgiven' on a stylistic level, his life is a different matter (*Lives*, iii. 221). By comparison with a lesser poet, the greater poet sinks as a man. For Johnson here establishes an inverse relationship between the glories of a writer and those of a human being; contrasting public abilities with private behaviour, he sets authorial against moral stature. To render Pope's words a compliment to one of his dunces suggests the existence of a scale of worth quite different from artistic gradations of merit. As Law put it, 'one seem[s] to be of this world, looking at the things that are temporal, and the other to be of another world, looking wholly at the things that are eternal'.[44] Potter unwittingly recognized that the *Lives* propose a hierarchy of ethical as well as of aesthetic merits: 'If the Man has the good fortune to escape, the Poet is almost sure to be condemned.'[45]

Johnson often pursues the 'silent reference of human works' to moral character, as well as to 'human abilities' ('Preface to Shakespeare', *Yale*, vii. 81). Pope is especially vulnerable to such a reference because he insistently proposed a correspondence between his public and his private self—'but his tongue and his heart were at variance' ('Life of Pope', *Lives*, iii. 188). The 'Life of Pope' fulfils the spurious promise made by Martinus Scriblerus in the *Dunciad Variorum*: 'thou wilt be enabled to draw reflections, not only of a critical, but a moral nature, by being let into many particulars of the Person as well as Genius, and of the Fortune as well as Merit, of our Author' ('TESTIMONIES OF AUTHORS: Concerning our POET and his WORKS', *Dunciad*, 23). Justifying *Peri Bathous* and *The Dunciad* to Swift, Pope had himself invoked *An Essay on Criticism*. By altering '*Ill Author*' to '*bad Author*', he further endorsed the contrasting notion of himself as a *bonus orator*, embodying the Longinian idea that superior art necessarily derives from a superior life:[46]

I despise the world yet, I assure you, more than either Gay or you, and the Court more than all the rest of the world. As for those Scriblers for whom you

---

[43] Richard Blackmore, *Prince Arthur: 1695* (Menston: Scolar Press, 1971), 'The Preface', [p. viii].

[44] Law, *A Serious Call*, 12.   [45] Potter, *Inquiry*, 9.

[46] See Folkenflik, *Samuel Johnson, Biographer*, 118–19.

apprehend I would suppress my *Dulness*, (which by the way, for the future you are to call by a more pompous name, The *Dunceiad*) how much that nest of Hornets are my regard, will easily appear to you when you read the Treatise of the Bathos ... As the obtaining the love of valuable men is the happiest end I know of this life, so the next felicity is to get rid of fools and scoundrels; which I can't but own to you was one part of my design in falling upon these Authors, whose incapacity is not greater than their insincerity, and of whom I have always found (if I may quote myself)

> *That each bad Author is as bad a Friend.*

This Poem will rid me of those Insects ... if it silence these fellows, it must be something greater than any Iliad in Christendome. (*Correspondence*, ii. 481)[47]

To this strain of 'pretended discontent' with the great world, and an equally pretended indifference to the little world, Johnson objects that 'Swift's resentment was unreasonable, but it was sincere; Pope's was the mere mimickry of his friend, a fictitious part' (*Lives*, iii. 211). Blackmore himself had been a friend or acquaintance of Pope's, at least in 1714, when the latter asked John Hughes to 'make my most humble service acceptable to Sir Richard Blackmore' (*Correspondence*, i. 218). They quarrelled in 1716, when Blackmore accused Pope of writing a profane travesty of the first psalm.[48] Johnson alludes to the dispute in the *Lives* of Pope and of Blackmore, rightly identifying it as the root cause of Pope's enmity, and rightly suspecting that Blackmore's claim was well founded: 'he speaks with becoming abhorrence of a "godless author" who has burlesqued a Psalm. This author was supposed to be Pope, who published a reward for any one that would produce the coiner of the accusation, but never denied it, and was afterwards the perpetual and incessant enemy of

---

[47] Pope also quoted the reworked version of this line in a dedication to 'a Collection of Pieces relating to the *Dunciad*', which Savage 'was prevailed upon to sign, though he did not write it, and in which there are some Positions, that the true Author would perhaps not have published under his own Name' (*Savage*, 46–7). The dedication states that the ensuing works 'cannot but be of some Use, to shew the *different Spirit* with which good and bad Authors have ever *acted*, as well as *written*; and to evince a Truth, a greater than which was never advanced, that—*Each bad Author is as bad a Friend.*' See *Savage*, 46–9n. Johnson remarks disapprovingly on the content of and motives behind this dedication, and on Savage's part in concealing Pope's authorship (pp. 46–51). He dismisses the claim made in the dedication 'that the Letters annexed to each Species of bad Poets in the *Bathos*, were, as [Savage] was directed to assert, *set down at Random*' (*Savage*, 49–50). See also 'Life of Pope', *Lives*, iii. 147–50; 'nobody believes that the letters in The Bathos were placed at random' (*Lives*, iii. 150).

[48] See Jemielity, 'A Mock-Biblical Controversy', for a detailed description of this argument.

Blackmore' ('Life of Blackmore', *Lives*, ii. 247; see also 'Life of Pope', *Lives*, iii. 214–15).

This argument, based on religious as well as on literary principles, is the likeliest reason for Blackmore's centrality to all versions of *The Dunciad*. If Johnson felt conscious of his own inability to write *The Rape of the Lock* or Addisonian journalism, Pope's deficiency lay in his inability to complete a native, blank-verse epic (*Brutus* never got beyond a sketchy plan and an eight-line invocation, Johnson thinks 'perhaps without much loss to mankind', *Lives*, iii. 188), the form in which Blackmore, who 'did not fetch his heroes from foreign countries' (*Lives*, ii. 249), had made his name from the start. (See *Peri Bathous*, Pope, *Prose*, 180, for evidence of Pope's annoyance at Blackmore's 'Facility', and his 'five or six Epick Poems'.) In so doing, Blackmore repeatedly emphasized the religious commitment and curative moral powers of his writing—as befitted a medical doctor and a quondam teacher: '*I believe a* Christian Poet *has as great advantages as the* Pagan *had; and that our* Theology *may enter into an Epick Poem, and* raise *the Subject without being it self* debas'd.'[49]

Pope styled Blackmore a 'metaphorically debased' anti-hero in *Peri Bathous*, an 'incomparable' writer 'distinguish'd in the *true Profound*', indeed 'the Father of the *Bathos*' (*Prose*, 182, 184, 175, 180). With a determined literalism, and an enforced comparison between moral and authorial greatness and littleness, Johnson suggests another art of sinking in poetry which Pope 'might have *condescended* to learn' from Blackmore, 'the art of uniting ornament with strength, and ease with closeness' in his *Essay on Man* ('Life of Blackmore', *Lives*, ii. 254; my emphasis). Potter, as was previously noted, singled out this passage for attack: '[Johnson] has the peculiar felicity of discovering that Blackmore "finds the art of uniting ornament with strength, and ease with closeness. This, he tells us is a skill which Pope might have condescended to learn from him, when he needed it so much in his Moral Essays".' But one pertinent element of the definition of 'To CONDESCEND' in the *Dictionary* is 'to *sink* willingly to equal terms with inferiours' (my emphasis)—to stoop to the acknowledgement that you might learn something from them—whereas *An Essay on Man*, once its 'wonder-working sounds *sink* into sense', reveals 'a penury of knowledge and vulgarity of sentiment' that *Peri Bathous* might have ridiculed ('Life of Pope', *Lives*, iii. 243; my emphasis).

Johnson gives earnest consideration to *Peri Bathous'* argument that 'It is therefore manifest that *Mediocrity* ought to be allow'd, yea indulg'd . . .

---

[49] See Mack, *Alexander Pope*, 771–4; Blackmore, *Prince Arthur: 1695*, 'The Preface', [p. xv].

Why should the *Golden Mean*, and Quintessence of all Virtues, be deem'd so offensive only in this Art? Or *Coolness* and *Mediocrity* be so amiable a Quality in a Man, and so detestable in a Poet?' (Pope, *Prose*, 174). In spite of his comments on what Pope might have borrowed from Blackmore when he came to write *An Essay on Man*, it is chiefly in the realm of 'a Man' and not in that of 'a Poet' that Pope could have learned from Blackmore's '*Coolness* and *Mediocrity*'—from the latter's response to criticism, for instance: 'As an author [Blackmore] may justly claim *the honours* of magnanimity. The incessant attacks of his enemies, whether serious or merry, are never discovered to have disturbed his quiet . . . they neither provoked him to petulance nor depressed him to complaint' (*Lives*, ii. 253; my emphasis). Unlike Pope, Blackmore 'studied no niceties of versification' (*Lives*, ii. 253). But also unlike Pope, Blackmore studied no niceties of malice: 'He seems to have been more delighted with praise than pained by censure.' Johnson notes of Pope's hostile relationship with Dennis (to whose rapacious insolence Blackmore had responded with good grace, so that 'he and his critick were afterwards friends') that: 'Pope seems, at first, to have attacked him wantonly; but though he always professed to despise him, he discovers, by mentioning him very often, that he felt his force or his venom' ('Life of Blackmore', *Lives*, ii. 239; 'Life of Pope', *Lives*, iii. 98). Nor is Dryden exempt from the charge of pettiness. Johnson comments that he 'lived long enough to ridicule' Blackmore's *Paraphrase on the Book of Job* (1700), a formulation which makes it sound as if vilification of a lesser poet were the predominant reason that Dryden clung to life. Johnson later writes of one of Blackmore's epic poems that it was 'known enough to be ridiculed' ('Life of Blackmore', *Lives*, ii. 240, 250).

Oldmixon, one of Pope's victims who stands degraded 'In naked majesty' in *The Dunciad*'s diving contest, and 'Who but to *sink* the deeper, *rose* the higher' (II. 283, 290; my emphases), sketched an answer to *Peri Bathous* in a projected treatise 'On the Art of Sinking in Reputation'.[50] Johnson's inverted line from *An Essay on Man* quietly endorses such counter-attacks—from another perspective, no more than laughably damp, amphibians' squibs: 'This satire had the effect which he intended, by blasting the characters which it touched. [James] Ralph . . . complained that for a time he was in danger of starving, as the booksellers had no longer any confidence in his capacity' ('Life of Pope', *Lives*, iii. 146).[51] He

---

[50] See Rogers, *Grub Street*, 206.
[51] See also *Lives*, iii. 146 n. 3, in which G. B. Hill cites William Warburton's remark that Ralph 'ended . . . in the common sink of all such writers, a political newspaper, and

writes that 'Pope appears . . . to have contemplated his victory over the Dunces with great exultation', yet he was also morally 'reduced' by the covert attacks of his poem: 'Aaron Hill, who was represented as diving for the prize, expostulated with Pope in a manner so much superior to all mean solicitation, that Pope was reduced to sneak and shuffle, sometimes to deny and sometimes to apologize: he first endeavours to wound, and is then afraid to own that he meant a blow' (*Lives*, iii. 150, 151).

Here, Johnson turns another of Pope's lines against him, reflecting the character of 'Atticus' (Addison) back on its creator: 'Willing to wound, and yet afraid to strike, | Just hint a fault, and hesitate dislike' (*Arbuthnot*, ll. 203–4). In so doing, he reconstructs a dunce's eye view of Pope's attempt to impose the 'danger of starving' on authors who had done nothing to deserve it. In *The Dunciad*, 'one of his greatest and most elaborate performances', Pope may have 'endeavoured to sink into contempt all the writers by whom he had been attacked', but he also singled out 'some others whom he thought unable to defend themselves'. His 'incessant and unappeasable malignity', when placed alongside the temperate and conciliatory reactions of some of his victims, seems morally indefensible (*Lives*, iii. 145–6, 185).

Of the 1728 *Dunciad*, Johnson remarks that: 'At the head of the Dunces he placed poor Theobald, whom he accused of ingratitude, but whose real crime was supposed to be that of having revised Shakespeare more happily than himself' (*Lives*, iii. 145–6). 'Supposed' allows us to retain a measure of uncertainty about whose supposition this might have been. But when Pope publishes the fourth book of *The Dunciad* in 1742, Johnson's censures become more severe. Cibber, having intermittently appeared in the original poem, complained that he had never insulted Pope and therefore did not deserve to be singled out for ridicule: 'It might have been expected that Pope should have been, in some degree, mollified by this submissive gentleness; but no such consequence appeared. Though he *condescended* to commend Cibber once, he mentioned him afterwards contemptuously . . . and in the fourth book of *The Dunciad* attacked him with acrimony, to which the provocation is not easily discoverable' (*Lives*, iii. 184; my emphasis). The ensuing quarrel between Cibber and Pope, which resulted in Cibber taking Lewis Theobald's place in the poem, incurs Johnson's strongest criticism:

Pope's irascibility prevailed, and he resolved to tell the whole English world that he was at war with Cibber; and to shew that he thought him no common

received a small pittance for pay'. Sutherland quotes another contemporary assertion that Ralph 'greatly suffer'd with his Booksellers, Printers and Hawkers' (*Dunciad*, 452).

adversary he prepared no common vengeance: he published a new edition of *The Dunciad*, in which he degraded Theobald from his painful pre-eminence, and enthroned Cibber in his stead. Unhappily the two heroes were of opposite characters, and Pope was unwilling to lose what he had already written; he has therefore depraved his poem by giving to Cibber the old books, the cold pedantry and sluggish pertinacity of Theobald … Pope confessed his own pain by his anger, but he gave no pain to those who had provoked him. He was able to hurt none but himself: by transferring the same ridicule from one to another he destroyed its efficacy; for, by shewing that what he said of one he was ready to say of another, he reduced himself to the insignificance of his own magpye, who from his cage calls cuckold at a venture. (*Lives*, iii. 186–7)

Pope's 'Eagle-flight' again descends to 'a perch', one that is doubly of his own making ('RICHARDUS ARISTARCHUS OF THE HERO OF THE POEM', *Dunciad*, 255): driven by an insatiable private hostility, he is himself 'degraded' to the level of his 'coxcomb bird', who 'from his cage cries Cuckold, Whore, and Knave, | Tho' many a passenger he rightly call, | You hold him no Philosopher at all' (*Epistle I. To Sir Richard Temple, Lord Viscount Cobham* (1733), ll. 5–8). By pointing his reader in the direction of these lines, Johnson perhaps intended an additional reflection on the *Essay on Man*'s philosophical vacuity, padded out with a magpie's abundance of glitz. The description of Theobald as 'degraded from his painful pre-eminence' (he appears in only two lines of the 1743 *Dunciad*: I. 133 and I. 286) beautifully captures the sense in which excision from the poem oddly debases his standing, as well as relieving him from the agonies of public contempt. In Johnson's eyes, to be censured is always better than to be ignored: 'I would rather be attacked than unnoticed. For the worst thing you can do to an authour is to be silent as to his works. An assault upon a town is a bad thing; but starving it is still worse; an assault may be unsuccessful … but if you starve the town, you are sure of victory'; 'There is nothing more dreadful to an author than neglect, compared with which reproach, hatred, and opposition, are names of happiness'; 'it is surely better a man should be abused than forgotten' (Johnson in *Life*, iii. 375; *Rambler* 2, *Yale*, iii. 13; Johnson in *Miscellanies*, i. 270–1).

Johnson's criticism of Pope for foisting Theobald's character onto Cibber weakens Pat Rogers's argument that we need to recognize *The Dunciad*'s historical specificity. For if Pope voluntarily transferred his lines from one person to the other, it suddenly seems as if he cared less about the integrity or 'efficacy' of his gibes than he did about the beauty of his writing. Scriblerus had rashly argued in 1729 that, in *The Dunciad*, 'The manners are so depicted, and the sentiments so peculiar to those to whom applied, that surely to transfer them to any other ... personages, wou'd be exceeding difficult' ('MARTINUS SCRIBLERUS, OF THE POEM', *Dunciad*, 52). Once Johnson considers the waning applicability of the poem to its moving targets, Pope has left something else 'to be forgiven'. Rogers is at his least convincing when he endeavours to justify the 1743 substitution of Oldmixon for Dennis by a glancing reference to the switch in leading men—'It was *almost as if* Cibber, to augment his earlier crimes, had *actually produced* an edition of Shakespeare, the better to fit Theobald's shoes.'[52] But Cibber did no such thing, and the shoes remain ill-fitting.

Quoting another of Pope's lines, 'All, all but Truth, drops dead-born from the Press' (*Epilogue to the Satires* (1738), II. 226), Johnson considers Blackmore as one of that unfortunate and neglected fraternity of writers to father 'still-born Work' (*Tatler* 110, ii. 167). This plight is made the more pitiable in view of his medical profession, and in view of Pope's 'parental attention' to his publications, which 'never abandoned them' ('Life of Pope', *Lives*, iii. 221)—in spite of William Cleland's description of *The Dunciad* as 'an orphan of so much genius and spirit, which its parent seems to have abandoned from the very beginning' ('A LETTER TO THE PUBLISHER, Occasioned by the Present Edition of the DUNCIAD' (1729), *Dunciad*, 11):

His head still teemed with heroick poetry, and (1705) he published *Eliza* in ten books. I am afraid that the world was now weary of contending about Blackmore's heroes, for I do not remember that by any author, serious or comical, I have found *Eliza* either praised or blamed. She 'dropped', as it seems, 'dead-born from the press.' It is never mentioned, and was never seen by me till I borrowed it for the present occasion. ('Life of Blackmore', *Lives*, ii. 242)

Johnson's solicitude makes itself felt in his hesitant consideration of neglected literary endeavour, denied even the compliment of an attack ('I am afraid ... I do not remember'). He restores to Blackmore a degree of praise (for the work) and of honour (for the life), and in so doing adopts him into 'that order of men which deserves our kindness though not our reverence' (*Rambler* 145, *Yale*, v. 11). For, as he had remarked in *Idler* 51, 'though where there is vice there must be want of reverence, it is not reciprocally true, that where there is want of reverence there is always vice' (*Yale*, ii. 159):

BLACKMORE by the unremitted enmity of the wits, whom he provoked more by his virtue than his dulness, has been exposed to worse treatment than he deserved;

---

[52] Rogers, *Grub Street*, 194 (my emphases)

his name was so long used to point every epigram upon dull writers that it became at last a bye-word of contempt: but it deserves observation that malignity takes hold only of his writings, and that his life passed without reproach, even when his boldness of reprehension naturally turned upon him many eyes desirous to espy faults, which many tongues would have made haste to publish. But those who could not blame could at least forbear to praise, and therefore of his private life and domestick character there are no memorials. (*Lives*, ii. 252–3)

Another name fated to become a 'bye-word' (besides Boswell's), and to 'point' an 'epigram', was that of Charles XII: 'He left the Name, at which the World grew pale, | To point a Moral, or adorn a Tale' (*The Vanity of Human Wishes*, ll. 221–2). The lines up to and including 'To' sound as if they might be about to describe a fittingly grand reason for Charles bequeathing his name to the world—*in order to* fulfil some purpose. But that 'To' enacts a turn towards a wholly different perspective. Boundless individual ambition, apparently reinforced by the impressive pair of definite articles attached to 'Name' and 'World', is checked by the pair of indefinite articles attached to nouns describing the uses to which that name is put in the world: 'To point a Moral, or adorn a Tale.' The two lines serve reciprocally to test the claims of one another, as if one side of Johnson is in conversation with the other, and admiration is yielding to enquiry, panegyric to truth, and pride to humility. Similarly, at the end of the *Life of Savage*, once Johnson's subject has ceased to be a friend and becomes an exemplar, he also becomes potentially 'contemptible'. Charles's name has this much in common with the Scottish window-frames on which Johnson made his 'diminutive observations': both are from one perspective or in one literary mode great, important, and respectable; from or in the other, they are not. Blackmore's name, 'so long used to point every epigram upon dull writers that it became at last a bye-word of contempt', becomes in Johnson's hands a pointed moral on the shortcomings of what he recognized as a far greater literary mind.

If Pope is the petty virtuoso of domestic trivia, nursing his enmities as carefully as his ailments and his saucepan, his opposite in the *Lives* is Milton. Johnson pauses in the 'Life of Milton' to praise his subject for having stooped, in a rare act of humility, from the grandeur of *Paradise Lost* to the composition of a useful 'little book': '*Accidence commenced Grammar* [is] a little book which has nothing remarkable, but that its author, who had been lately defending the supreme powers of his country and was then writing *Paradise Lost*, could descend from his elevation to rescue children from the perplexity of grammatical confusion, and the trouble of lessons unnecessarily repeated' (*Lives*, i. 132). Milton is later commended for 'having … descended', in this work, 'to accommodate children', and thus for 'a kind of humble dignity, which did not disdain the meanest services to literature' (*Lives*, i. 147). His descent 'from his elevation' is an echo of Christ's incarnation, embodied in the exemplary paradox of 'humble dignity': another version of Johnson's claim to have composed biographical 'trifles with dignity' (*Life*, iv. 34 n. 5), and similar to the oxymoronic 'proud humility' with which Hazlitt distinguished Wordsworth's literary condescension, as well as to the 'sublime humility' whose absence from his father's religious character Edmund Gosse lamented.[53] Piozzi remembered that 'no man was more struck than Mr. Johnson with voluntary descent from possible splendour to painful duty' (*Miscellanies*, i. 157). She was probably alluding to this passage on 'little poems' from the 'Life of Watts':

> His tenderness appeared in his attention to children and to the poor. To the poor, while he lived in the family of his friend, he allowed the third part of his annual revenue, though the whole was not a hundred a year; and for children he condescended to lay aside the scholar, the philosopher, and the wit, to write little poems of devotion and systems of instruction, adapted to their wants and capacities, from the dawn of reason through its gradations of advance in the morning of life. Every man acquainted with the common principles of human action will look with veneration on the writer who is at one time combating Locke, and at another making a catechism for children in their fourth year. A voluntary descent from the dignity of science is perhaps the hardest lesson that humility can teach. (*Lives*, iii. 307–8)

'There is no employment in which men are more easily betrayed to indecency and impatience, than in that of teaching; in which they necessarily converse with those, who are their inferiours' (Sermon 8, *Yale*, xiv. 92). Just as humility taught Watts a lesson, so he can teach us a lesson about humility ('no man can teach what he has never learned', Sermon 8, *Yale*, xiv. 90). In the last sentence cited from the 'Life of Watts', Johnson comes close to quoting his definition of 'CONDESCENSION' in the *Dictionary*: 'Voluntary humiliation; descent from superiority; voluntary submission to equality with inferiours.' Watts was a friend and literary associate of Blackmore's, both men were teachers ('Life of Watts', *Lives*, iii. 304), and it is not surprising to discover that Pope alluded to Watts in most of the six 1728 editions of *The Dunciad*. In Book I, he is seen as one of those authors guilty of purging 'Greece and Rome' from the realms of learning: 'W—y, W—s, and Bl—' (Samuel Wesley, Watts,

---

[53] Edmund Gosse, *Father and Son: A Study of Two Temperaments* (1907), ed. Peter Abbs (Harmondsworth: Penguin, 1989), 113.

and Richard Blome, *Dunciad Variorum*, I. 125–6, *1728a–c*). Book III includes him in another list, 'W—s, B—r, M—n', whose members were identified by Curll as Watts, Henry Baker, and Luke Milbourne (*Dunciad Variorum*, III. 188, *1728a–f* and n.). Pope was subsequently persuaded to excise Watts's name from *The Dunciad*—either by Watts's own 'serious, though gentle remonstrance', or at the request of Jonathan Richardson. In any event, a shifty note in *The Dunciad Variorum* insists that Wesley and Watts have been targeted only in 'surreptitious Editions' of the poem. The 'editor' claims to have 'restor'd' the line 'according to its Original', by removing the names of two 'Persons eminent for good life; the one [Wesley] writ the Life of Christ in verse; the other [Watts] some valuable pieces in the lyrick kind on pious subjects' (*Dunciad Variorum*, I. 126n.).

Sutherland thinks it was probably Watts's 'popularity with humble readers' that saw him land in *The Dunciad* (*Dunciad Variorum*, I. 126n.). But the phrase 'eminent for good life' is central to the reason for Watts's inclusion in the *Lives of the Poets* ('It was not only in his book but in his mind that orthodoxy was united with charity', 'Life of Watts', *Lives*, iii. 308), as it is central to his removal from post-1728 editions of Pope's poem. Notwithstanding his assertion in the 'Life of Halifax' that 'in this collection poetical merit is the claim to attention', for Johnson, Watts acts (like Blackmore) as an ethical, not as an aesthetic contrast to deservedly greater literary reputations (*Lives*, ii. 41). The emphasis on 'poetical merit' in the 'Life of Halifax' perhaps also derives from the fact that Johnson had no choice but to write about Montague, 'an artful and active statesman' and meagre versifier, whereas Blackmore and Watts's presence in the *Lives* was determined by him (*Lives*, ii. 41). Watts was not primarily a poet, and the verses he did write were of the pious variety for which Johnson expressed a dislike in the 'Life of Waller', as well as in that of Watts: 'poetical devotion cannot often please . . . The ideas of Christian Theology are too simple for eloquence, too sacred for fiction, and too majestick for ornament'; 'his devotional poetry is, like that of others, unsatisfactory. The paucity of its topicks enforces perpetual repetition, and the sanctity of the matter rejects the ornaments of figurative diction. It is sufficient for Watts to have done better than others what no man has done well' ('Life of Waller', *Lives*, i. 291–2; 'Life of Watts', iii. 310). Johnson even told Boswell that he would be unable in his 'Life of Watts' to 'praise his poetry itself highly'. As in the letter he sent in 1777 to one W. Sharp, requesting information about Watts, 'a man who never wrote but for a good purpose', it was the 'design' behind the writing that, he felt confident, 'I can praise'. For it was the same design as that which had governed the *Prefaces Biographical and Critical,* 'written I hope in such a manner, as may tend to the promotion of Piety' (*Life,* iii. 358; *Letters,* iii. 38; *Yale,* i. 294).

Watts's pedagogical art of sinking is a voluntary condescension from 'different gradations of excellence' (*Life,* ii. 351) to attend to 'gradations of advance in the morning of life', framed in language 'adapted to [the] wants and capacities' of children. As he graciously lowers himself to instruction, Watts's pupils rise up to meet him. In the 'Preface' to *Divine Songs attempted in Easy Language, for the Use of Children* (1715), the work to which Johnson is referring when he commends Watts's descent from the pinnacles of learning—and which Watts himself called his '*little book*'—the author wrote that he had '*endeavoured to sink the Language to the Level of a Child's Understanding, and yet to keep it (if possible) above Contempt*'; the subjoined 'Slight SPECIMEN of MORAL SONGS' expressed the wish for a '*condescending Genius*' (*Divine Songs,* 147, 193). Of his *Hymns and Spiritual Songs* (1707), Watts advised the reader that 'The Metaphors are generally sunk to the Level of vulgar Capacities. I have . . . endeavoured to make the Sense plain and obvious. If the Verse appear so gentle and flowing as to incur the Censure of Feebleness, I may honestly affirm, that sometimes it cost me Labour to make it so: Some of the Beauties of Poesy are neglected, and some willingly defac'd.' The 'best' of his *Horæ Lyricæ* (1706), he wrote, 'sinks below . . . a Divine or Moral Ode' (*Hymns,* pp. vii–viii; *Divine Songs,* app. 1, p. 106).

Watts would have taken Johnson's 'condescended' as the highest compliment to his literary endeavours; as was previously mentioned, the OED credits him with the first recorded use of the word 'condescending', in the positive sense, in one of his *Hymns* (although there are earlier examples within this volume; on p. 143, for instance): 'How condescending and how kind, | Was God's Eternal Son! | Our Mis'ry reach'd his heav'nly mind, | And pity brought him down' ('Christ's dying Love: Or, Our Pardon bought at a dear Price', *Hymns,* 325). The *Hymns* are full of such images of Christ's incarnation. Casting Watts's descent to children in the same mould, Johnson sees it as an exemplary imitation of divine humility: 'But O what gentle condescending Ways | He takes to teach his heav'nly Grace!' ('The Offices of Christ, from several Scriptures', *Hymns,* 143). 'Teach' is a central word here. There is a solitary citation, from Watts, under 'TEACHABLE' ('Docile; susceptive of instruction') in Johnson's *Dictionary*: 'We ought to bring our minds free, unbiassed, and *teachable* to learn our religion from the word of God.' Gosse complained, in terms which echo Watts, that his father (who greatly admired Watts's hymns and psalms)[54] was incapable, when teaching him, of sinking to the level of a child: 'Such metaphysical ideas as "laying again the foundation of repentance from dead works" and "crucifying the Sons of God afresh" were not successfully brought down to the level of my understanding'; 'My Father, without realizing it, had been talking on his own level, not on mine, and now he condescended to me. But without very great success.'[55] The positive associations of condescension with teaching still crop up in unexpected places. William Myers recently recalled of his tutor, Wallace Robson, that: 'Once, having referred to the lines about the Incarnation in Dryden's "Religio Laici", he asked if we realized they were about the Divine Condescension. There was a pause—one learnt to respect them. " 'Condescension': a beautiful word until they ruined it." '[56]

Johnson may have had Watts in mind when he wrote of Milton that he 'never learned the art of doing little things with grace; he overlooked the milder excellence of suavity and softness: he was a "Lion" that had no skill "in dandling the Kid" '—a criticism he reiterated in conversation: 'Milton, Madam, was a genius that could cut a Colossus from a rock; but could not carve heads upon cherry-stones' ('Life of Milton', *Lives*, i. 163; *Life*, iv. 305). Johnson often described his response to Milton in terms of imprisonment. Late in his 'Life', he remarks that 'such is the power of his poetry that his call is obeyed without resistance, the reader feels himself in captivity to a higher and a nobler mind, and criticism sinks in admiration' (*Lives*, i. 190). There is something liberating, then, in a brief sojourn from the overwhelming grandeur of *Paradise Lost*, whose sublime elements Johnson repeatedly emphasized over and above the adventitious contributions of elegance and grace. *Accidence commenced Grammar*, like Watts's *Divine Songs*, represents one virtuous descent (Milton's own) from such sublimity. John Philips's Miltonic parody, *The Splendid Shilling* (1701), descends still further, demeaning 'Milton's phrase to the gross incidents of common life':

To degrade the sounding words and stately construction of Milton, by an application to the lowest and most trivial things, gratifies the mind with a momentary triumph over that grandeur which hitherto held its captives in admiration; the words and things are presented with a new appearance, and novelty is always grateful where it gives no pain. ('Life of John Philips', *Lives*, i. 317)

---

[54] See Ann Thwaite, *Glimpses of the Wonderful: The Life of Philip Henry Gosse* (London: Faber and Faber, 2002), 18, 52, 305.

[55] Gosse, *Father and Son*, 92–3.

[56] William Myers, letter to the *London Review of Books*, 23 Jan. 2003, p. 4.

The first two phrases of this sentence ('To degrade the sounding words and stately construction of Milton', 'by an application to the lowest and most trivial things') are equipollent, with sixteen syllables each—as if to hold in judicial suspension a grand style and its base (albeit novel) replica. But the dignified adjective–noun balance of 'sounding words' and 'stately construction' dwindles to the comparatively asymmetrical and superlative 'lowest and most trivial things'. The sentence, like the literary work it is describing, moves towards a sundering of high style from demeaning content, towards an unequal relationship between words and things. It is characteristic of Johnson that, having dwelt on its brief attractions, he should diminish a transitory pleasure he shares with his audience. The triumph that 'gratifies the mind' on reading *The Splendid Shilling* is in the present tense, because it is 'momentary'. If Milton has 'hitherto held [his] captives in admiration', we can presume his supremacy will endure the assaults of novelty, however pleasing. 'One excellence of *The Splendid Shilling*', as Johnson noted at the close of his brief 'Life of Somervile', 'is that it is short' (*Lives*, ii. 320).

Yet in Milton's 'Life', a perceived literary preference for 'new modes of existence' at the cost of 'things visible and known' and 'the occurrences of life' is brought to bear on a neglect of *all* 'sublunary care or pleasures', facilitated by Johnson's readiness to compare 'The regal and parental tyrant', who 'differ only in the extent of their dominions, and the number of their slaves' (*Lives*, i. 177–8; *Rambler* 148, *Yale*, v. 25). He collapses the public author into the domestic figure by referring to Milton's attacks on royal arbitration. Johnson might here be remembering the instances of private tyranny introduced to Watts's *Humility*, as quoted in Chapter 3:

It has been observed that they who most loudly clamour for liberty do not most liberally grant it. What we know of Milton's character in domestick relations is, that he was severe and arbitrary. His family consisted of women; and there appears in his books something like a Turkish contempt of females, as subordinate and inferior beings. That his own daughters might not break the ranks, he suffered them to be depressed by a mean and penurious education. He thought woman made only for obedience, and man only for rebellion. (*Lives*, i. 157)

Moving with silent ease from literary to biographical evidence ('there appears in his work . . . he suffered them to be depressed . . . he thought'), Johnson concludes with a trenchant summary broadly applicable to art and to life. The semi-chiastic formulation 'they who most loudly clamour for liberty do not most liberally grant it' calls for a correspondence between claims and practice that it does not find; and it therefore seems to be complaining of inconsistency. But in fact, it is a mark of unfortunate consistency in Milton as father and as poet that he failed to condescend to domestic arts just as he failed, in Johnson's words, 'to *condescend to rhyme*' (*Lives*, i. 194; my emphasis). His overwhelming majesty, seen on this homely scale, compares unfavourably with Watts's authorial descent to children, which is in its turn compatible with the deliberate 'Feebleness' of Watts' rhymes, and with his private descent to charity. Such compatibility might also recall the potential link between Swift's literary descent to low, sordid detail, and his benevolence to the needy. While Milton can make the rare boast of having lived *up* to the reputation of his works, he failed to live *down* to his family or to the lesser graces of verse. His mind is habitually 'too elevated to descend to minuteness' (*Idler* 69, *Yale*, ii. 216). Hence, perhaps, Johnson's enlisting of *Paradise Lost* beneath the second sense of the adverb 'LOWLY' ('Humbly; meekly; modestly') in the *Dictionary*: 'Heav'n is for thee too high | To know what passes there; be *lowly* wise: | Think only what concerns thee, and thy being.'[57]

4. DR JOHNSON AND DR LEVET: THE LIKENESS OF MEN

Johnson's commemorative verses 'On the Death of Dr. Robert Levet' sprang from a friendship of nearly forty years. In a journal entry of 1782, ten months after the *Lives* were completed, he recorded Levet's death and funeral: 'Robert Levett was buried in the church-yard of Bridewell, between one and two in the afternoon. He died on Thursday 17, about seven in the morning, by an instantaneous death. He was an old and faithful friend; I have known him from about 46 . . . May God have had mercy on him. May he have mercy on me' (*Yale*, i. 311). An ambiguity of tense in this brief entry contrives to bring the living and the dead into closer proximity. Johnson does not write that he once knew or 'had known' Levet, but that he *has* known him since 1746 or thereabouts. The perfect tense intimates a continuing relationship with 'an old and faithful friend' whose loss has not, as yet, quite registered in the mind—and whose remaining existence is bound up with that of the friend who has known and yet survives him. The auxiliaries 'he was' and 'I have' are put to work to sustain their previous kinship, by conjugating a new one beyond the grave. Precise details concerning Levet's death and funeral, on 'Thursday 17' and 'between one and two in the afternoon', sit alongside uncertainties concerning the year his and Johnson's friendship

---

[57] Milton, *Paradise Lost*, VIII. 172–4.

commenced ('about 46') and the exact moment it was terminated in Johnson's absence ('about seven in the morning'). The entry begins with 'Robert Levett' and dwindles expectantly to 'me'. 'It is good to speak dubiously about futurity', as Johnson had written four years earlier to Hester Thrale; 'It is likewise not amiss to hope' (*Letters*, iii. 144).

Boswell could not understand what Johnson saw in Levet. The *Life* dismisses him as:

an obscure practiser in physick amongst the lower people, his fees being sometimes very small sums, sometimes whatever provisions his patients could afford him; but of such extensive practice in that way, that Mrs. Williams has told me, his walk was from Houndsditch to Marybone ... such was Johnson's predilection for him, and fanciful estimation of his moderate abilities, that I have heard him say he should not be satisfied, though attended by all the College of Physicians, unless he had Mr. Levet with him. Ever since I was acquainted with Dr. Johnson, and many years before, ... Mr. Levet had an apartment in his house, or his chambers, and waited upon him every morning, through the whole course of his late and tedious breakfast. He was of a strange grotesque appearance, stiff and formal in his manner, and seldom said a word while any company was present. (*Life*, i. 243)

Boswell frequently ran into difficulties when he tried to account for Johnson's attentiveness to obscure and unappealing characters. He was disinclined to appreciate, at least in Johnson's case, the descent from authorial greatness to common life that his friend was so delighted to find in a 'little book' for children by the unlikeliest of subjects, Milton. He betrays his disdain for Levet by misconstruing Johnson's fondness as a 'predilection', his admiration as a 'fanciful estimation of ... moderate abilities', as if nothing but the great man's whimsy could account for such an attachment. Yet it might not be for reasons purely professional that Johnson would not be satisfied under the supervision of 'all the College of Physicians, unless he had Mr. Levet with him'. As he wrote to Dr Brocklesby towards the end of his life, 'If the virtue of medicines could be enforced by the benevolence of the Prescriber how soon should I be well' (*Letters*, iv. 371). 'Virtue' has a double sense here—'Moral goodness' and 'Medicinal efficacy' (senses 1 and 4 of 'VIRTUE' in the *Dictionary*)—exhibiting, once again, what Davie perceives as a characteristically eighteenth-century conjunction of the ethical with the scientific.

In the criticism on epitaphs that Johnson appended to his 'Life of Pope', he singled out for particular praise the lines '*On Mrs.* CORBET, *who died of a Cancer in her Breast*':

I have always considered this as the most valuable of Pope's epitaphs; the subject of it is a character not discriminated by any shining or eminent peculiarities, yet that which really makes, though not the splendour, the felicity of life, and that which every wise man will choose for his final and lasting companion in the languor of age, in the quiet of privacy, when he departs weary and disgusted from the ostentatious, the volatile, and the vain. Of such a character, which the dull overlook and the gay despise, it was fit that the value should be made known, and the dignity established. Domestick virtue, as it is exerted without great occasions or conspicuous consequences in an even unnoted tenor, required the genius of Pope to display it in such a manner as might attract regard, and enforce reverence. (*Lives*, iii. 262)

Pope's non-satirical elevation of a lowly character gains high praise: he descends beneath himself for charitable purposes, rather than sinking to attack his poetic and social inferiors. Johnson's appreciation of *The Rape of the Lock*, in which 'familiar things are made new', here finds, at last, its moral counterpart. Recommending obscure virtue to the attention of a jaded audience is an act that deserves readers' respect. This passage might also serve as an appraisal of Levet. Johnson, though 'fond of discrimination' (Reynolds in *Life*, ii. 306), delighted equally in memorials of characters 'not discriminated by any shining or eminent peculiarities'. That his protection of Levet did not cease with the death of his friend is indicated by the terse continuity of regard inscribed in the journal entry for 1782. The instantaneous nature of Levet's end—'I suppose not one minute passed between health and death'—continued to impress his more renowned friend with the uncertainty of 'human things' (*Letters*, iv. 15; 'human things' is itself a typically uncertain formulation).

As he wrote to Bennet Langton, on the night of Levet's death Johnson had

thought with uncommon earnestness, that however I might alter my mode of life, or whithersoever I might remove, I would endeavour to retain Levet about me, in the morning my servant brought me Word that Levet was brought to another state, a state for which, I think, he was not unprepared, for he was very useful to the poor. How much soever I valued him, I now wish that I had valued him more. (*Letters*, iv. 23)

Syntactically, this letter, like the journal entry on Levet's funeral, embodies continuity of feeling and mutual experience of death: there is no sentence break between Johnson's night thoughts and the realities of the morning, merely a series of commas. As Johnson was 'brought . . . Word' of his friend's death, so too that friend was 'brought to another state'.

If he could no longer preserve the living Levet, Johnson endeavoured vigorously to retain his presence and useful example 'about' him. 'On the Death of Dr. Robert Levet' is concerned with how a writer might recommend in verse the conduct of a man who not only never read poetry, but also failed (according to Johnson) to reveal 'any power by which he can be supposed to judge of an author's merit' (*Miscellanies*, ii. 110). The 'degree of exaggerated praise' that Johnson allowed himself when he described Garrick's death as having 'eclipsed the gaiety of nations' was not permissible here (*Life*, ii. 407; 'Life of Smith', *Lives*, ii. 21; see also *Life*, iii. 387). Borrowing instead the method of his obscure companion, whose 'vig'rous remedy display'd | The power of art without the show' ('Levet', ll. 15–16), Johnson exhibits the doctor's virtues in a language whose force derives from its lack of ostentation. In spite of his caricatures of Thomas Percy's modern ballads ('I put my hat upon my head | And walk'd into the Strand, | And there I met another man | Who's hat was in his hand', 'Parodies of Bishop Percy's *Hermit of Warkworth*', I), Johnson chose the stanzaic lyric in order to create a commemorative poem 'above grossness and below refinement, where propriety resides' ('Preface to Shakespeare', *Yale*, vii. 70). His attempt to create a mediocre literary vehicle in 'Levet', one that is 'above' and 'below' two possible extremes, recalls Addison and Watts. If Addison aspired to 'have brought Philosophy out of Closets and Libraries, Schools and Colleges, to dwell in Clubs and Assemblies, at Tea-Tables, and in Coffee-Houses' (*Spectator* 10, i. 44), Watts hoped he might 'assume this pleasure of being the first who hath brought down the royal author [David] into the common affairs of the christian life', rendering 'the sense and language . . . level to the lowest capacity' and to the 'meanest Christian'.[58] Yet he also strove to keep such language '*above Contempt*' (*Divine Songs*, 147).

One of Addison's boldest critical descents was his attempt to generate esteem for the popular ballad. *Spectator* 70 and 74 defend 'Chevy Chase' from the charge of risible mawkishness and compare it favourably with the performances of 'the greatest ancient Poets' (*Spectator* 74, i. 320): 'an ordinary Song or Ballad that is the Delight of the common People, cannot fail to please all such Readers as are not unqualified for the Entertainment by their Affectation or Ignorance' (*Spectator* 70, i. 297). Addison went on to recommend in pathetic terms 'The Babes in the Wood' as 'a plain simple Copy of Nature, destitute of all the Helps and

---

[58] Isaac Watts, 'Preface' to *The Psalms of David* (1719), in *The Works of the Late Reverend and Learned Isaac Watts, D.D.*, ed. D. Jennings and P. Doddridge, 6 vols. (London: for T. and T. Longman et al., 1753), iv, p. xxi.

Ornaments of Art. The Tale of it is a pretty Tragical Story, and pleases for no other Reason, but because it is a Copy of Nature. There is even a despicable Simplicity in the Verse; and yet, because the Sentiments appear genuine and unaffected, they are able to move the Mind of the most polite Reader'; 'The Author of it (whoever he was) has delivered it in such an abject Phrase, and Poorness of Expression, that the quoting any part of it would look like a Design of turning it into Ridicule ... those only who are endowed with a true Greatness of Soul and Genius, can divest themselves of the little Images of Ridicule, and admire Nature in her Simplicity and Nakedness' (*Spectator* 85, i. 362).

With seeming inevitability, a parody of Addison's high regard for 'the Darling Songs of the common People', published under the name of 'William Wagstaffe', took this to mean that we should apply ourselves 'to the Study of Ballads' rather than 'to the Classicks', noting with mock-surprise that 'some of the best things that are extant in our Language shou'd pass unobserv'd amidst a Croud of inferiour Productions'.[59] This observation could have been made in all seriousness. In the 'Life of Addison', however, Johnson sides with Wagstaffe: '[Addison] descended now and then to lower disquisitions; and by a serious display of the beauties of *Chevy Chase* exposed himself to the ridicule of "Wagstaff," who bestowed a like pompous character on *Tom Thumb* ... In *Chevy Chase* there is not much of either bombast or affectation; but there is chill and lifeless imbecility. The story cannot possibly be told in a manner that shall make less impression on the mind' (*Lives*, ii. 147–8). Johnson might, in another context, have classed Wagstaffe's response as typical of the dull ignorance or gay derision he reprimanded in his comments on epitaphs in the 'Life of Pope'.

Addison's defence (albeit with some grave reservations) of a 'plain simple Copy of Nature' anticipates by almost a century Wordsworth's 1802 preface to *Lyrical Ballads*. As if to highlight Addison's emphasis on stylistic destitution, and his refusal to quote the poem, Wordsworth cites the first stanza of 'Babes in the Wood', setting it against Johnson's parody of Percy and questioning why it is that 'the one stanza we admit as admirable, and the other as a fair example of the superlatively contemptible'. His answer draws a distinction between form and content: our distaste for ballads arises not from the poverty of their metre,

---

[59] 'William Wagstaffe' and George Canning, *Parodies of Ballad Criticism (1711–1781): William Wagstaffe, A Comment upon the History of Tom Thumb, 1711; George Canning, The Knave of Hearts, 1787*, ed. William K. Wimsatt, Jr. (Berkeley and Los Angeles: University of California, 1957), 3–4.

language, or syntax, but from the contemptible '*matter*' expressed in stanzas such as Johnson's. It is unfair, he argues, to dismiss the verse-form as a result of the fact that some ballads dwell on trivial subjects. If Johnson's only exercises in this genre had issued from contempt, Wordsworth would have been justified in summarizing that Johnson thought 'Poetry in which the language closely resembles that of life and nature' to be 'a bad kind of poetry, or . . . not poetry'.[60] But Johnson evidently felt drawn in one mood to poke fun at the laborious vacuity of ballads; in another, to sense the aptness of the form for expressing the laborious vacuity of life.

'It ought . . . to be the care of learning when she quits her exaltation', Johnson remarked, 'to descend with dignity' (*Rambler* 173, *Yale*, v. 153). His own lines on Levet's descent to the grave take care to do just that:

> Condemn'd to hope's delusive mine,
>   As on we toil from day to day,
> By sudden blasts, or slow decline,
>   Our social comforts drop away.
>
> Well tried through many a varying year,
>   See LEVET to the grave descend;
> Officious, innocent, sincere,
>   Of ev'ry friendless name the friend.
>   (ll. 1–8)[61]

Rachel Trickett cautiously observes that the 'style and mood' of this poem are 'not unlike Watts'.[62] The similarity, conscious or unconscious, goes further than this: Johnson seems to have caught the spirit of Watts's condescending art, eschewing the complex metaphors beloved of 'letter'd arrogance' for 'hope's delusive mine' and 'misery's darkest caverns' (ll. 1, 17). The first image of 'Levet' may recall, among other things, Watts's

---

[60] *Wordsworth: The Major Works*, 612–13.

[61] The poem exists in several versions. Because it is about a semi-literate character, there is a case for preferring Boswell's text (*Life*, iv. 137–9), since J. D. Fleeman and the *Yale* editors, following the *Gentleman's Magazine* text, omit his capitalization of certain abstract nouns ('Hope', 'Affection', 'Nature', 'Death', 'Misery', 'Anguish', and 'Want'), 'that Restoration and Augustan habit of visual literacy' as Barbara Everett calls it ('Rochester: The Sense of Nothing', in *Poets in their Time*, 88–119 (p. 99)). Although the sense of animated generalization operating within the lines is lessened by the removal of capitals, Boswell's 'Levet' is less authoritative than the *Gentleman's*. For a full presentation of variant readings, see S. C. Roberts, 'On the Death of Dr. Robert Levet: A Note on the Text', *Review of English Studies*, 3 (1927), 442–5.

[62] Rachel Trickett, *The Honest Muse: A Study in Augustan Verse* (Oxford: Clarendon Press, 1967), 251.

'The Invitation of the Gospel: Or, Spiritual Food and Cloathing' and 'The rich Sinner dying' which have the verses 'Dear God! The Treasures of thy Love | Are everlasting Mines, | Deep as our helpless Miseries are, | And boundless as our Sins!' and (as opening lines) 'In vain the wealthy Mortals toil, | And heap their shining Dust in vain' (*Hymns*, 9, 25), as well as a cancelled line from Johnson's early work 'The Young Author' (1743; written *c.* 1729): 'In blissful dreams he digs the golden mine' (see *Poems*, 190n.). The last poem describes the writer's 'pleasing hope of endless fame', which ends in his wish for 'a less distinguish'd lot' (ll. 12, 29). '[M]isery's darkest caverns' echoes the 'gloomy Caverns' and 'Caves of Darkness and of Doubt' in Watts's 'The Church saved, and her Enemies disappointed' and 'Christ inviting, and the Church answering the Invitation' (*Hymns*, 245, 63).

The internal rhymes of 'Levet'—'*still* he *fills* affection's eye' and 'No petty *gain* dis*dain*ed by pride' (ll. 9, 22; my emphases)—accentuate the later reference to the doctor's 'narrow round' (l. 25), a round that was in one sense remarkably extensive: 'from Houndsditch to Marybone', as Boswell tells us. Again, the image may owe something to Watts: ''Tis but at best a *narrow Bound* | That Heav'n allows to Men, | And Pains and Sins run thro' *the Round* | Of Threescore Years and Ten' ('The Shortness and Misery of Life', *Hymns*, 189; my emphases). Levet also exceeds the boundaries of this 'round', dying well after his seventieth birthday. 'Yet *still* he *fills* affection's eye' recalls Watts's vision of a descending deity, introduced with the same internal rhyme: 'God's Condescension to our Worship' has the lines '*Still* might he *fill* his starry Throne ... But th' heav'nly Majesty comes down' (*Hymns*, 194; my emphases). Johnson has a similar internal repetition, a form of shorthand to express a life restricted or curtailed by penury (and hence associated with a God who humbly contracted his omnipotence), in his commemoration of an itinerant Welsh violinist: 'Phillips, whose touch harmonious could remove | The pangs of guilty pow'r, and hapless love, | *Rest* here dist*ress'd* by poverty no more' ('An Epitaph on Claudy Phillips, A Musician' (1740), ll. 1–3; my emphases). Repetition is particularly effective in the last of these lines, where the word 'rest' is contained within 'distress'd'. Although it does not actually stand in the same relation to 'rest' as, say, 'dis-enchant' does to 'enchant', 'dist-ress'd' sounds as if it does: the repetition of 'rest' softens the privative action of 'distress'd', and hence of poverty (this sense is the more apparent in the text followed by the *Yale* editors, in which 'distress'd' is spelt 'distrest', *Yale*, vi. 68).

Johnson's description of his friend as 'Obscurely wise, and coarsely kind' (l. 10) does not flinch at the fact that Levet was difficult to like, or to distinguish. The line might allude to Pope's *Essay on Man*, which Johnson thought of as characterized by a different kind of 'penury'—that of 'knowledge'—and this could have seemed in its own way appropriate for a man who failed to exhibit any powers of literary discrimination. Pope describes man in general as 'A being darkly wise, and rudely great' (*Essay on Man*, II. 5), but it is the individual Levet who, for Johnson, is 'Obscurely wise'. He attends to those aspects of his friend which were unregarded even by himself (busy days and peaceful nights, l. 29)—let alone by onlookers, such as Boswell, more habituated to attending to greatness. Four days before Johnson gave the first recital of 'On the Death of Dr. Robert Levet' (to Boswell, 'with an emotion which gave [it] full effect', *Life*, iv. 165), he noted in his journal: 'It occurred to me that though my time might pass unemployed, no more should pass uncounted, and this has been written to day in consequence of that thought' (*Yale*, i. 313). Johnson's self-directed injunction to count his time, contrasted with Levet's 'Unfelt, uncounted' days and nights, reflects a larger contrast between the unconscious possession of a 'single talent' and Johnson's painful awareness of multiple intellectual gifts (ll. 30, 28). The only direct literary allusion of the poem—to the parable of the talents—is introduced by a colloquialism, 'sure' (l. 27), which serves to remind us of its domestic context, and hence to reflect once again on the presumption of 'letter'd arrogance' when it denies its praise to 'merit unrefin'd' (ll. 11–12)—however ill adapted that might be to consider artistic 'merit'. Johnson may have spent his professional life in adjusting the merits of literature, but, as he wrote in *Rambler* 68, 'To be happy at home is the ultimate result of all ambition' (*Yale*, iii. 360).

If Johnson chose to focus on the unregarded aspects of Levet's life, he excluded one shady and ludicrous episode from his poem. The anonymous 'Anecdotes of Mr. *Levett*', published after Johnson's death in the *Gentleman's Magazine* (1785), reveal that:

Before [Levet] became a constant inmate of the Doctor's house, he married, when he was near sixty, a woman of the town, who had persuaded him (notwithstanding their place of congress was a small coal-shed in Fetter-lane) that she was nearly related to a man of fortune, but was injuriously kept by him out of large possessions ... Compared with the marvels of this transaction, as Johnson himself declared when relating them, the tales in the Arabian Nights' Entertainments seem familiar occurrences. Never was infant more completely duped than our hero. He had not been married four months, before a writ was taken out against him, for debts incurred by his wife ... In a short time afterwards, she ran away from him, and was tried, providentially, in his opinion, for picking pockets at the Old Bailey. Her husband was, with difficulty, prevented from attending the court, in the hope she would be hanged. She pleaded her own cause, and was acquitted; a separation between this ill-starred couple took place; and Dr. Johnson then took Levett home, where he continued till his death, which happened suddenly, without pain, Jan. 17, 1782. His vanity in supposing that a young woman of family and fortune should be enamoured of him, Dr. Johnson thought, deserved some check. (*Miscellanies*, ii. 110–11)

If the writer intended to ridicule Levet when, in pseudo-romance strain, he zestfully compared his 'hero' to a duped infant, the effect is, in fact, slightly different. For the comment serves to point up Johnson's paternal solicitude (he took Levet home not only for a ticking-off, but for life), which might remind us of Watts's praiseworthy descent to the instruction of children, as well as of Addison's commendation to our regard of the forlorn and despised Babes in the Wood. Piozzi reports that Johnson would often retail similar anecdotes of 'tragicomical distresses', of indigence and wretched marriages, in order to raise 'contributions for some distressed author, or wit in want'. Johnson, she writes, 'made us all more than amends by diverting descriptions of the lives they were then passing in corners unseen by anyone but himself and that odd old surgeon whom he kept in his house' (*Miscellanies*, i. 226–7, 229).

As the poem tells us, Levet was (like Johnson) privy to the largely 'unseen' miseries of 'hopeless anguish' and 'lonely want' (ll. 19–20); 'The eye of wealth', *Rambler* 166 argues (in contrast to 'affection's eye'), 'is elevated towards higher stations, and seldom descends to examine the actions of those who are placed below the level of its notice' (*Yale*, v. 116). The poem eschews any direct reference to Levet's foolhardy marriage, but Johnson's tactfully averted gaze does not mean that it was necessarily absent from his thoughts. We might number it, and the 'check' he thought Levet's vanity deserved, among the delusive hopes to which we are collectively condemned at the beginning of the poem, or see in 'misery's darkest caverns' a discreet periphrasis for the 'small coal-shed in Fetter-lane'. The narrative of Levet's unfortunate alliance might have struck a chord for another reason: the young Johnson had himself been closely attached to (perhaps duped by) a character who claimed to be 'nearly related to a man of fortune, but ... injuriously kept by him out of large possessions' (see Boswell on Savage in *Life*, i. 169–74).

Levet is a shadowy actor in the poem celebrating his hitherto unsung achievements. Johnson employs an assemblage of synecdochic constructions ('His vig'rous remedy', 'useful care', and 'virtues', ll. 15, 18, 25) to act out the scenes of his life in place of Levet himself. These abstracted agencies contribute to a sense of diminished capabilities, of a character scarcely at the helm of his own life or visible in his own poem. Although we are enjoined to 'See LEVET to the grave descend' (l. 6), it is difficult to do just that: how are we to distinguish the obscurely wise subject of his own poetic commemoration in misery's darkest caverns, where lonely want retired from view to die? One way in which we can attempt to do so is by thinking about the complex word 'Officious', as he is described at the beginning of the next line. 'See LEVET to the grave descend' sounds oddly as if Levet is electively stooping to his own mortality. Like Dickinson's Christ, he bends 'as low as Death', and it seems as if we might therefore *see* him do so, because it is a gradual process of decline. Yet the point of Levet's death is that it was sudden, as imperceptible to him as it was to Johnson, and this was a reward for a virtuous life—one in which he *had* descended to the grave in the sense of ministering to the mortally ill. It is in Johnson's poem that we see the link between the two forms of descent: between an 'Officious' stooping to those on the brink of death, and a mercifully painless demise.

Piozzi quoted the second verse of 'On the Death of Dr. Robert Levet' under 'OFFICIOUS, FORWARD TO RENDER UNDESIRED SERVICES, IMPORTUNATELY KIND, TROUBLESOME' in her *British Synonymy* (1794):

The first word here is commonly used in a bad sense certainly, and so Johnson understood it in his Dictionary; yet we find him many years after considering it more tenderly, when speaking of a dead dependant whom he loved, he says,

> Well tried through many a varying year,
>   See Levett to the grave descend;
> OFFICIOUS, innocent, sincere,
>   Of every friendless name the friend.

Johnson, indeed, always thinking neglect the worst misfortune that could befall a man, looked on a character of this description with less aversion than I do, who am apt to think that among the petty pests of society, after a weak foe comes an OFFICIOUS friend.[63]

Piozzi fails here to see that 'tenderly' considering an unattractive word might act as a vehicle for the tender commemoration of a friend

---

[63] Hester Lynch Piozzi, *British Synonymy: or, an Attempt at Regulating the Choice of Words in Familiar Conversation*, 2 vols. (London: for G. G. and J. Robinson, 1794), ii. 79–80.

whom others found despicable. Indeed, in *Rambler* 137, intellectual condescension such as that practised by Johnson in 'Levet', and charitable condescension such as that practised by Levet himself, is described as 'tender officiousness' (*Yale*, iv. 364). To class Levet amongst 'the petty pests of society', and to describe him as a 'dead dependant', is to overlook the fact that 'Johnson . . . never wished him to be regarded as an inferior, or treated him like a dependent' (*Miscellanies*, ii. 109–10). Arthur Murphy understood the word 'officious' quite differently: '[Johnson's] friend Levett, his physician in ordinary, . . . was mute, officious, and ever complying' (*Life*, ii. 5 n. 1). The primary sense of 'OFFICIOUS' in the *Dictionary* is, in fact, not Piozzi's, but that of *Rambler* 137: 'Kind; doing good offices.' Only secondarily is it defined as 'Importunately forward'.

Johnson's restoration of 'Officious' to its more lenient sense might itself, then, be construed as a kindly office to the language, undertaken in parallel with the celebration of a dead friend (he had already viewed the quality of officiousness in a negative frame in the *Life of Savage*, 16, 19, 95). For his 'Officious' harbours the twin strains of praise and blame, of elevation and degradation, that characterize the word 'little'—as well as the full range of possible reactions to Levet, from Thrale and Boswell's to Johnson and Murphy's. The 'innocent' and 'sincere' with which Johnson immediately qualifies 'Officious' (this is the only line in the poem to consist solely of adjectives) are directions as to how we should understand the preceding word, and hence a further hint of Levet's hidden qualities. Conjoining the medical with the moral, they also refer to his virtuously condescending profession. To be 'INNOCENT' is, according to the *Dictionary*, to be 'Unhurtful; harmless in effects' (sense 3), no mean feat for an eighteenth-century doctor, while the primary sense of its companion word in this poem, 'SINCERE', is 'Unhurt, uninjured'—reflecting the consequences of those harmless offices on his patients. Such local acts of restoration, a curative force of Johnson's own, should prompt us to look beyond the 'offensive particulars' of Levet's character which disgusted Boswell, for '[Levet's] brutality is in his manners, not his mind' (Johnson in *Life*, app. D, iii. 462). Just so, we should see beyond the pejorative implications of 'Officious' to its innocent properties, not confuse Piozzi's 'IMPORTUNATELY KIND' with Johnson's 'coarsely kind'. Austen, whose favourite 'moral' author 'in prose' was Johnson, well understood the distinction, and accordingly made the rehabilitation in Emma's mind of Miss Bates—an officious friend if ever there was one—the pivotal ethical lesson of *Emma* (Henry Austen in Austen, *Works*, v. 7; Austen, *Works*, iv. 374–84).

Johnson's poem begins in a collective state of being 'Condemn'd' and closes in Levet's 'soul' being individually 'free'd' from the 'vital chain' (ll. 35–6). Resembling Watts's depiction of 'The Lamb that freed my captive Soul | From *Satan*'s heavy Chains' ('Redemption by Price and Power', *Hymns*, 179), Johnson's final image presents a Christian escape from the desolate pagan eternity of the last two lines of a translation he completed, weeks before his own death in 1784, of Horace's 'Diffugere nives': 'Nor can the might of Theseus rend | The chains of hell that hold his friend' (ll. 27–8). Reflecting on lives such as Levet's served, temporarily, to combat Johnson's terror of divine judgement. It did so because 'Bless'd are the humble Souls that see | Their Emptiness and Poverty' (Watts, 'The Beatitudes', *Hymns*, 96). The poem's descent to Levet, like Levet's descent to the grave, is an earthly imitation of that descending God who 'emptied himself, and took upon him the form of a servant, and was made in the likeness of men' (Philippians 2: 8). Johnson deserves the honour he bestowed on George III (*Prefaces*, 3): 'It is the privilege of real greatness not to be afraid of diminution by condescending to the notice of little things.'

Bibliography: Works Cited

PRIMARY SOURCES

ADDISON, JOSEPH, et al., *The Spectator*, ed. Donald F. Bond, 5 vols., 2nd edn. (Oxford: Clarendon Press, 1987).

ANON., *The Whores Rhetorick (1683): A Facsimile Reproduction*, introd. James R. Irvine and G. Jack Gravlee (Delmar, NY: Scholars' Facsimiles and Reprints, 1979).

ANON., *Ad C. Herennium: De Ratione Dicendi (Rhetorica ad Herennium)*, trans. Harry Caplan (Cambridge, Mass.: Harvard University Press, 1954; repr. 1989).

ARBUTHNOT, JOHN, *An Essay concerning the Nature of Aliments, and the Choice of Them, according to the different Constitutions of Human Bodies. In which the different Effects, Advantages and Disadvantages of Animal and Vegetable Diet are Explain'd* (London: for J. Tonson, 1731).

ARISTOTLE, *The 'Art' of Rhetoric*, trans. John Henry Freese (London: Heinemann, 1926; repr. 1947).

——— 'LONGINUS', and DEMETRIUS, *Aristotle: The Poetics, Longinus: On the Sublime, Demetrius: On Style*, trans. W. Hamilton Ffye and W. Rhys Roberts (Cambridge, Mass.: Harvard University Press, 1927; repr. 1991).

ASTREY, FRANCIS, *Humility Recommended. In a Sermon Preach'd before the Right Honourable the Lord Mayor and the Court of Aldermen in the Cathedral Church of St. Paul* (London: for Henry Clements, 1716).

AUSTEN, JANE, *The Works of Jane Austen*, ed. R. W. Chapman, 6 vols., 3rd edn. (Oxford: Oxford University Press, 1988).

——— *Jane Austen's Letters*, ed. Deirdre Le Faye, 3rd edn. (Oxford: Oxford University Press, 1996).

[BAKER, DAVID ERSKINE], *The Companion to the Play-House: or, an Historical Account of all the Dramatic Writers (and their Works) that have appeared in Great Britain and Ireland, from the Commencement of our Theatrical Exhibitions, down to the present year 1764. Composed in the form of a Dictionary*, 2 vols. (London: for T. Becket and P. A. Dehondt; C. Henderson, and T. Davies, 1764).

BARETTI, GIUSEPPE, *Easy Phraseology, for the Use of Young Ladies, who intend to learn the Colloquial Part of the Italian Language* (London: for G. Robinson and T. Cadell, 1775).

BEATTIE, JAMES, *Essays* (Edinburgh: for William Creech, 1776).

BLACKMORE, SIR RICHARD, *King Arthur: An Heroick Poem in Twelve Books* (London: for Awnsham and John Churchil[l] and Jacob Tonson, 1697).

244 Bibliography

BLACKMORE, SIR RICHARD, *Prince Arthur: 1695* (Menston: Scolar Press, 1971).

BLACKWALL, ANTHONY, *The Sacred Classics Defended and Illustrated: Or, An Essay humbly offer'd towards proving the Purity, Prosperity, and true Eloquence of the Writers of the New-Testament* (London: for C. Rivington and W. Cantrell, 1725).

——*An Introduction to the Classics: Containing a Short Discourse on their Excellencies; and Directions how to Study them to Advantage*, 4th edn., with additions (London: for Charles Rivington, 1728).

BLOOM, EDWARD A., and BLOOM, LILLIAN D. (eds.), *Addison and Steele: The Critical Heritage* (London Routledge, 1995).

BOLINGBROKE, HENRY ST JOHN, LORD, *The Works of the late Right Honourable Henry St. John, Lord Viscount Bolingbroke*, ed. David Mallet, 5 vols. (London: for the editor, 1754).

BORUSLAWSKI, JOSEPH, *Memoirs of the Celebrated Dwarf, Joseph Boruslawski: a Polish Gentleman; Containing a Faithful and Curious Account of his Birth, Education, Marriage, Travels and Voyages; Written by Himself*, trans. Mr Des Carrieres (London: [n.p.], 1788).

BOSWELL, JAMES, *Boswell's Journal of a Tour to the Hebrides with Samuel Johnson, LL.D*, ed. Frederick A. Pottle and Charles H. Bennett (London: Heinemann, 1936).

——*Boswell's London Journal: 1762–1763*, ed. Frederick A. Pottle (London: Heinemann, 1950).

——*Boswell on the Grand Tour: Germany and Switzerland, 1764*, ed. Frederick A. Pottle (London: Heinemann, 1953).

——*Boswell in Search of a Wife: 1766–1769*, ed. Frank Brady and Frederick A. Pottle (London: Heinemann, 1958).

——*Boswell, The Ominous Years: 1774–1776*, ed. Charles Ryskamp and Frederick A. Pottle (London: Heinemann, 1963).

——*Boswell's Life of Johnson; Together with Boswell's Journal of a Tour to the Hebrides*, ed. George Birkbeck Hill, rev. and enlarged L. F. Powell, 6 vols., 2nd edn. (Oxford: Clarendon Press, 1971).

——*James Boswell's Life of Johnson: An Edition of the Original Manuscript in Four Volumes* (Edinburgh: Edinburgh University Press, 1994–).

——*The Correspondence and Other Papers of James Boswell Relating to the Making of the Life of Johnson*, ed. Marshall Waingrow, 2nd edn. (Edinburgh: Edinburgh University Press, 2001).

BROOKE, HENRY, *The Poetical Works of Henry Brooke, Esq.*, ed., rev., and corrected by Miss Brooke, 4 vols., 3rd edn. (Dublin: for the editor, 1792).

BURKE, EDMUND, *A Philosophical Enquiry into the Origins of our Ideas of the Sublime and the Beautiful*, ed. James T. Boulton (Oxford: Basil Blackwell, 1987).

BURNEY, FRANCES, *Dr Johnson & Fanny Burney: Extracts from Fanny Burney's Prose 1777–84*, ed. Nigel Wood (Bristol: Bristol Classical Press, 1989).

BYRON, GEORGE GORDON, LORD, *Byron's Letters and Journals*, ed. Leslie Marchand, 12 vols. (Cambridge, Mass.: The Belknap Press of Harvard University Press, 1973–82).

[CALLENDER, JAMES THOMSON], *Deformities of Dr Samuel Johnson*, 2nd edn. (Berkeley and Los Angeles: University of California, 1971).

[CAMPBELL, ARCHIBALD], *Lexiphanes, a Dialogue. Imitated from Lucian, and suited to the Present Times. Being an Attempt to restore the English Tongue to its Ancient Purity, and to correct, as well as to expose, the affected Style, hard Words, and absurd Phraseology of many late Writers, and particularly of our English Lexiphanes, The Rambler*, 2nd edn., corrected (London: for J. Knox, 1767).

CHAUCER, GEOFFREY, *The Riverside Chaucer*, ed. Larry D. Benson, 3rd edn. (Oxford: Oxford University Press, 1987; repr. 1992).

CICERO, MARCUS TULLIUS, *Brutus and Orator*, trans. G. L. Hendrickson and H. M. Hubbell, rev. edn. (Cambridge, Mass.: Harvard University Press, 1939; repr. 1962).

—— *De Oratore*, trans. E. W. Sutton and H. Rackham, 2 vols. (London: Heinemann, 1942; repr. 1959).

COMPTON-BURNETT, IVY, *A Family and a Fortune* (Harmondsworth: Penguin, 1983).

—— *Two Worlds and their Ways* (London: Virago, 1990).

COURTENAY, JOHN, *A Poetical Review of the Literary and Moral Character of the late Samuel Johnson* (Los Angeles: William Andrews Clark Memorial Library, 1969).

COWPER, WILLIAM, *The Poems of William Cowper*, ed. John D. Baird and Charles Ryskamp, 3 vols. (Oxford: Clarendon Press, 1980–95).

CRISPIN, EDMUND (Bruce Montgomery), *The Long Divorce* (Harmondsworth: Penguin, 1958).

DE LA MARE, WALTER, *Memoirs of a Midget* (Harmondsworth: Penguin, 1955).

DICKINSON, EMILY, *The Complete Poems*, ed. Thomas H. Johnson (London: Faber and Faber, 1970; repr. 1982).

DIONYSIUS OF HALICARNASSUS, *The Critical Essays*, trans. Stephen Usher, 2 vols. (Cambridge, Mass.: Harvard University Press, 1974–85).

DODWELL, WILLIAM, *Practical Discourses on Moral Subjects*, 2 vols. (London: for Sam. Birt, 1748–9).

DRYDEN, JOHN, *The Works of John Dryden*, ed. Edward Niles Hooker, H. T. Swedenberg, Jr., and Alan Roper, 20 vols. (Berkeley and Los Angeles: University of California Press, 1956–2000).

DUCK, STEPHEN, *Poems on Several Occasions* (London: for the author, 1736).

ELIOT, T. S., *Eeldrop and Appleplex* (London: Foundling Press, 1992).

FIELDING, HENRY, *The Wesleyan Edition of the Works of Henry Fielding* (Oxford: Clarendon Press, 1967–).

—— *The Criticism of Henry Fielding*, ed. Ioan Williams (London: Routledge & Kegan Paul, 1970).

FIELDING, HENRY, *The History of the Adventures of Joseph Andrews and of his Friend Mr. Abraham Andrews and An Apology for the Life of Mrs. Shamela Andrews*, ed. Douglas Brooks (Oxford: Oxford University Press, 1971).

FREUD, SIGMUND, *The Standard Edition of the Complete Psychological Works of Sigmund Freud*, ed. and trans. James Strachey et al., 24 vols. (London: Hogarth Press and the Institute of Psycho-Analysis, 1953–74).

GASKELL, ELIZABETH, *Cranford*, ed. Elizabeth Porges Watson (Oxford: Oxford University Press, 1980).

GIBBON, EDWARD, *The History of the Decline and Fall of the Roman Empire*, ed. David Womersley, 3 vols. (Harmondsworth: Penguin, 1995).

GOLDSMITH, OLIVER, *Collected Works of Oliver Goldsmith*, ed. Arthur Friedman, 5 vols. (Oxford: Clarendon Press, 1966).

[GORDON, THOMAS], *A Dedication to a Great Man, Concerning Dedications* (London: for James Roberts, 1718).

GOSSE, EDMUND, *Father and Son: A Study of Two Temperaments*, ed. Peter Abbs (Harmondsworth: Penguin, 1989).

GRAY, THOMAS, and MASON, WILLIAM, *The Poems of Mr Gray. To which are prefixed Memoirs of his Life and Writings by W. Mason, M.A.* (York: J. Todd, 1775).

HAUPTMANN, GERHART, *Die Jungfern von Bischofsberg* (Berlin: Fischer, 1907).

HAZLITT, WILLIAM, *The Complete Works of William Hazlitt in Twenty-One Volumes: Centenary Edition*, ed. P. P. Howe (London: J. M. Dent, 1930–4).

HILL, GEORGE BIRKBECK (ed.), *Johnsonian Miscellanies*, 2 vols. (New York: Barnes & Noble, 1966; repr. 1970).

JAMES, HENRY, *Roderick Hudson*, introd. Tony Tanner (Oxford: Oxford University Press, 1980; repr. 1988).

—— *The Critical Muse: Selected Literary Criticism*, ed. Roger Gard (London: Penguin, 1987).

JEFFREY, DAVID LYLE (ed.), *English Spirituality in the Age of Wesley* (Grand Rapids, Mich.: William B. Eerdmans, 1987).

JOHNSON, SAMUEL, *Samuel Johnson's Prefaces & Dedications*, ed. Allen T. Hazen (Port Washington, NY: Kennikat, 1937; repr. 1973).

—— *The Yale Edition of the Works of Samuel Johnson*, ed. John H. Middendorf et al. (New Haven: Yale University Press, 1956–   ).

—— *Dr Johnson: Prose and Poetry*, ed. Mona Wilson (London: Rupert Hart-Davis, 1969).

—— *An Account of the Life of Mr Richard Savage, Son of the late Earl Rivers*, ed. Clarence Tracy (Oxford: Clarendon Press, 1971).

—— *Early Biographical Writings of Dr. Johnson*, ed. J. D. Fleeman (Farnborough: Gregg International, 1973).

—— *The Complete English Poems*, ed. J. D. Fleeman (Harmondsworth: Penguin, 1971; repr. 1982).

—— *The Letters of Samuel Johnson*, ed. Bruce Redford, 5 vols. (Princeton: Princeton University Press, 1992–4).

_____ *A Dictionary of the English Language*, ed. Anne McDermott (Cambridge: Cambridge University Press, 1996) [on CD-Rom].

_____ *The Lives of the English Poets*, ed. George Birkbeck Hill, 3 vols., 2nd edn. (Oxford: Clarendon Press, 1996).

JOYCE, STANISLAUS, *My Brother's Keeper*, ed. Richard Ellmann, introd. T. S. Eliot (London: Faber and Faber, 1982).

JUVENAL, DECIMUS IUNIUS, and JOHNSON, SAMUEL, *Johnson's Juvenal: London and The Vanity of Human Wishes*, ed. Niall Rudd (Bristol: Bristol Classical Press, 1981; repr. 1988).

KAFKA, FRANZ, *Briefe*, ed. Hans-Gerd Koch (Frankfurt a. M.: Fischer, 1999–).

_____ *Tagebücher*, ed. Hans-Gerd Koch, Michael Müller, and Malcolm Pasley, 3 vols. (Frankfurt a. M.: Fischer, 1983).

LAMB, CHARLES, *Selected Prose*, ed. Adam Philips (Harmondsworth: Penguin, 1985).

LAW, WILLIAM, *A Serious Call to a Devout and Holy Life. Adapted to the State and Condition of all Orders of Christians*, 2nd edn., corrected (London: for William Innes, 1732).

LENNOX, CHARLOTTE, *The Female Quixote, or, The Adventures of Arabella*, ed. Margaret Dalziel, introd. Margaret Anne Doody (Oxford: Oxford University Press, 1989).

LOCKE, JOHN, *An Essay concerning Human Understanding*, ed. Peter Nidditch (Oxford: Clarendon Press, 1975; repr. 1979).

'LONGINUS', *Longinus, On the Sublime: The Peri Hupsous in Translations by Nicholas Boileau-Despréaux, 1674, and William Smith, 1739: Facsimile Reproductions*, introd. William Bruce Johnson (Delmar, NY: Scholars' Facsimiles & Reprints, 1975).

LONSDALE, ROGER (ed.), *The New Oxford Book of Eighteenth-Century Verse* (Oxford: Oxford University Press, 1984).

MILL, JOHN STUART, *The Collected Works of John Stuart Mill*, ed. John M. Robson et al., 32 vols. (Toronto: University of Toronto Press, 1963–91).

MILTON, JOHN, *Paradise Lost*, ed. Alastair Fowler (London: Longman, 1968; repr. 1990).

MONTAGU, ELIZABETH, *An Essay on the Writings and Genius of Shakespear, Compared with the Greek and French Dramatic Poets* (London: Frank Cass, 1970).

NORRIS, JOHN, *A Practical Treatise Concerning Humility. Design'd for the Furtherance of that Great Christian Vertue, both in the Minds and Lives of Men* (London: for S. Manship, 1707).

NORTH, ROGER, *The Life of the Honourable Sir Dudley North: Commissioner of the Customs, and afterwards of the Treasury to His Majesty King Charles the Second. And of the Honourable and Reverend Dr. John North, Master of Trinity College in Cambridge, and Greek Professor* (London: for the editor, 1744).

The Oxford English Dictionary Online, http://dictionary. oed.com/.

PAGE, NORMAN (ed.), *Dr Johnson: Interviews and Recollections* (Totowa, NJ: Barnes & Noble, 1987).

PEACHAM, HENRY, *The Garden of Eloquence*, ed. R. C. Alston (Menston: Scolar Press, 1971).

PINDAR, PETER (John Wolcot), *The Works of Peter Pindar*, 4 vols. (London: for Walker, Edwards et al., 1816).

PIOZZI, HESTER LYNCH, *British Synonymy: or, an Attempt at Regulating the Choice of Words in Familiar Conversation*, 2 vols. (London: for G. G. and J. Robinson, 1794).

_____ *Thraliana: The Diary of Mrs. Hester Lynch Thrale, Later Mrs Piozzi, 1776–1809*, ed. Katherine C. Balderston, 2 vols., 2nd edn. (Oxford: Clarendon Press, 1951).

_____ and JOHNSON, SAMUEL, *Letters to and from the late Samuel Johnson, LL.D.*, 2 vols. (London: for A. Strahan and T. Cadell, 1788).

POPE, ALEXANDER, *The Correspondence of Alexander Pope*, ed. George Sherburn, 5 vols. (Oxford: Oxford University Press, 1956).

_____ *The Twickenham Edition of the Poems of Alexander Pope*, ed. John Butt, 11 vols. (London: Methuen, 1939–69).

_____ *Selected Prose of Alexander Pope*, ed. Paul Hammond (Cambridge: Cambridge University Press, 1987).

POTTER, ROBERT, *An Inquiry into some Passages in Dr. Johnson's Lives of the Poets: Particularly his Observations on Lyric Poetry, and the Odes of Gray* (London: for J. Dodsley, 1783).

PUTTENHAM, GEORGE, *The Arte of English Poesie*, ed. George Doidge Willcock and Alice Walker (Cambridge: Cambridge University Press, 1936; repr. 1970).

REYNOLDS, JOSHUA, *Discourses on Art*, ed. Robert Wark (New Haven: Yale University Press, 1975).

RICHARDSON, SAMUEL, *Selected Letters of Samuel Richardson*, ed. John Carroll (Oxford: Clarendon Press, 1964).

_____ *Pamela; or, Virtue Rewarded*, ed. Peter Sabor, introd. Margaret Anne Doody (Harmondsworth: Penguin, 1985).

_____ *Pamela; or, Virtue Rewarded*, ed. Thomas Keymer and Alice Wakely (Oxford: Oxford University Press, 2001).

RUFFHEAD, OWEN, 'The Prince of Abissinia. A Tale', *Monthly Review*, 20 (1759), 428–37.

SCOTT, SARAH, *The History of Sir George Ellison*, 2nd edn. (London: F. Noble, 1770).

SENECA, LUCIUS ANNAEUS, *Seneca: Tragedies*, trans. Frank Justus Miller, 2 vols., rev. edn. (London: Heinemann, 1929; repr. 1968).

SHAFTESBURY, ANTHONY ASHLEY COOPER, third Earl of, *Characteristics of Men, Manners, Opinions, Times*, ed. Lawrence Klein (Cambridge: Cambridge University Press, 1999; repr. 2001).

SHAKESPEARE, WILLIAM, *The Complete Works: Compact Edition*, ed. Stanley Wells, Gary Taylor, John Jowett, and William Montgomery (Oxford: Oxford University Press, 1994; repr. 1995).

SMITH, ADAM, *The Glasgow Edition of the Works and Correspondence of Adam Smith*, 7 vols., ed. R. H. Campbell, D. D. Raphael, and A. S. Skinner (Oxford: Clarendon Press, 1976–83).

SMITH, JOHN, *The Mystery of Rhetorick Unveil'd. Wherein above 130 of the Tropes and Figures are severally derived from the Greek into English; together with lively Definitions, and Variety of Latin, English, Scriptural Examples, pertinent to each of them apart. Eminently delightful and profitable for young Scholars, and others of all sorts, enabling them to discern and imitate the Elegancy in any Author they read, & c.* (London: for George Eversden, 1683).

SPENCE, JOSEPH, *An Essay on Pope's Odyssey: in which Some Particular Beauties and Blemishes of that Work are Consider'd*, 2 vols. (London: for James and J. Knapton et al., 1726–7).

_____ *Observations, Anecdotes, and Characters of Books and Men Collected from Conversation*, ed. James M. Osborn, 2 vols. (Oxford: Clarendon Press, 1966).

STATIUS, PUBLIUS PAPINIUS, *Statius*, trans. J. H. Mozley, 2 vols. (London: Heinemann, 1928; repr. 1957).

STEELE, RICHARD, *The Christian Hero: An Argument Proving that no Principles but those of Religion are sufficient to make a Great Man*, 2nd edn., with additions (London: for Jacob Tonson, 1701).

_____ et al., *The Tatler*, ed. Donald F. Bond, 3 vols. (Oxford: Clarendon Press, 1987).

STIRLING, JOHN, *A System of Rhetoric*, ed. R. C. Alston (Menston: Scolar Press, 1968).

SWIFT, JONATHAN, *The Prose Works of Jonathan Swift*, ed. Herbert Davis, 16 vols. (Oxford: Basil Blackwell for Shakespeare Head, 1939–74).

_____ *The Poems of Jonathan Swift*, ed. Harold Williams, 3 vols., 2nd edn. (Oxford: Clarendon Press, 1958).

THACKERAY, WILLIAM, *Vanity Fair* (Harmondsworth: Penguin, 1994).

'WAGSTAFFE, WILLIAM', and CANNING, GEORGE, *Parodies of Ballad Criticism (1711–1781): William Wagstaffe, A Comment upon the History of Tom Thumb, 1711; George Canning, The Knave of Hearts, 1787*, ed. W. K. Wimsatt, Jr. (Berkeley and Los Angeles: University of California, 1957).

WARTON, THOMAS, *The Life of Sir Thomas Pope* (London: T. Davies, 1772).

WATTS, ISAAC, *A Guide to Prayer. Or, A Free and Rational Account of the Gift, Grace and Spirit of Prayer; with Plain Directions how Every Christian may attain them* (London: for Emanuel Matthews and Sarah Cliff, 1715).

_____ *Humility Represented in the Character of St. Paul, the Chief Springs of it opened, and its Various Advantages display'd; together with some Occasional Views of the Contrary Vice* (London: for R. Ford and R. Hett, 1737).

WATTS, ISAAC, *The Works of the Late Reverend and Learned Isaac Watts, D.D.*, ed. D. Jennings and P. Doddridge, 6 vols. (London: for T. and T. Longman et al., 1753).

—— *Hymns and Spiritual Songs. In Three Books. I. Collected from the Scriptures. II. Composed on Divine Subjects. III. Prepar'd for the Lord's Supper*, 19th edn. (London: for R. Ware et al., 1755).

—— *Divine Songs attempted in Easy Language for the Use of Children: Facsimile Reproductions of the First Edition of 1715 and an Illustrated Edition of circa 1840*, introd. J. H. P. Papford (London: Oxford University Press, 1971).

WELSTED, LEONARD, *The Works, in Verse and Prose, of Leonard Welsted, Esq*, ed. John Nichols (London: for the editor, 1787).

WHITMAN, WALT, *Complete Poetry and Collected Prose*, ed. Justin Kaplan (New York: Viking Press, 1982).

WORDSWORTH, WILLIAM, *The Major Works*, ed. Stephen Gill (Oxford: Oxford University Press, 1984; repr. 2000).

SECONDARY SOURCES

ACKROYD, PETER, *Albion: The Origins of the English Imagination* (London: Chatto & Windus, 2002).

ANDERSON, BENEDICT, *Imagined Communities: Reflections on the Origin and Spread of Nationalism*, rev. edn. (London: Verso, 1991).

ANDERSON, DAVID R., and KOLB, GWIN J. (eds.), *Approaches to Teaching the Works of Samuel Johnson* (New York: MLA, 1993).

ANTCZAK, FREDERICK, COGGINS, CINDA, and KLINGER, GEOFFREY D. (eds.), *Professing Rhetoric: Selected Papers from the 2000 Rhetoric Society of America Conference* (Mahwah, NJ: Lawrence Erlbaum Associates, 2002).

AUERBACH, ERIC, *Literary Language and its Public in Late Latin Antiquity and in the Middle Ages*, trans. Ralph Mannheim (London: Routledge & Kegan Paul, 1965).

—— *Mimesis: The Representation of Reality in Western Culture*, trans. Willard R. Trask, 10th edn. (Princeton: Princeton University Press, 1991).

BAILEY, JOHN, *Walt Whitman* (London: Macmillan, 1926).

BARCHAS, JANINE, *Graphic Design, Print Culture, and the Eighteenth-Century Novel* (Cambridge: Cambridge University Press, 2003).

BARRELL, JOHN, *The Dark Side of the Landscape: The Rural Poor in English Painting, 1730–1840* (Cambridge: Cambridge University Press, 1980).

—— *English Literature in History 1730–80: An Equal, Wide Survey* (London: Hutchinson, 1983).

BASKER, JAMES G., 'Dancing Dogs, Women Preachers and the Myth of Johnson's Misogyny', *Age of Johnson*, 3 (1990), 63–90.

—— 'Myth upon Myth: Johnson, Gender, and the Misogyny Question', *Age of Johnson*, 8 (1997), 175–87.

BATE, W. JACKSON, *Samuel Johnson* (London: Chatto & Windus, 1978).

BAXANDALL, MICHAEL, *Patterns of Intention: On the Historical Explanation of Pictures* (New Haven: Yale University Press, 1985).

BEDFORD, EMMETT G., and DILLIGAN, ROBERT J., *A Concordance to the Poems of Alexander Pope*, 2 vols. (Detroit: Gale Research Company, 1974).

BENJAMIN, WALTER, *Illuminations*, ed. Hannah Arendt, trans. Harry Zohn (New York: Schocken, 1969).

BOULTON, JAMES T. (ed.), *Johnson: The Critical Heritage* (London: Routledge & Kegan Paul, 1971).

BOYS, RICHARD C., *Contributions in Modern Philology*, 13: *Sir Richard Blackmore and the Wits: A Study of "Commendatory Verses on the Author of the Two Arthurs and the Satyr against Wit" (1700)* (Michigan: University of Michigan Press, 1949).

BUTLER, MARILYN, *Romantics, Rebels and Reactionaries: English Literature and its Background, 1760–1830* (Oxford: Oxford University Press, 1981; repr. 1990).

_____ 'Oxford's Eighteenth-Century Versions', *Eighteenth-Century Life*, 12 (1988), 128–36.

CAFARELLI, ANNETTE WHEELER, 'Johnson and Women: Demasculinizing Literary History', *Age of Johnson*, 5 (1992), 61–114.

CAFFI, CLAUDIA, 'Litote', *Journal of Pragmatics*, 13 (1989), 903–12.

CASEY, JOHN, *Pagan Virtue: An Essay in Ethics* (Oxford: Clarendon Press, 1990).

CLARK, JONATHAN, and ERSKINE-HILL, HOWARD (eds.), *Samuel Johnson in Historical Context* (Basingstoke: Palgrave, 2002).

CLARKE, NORMA, *Dr Johnson's Women* (London: Hambledon, 2001).

CLIFFORD, JAMES, *Young Sam Johnson* (New York: McGraw-Hill, 1955).

CLINGHAM, GREG (ed.), *The Cambridge Companion to Samuel Johnson* (Cambridge: Cambridge University Press, 1997).

CRAWFORD, THOMAS (ed.), *Boswell in Scotland and Beyond* (Glasgow: Association for Scottish Literary Studies, 1997).

CURLEY, THOMAS, *Samuel Johnson and the Age of Travel* (Athens: University of Georgia Press, 1976).

DAVIE, DONALD A., 'Berkeley's Style in *Siris*', *Cambridge Journal*, 4 (1950–1), 427–33.

_____ *Purity of Diction in English Verse and Articulate Energy* (London: Penguin Books, 1992).

DOUGLAS, MARY, *Purity and Danger: An Analysis of the Concepts of Pollution and Taboo* (London: Routledge & Kegan Paul, 1966; repr. 1976).

DUSSINGER, JOHN A., 'Style and Intention in the *Life of Savage*', *ELH* 37 (1970), 564–80.

EAGLETON, TERRY, *After Theory* (London: Allen Lane, 2003).

EAVES, T. C. DUNCAN, and KIMPEL, BEN D., *Samuel Richardson: A Biography* (Oxford: Clarendon Press, 1971).

EDINGER, WILLIAM, *Samuel Johnson and Detailed Representation: The Significance of the Classical Sources* (Victoria: English Literary Studies, University of Victoria, 1997).

ELIAS, NORBERT, *The Civilizing Process: The History of Manners and State Formation and Civilization*, trans. Edmund Jephcott (Oxford: Blackwell, 1994).

ELIOT, T. S., *On Poetry and Poets* (London: Faber and Faber, 1957; repr. 1990).

—— *Selected Prose of T. S. Eliot*, ed. Frank Kermode (London: Faber and Faber, 1975).

EMPSON, WILLIAM, *Seven Types of Ambiguity* (London: Hogarth Press, 1991).

—— *Some Versions of Pastoral* (London: Hogarth Press, 1986).

—— *The Structure of Complex Words* (Harmondsworth: Penguin, 1995).

ERSKINE-HILL, HOWARD, 'Johnson and the Petty Particular', *Transactions of the Johnson Society of Lichfield* (1976), 40–7.

—— (ed.), *Proceedings of the British Academy*, 91: *Alexander Pope: World and Word* (Oxford: Oxford University Press for the British Academy, 1998).

EVERETT, BARBARA, *Poets in their Time: Essays on English Poetry from Donne to Larkin* (Oxford: Clarendon Press, 1991).

FAIRER, DAVID (ed.), *Pope: New Contexts* (Hemel Hempstead: Harvester Wheatsheaf, 1990).

FLEEMAN, J. D. (ed.), *The Sale Catalogue of Johnson's Library: A Facsimile Edition* (Victoria: English Literary Studies, 1975).

FOLKENFLIK, ROBERT, *Samuel Johnson, Biographer* (Ithaca, NY: Cornell University Press, 1978).

FORD, BORIS (ed.), *The Cambridge Cultural History of Britain*, V: *Eighteenth-Century Britain* (Cambridge: Cambridge University Press, 1992).

FRYE, NORTHROP, *The Secular Scripture: A Study of the Structure of Romance* (Cambridge, Mass.: Harvard University Press, 1976).

FUSSELL, PAUL, *The Rhetorical World of Augustan Humanism: Ethics and Imagery from Swift to Burke* (Oxford: Clarendon Press, 1965).

—— *Samuel Johnson and the Life of Writing* (London: Chatto & Windus, 1972).

GENETTE, GÉRARD, *Paratexts: Thresholds of Interpretation*, trans. Jane E. Lewin (Cambridge: Cambridge University Press, 1997).

GOLDHAGEN, DANIEL JONAH, *Hitler's Willing Executioners: Ordinary Germans and the Holocaust* (London: Abacus, 1996).

GRAY, JAMES, *Johnson's Sermons: A Study* (Oxford: Clarendon Press, 1972).

GRIFFIN, DUSTIN, *Literary Patronage in England, 1650–1800* (Cambridge: Cambridge University Press, 1996).

GRIFFITHS, ERIC, 'Dryden's Past', *Proceedings of the British Academy*, 84 (1992), 113–49.

GRUNDY, ISOBEL, *Samuel Johnson and the Scale of Greatness* (Leicester: Leicester University Press, 1986).

—— 'Samuel Johnson as Patron of Women', *Age of Johnson*, 1 (1987), 59–77.

HAGSTRUM, JEAN H., *Samuel Johnson's Literary Criticism* (Minneapolis: University of Minnesota Press, 1952).

HAMMOND, BREAN, *Professional Imaginative Writing in England, 1670–1740: 'Hackney for Bread'* (Oxford: Clarendon Press, 1997).

HART, KEVIN, *Samuel Johnson and the Culture of Property* (Cambridge: Cambridge University Press, 1999).

HINNANT, CHARLES H. (ed.), *Johnson and Gender: Special Issue of South Central Review*, 9: 4 (1992).

HOGAN, C. B., 'Jane Austen and her Early Public', *Review of English Studies*, NS 1 (1950), 39–54.

HOLLAND, TOM, *Rubicon: The Triumph and Tragedy of the Roman Republic* (London: Little, Brown, 2003).

HOWELL, WILBUR S., *Eighteenth-Century British Logic and Rhetoric* (Princeton: Princeton University Press, 1971).

INGHAM, PATRICIA, 'Dr. Johnson's "Elegance"', *Review of English Studies*, NS 19 (1968), 271–8.

JARVIS, SIMON, *Scholars and Gentlemen: Shakespearian Textual Criticism and Representations of Scholarly Labour, 1725–1765* (Oxford: Clarendon Press, 1995).

JEMIELITY, THOMAS, 'A Mock-Biblical Controversy: Sir Richard Blackmore in the *Dunciad*', *Philological Quarterly*, 74 (1995), 249–77.

JURAFSKY, DANIEL, 'Universal Tendencies in the Semanties of the Diminutive', *Language: Journal of the Linguistic Society of America*, 72 (1996), 533–78.

JUSTICE, GEORGE, and TINKER, NATHAN (eds.), *Women's Writing and the Circulation of Ideas: Manuscript Publication in England, 1550–1800* (Cambridge: Cambridge University Press, 2002).

KEATES, JONATHAN, *Purcell : A Biography* (London: Chatto & Windus, 1995).

KEMMERER, KATHLEEN NULTON, *'A Neutral Being between the Sexes': Samuel Johnson's Sexual Politics* (Lewisburg, Pa.: Bucknell University Press, 1998).

KETCHAM, MICHAEL G., *Transparent Designs: Reading, Performance, and Form in the Spectator Papers* (Athens: University of Georgia Press, 1985).

KNOBLAUCH, CYRIL, 'Samuel Johnson and the Composing Process', *Eighteenth-Century Studies*, 13 (1980), 243–62.

KORSHIN, PAUL, and ALLEN, ROBERT R. (eds.), *Greene Centennial Studies: Essays Presented to Donald Greene in the Centennial Year of the University of Southern California* (Charlottesville: University of Virginia Press, 1984).

LAKOFF, GEORGE, 'Hedges: A Study in Meaning Criteria and the Logic of Fuzzy Concepts', *Journal of Philosophical Logic*, 2 (1973), 458–508.

LIPKING, LAWRENCE, *Samuel Johnson: The Life of an Author* (Cambridge, Mass.: Harvard University Press, 1998).

LYNN, STEVEN, 'Johnson's *Rambler* and Eighteenth-Century Rhetoric', *Eighteenth-Century Studies*, 19 (1986), 461–79.

MCCUTCHEON, ELIZABETH, 'Denying the Contrary: More's Use of Litotes in the *Utopia*', *Moreana: Bulletin Thomas More*, 8 (1971), 107–21.

MACHEREY, PIERRE, *A Theory of Literary Production*, trans. Geoffrey Wall (London: Routledge & Kegan Paul, 1978).

MACK, MAYNARD, *Alexander Pope: A Life* (New Haven: Yale University Press, in association with W. W. Norton, 1985).

McLEAN, MARIE, 'Pretexts and Paratexts: The Art of the Peripheral', *New Literary History*, 22 (1991), 273–9.

MIDDENDORF, JOHN H. (ed.), *English Writers of the Eighteenth Century* (New York: Columbia University Press, 1971).

MIDGLEY, MARY, *Wickedness: A Philosophical Essay* (London: Routledge, 1984; repr. 1997).

MORRISON, SARAH R., 'Samuel Johnson, Mr. Rambler, and Women', *Age of Johnson*, 14 (2003), 23–50.

MURPHY, FRANCIS (ed.), *Walt Whitman: A Critical Anthology* (Harmondsworth: Penguin, 1969).

NUTTALL, A. D., 'Auerbach's *Mimesis*', *Essays in Criticism*, 54 (2004), 60–74.

PAGE, NORMAN, *The Language of Jane Austen* (Oxford: Basil Blackwell, 1972).

PARKER, FRED, *Scepticism and Literature: An Essay on Pope, Hume, Sterne, and Johnson* (Oxford: Oxford University Press, 2003).

PAULSON, RONALD, *Breaking and Remaking: Aesthetic Practice in England, 1700–1820* (New Brunswick, NJ: Rutgers University Press, 1989).

PERRY, SEAMUS, *Coleridge and the Uses of Division* (Oxford: Clarendon Press, 1999).

PRESTON, THOMAS R., 'Homeric Allusion in *A Journey to the Western Islands of Scotland*', *Eighteenth-Century Studies*, 5 (1972), 545–8.

RAWSON, CLAUDE, *God, Gulliver, and Genocide: Barbarism and the European Imagination* (Oxford: Oxford University Press, 2001).

REDFORD, BRUCE, *Designing the Life of Johnson: The Lyell Lectures, 2001–2* (Oxford: Oxford University Press, 2002).

REINERT, THOMAS, *Regulating Confusion: Samuel Johnson and the Crowd* (Durham, NC: Duke University Press, 1996).

RIBEIRO, ALVARO, and BASKER, JAMES G. (eds.), *Tradition in Transition: Women Writers, Marginal Texts, and the Eighteenth-Century Canon* (Oxford: Clarendon Press, 1996).

RICKS, CHRISTOPHER, *Keats and Embarrassment* (Oxford: Clarendon Press, 1974; repr. 1984).

——— *Milton's Grand Style* (Oxford: Clarendon Press, 1978; repr. 1985).

RIGOLOT, FRANÇOIS, 'Tolérance et condescendance dans la littérature française du XVIe siècle', *Bibliothèque d'humanisme et renaissance*, 62 (2000), 25–47.

ROBERTS, S. C., 'On the Death of Dr. Robert Levet: A Note on the Text', *Review of English Studies*, 3 (1927), 442–5.

ROBINSON, PETER, *In the Circumstances: About Poems and Poets* (Oxford: Clarendon Press, 1992).

ROGERS, PAT, *Grub Street: Studies in a Subculture* (London: Methuen, 1972).

——— *Henry Fielding: A Biography* (London: Paul Elek, 1979).

ROSENBERG, ALBERT, *Sir Richard Blackmore: A Poet and Physician of the Augustan Age* (Lincoln: University of Nebrasha Press, 1953).

ROUSSEAU, G. S. (ed.), *Goldsmith: The Critical Heritage* (London: Routledge & Kegan Paul, 1974).

RUSSELL, D. A., *Criticism in Antiquity* (London: Duckworth, 1981).

SHIPLEY, WILLIAM (ed.), *In Honor of Mary Haas: From the Haas Festival Conference on Native American Linguistics* (Berlin: Mouton de Gruyter, 1988).

SISMAN, ADAM, *Boswell's Presumptuous Task* (London: Hamish Hamilton, 2000).

SKINNER, QUENTIN, *Reason and Rhetoric in the Philosophy of Hobbes* (Cambridge: Cambridge University Press, 1996).

SPADAFORA, DAVID, *The Idea of Progress in Eighteenth-Century Britain* (New Haven: Yale University Press, 1990).

SPERBER, DAN, and WILSON, DEIRDRE, *Relevance: Communication and Cognition* (Oxford: Basil Blackwell, 1986).

STALLYBRASS, PETER, and WHITE, ALLON, *The Politics and Poetics of Transgression* (Ithaca, NY: Cornell University Press, 1986).

THWAITE, ANN, *Glimpses of the Wonderful: The Life of Philip Henry Gosse* (London: Faber and Faber, 2002).

TODOROV, TZVETAN (ed.), *French Literary Theory Today: A Reader* (Cambridge: Cambridge University Press, 1982).

TRACY, CLARENCE, *The Artificial Bastard: A Biography of Richard Savage* (Toronto: University of Toronto Press in co-operation with the University of Saskatchewan, 1953).

TRICKETT, RACHEL, *The Honest Muse: A Study in Augustan Verse* (Oxford: Clarendon Press, 1967).

TROTTER, DAVID, *Cooking with Mud: The Idea of Mess in Nineteenth-Century Art and Fiction* (Oxford: Oxford University Press, 2000).

VANCE, JOHN A. (ed.), *Boswell's 'Life of Johnson': New Questions, New Answers* (Athens: University of Georgia Press, 1985).

VICKERS, BRIAN, *In Defence of Rhetoric* (Oxford: Clarendon Press, 1988).

VOITLE, ROBERT, *Samuel Johnson the Moralist* (Cambridge, Mass.: Harvard University Press, 1961).

WATT, IAN, *The Rise of the Novel: Studies in Defoe, Richardson and Fielding* (Harmondsworth: Penguin, 1972).

WECHSELBLATT, MARTIN, 'Finding Mr. Boswell: Rhetorical Authority and National Identity in Johnson's *Journey to the Western Islands of Scotland*', *ELH* 60 (1993), 117–48.

WEINBROT, HOWARD D., *Britannia's Issue: The Rise of British Literature from Dryden to Ossian* (Cambridge: Cambridge University Press, 1993).

WILLIAMS, CAROLYN D., *Pope, Homer, and Manliness: Some Aspects of Eighteenth-Century Classical Learning* (London: Routledge, 1993).

WIMSATT, Jr., W. K., *The Prose Style of Samuel Johnson* (New Haven: Yale University Press, 1941; repr. 1963).

Index